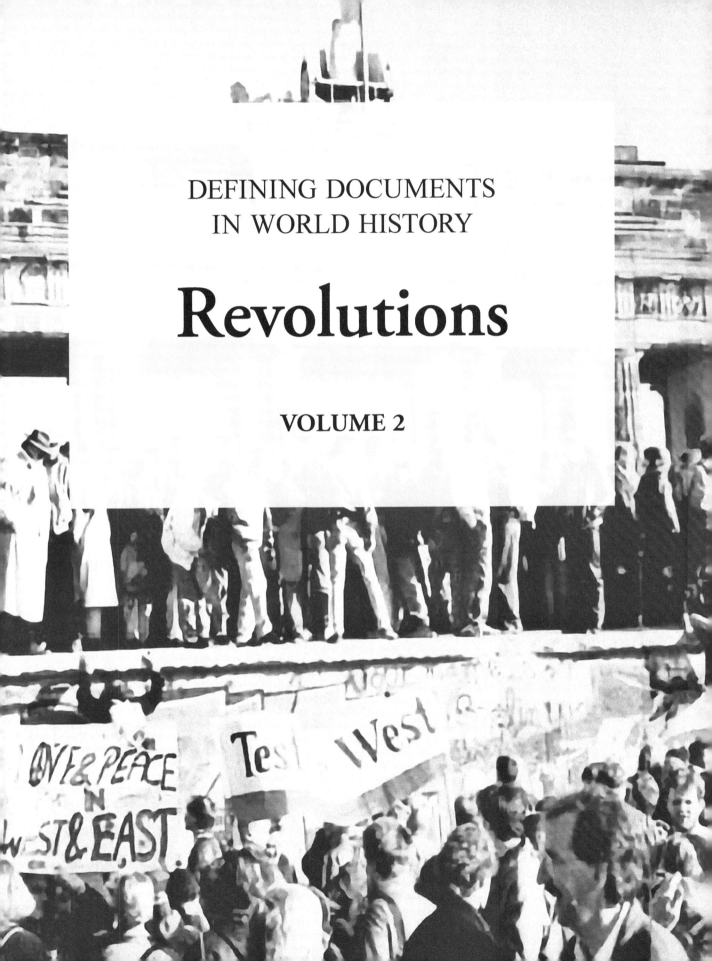

DEFINING DOCUMENTS IN WORLD HISTORY

Revolutions

VOLUME 2

DEFINING DOCUMENTS
IN WORLD HISTORY

Revolutions

Editor
Michael Shally-Jensen, PhD

Volume 2

SALEM PRESS
A Division of EBSCO Information Services, Inc.
Ipswich, Massachusetts

GREY HOUSE PUBLISHING

Cover: Image via iStock.com

Copyright © 2023 by EBSCO Information Services, Inc., and Grey House Publishing, Inc.

Defining Documents in World History: Revolutions, published by Grey House Publishing, Inc., Amenia, NY, under exclusive license from EBSCO Information Services, Inc.

All rights reserved. No part of this work may be used or reproduced in any manner whatsoever or transmitted in any form or by any means, electronic or mechanical, including photocopy, recording, or any information storage and retrieval system, without written permission from the copyright owner. For information, contact Grey House Publishing/Salem Press, 4919 Route 22, PO Box 56, Amenia, NY 12501.

∞ The paper used in these volumes conforms to the American National Standard for Permanence of Paper for Printed Library Materials, Z39.48 1992 (R2009).

Publisher's Cataloging-in-Publication Data
(Prepared by Parlew Associates, LLC)

Names: Shally-Jensen, Michael, editor.
Title: Revolutions / editor, Michael Shally-Jensen, PhD.
Other titles: Defining documents in world history (Salem Press)
Description: Ipswich, MA : Salem Press, a division of EBSCO Information Services, Inc. ; Amenia, NY : Grey House Publishing, 2023. | Includes bibliographical references and index. | Includes b&w photos and prints.
Identifiers: ISBN 9781637004043 (2 v. set) | ISBN 9781637004050 (v. 1) | ISBN 9781637004067 (v. 2) | ISBN 9781637004074 (ebook)
Subjects: LCSH: Revolutions. | Revolutions — History. | World politics. | World history. | BISAC: HISTORY / Military / Revolutions & Wars of Independence. | HISTORY / Modern / General. | HISTORY / World.
Classification: LCC HM876.R48 2023 (print) | LCC HM876 (ebook) | DDC 303.64 R—dc23

FIRST PRINTING
PRINTED IN THE UNITED STATES OF AMERICA

Table of Contents

Volume 2

Full Table of Contents ix

India 411
Karl Marx on British Rule in India 413
Government of India Act 424
Mohandas Gandhi: Statement at Trial 443
Jawaharlal Nehru's Speech on the Occasion of Indian Independence 453

China 461
Sun Yat-sen: "The Three Stages of Revolution" 463
"The Chinese People Have Stood Up!" 469
Mao Zedong on Communism and Counterrevolution 477
Letter from a Chinese "Rusticant" 491
U.S. Embassy Cables Concerning the Crackdown in Tiananmen Square 497

Mid-Century Rebels 505
¡No Pasarán! ("They Shall Not Pass!") 507
Mau Mau Warrior Oath 513
Fidel Castro's Speech at Twenty-One Nations Conference 516
Second Declaration of Havana 523

Vietnam—and Cambodia 529
Geneva Accords on Indochina 531
"The Path of Revolution in the South" 550
CIA Memo on National Liberation Front Methods 559
Message from Ho Chi Minh 566
The Paris Peace Accords 571
Story from the Khmer Rouge Killing Fields 581

Mid-East Revolts and Revolutions in the Twentieth Century 587
Proclamation of the Young Turks 589
Proclamation of the Algerian National Liberation Front 596
CIA Summary of the Overthrow of Premier Mossadeq of Iran 604
Gamal Abdel Nasser on the Nationalization of the Suez Canal 614
Ayatollah Khomeini on "The Great Satan" 623
Diary Excerpts of an American Hostage in Iran 633

The Revolt against Communism in Europe 639
Resolution of Hungarian Student Protestors 641
The "Two Thousand Words" Manifesto 648
Charter 77 655
CIA Cable on the Situation in Poland 663
Egon Krenz Letter to Mikhail Gorbachev 670
Gorbachev's Farewell Address 675

Other Modern Revolutionary Changes 683
Corazon Aquino on Achieving Peace through Peaceful Means 685
Nelson Mandela—Nobel Peace Prize Acceptance Speech 692
Hugo Chávez Speech in Havana 700

Ukraine—the Orange Revolution 709
Inaugural Speech by Ukrainian President Viktor Yushchenko 711
Remarks by Yulia Tymoshenko after Her Release from Prison 717

Arab Spring—and ISIS 723
Tawakkol Karman—Nobel Lecture 725
Egyptian President-Elect Mohamed Morsi's Acceptance Speech 736
Islamic State—Proclamation of the Caliphate 744
The Tunisian National Dialogue Quartet—Nobel Lecture 752

Recent Revolutionary Disturbances 763
Resolution Establishing the House Select Committee to Investigate the January 6th Attack on the U.S. Capitol 765
Summary of Terrorism Threat to the U.S. Homeland 775
Remarks by President Biden One Year after the January 6 Assault on the U.S. Capitol 783
Global Leaders Condemn Assault on Brazilian Government Buildings 796

Appendixes
Chronological List 807
Web Resources 809
Bibliography 815

Index 829

■ Full Table of Contents

Volume 1

Publisher's Note vii
Editor's Introduction ix
Contributors. xi
Full Table of Contents xiii

The Dutch Revolt 1
Dutch Declaration of Independence 3

The English Revolution 21
Resolves by the English House of Commons regarding King Charles I and the Authority of the People. . . . 23
Reflection on the Glorious Revolution of 1688. 29

The American Revolution 35
John Hancock's Boston Massacre Oration 37
Declaration of the Causes and Necessity of Taking Up Arms 51
Give Me Liberty or Give Me Death 63
The Dominion of Providence over the Passions of Men. 74
Common Sense 85
Declaration of Independence 98
From the Commissioners for Negotiating a Peace with Great Britain 111

The French Revolution 125
Declaration of the Rights of Man and of the Citizen 127
Reflections on the Revolution in France. 138
Olympe de Gouges: Declaration of the Rights of Woman and of the Female Citizen 153
Maximilien Robespierre on the Ideals of the French Revolution 164

The Wider Americas in the Nineteenth Century. 179
Haitian Declaration of Independence. 181
Cartagena Manifesto 190
Simón Bolívar: Address at Angostura 205

Treaty of Córdoba..212
Documents relating to the Canadian Rebellions, 1837-1838.........................220
Benito Juárez on *La Reforma*..233
Montecristi Manifesto...241

The European Revolutions of 1848—Before and After..............................253
June Rebellion of 1832 as described in *Les Misérables* (1862)....................255
The Communist Manifesto..270
Louis Kossuth—Speech at a Dinner Given in His Honor by the U.S. Congress in Washington, D.C.....281
Manifesto of the Paris Commune...290
King Victor Emmanuel II: Address to Parliament..................................299

Japan and Korea..307
Meiji Charter Oath..309
Korean Declaration of Independence..315

The Mexican Revolution..323
Plan de San Luis de Potosi...325
Plan of Ayala..332

Ireland..341
John Morley on Irish Home Rule..343
Proclamation of the Provisional Government of the Irish Republic..........361

The Russian Revolution..369
What Is to Be Done?..371
Vladimir Lenin on the Tasks of the Soviet Government.......................389
Soviets in Action..395

Volume 2

Full Table of Contents ix

India 411
Karl Marx on British Rule in India 413
Government of India Act 424
Mohandas Gandhi: Statement at Trial 443
Jawaharlal Nehru's Speech on the Occasion of Indian Independence 453

China 461
Sun Yat-sen: "The Three Stages of Revolution" 463
"The Chinese People Have Stood Up!" 469
Mao Zedong on Communism and Counterrevolution 477
Letter from a Chinese "Rusticant" 491
U.S. Embassy Cables Concerning the Crackdown in Tiananmen Square 497

Mid-Century Rebels 505
¡No Pasarán! ("They Shall Not Pass!") 507
Mau Mau Warrior Oath 513
Fidel Castro's Speech at Twenty-One Nations Conference 516
Second Declaration of Havana 523

Vietnam—and Cambodia 529
Geneva Accords on Indochina 531
"The Path of Revolution in the South" 550
CIA Memo on National Liberation Front Methods 559
Message from Ho Chi Minh 566
The Paris Peace Accords 571
Story from the Khmer Rouge Killing Fields 581

Mid-East Revolts and Revolutions in the Twentieth Century .587
Proclamation of the Young Turks 589
Proclamation of the Algerian National Liberation Front 596
CIA Summary of the Overthrow of Premier Mossadeq of Iran 604
Gamal Abdel Nasser on the Nationalization of the Suez Canal 614
Ayatollah Khomeini on "The Great Satan" 623
Diary Excerpts of an American Hostage in Iran 633

The Revolt against Communism in Europe 639
Resolution of Hungarian Student Protestors 641
The "Two Thousand Words" Manifesto 648
Charter 77 655
CIA Cable on the Situation in Poland 663
Egon Krenz Letter to Mikhail Gorbachev. 670
Gorbachev's Farewell Address 675

Other Modern Revolutionary Changes 683
Corazon Aquino on Achieving Peace through Peaceful Means 685
Nelson Mandela—Nobel Peace Prize Acceptance Speech 692
Hugo Chávez Speech in Havana 700

Ukraine—the Orange Revolution 709
Inaugural Speech by Ukrainian President Viktor Yushchenko 711
Remarks by Yulia Tymoshenko after Her Release from Prison. 717

Arab Spring—and ISIS. 723
Tawakkol Karman—Nobel Lecture 725
Egyptian President-Elect Mohamed Morsi's Acceptance Speech 736
Islamic State—Proclamation of the Caliphate 744
The Tunisian National Dialogue Quartet—Nobel Lecture 752

Recent Revolutionary Disturbances. 763
Resolution Establishing the House Select Committee to Investigate the January 6th Attack on the
    U.S. Capitol. 765
Summary of Terrorism Threat to the U.S. Homeland. 775
Remarks by President Biden One Year after the January 6 Assault on the U.S. Capitol 783
Global Leaders Condemn Assault on Brazilian Government Buildings 796

Appendixes
Chronological List 807
Web Resources. 809
Bibliography 815

Index 829

India

Having been founded in 1600, by the mid-1700s the British East India Company was a dominant force in India, particularly as the Moghul empire began to decline. In 1857 a mutiny against the company, which maintained its own army, led to a wider rebellion that caused the British government to force the company's closure and assume direct responsibility for the vast colonial apparatus it had built up in India over the past two centuries. The British Raj, as it was called, introduced massive changes to Indian society, especially in the areas of civil administration, education, and business enterprise; and yet India remained resolutely Indian, in all its complexity. Discontent with British rule grew as the twentieth century progressed.

In 1919 the country's largest political party, the Indian National Congress, in league with the independence leader Mohandas K. Gandhi, succeeded in winning some key concessions from Britain in the form of the Government of India Act. Still, self-government was the goal of Gandhi's nonviolent resistance movement. He was aided in the Congress party by Jawaharlal Nehru, and both leaders also liaised with the head of the next most influential party, the Muslim League's Muhammad Ali Jinnah. Gandhi was put on trial by British authorities for some of his civil disobedience actions, but this only heightened the resolve of his followers to achieve independence. A broad Quit India movement took hold during World War II, even as the British crown instituted a set of power-sharing arrangements.

By the end of the war Britain was ready to be rid of its largest colonial enterprise. The question of independence was complicated, however, by the Muslim League's insistence that a separate state for Muslim's be established, in order to secure their future in the predominantly Hindu subcontinent. Independence finally came in 1947, along with the partition of India. Nehru headed the new Indian nation, and Jinnah ruled the newly created Pakistan. In the mass migration of populations that the split entailed, over a million people died due to ethnic and/or sectarian clashes.

Karl Marx on British Rule in India

Date: June 25 and August 8, 1853
Author: Karl Marx
Genre: newspaper articles

Summary Overview

In 1853, the future of the British East India Company was debated in the British Parliament. The government had long been concerned that the company's profit-making motives conflicted with its ability to rule the subcontinent fairly and in the interests of the Indian people. Eventually the government passed the Charter Act of 1853, limiting the power and the future of the East India Company in its governance of India.

Karl Marx was working at the time as the London correspondent for the New-York Daily Tribune, *his notoriety then only barely established outside academic circles. The* Tribune *articles often served as outlets for expressions of his political viewpoints, and the debate over the future of British rule in India excited his philosophical sensibilities. Aggravated with the hypocrisy of the debate—a debate he saw, not incorrectly, as one about whether the pillage of South Asia would be continued under the aegis of a private company or by the British government—Marx poured his vitriol into several articles detailing the nature of British colonialism, of which this one is the most famous and representative. Despite his displays of bigotry, hyperbole, and ignorance of Indian culture, Marx was an incisive commentator on the British Empire in general, and these articles contributed to his critique of imperialism as a function of the exploitation of capitalism.*

Defining Moment

The Company of Merchants of London Trading into the East Indies – the English (later British) East India Company – won a royal charter from Queen Elizabeth I in 1600, established with the goal of exploiting the lucrative spice trade to be found among South Asia's many kingdoms and principalities. The company built several "factories", or protected trading stations, along the Indian coastline, and located its lead factory in Calcutta, a town they built largely themselves for the purpose. The Company became prosperous bringing cotton cloth, spices, teas, opium and gems out of India and introducing other crops to the subcontinent, despite wars and famines in India and the anger of wool merchants in Britain itself. By the mid-eighteenth century, the British East India Company (BEIC) was the most prosperous corporation in India, and perhaps the world.

The Company's position in India was always precarious, however. Despised by the Mughal emperor Aurangzeb and facing competition from other European corporations, the BEIC negotiated its way between warring factions among the Indians and had to maintain an army of its own to protect itself. In 1757, a Company soldier named Robert Clive won a battle over the Nawab of Bengal at Plassey, outside Calcutta, to assert the BEIC as the dominant European company left trading in India. However, since the Nawab was now displaced, the Company had to assert

Flag of the East India Company, 1801-1858. Image via Wikimedia Commons. [Public domain.]

Coat of arms of the East India Company. Image via Wikimedia Commons. [Public domain.]

governmental responsibility over Bengal in order to maintain a steady and peaceful trade in the region. Like any government, the Company levied taxes; unlike every government, these taxes crushed the impoverished population of Bengal, many of whom were left landless and thus starving in a famine of the Company's making. As a result, the British government altered its charter with the British East India Company and began appointing governors-general to watch over the Company's affairs and the people they ruled over. The British Empire in India had become formal.

Over the next century, the British East India Company fought wars in India, forged alliances, established new trading relationships and picked up new populations to govern; by 1849, the Company was the most powerful governing entity in the subcontinent. It dominated a swathe of territory from the borders of modern-day Iran to modern-day Thailand, and from Tibet south to the Indian Ocean, and the Company held protective rights over those principalities that it did not govern directly. At the same time, the British government back in London became increasingly uncomfortable with the Company's government over the world's second largest population in its name – as if Exxon ran Saudi Arabia, Iraq, and Iran today in the name of the United States. In 1813 they ended the Company's monopoly on British trade from India; in 1833 they demanded that the Company cease trading altogether and concentrate on the proper governance of the Indian people. Concern over responsibility for such an impoverished population was intense in Victorian Britain, a state which saw its empire as an outgrowth of a Christian mission to extend the benefits of Western civilization to peoples all over the world. Yet no one talked about leaving the Indian people to govern themselves; the idea of decolonization was unthinkable in an era of European power politics where colonies were the measure of great power status.

In 1853, debate over the Company's future centered on a renewal of its charter, a regular action taken every twenty years over the course of the Company's history since 1600. No major changes were made to the charter, but debate centered around how long the charter should last – many politicians believed it was time for the British crown to pay off the Company's investors and take over the permanent management of India themselves. The idea of a profit-making entity, however emasculated, governing a vast section of the world's population was unseemly. In the end, the Company's charter was renewed, but without an expiration date – meaning the Company could either last forever governing India with the expressed consent and protection of the British Empire, or – as proved to be the case – its contract could be canceled and the Company disbanded at any time. The Company's days were numbered.

However, no one seemed to think that Britain's days governing India were similarly limited. In reality, the replacement of the Company's rule with formal British rule from London meant only that India's riches could be exploited by many corporations operating in the subcontinent under the Union Jack's responsibility, as opposed to just one. This fact was ignored by most observers, but not by the London correspondent to the *New-York Daily Tribune*, Karl Marx.

At the time, Marx was a relatively little known philosopher, struggling to make a living by writing articles on events as he saw them reported in London, then the biggest and most important city in the world and Marx's home. In reporting on the debates over the Charter Act of 1853, Marx expounded on his ideas on colonial exploitation – that expansion into new markets was a function of the insistence on giving low wages to workers at home, making them an inadequate market for goods. Colonies were captive markets, established to create new outlets for the sale of product and avoid having to raise wages for workers closer to home. Furthermore, colonies provided outlets for surplus population, and sources of cheap natural resources to provide a means of further economic expansion. Though he never came up with a formal theory of colonialism, his articles addressing British India became famous among his works, especially in the postcolonial world, where they offered a template for describing why former colonies were still dependent upon the developed even after the colonizers had gone home.

Author Biography

Karl Marx was born May 5, 1818 in Trier, a city in the Prussian Rhineland near the French border. His father was a lawyer, and Karl himself went to school to study law as well, but became more interested in philosophy, obtaining a doctorate in philosophy in 1841. Instead of working at a university, Marx became a journalist, moving to Paris in 1843. There he met Friedrich Engels, a German whose interest in the concept of communism – an ideology dedicated to achieving economic equality in the context of a societal commune – mirrored his own. Marx and Engels would be associated as journalists, writers and underground politicians for the rest of Marx's life, and Engels became his long-time benefactor, funneling profits from the textile factory he managed in Manchester, England to support Marx while he wrote treatises and articles on communism.

In 1848, Marx and Engels published a pamphlet explaining the principles of communism to interested parties, The Communist Manifesto. According to them, the history of the world was a history of a struggle between different economic units in society, called classes, over who controlled the profits of the average person's labor. The time was rapidly approaching when the final conflict between classes was to occur, when industrial workers themselves would overthrow the power of their managers and owners and establish a society based in equality, or

Company painting depicting an official of the East India Company, c. 1760. Company paintings were made in India by Indian artists, many of whom worked for European patrons in 18th and 19th centuries, blending traditional and Western elements. Image via Wikimedia Commons. [Public domain.]

communism. The Manifesto was not a bestseller. Yet over the following two decades, Marx published more newspaper articles and books about his ideas on communism and became a prominent member of the International Workingmen's Association. With his growing public profile, the Communist Manifesto became a popular read, particularly as it had been published in 1848, a year of revolution in Europe. It remains Marx's easiest delineation of his ideas for the general public to digest.

In 1849, Marx moved to London, where he and his family spent the rest of their lives living in genteel poverty. Marx worked as a newspaper correspondent and editor, most famously for the *New-York Daily Tribune*, and Engels supplemented Marx's meager income with a stipend. During the 1850s and 1860s, he worked on a long-term study of the history of industrial economics and the working classes exploited within them, called *Capital* (or *Das Kapital* in Ger-

The East India House, painted by Thomas Malton, 1800. Image via Wikimedia Commons. [Public domain.]

man, the language in which it was written). The first volume came out in 1867. By that time, Marx had become a prominent member of the International Workingmen's Association, commonly called the First International, and was placed in charge of writing up the organization's political platform. In this role, he was able to expound on his ideas in *Capital* and *The Communist Manifesto* to a wide and sympathetic audience. It was in this manner that he became a socialist intellectual famous across Europe for his critique of capitalism.

In 1870, the people of Paris launched a revolt against their government for surrendering to the Prussians and ending the Franco-Prussian War. Since many of the rebels were artisans, factory workers and other urbanites whom Marx considered members of the working classes, he and other socialists held out some hope that the Parisians' establishment of what they called a "commune" was the beginning of the worldwide communist revolution. While the Parisians were probably influenced by the First International, however, they had no interest in communism and the revolt collapsed within six months. The First International fell apart itself in Europe by 1873; simultaneously, Marx's health went into decline. He died in 1883.

Historical Document

Karl Marx on British Rule in India

...How came it that English supremacy was established in India? The paramount power of the Great Mogul was broken by the Mogul Viceroys. The power of the Viceroys was broken by the Mahrattas. The power of the Mahrattas was broken by the Afghans, and while all were struggling against all, the Briton rushed in and was enabled to subdue them all. A country not only divided between Mahommedan and Hindoo, but between tribe and tribe, between caste and caste; a society whose framework was based on a sort of equilibrium, resulting from a general repulsion and constitutional exclusiveness between all its members. Such a country and such a society, were they not the predestined prey of conquest? If we knew nothing of the past history of Hindostan, would there not be the one great and incontestable fact, that even at this moment India is held in English thraldom by an Indian army maintained at the cost of India? India, then, could not escape the fate of being conquered, and the whole of her past history, if it be anything, is the history of the successive conquests she has undergone. Indian society has no history at all, at least no known history. What we call its history, is but the history of the successive intruders who founded their empires on the passive basis of that unresisting and unchanging society. The question, therefore, is not whether the English had a right to conquer India, but whether we are to prefer India conquered by the Turk, by the Persian, by the Russian, to India conquered by the Briton.

England has to fulfill a double mission in India: one destructive, the other regenerating the annihilation of old Asiatic society, and the laying the material foundations of Western society in Asia.

Arabs, Turks, Tartars, Moguls, who had successively overrun India, soon became Hindooized, the barbarian conquerors being, by an eternal law of history, conquered themselves by the superior civilization of their subjects. The British were the first conquerors superior, and therefore, inaccessible to Hindoo civilization. They destroyed it by breaking up the native communities, by uprooting the native industry, and by levelling all that was great and elevated in the native society. The historic pages of their rule in India report hardly anything beyond that destruction. The work of regeneration hardly transpires through a heap of ruins. Nevertheless it has begun.

The political unity of India, more consolidated, and extending farther than it ever did under the Great Moguls, was the first condition of its regeneration. That unity, imposed by the British sword, will now be strengthened and perpetuated by the electric telegraph. The native army, organized and trained by the British drill-sergeant, was the sine qua non of Indian self-emancipation, and of India ceasing to be the prey of the first foreign intruder. The free press, introduced for the first time into Asiatic society, and managed principally by the common offspring of Hindoos and Europeans, is a new and powerful agent of reconstruction. The Zemindari and Ryotwar themselves, abominable as they are, involve two distinct forms of private property in land—the great desideratum of Asiatic society. From the Indian natives, reluctantly and sparingly educated at Calcutta, under English superintendence, a fresh class is springing up, endowed with the requirements for government and imbued with European science. Steam has brought India into regular and rapid communication with Europe, has connected its chief ports with those of the whole south-eastern ocean, and has revindicated it from the isolated position which was the prime law of its stagnation. The day is not far distant when, by a combination of railways and steam-vessels, the distance between England and India, measured by time, will be shortened to eight days, and when that once fabulous country will thus be actually annexed to the Western world.

The ruling classes of Great Britain have had, till now, but an accidental, transitory and exceptional interest in the progress of India. The aristocracy wanted to conquer it, the moneyocracy to plunder it, and the millocracy to undersell it. But now the tables are turned. The millocracy have discovered that the transformation of India into a reproductive country has become of vital importance to them, and that, to that end, it is necessary, above all, to gift her with means of irrigation and of internal communication. They intend now drawing a net of railroads over India. And they will do it. The results must be inappreciable.

It is notorious that the productive powers of India are paralysed by the utter want of means for conveying and exchanging its various produce. Nowhere, more than in India, do we meet with social destitution in the midst of natural plenty, for want of the means of exchange. It was proved before a Committee of the British House of Commons, which sat in 1848, that

"when grain was selling from 6/- to 8/- a quarter at Khandesh, it was sold at 64/ to 70/- at Poona, where the people were dying in the streets of famine, without the possibility of gaining supplies from Khandesh, because the clay-roads were impracticable."

The introduction of railroads may be easily made to subserve agricultural purposes by the formation of tanks, where ground is required for embankment, and by the conveyance of water along the different lines. Thus irrigation, the sine qua non of farming in the East, might be greatly extended, and the frequently recurring local famines, arising from the want of water, would be averted. The general importance of railways, viewed under this head, must become evident, when we remember that irrigated lands, even in the districts near Ghauts, pay three times as much in taxes, afford ten or twelve times as much employment, and yield twelve or fifteen times as much profit, as the same area without irrigation.

Railways will afford the means of diminishing the amount and the cost of the military establishments. Col. Warren, Town Major of the Fort St. William, stated before a Select Committee of the House of Commons:

"The practicability of receiving intelligence from distant parts of the country, in as many hours as at present it requires days and even weeks, and of sending instructions, with troops and stores, in the more brief period, are considerations which cannot be too highly estimated. Troops could be kept at more distant and healthier stations than at present, and much loss of life from sickness would by this means be spared. Stores could not to the same extent he required at the various depots, and. the loss by decay, and the destruction incidental to the climate, would also be avoided. The number of troops might be diminished in direct proportion to their effectiveness."

We know that the municipal organization and the economical basis of the village communities has been broken up, but their worst feature, the dissolution of society into stereotype and disconnected atoms, has survived their vitality. The village isolation produced the absence of roads in India, and the absence of roads perpetuated the village isolation. On this plan a community existed with a given scale of low conveniences, almost without intercourse with other villages, without the desires and efforts indispensable to social advance. The British having broken up this self-sufficient inertia of the villages, railways will provide the new want of communication and intercourse. Besides,

"one of the effects of the railway system will he to bring into every village affected by it such knowledge of the contrivances and appliances of other countries, and such means of obtaining them, as will first put the hereditary and stipendiary village artisanship of India to full proof of its capabilities, and then supply its defects." (Chapman, *The Cotton and Commerce of India* [pp. 95-97].)

I know that the English millocracy intend to endow India with railways with the exclusive view of extracting at diminished expenses the cotton and other raw materials for their manufactures. But when you have once introduced machinery into the locomotion of a country, which possesses iron and coals, you are unable to withhold it from its fabrication. You cannot maintain a net of railways over an immense country without introducing all those industrial processes necessary to meet the immediate and current wants of railway locomotion, and out of which there must grow the application of machinery to those branches of industry not immediately connected with railways. The railway-system will therefore become, in India, truly the forerunner of modern industry. This is the more certain as the Hindoos are allowed by British authorities themselves to possess particular aptitude for accommodating themselves to entirely new labor, and acquiring the requisite knowledge of machinery. Ample proof of this fact is afforded by the capacities and expertness of the native engineers in the Calcutta mint, where they have been for years employed in working the steam machinery, by the natives attached to the several steam engines in the Burdwan coal districts, and by other instances. Mr. Campbell himself, greatly influenced as he is by the prejudices of the East India Company, is obliged to avow

"that the great mass of the Indian people possesses a great industrial energy, is well fitted to accumulate capital, and remarkable for a mathematical clearness of head and talent for figures and exact sciences." "Their intellects," he says, "are excellent."

Modern industry, resulting from the railway system, will dissolve the hereditary divisions of labor, upon which rest the Indian castes, those decisive impediments to Indian progress and Indian power.

All the English bourgeoisie may be forced to do will neither emancipate nor materially mend the social condition of the mass of the people, depending not only on the development of the productive powers, but on their appropriation by the people. But what they will not fail to do is to lay down the material premises for both. Has the bourgeoisie ever done more? Has it ever effected a progress without dragging individuals and people through blood and dirt, through misery and degradation?

The Indians will not reap the fruits of the new elements of society scattered among them by the British bourgeoisie, till in Great Britain itself the now ruling classes shall have been supplanted by the industrial proletariat, or till the Hindoos themselves shall have grown strong enough to throw off the English yoke altogether. ...

I cannot part with the subject of India without some concluding remarks.

The profound hypocrisy and inherent barbarism of bourgeois civilization lies unveiled before our eyes, turning from its home, where it assumes respectable forms, to the colonies, where it goes naked. They are the defenders of property, but did any revolutionary party ever originate agrarian revolutions like those in Bengal, in Madras, and in Bombay? Did they not, in India, to borrow an expression of that great robber, Lord Clive himself, resort to atrocious extortion, when simple corruption could not keep pace with their rapacity? While they prated in Europe about the inviolable sanctity of the national debt, did they not confiscate in India the dividends of the rajahs, 171 who had invested their private savings in the Company's own funds? While they combatted the French revolution under the pretext of defending "our holy religion," did they not forbid, at the same time, Christianity to be propagated in India, and did they not, in order to make money out of the pilgrims streaming to the temples of Orissa and Bengal, take up the trade in the murder and prostitution perpetrated in the temple of juggernaut? These are the men of "Property, Order, Family, and Religion."

The devastating effects of English industry, when contemplated with regard to India, a country as vast as Europe, and containing 150 millions of acres, are palpable and confounding. But we must not forget that they are only the organic results of the whole system of production as it is now constituted. That production rests on the supreme rule of capital. The centralization of capital is essential to the existence of capital as an independent power. The destructive influence of that centralization upon the markets of the world does but reveal, in the most gigantic dimensions, the inherent organic laws of political economy now at work in every civilized town. The bourgeois period of history has to create the material basis of the new world—on the one hand universal intercourse founded upon the mutual dependency of mankind, and the means of that intercourse; on the other hand, the development of the productive powers of man and the transformation of material production into a scientific domination of natural agencies. Bourgeois industry and commerce create these material conditions of a new world in the same way as geological revolutions have created the surface of the earth. When a great social revolution shall have mastered the results of the bourgeois epoch, the market of the world and the modern powers of production and subjected them to the common control of the most advanced peoples, then only will human progress cease to resemble that hideous, pagan idol, who would not drink the nectar but from the skulls of the slain.

Glossary

Hindoo: Hindu (in Marx's terms, anyone not a Muslim in the British colony)

Hindostan: India; the colloquial British term for the colony in South Asia. There was no such place as "India"—a Muslim term for the land of Hindus—until the British colony drew its boundaries in the eighteenth and nineteenth centuries

Mahommedan: Muslim

Millocracy: in this context, wealthy British producers of textiles, churned out in mills. Marx is condemning them for forcing Indian cotton textile producers out of business in order to force the Indian people to buy British cotton products

prated: babbled on and on

temple of juggernaut: a vastly large, moving wagon which Hindus prayed before as it moved, often crushing its devotees to death; from it, we gained the concept of a "juggernaut" as an unstoppable, powerful force sweeping everything before it beneath its wheels

Zemindari and Ryotwar: land taxes collected in various Hindu states

Document Analysis

It is interesting that the *New-York Daily Tribune*, a Whig and later Democratic Party organ in the United States, should publish an almost-obscure German communist philosopher's articles on news from Britain. Under Horace Greeley, the owner and editor of the *Tribune*, the paper was idealistic and responsible in tone, in comparison to its more sensationalist competitors. As a result of this reputation, in the 1850s, the *Tribune* was the most widely read newspaper in the United States. Greeley himself was somewhat Anglophobic, so his newspaper's relationship to the acerbic Marx was one of mutual support. Marx would remain the *Tribune*'s London correspondent for an astounding ten years, criticizing the economic society he saw around him, delineating his ideas on socialism, and apparently receiving editorial approval and a paycheck for doing it.

Marx opens by describing how the British came to be a major power in India in the eighteenth century. The Mughal Empire was the dominant Muslim empire in northern and central India from 1522 on. In the eighteenth century it faced rebellions from its allies and eventually was reduced in power when destroyed in an invasion by Punjabis from Afghanistan in 1733. Under these circumstances, the British East India Company remained neutral, lending money, weapons and even soldiers to any warring prince willing to put up his principality as collateral for the loan. When said loans defaulted, as they often did, the Company became the *de facto* ruler over numerous former principalities in South Asia. Marx notes that South Asia is politically, religiously, culturally and socially inclined toward entropy – in point of fact, there was no such place as "India" until the British colonized it with an army and drew its borders, because its people had generally divided into different empires, states, religions, castes, ethnicities and the like. Marx believes that such divisions inclined India to be ripe for conquest, that as a result, "Indian society has no history at all, at least no known history. What we call its history, is but the history of the successive intruders who founded their empires on the passive basis of that unresisting and unchanging society."

At least, in Marx's opinion, it was better that it be conquered by the British than by Turks, Persians or Russians. The British were a people of a higher civilization, the first to conquer India and not be assimilated into the Hindu population, religion and culture. Despite his prejudices, however, Marx sympathized with the Indian people, seeing their civilization destroyed "by breaking up the native communities, by uprooting the native industry, and by levelling all that was great and elevated in the native society." His hope and expectation was that unity under British rule would be enhanced by representations of modernity like the telegraph, the Indian Army, a free press, the introduction of private property, western education and steam power.

Yet he notes that unity is a condition that the British intend to design and exploit for their own profit. For example, crisscrossing the Indian countryside with railroads was merely a means of getting goods to and from market in India, with no intent to better the lot of the Indian people themselves. This was especially rapacious considering the regular famines that swept the subcontinent, as cheap food exchanges were impossible without railroads being built expressly for the purpose of food distribution (in Marx's example, between Khandesh and Poona). Likewise, irrigation canals could be built, particularly by army troops who would otherwise be sitting around doing nothing–"The number of troops might be diminished in direct proportion to their effectiveness"–yet creating the means to improve agricultural and textile production would create competition for British goods in Indian markets, and no official involved with British India wanted that.

Nevertheless, Marx believed that the railroad had the potential to break down British economic power in India by forcing railroad builders to use Indian resources to build the rails; "The railway-system will therefore become, in India, truly the forerunner of modern industry." The Indians themselves responded positively to the development of a rail system, however exploitative, and the rail system surely held the power to break down Hindu castes, "those decisive impediments to Indian progress and Indian power." Yet, as Marx notes, the Indian people–indeed the British working classes too–would never benefit truly from the development of the railroad until they overthrew the power of the ruling classes.

Marx concludes by damning the hypocrisy of British rule in India, whether it be by the British East India Company or the government itself, as seemed to be imminent in 1853. For all their complaints, members of parliament obviously had no intention of affecting land reform in South Asia, stemming corruption, reducing Indian debt (the 171 rajahs he referred to were princes who had lost their land to the Company as collateral for loans) or spreading Christianity–"These are the men of 'Property, Order, Family, and Religion.'" He makes a logical argument against the sanctity of capital and industrialism; he admits they were necessary to create a modern society. Yet once "a great social revolution shall have mastered the results of the bourgeois epoch, …then only will human progress cease to resemble that hideous, pagan idol, who would not drink the nectar but from the skulls of the slain."

Essential Themes

Four years after Marx wrote his articles, he would find himself commenting on a vast rebellion launched by Indian soldiers, or *sepoys*, in northern and central India in 1857. The British referred to the rebellion as a "mutiny", a somewhat contemptuous term in that it assumed that the Indian people owed the British their loyalty and obedience. British officers were able to command enough loyalty and obedience that the rebellion was put down by 1858, but British East India Company rule over India was over. The Company was dissolved and the British government made its territories in South Asia into a crown colony, which they would continue to exploit economically until 1947.

In his *Daily Tribune* articles on the rebellion, Marx held out little hope for its success, but it certainly signaled to him the Indian people's desire to throw off the shackles of British rule in favor of a more egalitarian political and economic organization of their resources, in line with his own ideas on socialism. He believed that modernization had improved Indian civilization, and in *Capital* he hoped for a continued breakdown of traditional Hindu caste structures and political despotism that might lead to revolution. Indeed, after the failure of the Paris Commune in 1871, he essentially gave up on the idea of a political revolution happening in favor of communism in the western world, at least any time soon. Places like India–and Russia, for that matter–seemed potentially more likely to rise in revolt than the industrial states of Britain or Germany that he had targeted earlier.

Marx died in 1883. Within two decades, his ideas on socialism and communist revolution had been marginalized to the radical fringe in European politics, while other socialists who were willing to work within parliamentary and legal structures became more prominent. It was only with the Bolshevik Revolution of 1917 that Marx's name regained renown in European intellectual circles–an "accident of history", as one historian referred to it. As adherents to communism began to dig into his writings, Marx's *Tribune* articles on India gained consideration as his most articulate pronouncements on imperialism, especially when coupled with the growing popularity of communism in the colonial world throughout the twentieth century.

—David Simonelli, PhD

Bibliography and Additional Reading

Anderson, Kevin B. *Marx at the Margins: On Nationalism, Ethnicity, and Non-Western Societies*. Chicago: University of Chicago Press, 2010.

Bartolovich, Crystal, and Neil Lazarus, eds. *Marxism, Modernity and Postcolonial Studies*. New York: Cambridge UP, 2002.

Husain, Iqbal, Editor. *Karl Marx on India: From the New York Daily Tribune (Including Articles by Frederick Engels)*. New Delhi: Tulika Books, 2006.

Marxists Internet Archive www.marxists.org/index.htm.

Government of India Act

Date: 1919
Authors: Edwin Montagu; Frederic John Napier Thesiger, 3rd Baron Chelmsford
Genre: law

Summary Overview

The Government of India Act of 1919 was the latest in a series of acts passed by the British parliament to define the structure of government and administration in Great Britain's chief colony, India. A total of sixteen other Government of India Acts were passed by Parliament. The chief purpose of the 1919 act was to allow the people of India greater participation in their own government. Toward this end, it created a dyarchy, or a dual form of government, with power shared by the Crown and provincial authorities. The Government of India Act of 1919 relinquished to provincial councils Britain's control of some areas of government, such as agriculture, education, and health, while other areas of government, such as foreign policy, justice, communications, and the military, remained under the authority of Great Britain through its appointed viceroy of India. The act also enlarged and reformed the Imperial Legislative Council, transforming it into a bicameral (two-house) legislature. Both the lower house, called the Legislative Assembly, and the upper house, called the Council of States, would consist of elected and appointed members. The 1919 legislation served to enact reforms that had been suggested by Edwin Montagu, the secretary of state for India, and Frederic Thesiger, Lord Chelmsford, the viceroy of India, in the wake of growing dissatisfaction with British rule and a blossoming independence movement in India.

Defining Moment

The context for the 1919 Government of India Act stretches back to the early years of the seventeenth century, when Queen Elizabeth I chartered the British East India Company and granted it perpetual trading rights in India. Throughout the seventeenth and eighteenth centuries, the East India Company drove out its French competitors, eclipsed its Dutch competitors, and defeated Bengalese forces that were allied with the French. When the dust settled, the East India Company had consolidated its hold on India and was the de facto ruler of some two-thirds of the nation. It carried on lucrative trade in such commodities as silk, cotton, indigo dye, tea, saltpeter, and opium, in large part by striking alliances with local rulers.

In the late eighteenth and early nineteenth centuries, however, charges of corruption, bribery, and abuse were leveled against the East India Company, causing Parliament to pass legislation designed to rein in the company's activities. Despite these attempts at reform, discontent with British rule in India simmered for years. It boiled over in 1857 when the *sepoys*, or Indian soldiers serving under the British, revolted in what is variously called the Sepoy Mutiny (or Sepoy Rebellion), the Great Rebellion, or, among Indians, the First War of Indian Independence. Indians believed that the British wanted to westernize them and convert them to Christianity. The revolt erupted on May 10, 1857, among sepoys stationed near Bengal, and soon sepoy garrisons at several other cities, notably Delhi and Kanpur, mutinied, in some instances with the backing of civilians. Over the following year, British forces regrouped, gained control of the cities where sepoys had revolted, and reasserted the authority of the East India Company, finally quashing the revolt on June 20, 1858. The conflict was bloody, and British forces felt justified in retaliating. Entire villages were wiped out, and mutineers were put to death.

In the aftermath of the Sepoy Rebellion, Britain abolished the East India Company and made efforts to create more of a cooperative relationship with Indians. The army was restructured to include more Indians, and no efforts were made to impose Christianity on Indians or to interfere further with traditional religious beliefs and social practices. The British created a complex governmental and administrative structure that came to be called the British *Raj*—a Hindustani word meaning "reign." A secretary of state for India and a Council of India oversaw the administration of the colony. India was governed by a viceroy, but other governmental officials oversaw affairs in India's various regions with the help of Indian officials who served in an advisory capacity. Additionally, a number of so-called princely states were recognized. Meanwhile, the Indian economy developed rapidly as the British built an economic infrastructure, including schools, irrigation projects, and roads. In 1876, England's Queen Victoria was given the title of empress of India.

Britain at this point had no intention of relinquishing control of India. The colony provided valuable raw materials and an export market for British-made goods. Nevertheless, concessions were made. The Indian Councils Act of 1892 allowed Indians a voice in provincial legislation. Matters began to turn sour, though, in 1895, when the British imposed an excise tax on Indian cotton, enriching Britain at India's expense. Then in 1899, George Curzon became India's viceroy. Curzon would unwittingly foment growing dissatisfaction through two measures.

The first of these was the Indian Universities Act of 1904, which gave Britain control over all Indian colleges and universities. The other measure was enacted in 1905, when Curzon partitioned Bengal into two provinces in an effort to curb the political activism—and acts of terrorism—there. The results of Curzon's arbitrary and heavy-handed decisions were demonstrations and a boycott of goods manufactured in Britain, particularly in England's cotton mills. More significant, the viceroy's actions started to turn the Indian National Congress, a political party established in 1885, into a nationalist movement. One of the chief figures in that movement was a young Mohandas K. Gandhi, who would become a worldwide symbol of nonviolent resistance to colonial rule.

In an effort to solve the crisis, the Crown replaced Curzon. After discussions in 1909 Parliament passed another Indian Councils Act, which is also referred to as the Morley-Minto reforms after its authors, John Morley, the secretary of state for India, and Gilbert Elliot-Murray-Kynynmond, Fourth Earl of Minto, India's governor-general. This act provided for Indian membership in provincial executive councils and enlarged the Imperial Legislative Council to give Indians greater political representation. In 1911 the partition of Bengal was reversed, and recommendations were made to increase Indians' participation in government and the military. World War I put issues of Anglo-Indian cooperation on hold, but it also increased calls for greater independence. India made major contributions to the war effort, including monetary contributions of millions of pounds and the lives of some forty thousand soldiers who fought and died for Britain.

Throughout the war and afterward, political unrest in India grew. Militant activists in Bengal and Punjab backed insurrections and brought the provincial governments to a standstill. As conspiracies came to light, Britain passed the Defence of India Act in 1915 in an effort to curb revolutionary activities. In 1918 a sedition committee, chaired by Sydney Rowlatt, was formed to investigate possible links between Indian militants on the one hand and both German and Russian revolutionaries on the other; one such link came to be called the Hindu-German Conspiracy. Out of these investigations came the Rowlatt Act, passed in March 1919. The purpose of this repressive act was to strengthen and extend the Defence of India Act by exposing conspiracies and quelling civil unrest, which was being fomented by a combination of inflation, high taxes, a devastating flu epidemic, and disruption of trade because of the war. Unrest led to violence in the northern Indian city of Amritsar, which had been placed under martial law as a result of bombings, arson, and protest. On April 13, 1919, British troops opened fire on a religious gathering, according to official British estimates killing some 379 people and wounding 1,100 others in what has been called the Amritsar Massacre or, after the name of the park where it occurred, the Jallianwala Bagh Massacre. Indian authorities put the casualty figures much higher.

In light of these events, the new secretary of state for India, Edwin Montagu, acknowledged that Britain was in India's debt. Earlier, in August 1917, he had signaled a change in British policy in a declaration before the House of Commons:

> *The policy of His Majesty's Government, with which the Government of India are in complete accord, is that of the increasing association of Indians in every branch of the administration and the gradual development of self-governing institutions with a view to the progressive realization of responsible government in India, as an integral part of the British Empire.* (qtd. in Alam, p. 48)

He collaborated with India's viceroy, Lord Chelmsford, and in 1918 the two issued the Montagu-Chelmsford Report, which was submitted to Parliament in May 1918 and again in June of that year. Their recommendations formed the basis of the Government of India Act, passed into law in December 1919.

Author Biography

As with most legislation, identifying a particular author is difficult, for any bill is likely to be the work of numerous legislators. Further, because the Government of India Act of 1919 was in large part an amendment of earlier acts of Parliament, it contains provisions written by the authors of those earlier acts. Nonetheless, two authors stand out, for the bill essentially enacted the reforms suggested by Edwin Montagu, the secretary of state for India, and Lord Chelmsford, India's viceroy at the time. Their conclusions were presented to the British Parliament as the Montagu-Chelmsford Report, which formed the core of the 1919 act.

Edwin Samuel Montagu, only the second Jew ever to serve in the British cabinet, was born in 1879. He entered politics in 1906, when he was elected to a seat in Parliament. In the years that followed he served in a variety of government posts, including undersecretary of state for India from 1910 to 1914. In 1917 he was appointed secretary of state for India, a post he held until 1922. Montagu died in 1924.

Lord Chelmsford was Frederic John Napier Thesiger, 3rd Baron Chelmsford; he was elevated to the position of 1st Viscount Chelmsford in 1921. He was born in 1868. After completing his education at Oxford University and succeeding his father as Baron Chelmsford, he was appointed governor first of Queensland, Australia, and then of neighboring New South Wales. During World War I he commanded a regiment in India, and he was appointed viceroy of India in 1916, a post he held until 1921. His service in India coincided with massive unrest and the Amritsar Massacre, and he returned to England amid charges of incompetence. He spent the last years of his life retired from politics before his death in 1933.

Historical Document

Whereas it is the declared policy of Parliament to provide for the increasing association of Indians in every branch of Indian administration, and for the gradual development of self-governing institutions with a view to the progressive realisation of responsible government in British India as an integral part of the empire:

And whereas progress in giving effect to this policy can only be achieved by successive stages, and it is expedient that substantial steps in this direction should now be taken:

And whereas the time and manner of each advance can be determined only by Parliament, upon whom responsibility lies for the welfare and advancement of the Indian peoples:

And whereas the action of Parliament in such matters must be guided by the co-operation received from those on whom new opportunities of service will be conferred, and by the extent to which it is found that confidence can be reposed in their sense of responsibility:

And whereas concurrently with the gradual development of self-governing institutions in the Provinces of India it is expedient to give to those Provinces in provincial matters the largest measure of independence of the Government of India, which is compatible with the due discharge by the latter of its own responsibilities:

Be it therefore enacted by the King's most Excellent Majesty, by and with the advice and consent of the Lords Spiritual and Temporal, and Commons, in this present Parliament assembled, and by the authority of the same, as follows:—

Part I. Local Governments

1. (*1*) Provision may be made by rules under the Government of India Act, 1915, as amended by the Government of India (Amendment) Act, 1916 (which Act, as so amended, is in this Act referred to as "the principal Act")—

(*a*) for the classification of subjects, in relation to the functions of government, as central and provincial subjects, for the purpose of distinguishing the functions of local governments and local legislatures from the functions of the Governor-General in Council and the Indian legislature;

(b) for the devolution of authority in respect of provincial subjects to local governments, and for the allocation of revenues or other moneys to those governments;

(c) for the use under the authority of the Governor-General in Council of the agency of local governments in relation to central subjects, in so far as such agency may be found convenient, and for determining the financial conditions of such agency; and

(d) for the transfer from among the provincial subjects of subjects (in this Act referred to as "transferred subjects") to the administration of the governor acting with ministers appointed under this Act, and for the allocation of revenues or moneys for the purpose of such administration.

(2) Without prejudice to the generality of the foregoing powers, rules made for the abovementioned purposes may—

(i) regulate the extent and conditions of such devolution, allocation, and transfer;

(ii) provide for fixing the contributions payable by local governments to the Governor-General in Council, and making such contributions a first charge on allocated revenues or moneys;

(iii) provide for constituting a finance department in any province, and regulating the functions of that department;

(iv) provide for regulating the exercise of the authority vested in the local government of a province over members of the public services therein;

(v) provide for the settlement of doubts arising as to whether any matter does or does not relate to a provincial subject or a transferred subject, and for the treatment of matters which affect both a transferred subject and a subject which is not transferred; and

(vi) make such consequential and supplemental provisions as appear necessary or expedient:

Provided that, without prejudice to any general power of revoking or altering rules under the principal Act, the rules shall not authorise the revocation or suspension of the transfer of any subject except with the sanction of the Secretary of State in Council.

(3) The powers of superintendence, direction, and control over local governments vested in the Governor-General in Council under the principal Act

shall, in relation to transferred subjects, be exercised only for such purposes as may be specified in rules made under that Act, but the Governor-General in Council shall be the sole judge as to whether the purpose of the exercise of such powers in any particular case comes within the purposes so specified.

(4) The expressions "central subjects" and "provincial subjects" as used in this Act mean subjects so classified under the rules.

Provincial subjects, other than transferred subjects, are in this Act referred to as "reserved subjects."...

3. (1) The presidencies of Fort William in Bengal, Fort St. George, and Bombay, and the provinces known as the United Provinces, the Punjab, Bihar and Orissa, the Central Provinces, and Assam, shall each be governed, in relation to reserved subjects, by a governor in council, and in relation to transferred subjects (save as otherwise provided by this Act) by the governor acting with ministers appointed under this Act.

The said presidencies and provinces are in this Act referred to as "governor's provinces" and the two first-named presidencies are in this Act referred to as the presidencies of Bengal and Madras.

(2) The provisions of section forty-six to fifty-one of the principal Act, as amended by this Act, shall apply to the United Provinces, the Punjab, Bihar and Orissa, the Central Provinces, and Assam, as they apply to the presidencies of Bengal, Madras, and Bombay: Provided that the governors of the said provinces shall be appointed after consultation with the Governor-General.

4. (1) The governor of a governor's province may, by notification, appoint ministers, not being members of his executive council or other officials, to administer transferred subjects and any ministers so appointed shall hold office during his pleasure.

There may be paid to any minister so appointed in any province the same salary as is payable to a member of the executive council in that province, unless a smaller salary is provided by vote of the legislative council of the province.

(2) No minister shall hold office for a longer period than six months, unless he is or becomes an elected member of the local legislature.

(3) In relation to transferred subjects, the governor shall be guided by the advice of his ministers, unless he sees sufficient cause to dissent from their opinion, in which case he may require action to be taken otherwise than in accordance with that advice: Provided that rules may be made under the principal Act for the temporary administration of a transferred subject where, in cases of emergency, owing to a vacancy, there is no minister in charge of the

subject, by such authority and in such manner as may be prescribed by the rules.

(4) The governor of a governor's province may at his discretion appoint from among the non-official members of the local legislature council secretaries, who shall hold office during his pleasure, and discharge such duties in assisting members of the executive council and ministers, as he may assign to them.

There shall be paid to council secretaries so appointed such salary as may be provided by vote of the legislative council.

A council secretary shall cease to hold office if he ceases for more than six months to be a member of the legislative council....

10. (1) The local legislature of any province has power, subject to the provisions of this Act, to make laws for the peace and good government of the territories for the time being constituting that province.

(2) The local legislature of any province may, subject to the provisions of the sub-section next following, repeal or alter as to that province any law made either before or after the commencement of this Act by any authority in British India other than that local legislature.

(3) The local legislature of any province may not, without the previous sanction of the Governor-General, make or take into consideration any law—

(a) imposing or authorising the imposition of any new tax unless the tax is a tax scheduled as exempted from this provision by rules made under the principal Act; or

(b) affecting the public debt of India, or the customs duties, or any other tax or duty for the time being in force and imposed by the authority of the Governor-General in Council for the general purposes of the government of India, provided that the imposition or alteration of a tax scheduled as aforesaid shall not be deemed to affect any such tax or duty; or

(c) affecting the discipline or maintenance of any part of His Majesty's naval, military, or air forces; or

(d) affecting the relations of the government with foreign princes or states; or

(e) regulating any central subject; or

(f) regulating any provincial subject which has been declared by rules under the principal Act to be, either in whole or in part, subject to legislation by the

Indian legislature, in respect of any matter to which such declaration applies; or

(g) affecting any power expressly reserved to the Governor-General in Council by any law for the time being in force; or

(h) altering or repealing the provisions of any law which, having been made before the commencement of this Act by any authority in British India other than that local legislature, is declared by rules under the principal Act to be a law which cannot be repealed or altered by the local legislature without previous sanction; or

(i) altering or repealing any provision of an Act of the Indian legislature made after the commencement of this Act, which by the provisions of that Act may not be repealed or altered by the local legislature without previous sanction:

Provided that an Act or a provision of an Act made by a local legislature, and subsequently assented to by the Governor-General in pursuance of this Act, shall not be deemed invalid by reason only of its requiring the previous sanction of the Governor-General under this Act.

(4) The local legislature of any province has not power to make any law affecting any Act of Parliament....

13. (1) Where a governor's legislative council has refused leave to introduce, or has failed to pass in a form recommended by the governor, any Bill relating to a reserved subject the governor may certify that the passage of the Bill is essential for the discharge of his responsibility for the subject, and thereupon the Bill shall, notwithstanding that the council have not consented thereto, be deemed to have passed, and shall, on signature by the governor, become an Act of the local legislature in the form of the Bill as originally introduced or proposed to be introduced in the council or (as the case may be) in the form recommended to the council by the governor.

(2) Every such Act shall be expressed to be made by the governor, and the governor shall forthwith send an authentic copy thereof to the Governor-General, who shall reserve the Act for the signification of His Majesty's pleasure and upon the signification of such assent by His Majesty in Council, and the notification thereof by the Governor-General, the Act shall have the same force and effect as an Act passed by the local legislature and duly assented to:

Provided that where, in the opinion of the Governor-General a state of emergency exists which justifies such action, he may, instead of reserving such Act, signify his assent thereto, and thereupon the Act shall have such force and effect as aforesaid, subject however to disallowance by His Majesty in Council.

(3) An Act made under this section shall, as soon as practicable after being made, be laid before each House of Parliament, and an Act which is required to be presented for His Majesty's assent shall not be so presented until copies thereof have been laid before each House of Parliament for not less than eight days on which that House has sat....

15. (*1*) The Governor-General in Council may after obtaining an expression of opinion from the local government and the local legislature affected, by notification, with the sanction of His Majesty previously signified by the Secretary of State in Council, constitute a new governor's province, or place part of a governor's province under the administration of a deputy-governor to be appointed by the Governor-General, and may in any such case apply, with such modifications as appear necessary or desirable, all or any of the provisions of the principal Act or this Act relating to governors' provinces, or provinces under a lieutenant governor or chief commissioner, to any such new province or part of a province.

(2) The Governor-General in Council may declare any territory in British India to be a "backward tract," and may, by notification, with such sanction as aforesaid, direct that the principal Act and this Act shall apply to that territory subject to such exceptions and modifications as may be prescribed in the notification Where the Governor-General in Council has, by notification, directed as aforesaid, he may, by the same or subsequent notification, direct that any Act of the Indian legislature shall not apply to the territory in question or any part thereof, or shall apply to the territory or any part thereof subject to such exceptions or modifications as the Governor-General thinks fit, or may authorise the governor in council to give similar directions as respects any Act of the local legislature....

Part II. Government of India

17. Subject to the provisions of this Act, the Indian legislature shall consist of the Governor-General and two chambers, namely, the Council of State and the Legislative Assembly.

Except as otherwise provided by or under this Act, a Bill shall not be deemed to have been passed by the Indian legislature unless it has been agreed to by both chambers, either without amendment or with such amendments only as may be agreed to by both chambers.

18. (*1*) The Council of State shall consist of not more than sixty members nominated or elected in accordance with rules made under the principal Act, of whom not more than twenty shall be official members.

(2) The Governor-General shall have power to appoint, from among the members of the Council of State, a president and other persons to preside in such circumstances as he may direct.

(3) The Governor-General shall have the right of addressing the Council of State, and may for that purpose require the attendance of its members.

19. (1) The Legislative Assembly shall consist of members nominated or elected in accordance with rules made under the principal Act.

(2) The total number of members of the Legislative Assembly shall be one hundred and forty. The number of non-elected members shall be forty, of whom twenty-six shall be official members. The number of elected members shall be one hundred:

Provided that rules made under the principal Act may provide for increasing the number of members of the Legislative Assembly as fixed by this section, and may vary the proportion which the classes of members bear one to another, so, however, that at least five-sevenths of the members of the Legislative Assembly shall be elected members, and at least one-third of the other members shall be nonofficial members.

(3) The Governor-General shall have the right of addressing the Legislative Assembly, and may for that purpose require the attendance of its members.

20. (1) There shall be a president of the Legislative Assembly, who shall, until the expiration of four years from the first meeting thereof, be a person appointed by the Governor-General, and shall thereafter be a member of the Assembly elected by the Assembly and approved by the Governor-General:

Provided that, if at the expiration of such period of four years the Assembly is in session, the president then in office shall continue in office until the end of the current session, and the first election of a president shall take place at the commencement of the ensuing session.

(2) There shall be a deputy-president of the Legislative Assembly, who shall preside at meetings of the Assembly in the absence of the president, and who shall be a member of the Assembly elected by the Assembly and approved by the Governor-General.

(3) The appointed president shall hold office until the date of the election of a president under this section, but he may resign his office by writing under his hand addressed to the Governor-General, or may be removed from office by order of the Governor-General, and any vacancy occurring before the expiration of his term of office shall be filled by a similar appointment for the remainder of such term.

(*4*) An elected president and a deputy-president shall cease to hold office if they cease to be members of the Assembly. They may resign office by writing under their hands addressed to the Governor-General, and may be removed from office by a vote of the Assembly with the concurrence of the Governor-General.

(*5*) A president and deputy-president shall receive such salaries as may be determined, in the case of an appointed president by the Governor-General, and in the case of an elected president and a deputy-president by Act of the Indian legislature....

22. (*1*) An official shall not be qualified for election as member of either chamber of the Indian legislature, and if any non-official member of either chamber accepts office in the service of the Crown in India, his seat in that chamber shall become vacant.

(*2*) If an elected member of either chamber of the Indian legislature becomes a member of the other chamber, his seat in such first-mentioned chamber shall thereupon become vacant.

(*3*) If any person is elected a member of both chambers of the Indian legislature, he shall, before he takes his seat in either chamber, signify in writing the chamber of which he desires to be a member, and thereupon his seat in the other chamber shall become vacant.

(*4*) Every member of the Governor-General's Executive Council shall be nominated as a member of one chamber of the Indian legislature, and shall have the right of attending in and addressing the other chamber, but shall not be a member of both chambers....

26. (*1*) Where either chamber of the Indian legislature refuses leave to introduce, or fails to pass in a form recommended by the Governor-General, any Bill, the Governor-General may certify that the passage of the Bill is essential for the safety, tranquillity or interests of British India or any part thereof, and thereupon—

(*a*) if the Bill has already been passed by the other chamber, the Bill shall on signature by the Governor-General, notwithstanding that it has not been consented to by both chambers, forthwith become an Act of the Indian legislature in the form of the Bill as originally introduced or proposed to be introduced in the Indian legislature, or (as the case may be) in the form recommended by the Governor-General; and

(*b*) if the Bill has not already been so passed, the Bill shall be laid before the other chamber and, if consented to by that chamber in the form recommended by the Governor-General, shall become an Act as aforesaid on the signification of the Governor-General's assent, or, if not so consented to, shall, on signature by the Governor-General become an Act as aforesaid.

(2) Every such Act shall be expressed to be made by the Governor-General, and shall, as soon as practicable after being made, be laid before both Houses of Parliament, and shall not have effect until it has received His Majesty's assent, and shall not be presented for His Majesty's assent until copies thereof have been laid before each House of Parliament for not less than eight days on which that House has sat; and upon the signification of such assent by His Majesty in Council, and the notification thereof by the Governor-General, the Act shall have the same force and effect as an Act passed by the Indian legislature and duly assented to:

Provided that, where in the opinion of the Governor-General a state of emergency exists which justifies such action, the Governor-General may direct that any such Act shall come into operation forthwith, and thereupon the Act shall have such force and effect as aforesaid, subject, however, to disallowance by His Majesty in Council....

Part III. Secretary of State in Council

1. The following amendments shall be made in section three of the principal Act in relation to the composition of the Council of India, the qualification, term of office, and remuneration of its members:—

(1) The provisions of sub-section (1) shall have effect as though "eight" and "twelve" were substituted for "ten" and "fourteen" respectively, as the minimum and maximum number of members, provided that the council as constituted at the time of the passing of this Act shall not be affected by this provision, but no fresh appointment or re-appointment thereto shall be made in excess of the maximum prescribed by this provision.

(2) The provisions of sub-section (3) shall have effect as if "one-half" were substituted for "nine" and "India" were substituted for "British India."

(3) In sub-section (4) "five years" shall be substituted for "seven years" as the term of office of members of the council, provided that the tenure of office of any person who is a member of the council at the time of the passing of this Act shall not be affected by this provision.

(4) The provisions of sub-section (8) shall cease to have effect and in lieu thereof the following provisions shall be inserted:

"There shall be paid to each member of the Council of India the annual salary of twelve hundred pounds: provided that any member of the council who was at the time of his appointment domiciled in India shall receive, in addition to the salary hereby provided, an annual subsistence allowance of six hundred pounds.

Such salaries and allowances may be paid out of the revenues of India or out of moneys provided by Parliament."

(5) Notwithstanding anything in any Act or rules, where any person in the service of the Crown in India is appointed a member of the council before completion of the period of such service required to entitle him to a pension or annuity, his service as such member shall, for the purpose of any pension or annuity which would be payable to him on completion of such period, be reckoned as service under the Crown in India whilst resident in India.

32. (1) The provision in section six of the principal Act which prescribes the quorum for meeting of the Council of India shall cease to have effect, and the Secretary of State shall provide for a quorum by directions to be issued in this behalf.

(2) The provision in section eight of the principal Act relating to meetings of the Council of India shall have effect as though "month" were substituted for "week."

(3) Section ten of the principal Act shall have effect as though the words "all business of the council or committees thereof is to be transacted" were omitted, and the words "the business of the Secretary of State in Council or the Council of India shall be transacted, and any order made or act done in accordance with such direction shall, subject to the provisions of this Act, be treated as being an order of the Secretary of State in Council" were inserted in lieu thereof.

33. The Secretary of State in Council may, notwithstanding anything in the principal Act, by rule regulate and restrict the exercise of the powers of superintendence, direction, and control, vested in the Secretary of State and the Secretary of State in Council, by the principal Act, or otherwise, in such manner as may appear necessary or expedient in order to give effect to the purposes of this Act.

Before any rules are made under this section relating to subjects other than transferred subjects, the rules proposed to be made shall be laid in draft before both Houses of Parliament, and such rules shall not be made unless both Houses by resolution approve the draft either without modification or addition, or with modifications or additions to which both Houses agree, but upon such approval being given the Secretary of State in Council may make such rules in the form in which they have been approved, and such rules on being so made shall be of full force and effect.

Any rules relating to transferred subjects made under this section shall be laid before both Houses of Parliament as soon as may be after they are made, and, if an Address is presented to His Majesty by either House of Parliament within the next thirty days on which that House has sat after the rules are laid before it praying that the rules or any of them may be annulled, His Majesty in Council may annul the rules or any of them, and those rules shall thenceforth be void, but without prejudice to the validity of anything previously done thereunder.

34. So much of section five of the principal Act as relates to orders and communications sent to India from the United Kingdom and to orders made in the United Kingdom, and sections eleven, twelve, thirteen and fourteen of the principal Act, shall cease to have effect and the procedure for the sending of orders and communications to India and in general for correspondence between the Secretary of State and the Governor-General in Council or any local government shall be such as may be prescribed by order of the Secretary of State in Council.

35. His Majesty may by Order in Council make provision for the appointment of a High Commissioner for India in the United Kingdom and for the pay pension powers, duties, and conditions of employment of the High Commissioner and of his assistants; and the Order may further provide for delegating to the High Commissioner any of the powers previously exercised by the Secretary of State or the Secretary of State in Council whether under the principal Act or otherwise in relation to making contractor and may prescribe the conditions under which he shall act on behalf of the Governor-General in Council or any local government.

Part IV. The Civil Services in India

36. (1) Subject to the provisions of the principal Act and of rules made thereunder, every person in the civil service of the Crown in India holds office during His Majesty's pleasure, and may be employed in any manner required by a proper authority within the scope of his duty, but no person in that service may be dismissed by any authority subordinate to that by which he was appointed, and the Secretary of State in Council may (except so far as he may provide by rules to the contrary) reinstate any person in that service who has been dismissed.

If any such person appointed by the Secretary of State in Council thinks himself wronged by an order of an official superior in a governor's province, and on due application made to that superior does not receive the redress to which he may consider himself entitled, he may, without prejudice to any other right of redress, complain, to the governor of the province in order to obtain justice and the governor is hereby directed to examine such complaint and require such action to be taken thereon as may appear to him to be just and equitable.

(2) The Secretary of State in Council may make rules for regulating the classification of the civil services in India, the methods of their recruitment, their conditions of service, pay and allowances, and discipline and conduct. Such rules may, to such extent and in respect of such matters as may be prescribed, delegate the power of making rules to the Governor-General in Council or to local governments, or authorise the Indian legislature or local legislatures to make laws regulating the public services:

Provided that every person appointed before the commencement of this Act by the Secretary of State in Council to the civil service of the Crown in India shall retain all his existing or accruing rights, or shall receive such compensation for the loss of any of them as the Secretary of State in Council may consider just and equitable.

(3) The right to pensions and the scale and conditions of pensions of all persons in the civil service of the Crown in India appointed by the Secretary of State in Council shall be regulated in accordance with the rules in force at the time of the passing of this Act. Any such rules may be varied or added to by the Secretary of State in Council and shall have effect as so varied or added to, but any such variation or addition shall not adversely affect the pension of any member of the service appointed before the date thereof.

Nothing in this section or in any rule thereunder shall prejudice the rights to which any person may, or may have, become entitled under the provisions in relation to pensions contained in the East India Annuity Funds Act, 1874.

(4) For the removal of doubts it is hereby declared that all rules or other provisions in operation at the time of the passing of this Act, whether made by the Secretary of State in Council or by any other authority, relating to the civil service of the Crown in India, were duly made in accordance with the powers in that behalf, and are confirmed, but any such rules or provisions may be revoked, varied, or added to by rules or laws made under this section.

37. (1) Notwithstanding anything in section ninety-seven of the principal Act the Secretary of State may make appointments to the Indian Civil Service of persons domiciled in India, in accordance with such rules as may be prescribed by the Secretary of State in Council with the concurrence of the majority of votes at a meeting of the Council of India.

Any rules made under this section shall not have force until they have been laid for thirty days before both Houses of Parliament.

(2) The Indian Civil Service (Temporary Provisions) Act, 1915 (which confers power during the war and for a period of two years thereafter to make appointments to the Indian Civil Service without examination), shall have effect as though "three years" were substituted for "two years."

Glossary

Bengal: today, the nation of Bangladesh and the Indian state of West Bengal

Bombay: today, Mumbai

Lords Spiritual and Temporal, and Commons: members of Parliament; at the time of the act, the lords spiritual were bishops and the lords temporal were members of the hereditary peerage; they comprised the House of Lords; "Commons," representatives of the towns and cities, sat in the House of Commons, as they do today

Punjab: today, the western part lies in the nation of Pakistan; East Punjab is an Indian state

Document Analysis

In 1915 the British parliament passed yet another act called the Government of India Act. The purpose of the 1915 act was to consolidate into one set of laws all earlier legislation concerning the government of India. That set of laws was amended by the Government of India Act of 1916. The 1919 legislation, in turn, was in large part a further amendment to the 1915 act. Throughout the 1919 act, the 1915 act, as amended by the 1916 act, is referred to as the "principal Act."

The act's *preamble* seems almost grudgingly to acknowledge the need "for the increasing association of Indians in every branch of Indian administration, and for the gradual development of self-governing institutions." Despite this acknowledgment, the act states that Indian self-government can be achieved only in "successive stages" and asserts that "the welfare and advancement of the Indian peoples" lies with Parliament.

Part I of the act amounts to the definition of terms. The chief point made in section 1 is the division between two types of concerns, central and provincial. "Central subjects" refers to those matters directly administered by the government of India whereby interests across the borders of provinces are predominant. "Provincial subjects" refers to matters in which individual provincial interests are predominant. Reference is also made to the governor-general, a title used in combination with viceroy to designate the Crown-appointed governor of India, and to the Council, meaning the governor-general's advisory Council of India. "Transferred subjects" are those matters being turned over to the provincial governments, while "reserved subjects" are those that would remain under the control of the governor-general. This division of provincial and central functions constituted the essence of the dyarchy formed by the act.

Section 1 goes on to specify legalities associated with the "devolution of authority" down to the provinces. In particular, it outlines how matters of taxation, funding, salaries, and the like are to be handled. But section 1 also makes clear that the act is in no wise turning India over to the Indians. It states that "the rules shall not authorise the revocation or suspension of the transfer of any subject except with the sanction of the Secretary of State in Council." It further states that "the Governor-General in Council shall be the sole judge as to whether the purpose of the exercise of such powers in any particular case comes within the purposes so specified." Section 3 specifies which provinces in India will remain under the control of British-appointed governors, called "governor's provinces." "United Provinces" refers to the United Provinces of Agra and Oudh, in northern India. Section 4 goes on to state that "in relation to transferred subjects, the governor shall be guided by the advice of his ministers, unless he sees sufficient cause to dissent from their opinion, in which case he may require action to be taken otherwise than in accordance with that advice." Put simply, the power to devolve authority down to the provinces remained in the hands of British authorities.

Transfer of some authority is accomplished in section 10: "The local legislature of any province has power, subject to the provisions of this Act, to make laws for the peace and good government of the territories for the time being constituting that province." Later, in a table appended to the act, the memberships of the local legislative councils are established. The largest was the province of Bengal, with 125 members, followed by Madras and the United Provinces, each with 118, and Bombay, with 111. Additionally, Bihar and Orissa would have 98, Punjab 83, the Central Provinces 70, and Assam 53.

Section 10 continues by specifying those areas in which local legislators cannot make laws. Among such restricted areas are the bodies of law related to taxation, customs duties, the public debt, the military, and foreign affairs. Additionally, emergency powers are reserved to the governor-general. Provisions are then made for the procedures to be followed for the enactment of laws by Indian legislatures. Interestingly, section 15 notes that the act does not apply to any portion of India that the governor-general deems a "backward tract." This provision gave the governor-general broad powers to retain control over areas regarded as recalcitrant.

Part II turns to the nuts and bolts of the national Indian government. It creates a bicameral legislature consisting of a Council of State and a Legislative Assembly. The Council of State is to consist of no more than sixty members, some of whom would be elected and some appointed. The Legislative Assembly is to consist of one hundred elected members and forty appointed members; the act outlines the duties of the assembly's president and deputy president and includes provisions relating to membership in the assembly. The governor-general would retain a hand in the deliberations and actions of the assembly, for, as noted in section 22, "every member of the Governor-General's Executive Council shall be nominated as a member of one chamber of the Indian legislature." Section 26 goes on to say that if either chamber of the Indian legislature refuses to introduce or pass bills in a form the governor-general recommends, "the Governor-General may certify that the passage of the Bill is essential for the safety, tranquillity or interests of British India." Finally, section 26 specifies that any bill passed by the Indian legislature must be submitted to the British parliament.

In Part III, Sections 31–35 of the act consist primarily of legalities as they pertain to the Council of India. Again, the 1919 act consists largely of amendments to the earlier "principal Act" of 1915 as amended in 1916. The 1919 act, then, specifies such matters as the terms of office of the Council of India, the members' salaries, eligibility for membership on the council, the powers of the council and of the secretary of state for India, and procedures to be followed by the council and Parliament for the enactment of the council's orders.

Part IV turns to the civil services. The civil service was already an important part of the Raj and would continue to be so after 1919. Attention had been paid to the civil service as early as 1886, when the Aitchison Commission was set up to address Indian demands for more extensive participation in the civil service at higher levels. Then, in 1912, the Royal Commission on the Public Services of India—often called the Islington Commission after the name of its chair, John Dickson-Poynder, Lord Islington—was formed to make further recommendations. In its report, issued in 1915, the commission called for appointments to high-level posts to be made in both England and India and recommended that a quarter of the highest posts should be filled by Indians. Because of World War I, however, no action was taken on the Islington Commission's report.

Section 36 begins by noting that any Indian who serves in the civil service does so "during His Majesty's pleasure" (the king of England at the time was George V—until that time the only British monarch who had ever visited India, in 1911). Again, this part of the act deals with legalities. It specifies conditions under which people could be dismissed from the civil service, but it also specifies how they could be reinstated. It vests in the secretary of state for India and the Council of India the power to determine the "rules for regulating the classification of the civil services in India, the methods of their recruitment, their conditions of service, pay and allowances, and discipline and conduct." Part IV goes on to address such issues as compensation and pensions.

Essential Themes

In the aftermath of the law's passage, the Indian National Congress expressed disappointment with the Government of India Act of 1919. Accordingly, under the leadership of Gandhi, agitation for independence continued. Gandhi was the leader of the "noncooperation movement," which urged Indians to refuse to pay taxes, to resign from government posts, to decline British honors and titles, and to boycott educational institutions and the court system. Throughout the 1920s numerous political parties calling for Indian independence emerged. Their activities culminated at a conference in Bombay in May 1928 that called for Indian resistance to British rule. Then in 1929, at a historic conference in Lahore, the Indian National Congress passed a resolution calling for complete independence from Britain.

The 1930s witnessed widespread civil disobedience. A key event was Gandhi's famous Salt March, which took place in March–April 1930 to protest British taxation on salt. Police and protesters clashed in Calcutta and Peshawar, and by the end of 1931 some one hundred thousand Indians had been arrested for various forms of civil disobedience. In 1935 Britain passed yet another Government of India Act, this one granting complete provincial authority to Indians. It was not enough, however. The nationalist "Quit India" movement continued to urge civil disobedience, and in 1946 the Royal Indian Navy mutinied. Finally, on August 15,

1947, the British colony was partitioned into India, primarily Hindu, and Pakistan, primarily Muslim, and both nations achieved complete independence.

The Government of India Act of 1919 was part of a mosaic of laws stretching back to the eighteenth century. The act was passed in the middle of an independence movement that had its roots in the early to mid-nineteenth century, accelerated in the late nineteenth century, and crescendoed throughout the first half of the twentieth century. In one sense, the act had little impact. If it was designed to appease Indian nationalists, it failed signally, for true power remained vested in British hands, and that fact was obvious to Indian nationalist leaders. Nevertheless, the act served as a wedge, a crack in British authority. It gave Indians a taste of government participation as well as forums in which they could express their aspirations. Less than three decades later, those aspirations would be realized. India today, with more than 1.4 billion people, remains the world's largest democratic nation.

—Michael J. O'Neal, PhD

Bibliography and Additional Reading

Baillie, Alexander Charles. *Call of Empire: From the Highlands to Hindostan.* Montreal: McGill-Queens University Press, 2017.

Ghosh, Durba. *Gentlemanly Terrorists: Political Violence and the Colonial State in India, 1919–1949.* New York: Cambridge University Press, 2017.

James, Lawrence. *Raj: The Making and Unmaking of British India.* New York: St. Martin's Press, 1998.

Kulke, Hermann, and Dietmar Rothermund. *A History of India.* 6th ed. New York: Routledge, 2016.

Moorhouse, Geoffrey. *India Britannica.* New York: Harper & Row, 1983.

Porter, Andrew, and Alaine M. Low, eds. *The Oxford History of the British Empire*, Vol. 3: *The Nineteenth Century.* Oxford, UK: Oxford University Press, 1999.

Wolpert, Stanley. *A New History of India.* 8th ed. New York: Oxford University Press, 2008.

Mohandas Gandhi: Statement at Trial

Date: March 1922
Author: Mohandas Gandhi
Genre: statement of principle

Summary Overview

As the unquestioned leader of the Indian independence movement in the 1920s (and after), Mohandas Gandhi—the Mahatma or "great soul" to his followers—was held responsible by British leaders for any public opposition to British rule in India. Despite his promotion of nonviolence, Gandhi's inability to control his followers' propensity to violence led to his arrest in 1922 on charges of inciting sedition. Standing before a British judge, Gandhi prepared a statement accepting his arrest and conviction, but denying the legitimacy of the British colonial authority that intended to jail him. Gandhi's written statement, as read out in court, amounted to an autobiography describing how events and experiences had transformed him from a loyal subject of the British crown in India to an implacable, if nonviolent opponent of British rule.

Defining Moment

Mohandas Gandhi (1869-1948) returned to India from South Africa in 1915. Trained as a lawyer at University College in London, he became famous for challenging Cape Colony's racial discrimination policies directed against South Asians. His campaigns for equal rights were committed to nonviolent protest, but also to displaying loyalty to the British Empire. British governance might be misguided in Gandhi's opinion, but it still conveyed the benefits of a just legal system and capitalist world trade on educated Indians like himself. Having traveled the Indian subcontinent in 1915, Gandhi joined India's most powerful political action group, the Indian National Congress (INC), and settled an ashram—a Hindu religious community—outside Ahmedabad near Bombay (Mumbai). He then dedicated himself to pursuing social and political justice within the confines of British rule.

The First World War had just begun at the point when Gandhi arrived home. Like most politically-minded Indians, Gandhi believed that Indian sacrifices made during the war would advance the cause of Indian self-government in the style of Canada or Australia once the war came to an end. In 1919, the Secretary of State for India, Edwin Montagu, and the Viceroy of India, Lord Chelmsford, proposed a series of governmental reforms for India, opening up the professions, local government and the civil service to Indian participation. Yet no effort was made to grant Indians a parliament of their own or any control over law and order. Worse, when the INC led protests against the inadequacy of the Montagu-Chelmsford reforms, the British government responded with the Rowlatt Acts, which banned major public demonstrations in India in an effort to shut down protests.

In April 1919, one such demonstration was scheduled to be held during a Sikh religious festival at Jallianwalla Bagh, a public parcel in the town of Amritsar in northern India. The week before the festival, an English missionary nun was pushed to the ground in Amritsar by an unknown assailant. The act of a dark-skinned Indian attacking a white woman enraged the local military commander, Brigadier General Reginald Dyer, who declared martial law and banned any gathering at Jallianwalla Bagh. In an era before radio, and when most Indians could not understand English, Dyer's declaration went unheeded; even those who knew of it assumed it applied only to the political demonstration and not the religious festival. Thousands of people gathered at Jallianwalla Bagh on the day of the festival, and some political speakers even organized to defy the ban. At that point, an armored car barreled into the parcel with Dyer himself in it, accompanied by soldiers of the British-officered Indian Army. Dyer read out, in English, a demand that the crowd disperse; when they did not, the soldiers opened fire, killing 379 unarmed civilians and wounding hundreds more. The soldiers drove everyone out of Jallianwala Bagh; when relatives came to claim the bodies of their loved ones, the soldiers refused to let them in, and instead allowed the bodies to be eaten by jackals and vultures. During the next week, on Dyer's orders, soldiers forced any Indian who wished to walk on the street where the nun had been attacked to crawl on their bellies to their destination.

The "Armritsar Massacre," as the event came to be called, was a savage act of repression that turned much of the INC against British rule in India, including Gandhi himself. His mode of launching protests against unjust laws was in the form of what he referred to as " *satyagraha*," loosely translated as "truth force." Gandhi and his followers would place themselves physically in direct opposition to the operation of the law and force British officials on the scene to respond, usually with violence, which exposed the repression and hypocrisy inherent in the system of British colonial rule. Gandhi also relied on traditional Hindu forms of protest, like fasting or organizing " *hartals*," work stoppages. Previously, Gandhi had used these tactics to try to get British colonial government to reform its ways and open up to Indian equality within the colonial system. After Amritsar, Gandhi was determined to end the colonial system in India altogether, and the direct, heroic and Hindu nature of his tactics made him the unquestioned leader of the Indian National Congress and the independence movement by the end of 1920.

Flush with power, Gandhi promised Indians that if they united and followed his nonviolent program, they could be rid of British rulership in a year. He launched a massive boycott of British industrial products, told his followers not to pay British taxes, and promoted Indian production over British goods, especially in textiles, where British producers had deliberately shut down the Indian cotton industry to kill competition. However, Gandhi found out fast that it was one thing to promote nonviolence, unity and noncooperation, and another thing entirely to get his followers to establish the discipline and courage to use them as tactics. A boycott of a visit by the Prince of Wales in 1921 turned into a riot in Bombay. Efforts to cross caste boundaries by accepting *dalits*, or untouchables, into his ashram were met with mystification by his Hindu followers. Hindus and Muslims set upon each other at numerous demonstrations, despite the fact that Gandhi promoted religious tolerance. Regardless of his support for the *Khilafat* movement—the effort to maintain the authority of the Ottoman Empire's Sultan as the Caliph of Islam—Indian Muslims in general did not trust Gandhi.

One *satyagraha* campaign was to be implemented in early 1922—the people of Uttar Pradesh were scheduled to demonstrate against taxation. On February 1, Gandhi sent a letter to the Viceroy of India announcing the campaign. Three days later, on February 4, peasant demonstrators set fire to a police station in Chauri Chaura, a small village in Gujarat, and 22 policemen were killed. Horrified, Gandhi blamed himself for not teaching his followers the principles of *ahimsa*, or nonviolence. He called off the *satyagraha* movement and went on a five day fast to discipline himself. This was hardly enough to satisfy British authorities, however, who arrested Gandhi at his ashram in March 1922 under Section 124 A of the Indian Penal Code, charging him with sedition.

Gandhi's trial was held on March 18, 1922, before the Honorable C. N. Broomfield, the District and Sessions Judge in Ahmedabad. Coupled with Gandhi was Shri Shankarlal Banker, the editor of Gandhi's newspaper and mouthpiece, *Young India*, who had published Gandhi's call for *satyagraha*. For trial, Gandhi prepared a written statement, which the judge allowed him to read off before the proceedings began. The statement has since been acclaimed as Gandhi's best articulation of his philosophy of nonviolent resistance to British colonial rule.

Author Biography

Mohandas Karamchand Gandhi was born in 1869 to a high caste and well-educated Hindu family in India. He went to university in India and then on to University College London to obtain a law degree. After returning to India, he accepted a job working as the representative of an Indian law firm in Cape Colony in South Africa. There, Gandhi's experience as a highly born Indian elite did not jibe with the officially-sanctioned discrimination he faced according to the prevailing racial laws. Gandhi dedicated himself to fighting injustice in Cape Colony and educating his fellow South Asians living in Cape Colony as to their rights as members of the British Empire.

While in South Africa, Gandhi read the essays of the Russian novelist Leo Tolstoy on the concept of Christian anarchy, espousing a doctrine of noncooperation with institutions that were upheld by violence. Gandhi corresponded with Tolstoy about these ideas toward the end of the novelist's life, and set up a series of Tolstoy Farms in Cape Colony with the goal of trying to implement Tolstoy's ideas. The farms, like the ashram at Ahmedabad, proved successful when Gandhi combined Tolstoy's ideas with more traditional Hindu culture and methods of protest, calling them *satyagraha*, or truth force. In Cape Colony, Gandhi's followers refused to pay taxes, went on strike, abandoned work and occasionally met violent attacks with passive resistance. *Satyagraha* proved moderately successful in South Africa, as the new Union government passed laws to accommodate its South Asian citizens in 1913.

Gandhi returned to India in 1915, and, after Amritsar, dedicated his movement to the cessation of British rule over the Indian subcontinent. In the process, he became the dominant figure in the Indian National Congress, and a hero to the average Hindu. Most Indians had never seen a British official in their lives, and Gandhi's insistence that they ignore British rule meant that, by simply living their lives, they were revolutionary heroes. On the other hand, his inability to convince his followers of the necessity of nonviolence in these campaigns brought the *satyagraha* movement to grief, and after his conviction for sedition in 1922, Gandhi appeared somewhat spent as a leader.

In 1928, Gandhi renewed his call for the complete independence of India; British officials halfheartedly negotiated with him, but the excitement level for his movement seemed abated. Then Gandhi alit on a brilliant *satyagraha* campaign to capture the world's atten-

Gandhi promoted the principle of ahimsa very successfully by applying it to all spheres of life, particularly to politics. Photo via Wikimedia Commons. [Public domain.]

tion—he would walk to the Indian Ocean and make salt. Salt was a necessity in India's equatorial climate for preserving food and maintain bodily hydration, and British businesses had controlled its production legally for more than 250 years. Gandhi walked to the Indian Ocean from his home in Ahmedabad, trailed by thousands of followers. More important, he was also followed by radio correspondents and newsreel cameras—the British government could not stand the exposure of the tyranny inherent in the salt-making laws, and agreed to discuss independence with Gandhi and the INC.

Between 1930 and 1932, a series of Round Table Conferences were held in London at which Gandhi negotiated for Indian self-government within the confines of the British Empire. However, upon the implementation of a provisional parliamentary system in 1947, fissures opened in the Indian independence movement between Hindus and Muslims. When the Second World War began, the British viceroy of India declared war in India's name, infuriating Indian opinions and reviving Gandhi's efforts to achieve independence. The pressure of the war and a famine in 1943 gave Gandhi's "Quit India" campaign a new urgency, and when the war ended, a new Labour Party government in Britain proved eager to effect Indian independence and end the headache of Gandhi's nonviolent protests. Negotiations resulted in the formation of two large new states in 1947, predominantly Hindu India and predominantly Muslim Pakistan. Population migrations resulted in a vast civil war in which more than half a million members of the former British colony were killed. Gandhi called for an end to the killings, but instead he was assassinated in January 1948 by a Hindu nationalist angered at the religious split of the old British colony.

Historical Document

Ghandi's Statement at Trial

Non-violence is the first article of my faith. It is also the last article of my creed. But I had to make my choice. I had either to submit to a system which I considered had done an irreparable harm to my country or incur the risk of the mad fury of my people bursting forth when they understood the truth from my lips. I know that my people have sometimes gone mad. I am deeply sorry for it and I am, therefore, here to submit not to a light penalty but to the highest penalty. I do not ask for mercy. I do not plead any extending act. I am here, therefore, to invite and cheerfully submit to the highest penalty that can be inflicted upon me for what in law is a deliberate crime, and what appears to me to be the highest duty of a citizen. The only course open to you, the Judge, is, as I am going to say in my statement, either to resign your post, or inflict on me the severest penalty if you believe that the system and law you are assisting to administer are good for the people. I do not accept that kind of conversion. But by the time I have finished with my statement you will have a glimpse of what is raging within my breast to run this maddest risk which a sane man can run.

[Gandhi then read out a written statement.]

I owe it perhaps to the Indian public and to the public in England, to placate which this prosecution is mainly taken up, that I should explain why from a staunch loyalist and co-operator, I have become an uncompromising disaffectionist and non-co-operator. To the court too I should say why I plead guilty to the charge of promoting disaffection towards the Government established by law in India.

My public life began in 1893 in South Africa in troubled weather. My first contact with British authority in that country was not of a happy character. I discovered that as a man and an Indian, I had no rights. More correctly I discovered that I had no rights as a man because I was an Indian.

But I was not baffled. I thought that this treatment of Indians was an excrescence upon a system that was intrinsically and mainly good. I gave the Government my voluntary and hearty co-operation, criticizing it freely where I felt it was faulty but never wishing its destruction.

Consequently when the existence of the Empire was threatened in 1899 by the Boer challenge, I offered my services to it, raised a volunteer ambulance corps and served at several actions that took place for the relief of Ladysmith.

Similarly in 1906, at the time of the Zulu 'revolt', I raised a stretcher-bearer party and served till the end of the 'rebellion'. On both the occasions I received medals and was even mentioned in dispatches. For my work in South Africa I was given by Lord Hardinge a Kaisar-i-Hind gold medal. When the war broke out in 1914 between England and Germany, I raised a volunteer ambulance corps in London, consisting of the then resident Indians in London, chiefly students. Its work was acknowledged by the authorities to be valuable. Lastly, in India when a special appeal was made at the War Conference in Delhi in 1918 by Lord Chelmsford for recruits, I struggled at the cost of my health to raise a corps in Kheda, and the response was being made when the hostilities ceased and orders were received that no more recruits were wanted. In all these efforts at service, I was actuated by the belief that it was possible by such services to gain a status of full equality in the Empire for my countrymen.

The first shock came in the shape of the Rowlatt Act, a law designed to rob the people of all real freedom. I felt called upon to lead an intensive agitation against it. Then followed the Punjab horrors beginning with the massacre at Jallianwala Bagh and culminating in crawling orders, public flogging and other indescribable humiliations. I discovered too that the plighted word of the Prime Minister to the Mussalmans of India regarding the integrity of Turkey and the holy places of Islam was not likely to be fulfilled. But in spite of the forebodings and the grave warnings of friends, at the Amritsar Congress in 1919, I fought for co-operation and working of the Montagu-Chelmsford reforms, hoping that the Prime Minister would redeem his promise to the Indian Mussalmans, that the Punjab wound would be healed, and that the reforms, inadequate and unsatisfactory though they were, marked a new era of hope in the life of India.

But all that hope was shattered. The Khilafat promise was not to be redeemed. The Punjab crime was whitewashed and most culprits went not only unpunished but remained in service, and some continued to draw pensions from the Indian revenue and in some cases were even rewarded. I saw too that not only did the reforms not mark a change of heart, but they were only a method of further draining India of her wealth and of prolonging her servitude.

I came reluctantly to the conclusion that the British connection had made India more helpless than she ever was before, politically and economically. A disarmed India has no power of resistance against any aggressor if she wanted to engage in an armed conflict with him. So much is this the case that some of our best men consider that India must take generations, before she can achieve Dominion Status. She has become so poor that she has little power of resisting famines. Before the British advent India spun and wove in her millions of cottages, just the supplement she needed for adding to her meager agricultural resources. This cottage industry, so vital for India's existence, has been ruined by incredibly heartless and inhuman processes as described by English witnesses.

Little do town dwellers know how the semi-starved masses of India are slowly sinking to lifelessness. Little do they know that their miserable comfort represents the brokerage they get for their work they do for the foreign exploiter, that the profits and the brokerage are sucked from the masses. Little do they realize that the Government established by law in British India is carried on for this exploitation of the masses. No sophistry, no jugglery in figures, can explain away the evidence that the skeletons in many villages present to the naked eye. I have no doubt whatsoever that both England and the town dweller of India will have to answer, if there is a God above, for this crime against humanity, which is perhaps unequalled in history. The law itself in this country has been used to serve the foreign exploiter. My unbiased examination of the Punjab Martial Law cases has led me to believe that at least ninety-five per cent of convictions were wholly bad. My experience of political cases in India leads me to the conclusion, in nine out of every ten, the condemned men were totally innocent. Their crime consisted in the love of their country. In ninety-nine cases out of hundred, justice has been denied to Indians as against Europeans in the courts of India. This is not an exaggerated picture. It is the experience of almost every Indian who has had anything to do with such cases. In my opinion, the administration of the law is thus prostituted, consciously or unconsciously, for the benefit of the exploiter.

The greater misfortune is that the Englishmen and their Indian associates in the administration of the country do not know that they are engaged in the crime I have attempted to describe. I am satisfied that many Englishmen and Indian officials honestly believe that they are administering one of the best systems devised in the world, and that India is making steady, though slow progress. They do not know that a subtle but effective system of terrorism and an organized display of force, on the one hand, and the deprivation of all powers of retaliation or self-defense, on the other, have emasculated the people and induced in them the habit of simulation. This awful habit has added to the ignorance and the self-deception of the administrators. Section 124 A, under which I am happily charged, is perhaps the prince among the political sections of the Indian Penal Code designed to suppress the liberty of the citizen. Affection cannot be manufactured or regulated by law. If one has no affection for a person or system, one should be free to give the fullest expression to his disaffection, so long as he does not contemplate, promote, or incite to violence. But the section under which Mr. Banker and I are charged is one under which mere promotion of disaffection is a crime. I have studied some of the cases tried under it; I know that some of the most loved of India's patriots have been convicted under it. I consider it a privilege, therefore, to be charged under that section. I have endeavored to give in their briefest outline the reasons for my disaffection. I have no personal ill-will against any single administrator, much less can I have any disaffection towards the King's person. But I hold it to be a virtue to be disaffected towards a Government which in its totality has done more harm to India than any previous system. India is less manly under the British rule than she ever was before. Holding such a belief, I consider it to be a sin to have affection for the system. And it has been a precious privilege for me to be able to write what I have in the various articles tendered in evidence against me.

In fact, I believe that I have rendered a service to India and England by showing in non-co-operation the way out of the unnatural state in which both are living. In my opinion, non-co-operation with evil is as much a duty as is co-operation with good. But in the past, non-co-operation has been deliberately expressed in violence to the evil-doer. I am endeavoring to show to my countrymen that violent non-co-operation only multiplies evil, and that as evil can only be sustained by violence, withdrawal of support of evil requires complete abstention from violence. Non-violence implies voluntary submission to the penalty for non-co-operation with evil. I am here, therefore, to invite and submit cheerfully to the highest penalty that can be inflicted upon me for what in law is deliberate crime, and what appears to me to be the highest duty of a citizen. The only course open to you, the Judge and the assessors, is either to resign your posts and thus dissociate yourselves from evil, if you feel that the law you are called upon to administer is an evil, and that in reality I am innocent, or to inflict on me the severest penalty, if you believe that the system and the law you are assisting to administer are good for the people of this country, and that my activity is, therefore, injurious to the common weal.

Glossary

excrescence: an unattractive growth on a body; metaphorically, an ugly abnormality found in an otherwise normal institution

Mussalmans: an old term for Muslims, antiquated today

sophistry: arguments made under false pretenses, or based on known lies

the common weal: the benefit of the public

Document Themes and Analysis

The presiding judge at Gandhi's trial, C. N. Broomfield, seemed to sympathize with Gandhi, showing him great respect in allowing him to read out a written statement. The only purpose for such a statement was to have it make it into the press, and any such statement would clearly be meant to embarrass the British government in India, so Broomfield was taking a calculated risk in allowing Gandhi to speak outside the boundaries of his case. Likely, Broomfield wanted to avoid controversy by allowing free speech; on the other hand, he also likely did not expect to be the subject of the speech.

The charges were read out, Gandhi being accused of violating the law by advocating sedition, and Shri Shankarlal Banker being accused of publishing seditious statements. Both of them pled guilty. Broomfield was prepared to pronounce sentence, but the government's Advocate-General, Sir Thomas Strangman, insisted on being allowed to delineate what the charges referred to, specifically the riots that had taken place due to the anti-tax campaign, and the deaths of the policemen in Chauri Chaura. Strangman pointed out to Gandhi, "you find that non-violence is insisted upon as an item of the campaign and of the creed, …[yet] of what value is it to insist on non-violence, if incessantly you preach disaffection towards the Government and hold it up as a treacherous Government, and if you openly and deliberately seek to instigate others to overthrow it?" Gandhi integrated these accusations into his statement, first admitting that he agreed entirely with Strangman's accusations, and took blame for the violence that had occurred as a result of his anti-tax *satyagraha*. Nevertheless, Gandhi insisted, "Non-violence is the first article of my faith. It is also the last article of my creed." He then allowed that the court should impose "the highest penalty" on him, unless Judge Broomfield was prepared to resign his post—which Gandhi clearly implied was the truly moral thing to do.

Gandhi then began to read from his prepared statement. He detailed his history in South Africa, where he had "discovered that I had no rights as a man because I was an Indian," but assumed that it was due to a flaw in the system of colonial government. When the Boer (or South African) War began in 1899, Gandhi loyally supported the British parliament's effort to suppress the Boer rebellion (Ladysmith was a major battle in the war), and when the Zulus rose in defiance of colonial control in 1906, he supported the British then too. He even won the Kaisar-i-Hind Medal, a rare award given to people in the Empire who had loyally served the British cause of colonial power. He especially supported Britain's efforts in the First World War, a war where the Empire's very existence was considered to be at stake by the British government.

Gandhi's efforts, however, were not made out of mere acceptance of the superiority of British authority in the Empire. He believed "that it was possible by such services to gain a status of full equality in the Empire for my countrymen." He found out after the First World War that this was not the case, the Montagu-Chelmsford reforms for further involvement in Indian government were inadequate, and the Rowlatt Act was repressive. The massacre at Jallianwala Bagh and Dyer's humiliating orders in Amritsar were simply accepted by the British government, and even rewarded—though Dyer was removed from his post, a newspaper back in Britain raised £26,000 as a subscription for him from the public to apply to his pension, and many members of the House of Lords stood up to applaud his efforts. Gandhi threw in a reference to the *Khilafat* movement to save the Ottoman caliphate as another British promise that went unmet.

The India Gandhi lived in was helpless politically, economically and militarily, had no possibility of "Dominion Status" or self-government within the empire, and had seen its cotton textiles industry destroyed. The division between the British-controlled cities and the masses who lived in the countryside was vast, where people starved and were susceptible to famine, a "crime against humanity, which is perhaps unequalled in history." Martial law as imposed by Dyer and the Rowlatt Act in the Punjab was still in place in 1922. Gandhi pointed to its injustice, believing that "in nine out of every ten [cases], the condemned men were totally innocent. Their crime consisted in the love of their country," and that Europeans received fairer justice in Indian courts than Indians did. Worst of all, most people involved in British government in India, both English and Indian, had little conception of how unjust their administration was to most Indians—they had no idea they upheld "a subtle but effective system of terrorism and an organized display of force, on the one hand, and the deprivation of all powers of retaliation or self-defense, on the other."

Gandhi was charged under Section 124 A of the Indian Penal Code, "perhaps the prince among the political sections of the Indian Penal Code designed to suppress the liberty of the citizen." Gandhi indeed preached sedition against the British government of India, but he believed this should be allowed so long as he did not advocate violence against British rule or any British official involved in the system. Because other Indian politicians had also been convicted of violating Section 124A of the Indian Penal Code for the same reasons, Gandhi "consider[ed] it a privilege, therefore, to be charged under that section." He claimed no ill will toward anyone propagating the law, but indeed considered it virtuous to oppose "a Government which in its totality has done more harm to India than any previous system. ...In fact, I believe that I have rendered a service to India and England by showing in non-co-operation the way out of the unnatural state in which both are living. In my opinion, non-co-operation with evil is as much a duty as is co-operation with good."

Finally, Gandhi "submit[ted] cheerfully to the highest penalty that can be inflicted upon me for what in law is deliberate crime, and what appears to me to be the highest duty of a citizen." He reiterated that Judge Broomfield had the choice to resign his post in sympathy with Gandhi and his arguments, or impose the highest penalty allowed by law.

In point of fact, Broomfield sentenced Gandhi to six years in prison. He only served two years in comparatively light circumstances, released when he had to undergo an appendectomy. In his time in prison, as the British government must have hoped, the INC lost focus in the independence movement, splitting between those who advocated outright independence and those who wanted dominion status, or self-government under the British crown. Gandhi himself returned to the tactics of Tolstoy upon leaving prison, calling for Indians to ignore British government by weaving their own cloth and refusing to pay taxes, but his efforts were weak in comparison to his reputation. Only when he decided to openly defy the British government, by launching the Salt March in 1930, did his independence movement regain momentum. It never lost that momentum again, eventually culminating in the independence of India and Pakistan in 1947. Even more, the tactics of nonviolent confrontation were copied around the world, in civil rights movements like that in the U.S. and Northern Ireland, in anticolonial efforts and in protests of all means and all ends.

—David Simonelli, PhD

Bibliography and Additional Reading

Brown, Judith M. *Gandhi: Prisoner of Hope*. New Haven, CT: Yale UP, 1989.

Fischer, Louis. *Gandhi: His Life and Message for the World*. New York: Mentor Press, 1954.

Haksar, Vinit. *Gandhi and Liberalism: Satyagraha and the Conquest of Evil*. London: Routledge, 2018.

Mahatma Gandhi Information Website. Mani Bhavan Gandhi Sangrahalaya www.gandhi-manibhavan.org/gandhicomesalive/speech3.htm .

Mahatma Gandhi One Spot Information Website. Bombay Sarvodaya Mandal–Gandhi Book Centre, Mumbai www.mkgandhi.org/main.htm .

Jawaharlal Nehru's Speech on the Occasion of Indian Independence

Date: August 14, 1947
Author: Jawaharlal Nehru
Genre: political speech

Summary Overview

One of the heroes of the Indian independence movement, Jawaharlal Nehru spoke to the colonial parliament on the night before the British government had scheduled its army and civil service to leave India and grant the subcontinental state its independence (Aug. 15, 1947). Nehru's "tryst with destiny" speech, as it came to be called, has gone down in Indian history as a brilliant oratorical transition from the period under British rule to the reclamation of India as a powerful player in world politics and the master of its own future.

Defining Moment

In the early seventeenth century, the first English merchants showed up in South Asia with the goal of making their way into the spice and gem trades. The empire they negotiated with for concessions, the Mughal Empire, was one of the most powerful states on earth, rulers of the majority of an ancient civilization, militarily advanced, religiously tolerant, wealthy, and internally peaceful. For good reason, the representatives of the English East India Company were obsequious in their dealings with the Mughals. However, the Mughals were only the most powerful of many states in South Asia, and the English merchants found, over time, that they could obtain a great deal of power and prestige themselves by exploiting divisions, handing out loans for the collateral of territory, and loaning out soldiers to provide the military balance in wars between states. By 1757, the British East India Company became the most powerful entity in South Asia, eclipsing the Mughals and making massive profits to support that power. British agents of the company built and ran their own capital city, Calcutta, they dominated the trades in cotton, spices, teas, opium and gems, and essentially established their own empire in South Asia, complicit with the support of the British government back in London – somewhat as if ExxonMobil dominated Arabia with the support of the American government. By the end of

Jawaharlal Nehru. Photo via Wikimedia Commons. [Public domain.]

the eighteenth century, it was Indian princes, politicians, and merchants who paid obsequious homage to the British as the dominant power in South Asia.

Yet the British East India Company's agents' sense of entitlement grew well beyond the boundaries of reason very quickly. The company shut down any industry that threatened its profits – Indian textiles, pharmaceutical, and salt manufacturers saw their businesses rendered illegal so the company could run them and profit from them. The Company levied crushing taxes over its territories, and did nothing to combat the regular famines that swept through South Asia. While the rapaciousness of these profits troubled the parliament back in London, their solution to the problem was to try to westernize and Christianize India, changing its laws, denigrating its medical practices, imposing western educational principles, and especially dismissing Hinduism and Islam as the religions of backwards and unenlightened peoples. Beneath a surface-level control over India, the policies of the company and the British government built resentment in a portion of the Indian population.

In 1857, that resentment exploded into rebellion. Indian soldiers, or *sepoys*, rose up against their officers, slaughtered hundreds of British people in the Ganges valley, and demanded the Mughal emperor return to power. The British referred to the rebellion as a "mutiny," a somewhat contemptuous term in that it assumed that the Indian people owed the British their loyalty and obedience. British officers were able to command enough loyalty and obedience that the rebellion was put down by 1858, but British East India Company rule over India was over. The company was eventually dissolved and the British government made its territories in South Asia into a crown colony. Queen Victoria declared that her government would end any efforts to Christianize any of her subjects. Yet nothing in India would ever be the same for its British colonizers – they perceived the people they ruled over as dangerous, brown-skinned, uncivilized, and inches away from destroying them at any provocation. British India was to be exploited, only, not improved, and Indians could never expect to contribute to their own governance, for fear of another rebellion and massacre.

Meanwhile, generations of wealthy Indians filtered through British universities, among them Jawaharlal Nehru and Mohandas Gandhi. They were schooled in the superiority of British civilization, in secular values, and in the meritocratic fairness of parliamentary democracy. And they wanted in. Instead of harboring anger over the westernization of their society, most educated Indians welcomed westernization as the improvement that the British always promised. These Indians came together in the Indian National Congress in 1885, to apply the kind of peaceful political pressure they had learned from British institutions would result in political change. They wanted to achieve self-governance, like that of Canada, Australia, or New Zealand – dominion status or Home Rule, as it was referred to in the British Empire – and they expected to prove themselves worthy of it. It was difficult for them to conceive of the idea that the British officials who had taught them the values of freedom, equality, meritocracy, and secularism had no intention of ever allowing Indians to achieve those things.

World War I brought these issues to a head. The Indian National Congress supported an Indian military presence in the First World War because they expected the sacrifice of Indian soldiers' lives to prove India's loyalty to the British Empire. In 1919, the Secretary of State for India, Edwin Montagu, and the Viceroy of India, Lord Chelmsford, proposed a series of governmental reforms for India, opening up the professions, local government, and the civil service to Indian participation. Yet no effort was made to grant Indians a parliament of their own or any control over law and order. Worse, when the INC led protests against the inadequacy of the Montagu-Chelmsford reforms, the British government responded with the Rowlatt Acts, which banned major public demonstrations in India in an effort to shut down protests.

In April 1919, a Sikh religious festival was scheduled for the Punjabi town of Amritsar, to be held in a stadium-like walled garden called Jallianwalla Bagh. When political speakers defied the British ban by going to the festival and making speeches against the colonial regime, the local military commander, Brigadier General Reginald Dyer, called in soldiers and had them open fire on the crowd, killing 379 unarmed civilians and wounding hundreds more. Weeks later, Nehru was riding in a covered sleeping compartment of a train car when a group of British soldiers entered the compartment, including, by coincidence, General Dyer. Apparently not knowing there was anyone else in the compartment, Dyer bragged about his actions at Jallianwala Bagh, claiming he had refrained only from laying waste to the entire town. Later, at a commission of inquiry, Dyer claimed the massacre had achieved "the necessary moral and widespread effect"; despite the fact he was dismissed from the service, many British subjects at home and in India agreed that he had done the right thing. Nehru was horrified, and came to the conclusion that racism like Dyer's was inherent and endemic in the British Empire; therefore, true independence was the only long-term solution worthy of India's future.

Over the course of the 1920s, Nehru, Mohandas Gandhi, and other members of the INC demonstrated for Indian self-government, whether under the British crown or outright independence. Nehru, Gandhi and others were jailed in the 1920s, but the focus of their demonstrations improved in the 1930s with Gandhi's Salt March. By defying the British ban on making salt, a bodily necessity in India's hot climate, Gandhi exposed the immorality behind the British imperial enterprise, and embarrassed the British government into negotiating for self-governance. Negotiations also brought about divisions in the independence movement, however. A rival political organization, the Muslim League, threatened to divide the British colony of India into a predominantly Hindu India and predominantly Muslim territories referred to as Pakistan. The British government exploited these divisions during the Second World War under Winston Churchill. India was considered vital to the British war effort, and while Nehru and Gandhi were jailed, Churchill fomented division in the ranks of the INC and the Muslim League over the future of self-governance in India, a future he had no intention of ever granting to the Indian people.

After the war, however, Churchill's government was replaced by a Labour Party government in London, a socialist government whose members had been committed to the independence of India since the time of the Salt March. Once British intentions became clear over independence – that India might finally overcome the racism of British dominance and run its own affairs apart from the British Empire – the INC and Muslim League began to bicker about legacies, and their respective Hindu and Muslim followers began to war in the streets of India's cities. Through hard negotiations and both the threat and reality of violence, British negotiators worked with Nehru and Gandhi to separate the old British colony into the separate states of India and Pakistan. Independence was expected in 1948, but once negotiations concluded, the British government moved up the date of independence to August 15, 1947, largely to hurry up and evacuate British officials before religious violence between Hindus and Muslims engulfed the two legacy states.

Regardless of its hard-won nature, India's independence was deserved. It was based in British principles of parliamentary government and capitalist world trade, but also pointed toward a future of freedom, equality and political participation that could never be achieved under British rule. Indians had reason to celebrate, and the major negotiator of their independence, Jawaharlal Nehru, gave that celebration words and life. Nehru addressed the pre-independence parliament on the last day of its colonial existence, August 14, 1947, trying to briefly define what independence had wrought and what it would bring in the coming years. His speech has gone down as one of the great speeches of the twentieth century.

Author Biography

Jawaharlal Nehru was born November 14, 1889 in Allahabad, India to a high caste Hindu family, the son of a major political figure in the newly former Indian National Congress. His family was wealthy enough to educate Jawaharlal in England, first at Harrow, then at Cambridge; he eventually earned a law degree at University College in London. Returning to India in 1912, he became a lawyer and member of the Indian National Congress, like his father. He and his wife Kamala were married in 1916, and had a daughter, Indira, in 1917.

Like most other members of the INC, Nehru wanted to achieve dominion status in the British Empire. His experience of hearing the racist pronunciations of General Dyer changed his opinions dramatically. Instead, Nehru turned to the leadership of Mohandas Gandhi, who was by 1920 the acknowledged leader of the INC and also a newly-minted advocate of Indian independence. Jailed with Gandhi in 1921 and 1922, Nehru studied Gandhi's principles of nonviolence and pledged himself to follow them. He was also impressed with the Russian Revolution, in which an agrarian people similar to those in India had overthrown an oppressive regime and were learning to govern themselves, and so became a committed socialist. Likewise, he agreed with Gandhi's efforts to break down the social barriers of caste and to find peace between the Hindu and Muslim populations of India. Nehru left jail committed to Gandhi and his nonviolent efforts; he became something of a liaison between Gandhi and the well-heeled INC while Gandhi himself rallied the impoverished Indian masses. The culmination of their joint efforts came with the 1930 Salt March in India, for which Nehru was arrested with Gandhi, and for which he also earned enough respect from his colleagues in the INC to became Gandhi's anointed choice as president of the INC. He would not leave the position for the rest of his life.

In the 1930s, he and Gandhi negotiated for a provisional Indian parliament under the British crown. However, their negotiations went for naught when the Viceroy of India, Lord Linlithgow, declared war in India's name in 1939, joining the British effort to defeat Germany without consulting anyone in the provisional parliament. British arrogance led Gandhi and Nehru to launch the "Quit India Movement" in 1942, demanding complete independence in the middle of the war. Nehru ended up arrested by the British government for a second time, this time staying in jail until the war was over in Europe in 1945. He then joined negotiations with the Labour Government in Britain that led to the ultimate independence of India and Muslim Pakistan in 1947.

Upon independence, Jawaharlal Nehru became India's first Prime Minister, as the leader of the Congress Party. He became the hero of independence, launching the nation's first Five Year Plan, declaring neutrality during the Cold War, and establishing secular principles and laws that reduced the political and economic power of the caste system in India. He continued to oppose imperialism in all its forms, becoming an icon of colonial independence as European empires fell apart around the globe. Nehru died in office in 1964; two years later, his daughter Indira became Prime Minister, launching a political dynasty in India whose importance lasts to the present day.

Historical Document

Jawaharlal Nehru's Speech on the Occasion of Indian Independence

Long years ago we made a tryst with destiny, and now the time comes when we shall redeem our pledge, not wholly or in full measure, but very substantially. At the stroke of the midnight hour, when the world sleeps, India will awake to life and freedom. A moment comes, which comes but rarely in history, when we step out from the old to the new, when an age ends, and when the soul of a nation, long suppressed, finds utterance. It is fitting that at this solemn moment we take the pledge of dedication to the service of India and her people and to the still larger cause of humanity.

At the dawn of history India started on her unending quest, and trackless centuries are filled with her striving and the grandeur of her success and her failures. Through good and ill fortune alike she has never lost sight of that quest or forgotten the ideals which gave her strength. We end today a period of ill fortune and India discovers herself again. The achievement we celebrate today is but a step, an opening of opportunity, to the greater triumphs and achievements that await us. Are we brave enough and wise enough to grasp this opportunity and accept the challenge of the future?

Freedom and power bring responsibility. The responsibility rests upon this Assembly, a sovereign body representing the sovereign people of India. Before the birth of freedom we have endured all the pains of labor and our hearts are heavy with the memory of this sorrow. Some of those pains continue even now. Nevertheless, the past is over and it is the future that beckons to us now.

That future is not one of ease or resting but of incessant striving so that we may fulfil the pledges we have so often taken and the one we shall take today. The service of India means the service of the millions who suffer. It means the ending of poverty and ignorance and disease and inequality of opportunity. The ambition of the greatest man of our generation has been to wipe every tear from every eye. That may be beyond us, but as long as there are tears and suffering, so long our work will not be over.

And so we have to labor and to work, and work hard, to give reality to our dreams. Those dreams are for India, but they are also for the world, for all the nations and peoples are too closely knit together today for any one of them to imagine that it can live apart. Peace has been said to be indivisible; so is freedom, so is prosperity now, and so also is disaster in this One World that can no longer be split into isolated fragments.

To the people of India, whose representatives we are, we make an appeal to join us with faith and confidence in this great adventure. This is no time for petty and destructive criticism, no time for ill-will or blaming others. We have to build the noble mansion of free India where all her children may dwell.

Document Themes and Analysis

Nehru's opening is striking, in that it paraphrases Franklin Delano Roosevelt's image of a "rendezvous with destiny" given in his second inaugural address in 1937. The phrase seems to provide resonance to Nehru's words, in the fact he is referring to a similar national overcoming of hard times (in Roosevelt's case, the Depression) to remake the known world into a new future. Nehru refers to this in his discussion of stepping from the old into the new, "when an age ends, and when the soul of a nation, long suppressed, finds utterance."

Nehru then gives a history lesson. As a writer, Nehru penned three books which gave an overview of India's history, mostly as a reminder to the world and the Indian people that they had once existed as a major civilization from a time before British rule. Nehru calls on Indians not to forget the past, especially as they need to "end today a period of ill fortune," in which the colony was split into India and Muslim-majority Pakistan, which culminated in an ongoing civil war. Nehru asks rhetorically of his people, in an effort to overcome the hatreds brewing in the division of the colony, "Are we brave enough and wise enough to grasp this opportunity and accept the challenge of the future?" In the next paragraph he dismisses the conflicts of the present as a relic of the colony's past.

Nehru continues with the rhetorical flourish that made his speech famous. He outlines the future of India, in an almost constitutional declaration of purpose for his future service as its prime minister – "The service of India means the service of the millions who suffer. It means the ending of poverty and ignorance and disease and inequality of opportunity." He credits this ambition to "the greatest man of our generation", Gandhi, and dedicates his state to ending the Indian people's impoverishment: "as long as there are tears and suffering, so long our work will not be over."

Finally, Nehru proclaims his intention to the world to overcome the divisions inherent in nation-states and to build "One World". Nehru would go on to be a founding member of the Non-Aligned Movement in 1955, along with the leaders of Ghana, Indonesia, Egypt and Yugoslavia. Their goal would be to avoid taking sides in the nuclear Cold War between the United States and the Soviet Union, a conflict that might destroy the modern world if allowed to "split [the world] into isolated fragments." And he calls on the Indian people to join him in the venture.

In the coming decade, Nehru would build on these promises; the Indian people's life expectancy would expand by almost twenty years, caste divisions would be broken down and India's power in world politics would grow as Nehru established a relationship with Mao Zedong's China. In 1962, that relationship would fray during the Sino-Indian War, and the resulting blow to Nehru's vision of a non-aligned world seemed to take a toll on his heart. He died two years later in 1964 as the revered hero of Indian independence.

—David Simonelli, PhD

Bibliography and Additional Reading

"Jawaharlal Nehru (1889-1964)." *BBC—History—Historical Figures* (2014). www.bbc.co.uk/history/historic_figures/nehru_jawaharlal.shtml.

Nehru, Jawaharlal. *Toward Freedom: The Autobiography of Jawaharlal Nehru*. New York: John Day Company, 1941.

Royle, Trevor. *The Last Days of the Raj*. London: Joseph, 1989.

"Shri Jawaharlal Nehru." *PMIndia*. www.pmindia.gov.in/en/former_pm/shri-jawaharlal-nehru.

Wolpert, Stanley. *A New History of India*. New York: Oxford University Press, 2009.

China

By the early twentieth century, the long-ruling Qing (Manchu) dynasty in China was in steep decline. An uprising in Wuchang (Hubei province) in 1911 sparked a number of other such revolts against the Qing. A republic was declared (1912) under the leadership of Sun Yat-sen, but under his successor a period of instability wracked the country as regional warlords returned to the scene. In an effort to oust them, the nationalist Kuomintang, under Chiang Kai-shek, allied themselves with the Chinese Communists and battled the warlords; by 1927, the former forces had succeeded. Once in power, however, Chiang Kai-shek disavowed the Communists. The latter undertook the Long March (1934–1935) to reassemble their forces in Shaanxi, after which, under their emerging leader Mao Zedong, they began to increase their base of support.

Meanwhile, Japan had occupied Manchuria in 1931, and in 1937 it launched a full-scale invasion of China from the north. It remained in control of much of northeastern China until the end of World War II. Again the Chinese Communists and the Kuomintang came together to fight the common enemy (Japan), but when the global conflict was over the two fought a bloody civil war for power in China. The United States backed Chiang Kai-shek, while the Soviet Union supported the Chinese Communists. In 1949, Beijing fell to the Communists, followed by other major urban centers. The Kuomintang fled to Taiwan (which became the Republic of China) while on the mainland the communist People's Republic of China was proclaimed, with Mao as its chairman and Zhou Enlai its premier.

The Communist leadership instituted major land reforms, rapid industrialization, and agricultural collectivization. The Chinese people experienced both selected improvements as well as harsh conditions under such programs as the Great Leap Forward (1958–1960) and the Cultural Revolution (1966–1976). China became a nuclear power in 1964 and remained a committed opponent of the United States until relations began to warm under the presidency of Richard Nixon. With Mao's death in 1976, the more moderate Deng Xiaoping took the helm and implemented major economic reforms, including policies favoring limited capitalist enterprise. By the 1980s China had one of the world's fastest-growing economies and had moderated many of its more hardline policies. In 1989 large demonstrations took place against corruption and for greater democratic reform, but the government brutally suppressed the demonstration in Beijing's Tiananmen Square. Since then the Chinese Communist Party has reaffirmed its supremacy in all matters and largely erased the Tiananmen uprising from the nation's history.

■ Sun Yat-sen: "The Three Stages of Revolution"

Date: 1918
Author: Sun Yat-sen
Genre: essay; political tract

Summary Overview

Sun Yat-sen is an unusual figure in modern Chinese history, in that he is revered in both the People's Republic of China and the Republic of China (Taiwan). This has made his writings an important part of twentieth-century Chinese political culture. For thirty years, Sun alternated between being a participant and an observer of the events that ended the Chinese Empire and created the opportunity for a variety of attempts to form a new government. Sun's views on the stages of a revolution were whole-heartedly accepted by the leaders of most of the factions in the struggle to unify China, including the leaders of both the Nationalists and Communists. These leaders made use of Sun's support for strong martial law during the initial stages of the revolution. What created a problem for them was the timing of the move from the first to the later stages of his proposals on revolution. However, by stating that they were following Sun's guidance, including his final goal during which all people would have full political rights, the leaders of various factions sought, and gained, the support of most Chinese.

Defining Moment

Although Sun Yat-sen had been working toward establishing a unified Chinese democracy for more than two decades, many of his thoughts on the subject had not been written down in a systematic fashion. While he had formed several organizations in his many attempts to achieve this goal, he had not been successful. Partial success had been obtained at the end of 1911, when the Qing Dynasty renounced any claim on power, allowing a new government to form. Although Sun announced the establishment of a Chinese republic in 1912, the military commander, Yuan Shikai, took control from Sun within a few weeks. After Yuan's attempt to become emperor, and then his death, in 1916, regional governors/military leaders held most of the power, with the general population still having no say in the government. In early 1918, Sun tried to move into the void of national leadership but failed. Sun then decided to outline his plans and goals for China. The work, from which the "Three Stages of Revolution" was taken, was written during this period in which Sun was an observer of the many governors and military commanders striving to gain power and to become the national ruler.

From 1894 to 1918, most of Sun's writing and speaking had been focused on trying to achieve near term goals, rather than a more philosophical long-term view. Even though Sun had mentioned these stages of revolution in 1905 during the formation of the Revolution League, it was only in 1918, while in "exile" in the French concession in Shanghai, that Sun had the luxury of including them when writing about his plans for the nation. His hope was that he could secure a base in China from which he could use these ideas to create a strong and stable Chinese nation. Even though part of the work had been completed with the overthrow of the Qing Dynasty, Sun hoped to give the general population an understanding of what lay ahead if he were given the needed support. He once again began an attempt to transform China from a feudal state to a modern nation in 1919, continuing it until his death. Much of this effort was based upon the ideals described in *A Program of National Reconstruction*. Having straddled the divide between Chinese nationalism and Chinese Communism, Sun's works and ideas, including these "Three Stages of Revolution," were incorporated by both as the two factions evolved into two rival governments claiming the same territory.

Author Biography

Sun Yat-sen (Sun Wen at birth; 1866-1925) was born into a poor, farming family. In 1879, his older brother took him to Hawaii, where Sun went to school and was exposed to Western ideas. He earned a medical degree in Hong Kong in 1892. In 1894 he became politically active, devising and trying to implement plans to help the Chinese people. Because of this, he was formally exiled, from 1895 to 1911, during which he tried ten times to change China's political system. Traveling widely in the West, Sun became known as the spokesperson for those trying to establish a republic in China. When a failed imperial economic policy fueled unrest in China in 1911, Sun returned to take advantage of the situation. He was elected president of the provisional government. After the emperor abdicated, the Republic's military commander forced Sun to resign, as the commander took the presidency. A few years later, Sun tried to regain leadership of the country, and failed. He spent the next two years writing and seeking new ways to unify a fractured China. Although during the early 1920s Sun had regained leadership in parts of southern China, he was never able to carry out his plan to develop a unified republic throughout China. In seeking his goal, Sun sought support from Chinese, Western and Communist sources. When he died, Sun was just one among many regional leaders in China, but he was seen as the leader of China by most of the world.

Sun Yat-sen, c. 1910s. Photo via Wikimedia Commons. [Public domain.]

Historical Document

The Three Stages of Revolution

The first stage is the period of destruction. During this period martial law is to be enforced. The revolutionary army undertakes to overthrow the Manchu tyranny, to eradicate the corruption of officialdom, to eliminate depraved customs, to exterminate the system of slave girls, to wipe out the scourge of opium, superstitious beliefs, and geomancy, to abolish the obstructive likin trade tax and so forth.

The second stage is a transitional period. It is planned that the provisional constitution will be promulgated and local self-government promoted to encourage the exercise of political rights by the people. The xian, or district, will be made the basic unit of local self-government and is to be divided into villages and rural districts—all under the jurisdiction of the district government.

The moment the enemy forces have been cleared and military operations have ceased in a district, the provisional constitution will be promulgated in the district, defining the rights and duties of citizens and the governing powers of the revolutionary government. The constitution will be enforced for three years, after which period the people of the district will elect their district officers.

In respect to such self-governing units the revolutionary government will exercise the right of political tutelage in accordance with the provisional constitution. When a period of six years expires after the attainment of political stability throughout the country, the districts that have become full-fledged self-governing units are each entitled to elect one representative to form the National Assembly. The task of the assembly will be to adopt a five-power constitution and to organize a central government consisting of five branches, namely, the Executive Branch the Legislative Branch, the Judicial Branch, the Examination Branch, and the Control Branch [Censorate]...

When the constitution is promulgated and the president and members of the National Assembly are elected, the revolutionary government will hand over its governing power to the president, and the period of political tutelage will come to an end.

The third phase is the period of the completion of reconstruction. During this period constitutional government is to be introduced, and the self-governing body in a district will enable the people directly to exercise their political rights. In regard to the district government the people are entitled to the rights of election, initiative, referendum, and recall. In regard to the national government, the people exercise the rights of suffrage, while the other rights are delegated to the representatives to the National Assembly. The period of constitutional government will mark the completion of reconstruction and the success of the revolution. This is the gist of the Revolutionary Program.

[Source: From *Sources of Chinese Tradition: From 1600 Through the Twentieth Century*, compiled by Wm. Theodore de Bary and Richard Lufrano, 2nd ed., vol. 2 (New York: Columbia University Press, 2000), 328-330].]

Glossary

control branch [censorate]: section of government that audits/monitors the other branches.

examination branch: section of government that judges the qualifications of potential government employees, who earned positions by passing exams.

geomancy: a form of divination based on geography or lines.

***likin* trade tax**: tax on items passing through a province.

Manchu: the original name of the Qing Dynasty.

Document Themes and Analysis

A successful revolution in any country necessitates changes in the government and other related aspects of society. However, in China, the push in the early twentieth-century was for the transformation of the government from a corrupt, absolute monarchy to a democratic republic. Thus, unlike some other nations where a rebellion simply caused one monarch to be replaced by another, or one president by another, China had to change the basic ways in which laws were created and enforced. Sun not only developed plans for the system of government he wanted in the new republic, but also plans for the transition from the old autocratic system to the new. These stages of revolution were to allow a smoother transition, by recognizing the steps that needed to be taken. Moving from destruction of the old to the implementation of the new was going to be part of any transformation. Sun was optimistic regarding the time it would take to complete this transition, although accurate in the process needed.

The first stage of the revolution was one that would be recognized by any revolutionary. The old had to be destroyed to make way for the new. Sun listed many of the evils that, from his perspective, needed to end. Although some were government policy, such as allowing duties to be charged on merchandise being shipped through a province, most could be seen as social issues that the old government either supported or ignored. These "depraved customs" needed to change for the betterment of China, according to Sun. While some were definite problems, such as the "slave girls" or use of opium, others might be seen as representing an impediment to China becoming a more Westernized nation (superstitious beliefs). As a youth, Sun was attracted to many Western ideals and he never wavered from this.

The second step being a "transitional period," Sun sought to encouragement the first steps toward a democratic republic. During the first stage, military rule would be the norm, as he believed that force would have to be used during the destruction of the old. Moving forward, Sun sought to implement a more democratic form beginning at the local level. He outlined how the provinces/districts would be subdivided for this purpose (many of these subdivisions already existed) and local elections would be the first phase of the second stage. This would take place "three years" after the eradication of the enemy forces, during which time other aspects of the new constitution "will be enforced." By beginning elections at the local level, Sun hoped that the voters would know the candidates better, and through the experience at the local level develop the skills necessary to select the best candidates running for office at the district or national level. Just as the first phase of this stage was for "three years," this next phase would last for "six years... after the attainment of political stability." Although many might look at this nine year period of transition as overly long, Sun had looked at past examples of successful change and seen that most went through periods of transitions. For example, in the United States it took more than a decade to move from the Continental Congress to the Articles of Confederation to the permanent system under the Constitution.

At the end of the second stage, a permanent constitution would be put in place, with a mixture of Western and Chinese political systems resulting in five branches of government: "the Executive Branch, the Legislative Branch, the Judicial Branch, the Examination Branch, and the Control Branch." The first three reflected mainstream Western political theory, while the last two were specific to Chinese culture. As implied in the first two stages, the third stage of revolution was to be the full implementation of the new constitutional system, including elections in which all people were eligible to vote. Members of the National Assembly, as the legislative branch, were to be elected by the people, would then pass the laws that would govern China. Although the details of the various branches were not given in this brief outline, Sun did assure the people greater rights at the local/district level, including what were popular progressive ideas of the period: "initiative, referendum, and recall." With the government in place, under the new constitution, Sun declared that this would mark the "success of the revolution." Although many of the political ideals outlined in his writing were incorporated in the background documents of both Chinese governments, only the Republic of China (Taiwan) incorporated the five branches he outlined in this text. The People's Republic of China developed a system that was closer to other Communist states of the 1940s.

—*Donald A. Watt, PhD*

Bibliography and Additional Reading

Asia for Educators. "Selections from A Program of National Reconstruction: 'The Three Stages of Revolution' (1918)" (Primary Source Documents with Questions) New York: Columbia University, 2018.

Linebarger, Paul Myron. *The Political Doctrines of Sun Yat-sen: An Exposition of the San Min Chu I.* (print original: Baltimore: The Johns Hopkins Press, 1937; second: Westport CT: Greenwood Press, Publishers, 1973.) Salt Lake City: Project Gutenberg, 2018.

Schiffrin, Harold Z. *Sun Yat-sen and the Origins of the Chinese Revolution.* Berkeley: University of California Press, 2010.

Sun Yat-sen. *Memoirs of a Chinese Revolutionary.* (original 1925) Agawam MA: Silver Street Media, 1912.

■ "The Chinese People Have Stood Up!"

Date: September 21, 1949
Author: Mao Zedong
Genre: speech

Summary Overview

"Victory has been achieved," was essentially what Mao Zedong told those gathered for the Chinese People's Political Consultative Conference in September 1949. Focusing on the military and political struggle in China since the end of World War II, Mao touted the basic ideology of the Chinese Communist Party (CCP), and what, ten days later, would become the People's Republic of China (PRC). He clearly identified those who had opposed the communists' drive to power as the Kuomintang (also transliterated at Guomindang), the Chinese nationalist party led by Chiang Kai-shek. The latter's ally, the United States, was also taken to task. In this self-congratulatory speech, Mao not only praises the efforts that led to the communist victory but also outlines an agenda for the Conference, which would create a new identity for the Chinese people and nation. In his vision of the future, Mao correctly foretold that the new state would need to continue to use its power to keep the nation moving toward the goals of the Communist Party.

Defining Moment

As China entered the 1920s, it was unclear if the hopes of creating a modern national democratic state, which many leaders of the 1911–1912 revolution desired, would be achieved. With the death of the last effective Qing Dynasty ruler in 1908, various regional leaders had gained greater power. When the move to create a Chinese republic began in 1911, the 1912 abdication by the Qing government allowed the creation of the Republic of China government—although it had limited power. The first president, Sun Yat-Sen, who was a strong supporter of a national republic, pragmatically stepped aside in order that a military leader, Yuan Shikai, could be the president of the new republic and attempt to hold it together by military means. However, Yuan Shikai became an autocratic ruler and, with his death in 1916, China essentially split into a collection of regional warlord governments.

In 1921, a group (including Mao) met in Shanghai to create the Chinese Communist Party (CCP), the goal being to plan the removal of the warlords and the creation of a unified state under communism. Until 1927, the communists (both Chinese and foreign) maintained a loose alliance with the Kuomintang, and their combined force was strong enough to make substantial progress toward elimination of the warlords. In April 1927, however, the Kuomintang attacked the communists, fearing that they were gaining too much power as the country moved toward unification. The two groups began to operate separately and to clash. In 1931, Mao, as an increasingly prominent figure in the Communist movement, was named chairman of the Chinese Soviet Republic, although this entity existed mainly on paper. Then, with Japan's incursions into China in the 1930s, the Kuomintang was forced to join forces with the communists again in order to defeat the

Flag of the People's Republic of China. Image via Wikimedia Commons. [Public domain.]

new common foe. As World War II began, Japan still held a large section of northern China and the animosity between the two Chinese groups resurfaced.

The three-year military struggle for the control of China was not as one-sided as Mao makes it out to be in his victory speech. Yet, the Communist forces, formed into the People's Liberation Army (PLA), were able slowly to secure control of the main political centers in the north, followed by a successful push to the south. With military victory at hand, Mao understood the need to develop a strong central government. Thus, with the formal proclamation of the People's Republic of China only ten days away, Mao gave the speech reproduced here to open the process of developing a government for the new state and to reaffirm the political ideology that would guide it.

Author Biography

Mao Zedong (1893–1976) was born in rural Hunan province, part of a fairly prosperous farming family. At a young age he began reading Western political philosophers rather than traditional Chinese Confucian texts. While in school, he wrote against the imperial system of government, supporting China becoming a republic. He adopted a socialist stance, eventually helping to form the CCP. He was always one of its leaders, although during the struggles of the 1920s it was not certain that he and his views would carry the day. During the Long March (1934–1935) he solidified his position as a military and political leader. With the creation of the People's Republic of China in 1949, Mao became its leader until his death. While an able revolutionary leader, Mao proved less successful as the head of a state. His initial program of agrarian reform was somewhat successful, but most of his later programs—the Great Leap Forward (1958–62), the Cultural Revolution (1966–1976)—were terrible human disasters, resulting in the deaths of many millions of people and generally failing to reach their goals.

Historical Document

Mao Zedong—"The Chinese People Have Stood Up!"

Fellow Delegates,

The Political Consultative Conference so eagerly awaited by the whole nation is herewith inaugurated.

Our conference is composed of more than six hundred delegates, representing all the democratic parties and people's organizations of China, the People's Liberation Army, the various regions and nationalities of the country and the overseas Chinese. This shows that ours is a conference embodying the great unity of the people of the whole country.

It is because we have defeated the reactionary Kuomintang government backed by U.S. imperialism that this great unity of the whole people has been achieved. In a little more than three years the heroic Chinese People's Liberation Army, an army such as the world has seldom seen, crushed all the offensives launched by the several million troops of the U.S.-supported reactionary Kuomintang government and turned to the counter-offensive and the offensive. At present the field armies of the People's Liberation Army, several million strong, have pushed the war to areas near Taiwan, Kwangtung, Kwangsi, Kweichow, Szechuan and Sinkiang, and the great majority of the Chinese people have won liberation. In a little more than three years the people of the whole country have closed their ranks, rallied to support the People's Liberation Army, fought the enemy and won basic victory. And it is on this foundation that the present People's Political Consultative Conference is convened.

Our conference is called the Political Consultative Conference because some three years ago we held a Political Consultative Conference with Chiang Kai-shek's Kuomintang.[1] The results of that conference were sabotaged by Chiang Kai-shek's Kuomintang and its accomplices; nevertheless the conference left an indelible impression on the people. It showed that nothing in the interest of the people could be accomplished together with Chiang Kai-shek's Kuomintang, the running dog of imperialism, and its accomplices. Even when resolutions were reluctantly adopted, it was of no avail, for as soon as the time was ripe, they tore them up and started a ruthless war against the people. The only gain from that conference was the profound lesson it taught the people that there is absolutely no room for compromise with Chiang Kai-shek's Kuomintang, the running dog of imperialism, and its accomplices—overthrow these enemies or be oppressed and slaughtered by them, either one or the other, there is no other choice. In a little more than three years the Chinese people, led by the Chinese Communist Party, have quickly awakened and organized themselves into a nation-wide united front against imperialism, feudalism, bureaucrat-capitalism and their general representative, the reactionary Kuomintang government, supported the People's War of Liberation, basically defeated the reactionary Kuomintang government, overthrown the rule of imperialism in China and restored the Political Consultative Conference.

The present Chinese People's Political Consultative Conference is convened on an entirely new foundation; it is representative of the people of the whole country and enjoys their trust and support. Therefore, the conference proclaims that it will exercise the functions and powers of a National People's Congress. In accordance with its agenda, the conference will enact the Organic Law of the Chinese People's Political Consultative Conference, the Organic Law of the Central People's Government of the People's Republic of China and the Common Program of the Chinese People's Political Consultative Conference; it will elect the National Committee of the Chinese People's Political Consultative Conference and the Central People's Government Council of the People's Republic of China; it will adopt the national flag and national emblem of the People's Republic of China; and it will decide on the seat of the capital of the People's Republic of China and adopt the chronological system in use in most countries of the world.

Fellow Delegates, we are all convinced that our work will go down in the history of mankind, demonstrating that the Chinese people, comprising one quarter of humanity, have now stood up. The Chinese have always been a great, courageous and industrious nation; it is only in modern times that they have fallen behind. And that was due entirely to oppression and exploitation by foreign imperialism and domestic reactionary governments. For over a century our forefathers never stopped waging unyielding struggles against domestic and foreign oppressors, including the Revolution of 1911 led by Dr. Sun Yat-sen, our great forerunner in the Chinese revolution. Our forefathers enjoined us to carry out their unfulfilled will. And we have acted accordingly. We have closed our ranks and defeated both domestic and foreign oppressors through the People's War of Liberation and the great people's revolution, and now we are proclaiming the founding of the People's Republic of China. From now on our nation will belong to the community of the peace-loving and freedom-loving nations of the world and work courageously and industriously to foster its own civilization and well-being and at the same time to promote world peace and freedom. Ours will no longer be a nation subject to insult and humiliation. We have stood up. Our revolution has won the sympathy and acclaim of the people of all countries. We have friends all over the world.

Our revolutionary work is not completed, the People's War of Liberation and the people's revolutionary movement are still forging ahead and we must keep up our efforts. The imperialists and the domestic reactionaries will certainly not take their defeat lying down; they will fight to the last ditch. After there is peace and order throughout the country, they are sure to engage in sabotage and create disturbances by one means or another and every day and every minute they will try to stage a come-back. This is inevitable and beyond all doubt, and under no circumstances must we relax our vigilance.

Our state system, the people's democratic dictatorship, is a powerful weapon for safeguarding the fruits of victory of the people's revolution and for thwarting the plots of domestic and foreign enemies for restoration, and this weapon we must firmly grasp. Internationally, we must unite with all peace-loving and freedom-loving countries and peoples, and first of all with the Soviet Union and the New Democracies, so that we shall not stand alone in our struggle to safeguard these fruits of victory and to thwart the plots of domestic and foreign enemies for restoration. As long as we persist in the people's democratic dictatorship and unite with our foreign friends, we shall always be victorious.

The people's democratic dictatorship and solidarity with our foreign friends will enable us to accomplish our work of construction rapidly. We are already confronted with the task of nation-wide economic construction. We have very favorable conditions: a population of 475 million people and a territory of 9,600,000 square kilometers. There are indeed difficulties ahead, and a great many too. But we firmly believe that by heroic struggle the people of the country will surmount them all. The Chinese people have rich experience in overcoming difficulties. If our forefathers, and we also, could weather long years of extreme difficulty and defeat powerful domestic and foreign reactionaries, why can't we now, after victory, build a prosperous and flourishing country? As long as we keep to our style of plain living and hard struggle, as long as we stand united and as long as we persist in the people's democratic dictatorship and unite with our foreign friends, we shall be able to win speedy victory on the economic front.

An upsurge in economic construction is bound to be followed by an upsurge of construction in the cultural sphere. The era in which the Chinese people were regarded as uncivilized is now ended. We shall emerge in the world as a nation with an advanced culture.

Our national defense will be consolidated and no imperialists will ever again be allowed to invade our land. Our people's armed forces must be maintained and developed with the heroic and steeled People's Liberation Army as the foundation. We will have not only a powerful army but also a powerful air force and a powerful navy.

Let the domestic and foreign reactionaries tremble before us! Let them say we are no good at this and no good at that. By our own indomitable efforts we the Chinese people will unswervingly reach our goal.

The heroes of the people who laid down their lives in the People's War of Liberation and the people's revolution shall live for ever in our memory!

Hail the victory of the People's War of Liberation and the people's revolution!

Hail the founding of the People's Republic of China!

Hail the triumph of the Chinese People's Political Consultative Conference!

NOTES: [1] "Smash Chiang Kai-shek's Offensive by a War of Self-Defence," Note 2, *Selected Works of Mao Tsetung*, Vol. IV.

[Source: china.usc.edu/Mao-declares-founding-of-peoples-republic-of-china-chinese-people-have-stood-up]

Glossary

Chiang Kai-shek: leader of the Kuomintang and the Republic of China(Taiwan) from 1928 until 1975

Kuomintang: the name of the dominant political party of the nationalist movement

Long March, the: a 370-day-long military retreat of over 5,600 miles westward from southeast China, then north through western China, ending in Shaanxi province in northern China; about ninety percent of the soldiers either died or left the army during the trek

New Democracies: a reference to post–World War II countries ruled by communist governments, primarily in Eastern Europe

people's democratic dictatorship: an authoritarian approach that, in Mao's view, the Communist Party should employ to keep the state from becoming one that serves the interests of the bourgeois

Sun Yat-Sen: leader of the revolution that, in 1912, ended the last imperial dynasty in China and instituted the Republic of China; he is honored by both the PRC and the Republic of China

Mao Zedong proclaiming the foundation of the People's Republic of China on October 1, 1949. Photo via Wikimedia Commons. [Public domain.]

Document Analysis

As Mao Zedong stood in front of the opening session of the People's Political Consultative Conference, he gave an inspirational speech, rather than outlining detailed plans for the conference to adopt. Although those gathered that day would have remembered the efforts of the post–World War II era, Mao went beyond retelling that story to hold up the prospect of a new, unified China under Communism. Unity is a key theme in his presentation. In addition, Mao castigates the Kuomintang as an enemy of the Chinese people, hindering the development of a strong postimperial state. Finally, Mao emphasizes his view that the strength of the Chinese people will help facilitate the massive sociopolitical transformation he envisions.

Mao claims that the unity of the people in their support for the PLA, and the Communist movement in general, has brought about a victory not only for the communists but for all of the people. Although the Kuomintang had thwarted previous efforts to create a joint government, the impending total communist victory meant that unification in China no longer depended on the Kuomintang. Mao saw the new government being created by the communists as representative of the whole country, in much the same way as the conference delegates themselves were representative. He charges the delegates with the tasks of establishing the framework of the new government, adopting its symbols, and electing the initial membership of the governing bodies. In this way China will become a viable member of the world community.

Mao speaks about the need to work to retain China's unique identity, its "advanced culture" (based on its long history). The new nation possessed population and territorial resources that would make it more than equal to other nations, and help it to develop economically. It also could rightfully celebrate its own culture and heritage. Mao believed that as the system of government assisted in the economic development of the nation, there would be enemies (reactionaries) both inside and outside the country who would attempt to sabotage such growth. Although he does not use the word *communist*, it is clear that he looks first to other communist states for assistance in international affairs.

Seeing economic development as the top priority, Mao advises potential enemies that the "Chinese people will unswervingly reach our goal." He asserts that the "people's democratic dictatorship" will act with great power to "thwart... the plots" of those trying to stop China's development. This speech, full of positive pronouncements for the future of China, and of the new government, serves as a synopsis of the "victory" and "triumph" that he believes he and other communist leaders had attained.

Essential Themes

Mao urges the members of the People's Political Consultative Conference to support his call to continue the unification of all areas and aspects of Chinese life. He places the Communist movement within the broader context of anti-imperial efforts by including Dr. Sun Yat-sen as a founder of the then current unification efforts. He makes it clear that the Kuomintang movement is a political movement that has lost its way, by rejecting opportunities to work with the communists in previous conferences. Thus, the masses are united against "imperialism, feudalism, bureaucrat-capitalism...the reactionary Kuomintang government."

Mao's analysis is that the Kuomintang's rejection of the communists planted the seeds of their own downfall, because, he believes, the general population supports communist ideals. Thus, the PLA was able to recruit millions of soldiers because the masses believed in the communist ideals, according to Mao. He shared the idea that the "true" revolution, initiated by Sun Yat-sen, was carried forward for the people by the "heroic and steeled People's Liberation Army." The newly awakened masses supported the effort which led to a swift victory by the PLA. While the PLA was victorious, Mao conveniently ignores the major defeats that it had suffered in some early battles.

While Mao calls upon the Conference to enact an "Organic Law" for the new nation, he suggests that the establishment of a new government will not be easy. There were then still several provinces that were yet to be fully occupied by the PLA; Mao notes that the overt military conflict was essentially over, but that new challenges lay ahead. He warns the delegates that it is highly likely that an ongoing "heroic" struggle would be necessary to "safeguard these fruits of victory." For Mao, prosperity for all people, not just for a few, would be the result of continuous vigilance by the people against the efforts of reactionaries to undercut it.

—Donald A. Watt, PhD

Bibliography and Additional Reading

Halsall, Paul. "Modern History Sourcebook: The Common Program of the Chinese People's Political Conference, 1949." *Internet History Sourcebook Project, Fordham University.*" New York: History Department, Fordham University, 1998.

Karl, Rebecca E. *Mao Zedong and China in the Twentieth Century World.: A Concise History.* Durham NC: Duke University Press, 2010.

Lary, Diana. *China's Republic.* Cambridge: Cambridge University Press, 2007.

Meisner, Maurice. *Mao Zedong: A Political and Intellectual Portrait.* Cambridge: Polity Press, 2006.

Ministry of Foreign Affairs of the People's Republic of China. "Formulation of Foreign Policy of New China on the Eve of its Birth." *Ministry of Foreign Affairs of the People's Republic of China.* Beijing: Ministry of Foreign Affairs of the People's Republic of China, 2014.

Office of the Historian. "The Chinese Revolution of 1949." *Milestones 1945–1952.* Washington, DC: Department of State, 2016.

Mao Zedong on Communism and Counterrevolution

Date: February 27, 1957
Author: Mao Zedong
Genre: speech

Summary Overview

A decade after the founding of the People's Republic of China, its leader, Mao Zedong, gave this speech as part of his Hundred Flowers Campaign. After Soviet leader Nikita Khrushchev gave a speech denouncing the brutal regime of dictator Joseph Stalin, Communist leaders around the world considered whether it was prudent to relax some of the restrictions imposed on their citizens, particularly intellectuals and students. Mao invited a renewed conversation about how conditions in China could be improved and offered to accept criticism. In the context of Mao's extremely repressive regime, this criticism was slow to materialize. Mao made this speech initially as a way to encourage his people to follow the unity-criticism-unity model for resolving internal conflicts. The speech was also intended to reinforce the idea that consensus could be reached without any structural change to the Communist government in China. Mao addressed the Hungarian Revolution of October 1956, in which students led an armed uprising against Hungary's Soviet-backed government. Mao made it clear that this was not an acceptable way to resolve internal conflicts in China. He claimed that it was a tool of the West, attempting to exploit "contradictions among the people" that should have been resolved through conversation and education.

Defining Moment

The Chinese Communist Party (CCP) was founded in 1921, and many of its original members, like Mao, were students and academics who had watched the Russian Revolution of 1917 with interest. The Communist government established in Russia was very appealing to Chinese intellectuals, who saw the same class struggle between peasants and landowners that existed in Russia. The nationalist Kuomintang party, led by Chiang Kai-shek, initially accepted the Chinese Communist Party, but in April 1927, thousands of Communists were killed in Shanghai as the Kuomintang purged them from their ranks. The two factions briefly cooperated to resist the Japanese invasion during World War II, but the relationship quickly deteriorated after Japan's defeat.

The Kuomintang under Chiang Kai-shek was heavily supported by the United States both during the war, as an ally against Japan, and after, as a barrier

Mao Zedong, 1959. Photo via Wikimedia Commons. [Public domain.]

to the spread of Communism. The Soviet Union invaded Manchuria in 1945 to fight the Japanese and only withdrew when the Chinese Communist Party was firmly in control of the territory. Despite negotiations between Mao Zedong and Chiang Kai-shek in 1945, within a year, civil war had broken out. After a series of strategic victories, Mao announced the creation of the People's Republic of China on October 1, 1949. Chiang Kai-shek and the Kuomintang faithful fled to Taiwan after his defeat.

Mao quickly began a program of sweeping land reforms, intended to consolidate support for the party among the rural peasantry. The 1950 Agrarian Reform Law reallocated land to peasants and led to organized meetings where landowners were often beaten and killed. In 1953, Mao accelerated the reallocation of land to the state and established rural communes. During the early years of his leadership, he also established the Campaign to Suppress Counterrevolutionaries, calling for the arrest of anyone accused of disloyalty to the Chinese Communist Party. Millions of Chinese citizens were killed during land reform and the purging of suspected opponents, and millions more were sent to forced labor camps, where many died of starvation and disease. Mao set quotas for local officials, insisting that public executions were necessary to root out enemies of the people. He encouraged citizens to inform on any suspicious behavior among their family members and friends. This information was used to purge businesspeople, political opponents, and members of Mao's own party that he suspected of disloyalty. Many suspected government officials were encouraged to commit suicide and did so to avoid public execution or death in the labor camps.

By 1953, China was firmly under Mao's control. His first five-year plan, launched that year along the Soviet model, focused on dramatically increased industrial production and massive civil engineering projects. In 1956, Mao introduced the Hundred Flowers Campaign, ostensibly to invite feedback and criticism, though many thought that this was an attempt by Mao to either demonstrate the extent of his support among the people or root out dissent. In any case, criticism was initially tolerated, but when it became clear that there were many complaints about Mao's leadership, the policy was reversed, and dissenters were brutally repressed.

Author Biography

Mao Zedong, later known as Chairman Mao, was born in Hunan Province, China, on December 26, 1893. He was from a prosperous farming family and received a rudimentary village education while working in his father's fields. A voracious reader, he left home when he was seventeen to pursue a secondary education in Hunan's capital city of Changsha, then a hotbed of antimonarchist rebellion. Mao briefly joined the nationalist revolutionary army, which overthrew the monarchy in 1912, then attended several different schools for various trades. He graduated from teacher training in 1918 and he moved to Beijing, where he worked in the Peking University library and followed the progress of the Russian Revolution. In 1921, he was one of the first leaders of the Chinese Communist Party. Though a committed Marxist-Leninist, Mao also joined the Kuomintang, believing that such an alliance would be expedient. He rose through the party ranks, working to organize rural peasants.

Kuomintang leader Sun Yat-sen died in March 1925 and was replaced by Chiang Kai-shek, who was not interested in mobilizing the rural peasantry or working with the Communists. Mao became a central figure in the resistance to Chiang Kai-shek, leading guerilla warfare from strongholds in the countryside. In 1937, the Japanese invaded China, and the Nationalist and Communist factions briefly reunited to fight the invaders. However, after the Japanese were defeated in 1945, the fragile coalition did not survive. In October 1949, Mao and the Communists established the People's Republic of China. Mao remained China's undisputed leader, with the exception of a brief period from 1962 to 1966, until his death on September 9, 1976. He was buried in a mausoleum in Beijing.

Historical Document

Mao Zedong on Communism and Counterrevolution

Our general subject is the correct handling of contradictions among the people. For convenience, let us discuss it under twelve sub-headings. Although reference will be made to contradictions between ourselves and the enemy, this discussion will centre on contradictions among the people.

I. Two Types of Contradictions Differing in Nature

Never before has our country been as united as it is today. The victories of the bourgeois-democratic revolution and of the socialist revolution and our achievements in socialist construction have rapidly changed the face of the old China. A still brighter future lies ahead for our motherland. The days of national disunity and chaos which the people detested are gone, never to return. Led by the working class and the Communist Party, our 600 million people, united as one, are engaged in the great task of building socialism. The unification of our country, the unity of our people and the unity of our various nationalities—these are the basic guarantees for the sure triumph of our cause. However, this does not mean that contradictions no longer exist in our society. To imagine that none exist is a naive idea which is at variance with objective reality. We are confronted with two types of social contradictions—those between ourselves and the enemy and those among the people. The two are totally different in nature.

To understand these two different types of contradictions correctly, we must first be clear on what is meant by "the people" and what is meant by "the enemy." The concept of "the people" varies in content in different countries and in different periods of history in a given country. Take our own country for example. During the War of Resistance Against Japan, all those classes, strata and social groups opposing Japanese aggression came within the category of the people, while the Japanese imperialists, their Chinese collaborators and the pro-Japanese elements were all enemies of the people. During the War of Liberation, the U.S. imperialists and their running dogs—the bureaucrat-capitalists, the landlords and the Kuomintang reactionaries who represented these two classes—were the enemies of the people, while the other classes, strata and social groups, which opposed them, all came within the category of the people. At the present stage, the period of building socialism, the classes, strata and social groups which favour, support and work for the cause of socialist construction all come within the category of the people, while the social forces and groups which resist the socialist revolution and are hostile to or sabotage socialist construction are all enemies of the people.

The contradictions between ourselves and the enemy are antagonistic contradictions. Within the ranks of the people, the contradictions among the working people are non-antagonistic, while those between the exploited and the exploiting classes have a non-antagonistic as well as an antagonistic aspect. There have always been contradictions among the people, but they are different in content in each period of the revolution and in the period of building socialism. In the conditions prevailing in China today, the contradictions among the people comprise the contradictions within the working class, the contradictions within the peasantry, the contradictions within the intelligentsia, the contradictions between the working class and the peasantry, the contradictions between the workers and peasants on the one hand and the intellectuals on the other, the contradictions between the working class and other sections of the working people on the one hand and the national bourgeoisie on the other, the contradictions within the national bourgeoisie, and so on. Our People's Government is one that genuinely represents the people's interests, it is a government that serves the people. Nevertheless, there are still certain contradictions between this government and the people. These include the contradictions between the interests of the state and the interests of the collective on the one hand and the interests of the individual on the other, between democracy and centralism, between the leadership and the led, and the contradictions arising from the bureaucratic style of work of some of the state personnel in their relations with the masses. All these are also contradictions among the people. Generally speaking, the fundamental identity of the people's interests underlies the contradictions among the people.

In our country, the contradiction between the working class and the national bourgeoisie comes under the category of contradictions among the people. By and large, the class struggle between the two is a class struggle within the ranks of the people, because the Chinese national bourgeoisie has a dual character. In the period of the bourgeois-democratic revolution, it had both a revolutionary and a conciliationist side to its character. In the period of the socialist revolution, exploitation of the working class for profit constitutes one side of the character of the national bourgeoisie, while its support of the Constitution and its willingness to accept socialist transformation constitute the other. The national bourgeoisie differs from the imperialists, the landlords and the bureaucrat-capitalists. The contradiction between the national bourgeoisie and the working class is one between exploiter and exploited, and is by nature antagonistic. But in the concrete conditions of China, this antagonistic contradiction between the two classes, if properly handled, can be transformed into a non-antagonistic one and be resolved by peaceful methods. However, the contradiction between the working class and the national bourgeoisie will change into a contradiction between ourselves and the enemy if we do not handle it properly and do not follow the policy of uniting with, criticizing and educating the national bourgeoisie, or if the national bourgeoisie does not accept this policy of ours.

Since they are different in nature, the contradictions between ourselves and the enemy and the contradictions among the people must be resolved by different methods. To put it briefly, the former entail drawing a clear distinction between ourselves and the enemy, and the latter entail drawing a clear distinction between right and wrong. It is of course true that the distinction between ourselves and the enemy is also one of right and wrong. For example, the question of who is in the right, we or the domestic and foreign reactionaries, the imperialists, the feudalists and bureaucrat-capitalists, is also one of right and wrong, but it is in a different category from questions of right and wrong among the people.

Our state is a people's democratic dictatorship led by the working class and based on the worker-peasant alliance. What is this dictatorship for? Its first function is internal, namely, to suppress the reactionary classes and elements and those exploiters who resist the socialist revolution, to suppress those who try to wreck our socialist construction, or in other words, to resolve the contradictions between ourselves and the internal enemy. For instance, to arrest, try and sentence certain counter-revolutionaries, and to deprive landlords and bureaucrat-capitalists of their right to vote and their freedom of speech for a certain period of time—all this comes within the scope of our dictatorship. To maintain public order and safeguard the interests of the people, it is necessary to exercise dictatorship as well over thieves, swindlers, murderers, arsonists, criminal gangs and other scoundrels who seriously disrupt public order. The second function of this dictatorship is to protect our country from subversion and possible aggression by external enemies. In such contingencies, it is the task of this dictatorship to resolve the contradiction between ourselves and the external enemy. The aim of this dictatorship is to protect all our people so that they can devote themselves to peaceful labour and make China a socialist country with modern industry, modern agriculture, and modern science and culture. Who is to exercise this dictatorship? Naturally, the working class and the entire people under its leadership. Dictatorship does not apply within the ranks of the people. The people cannot exercise dictatorship over themselves, nor must one section of the people oppress another. Law-breakers among the people will be punished according to law, but this is different in principle from the exercise of dictatorship to suppress enemies of the people. What applies among the people is democratic centralism. Our Constitution lays it down that citizens of the People's Republic of China enjoy freedom of speech, the press, assembly, association, procession, demonstration, religious belief, and so on. Our Constitution also provides that the organs of state must practice democratic centralism, that they must rely on the masses and that their personnel must serve the people. Our socialist democracy is the broadest kind of democracy, such as is not to be found in any bourgeois state. Our dictatorship is the people's democratic dictatorship led by the working class and based on the worker-peasant alliance. That is to say, democracy operates within the ranks of the people, while the working class, uniting with all others enjoying civil rights, and in the first place with the peasantry, enforces dictatorship over the reactionary classes and elements and all those who resist socialist transformation and oppose socialist construction. By civil rights, we mean, politically, the rights of freedom and democracy.

But this freedom is freedom with leadership and this democracy is democracy under centralized guidance, not anarchy. Anarchy does not accord with the interests or wishes of the people.

Certain people in our country were delighted by the Hungarian incident. They hoped that something similar would happen in China, that thousands upon thousands of people would take to the streets to demonstrate against the People's Government. Their hopes ran counter to the interests of the masses and therefore could not possibly win their support. Deceived by domestic and foreign counter-revolutionaries, a section of the people in Hungary made the mistake of resorting to violence against the people's government, with the result that both the state and the people suffered. The damage done to the country's economy in a few weeks of rioting will take a long time to repair. In our country there were some others who wavered, on the question of the Hungarian incident because they were ignorant of the real state of affairs in the world. They think that there is top little freedom under our people's democracy and that there is more, freedom under Western parliamentary democracy. They ask for a two-party system as in the West, with one party in office and the other in opposition. But this so-called two-party system is nothing but a device for maintaining the dictatorship of the bourgeoisie; it can never guarantee freedoms to the working people. As a matter of fact, freedom and democracy exist not in the abstract, but only in the concrete. In a society where class struggle exists, if there is freedom for the exploiting classes to exploit the working people, there is no freedom for the working people not to be exploited. If there is democracy for the bourgeoisie, there is no democracy for the proletariat and other working people. The legal existence of the Communist Party is tolerated in some capitalist countries, but only to the extent that it does not endanger the fundamental interests of the bourgeoisie; it is not tolerated beyond that. Those who demand freedom and democracy in the abstract regard democracy as an end and not as a means. Democracy as such sometimes seems to be an end, but it is in fact only a means. Marxism teaches us that democracy is part of the superstructure and belongs to the realm of politics. That is to say, in the last analysis, it serves the economic base. The same is true of freedom. Both democracy and freedom are relative, not absolute, and they come into being and develop in specific historical conditions. Within the ranks of the people, democracy is correlative with centralism and freedom with discipline. They are the two opposites of a single entity, contradictory as well as united, and we should not one-sidedly emphasize one to the exclusion of the other. Within the ranks of the people, we cannot do without freedom, nor can we do without discipline; we cannot do without democracy, nor can we do without centralism. This unity of democracy and centralism, of freedom and discipline, constitutes our democratic centralism. Under this system, the people enjoy broad democracy and freedom, but at the same time they have to keep within the bounds of socialist discipline. All this is well understood by the masses.

In advocating freedom with leadership and democracy under centralized guidance, we in no way mean that coercive measures should be taken to settle ideological questions or questions involving the distinction between right and wrong among the people. All attempts to use administrative orders or coercive measures to settle ideological questions or questions of right and wrong are not only ineffective but harmful. We cannot abolish religion by administrative order or force people not to believe in it. We cannot compel people to give up idealism, any more than we can force them to embrace Marxism. The only way to settle questions of an ideological nature or controversial issues among the people is by the democratic method, the method of discussion, criticism, persuasion and education, and not by the method of coercion or repression. To be able to carry on their production and studies effectively and to lead their lives in peace and order, the people want their government and those in charge of production and of cultural and educational organizations to issue appropriate administrative regulations of an obligatory nature. It is common sense that without them the maintenance of public order would be impossible. Administrative regulations and the method of persuasion and education complement each other in resolving contradictions among the people. In fact, administrative regulations for the maintenance of public order must be accompanied by persuasion and education, for in many cases regulations alone will not work.

This democratic method of resolving contradictions among the people was epitomized in 1942 in the formula "unity—criticism—unity." To elaborate, that means starting from the desire for unity, resolving contradictions through criticism or struggle, and arriving at a new unity on a new basis. In our experience this is the correct method of resolving contradictions among the people. In 1942 we used it to resolve contradictions inside the Communist Party, namely, the contradictions between the dogmatists and the great majority of the membership, and between dogmatism and Marxism. The "Left" dogmatists had resorted to the method of "ruthless struggle and merciless blows" in inner-Party struggle. It was the wrong method. In criticizing "Left" dogmatism, we did not use this old method but adopted a new one, that is, one of starting from the desire for unity, distinguishing between right and wrong through criticism or struggle, and arriving at a new unity on a new basis. This was the method used in the rectification movement of 1942. Within a few years, by the time the Chinese Communist Party held its Seventh National Congress in 1945, unity was achieved throughout the Party as anticipated, and consequently the people's revolution triumphed. Here, the essential thing is to start from the desire for unity. For without this desire for unity, the struggle, once begun, is certain to throw things into confusion and get out of hand. Wouldn't this be the same as "ruthless struggle and merciless blows"?

And what Party unity would there be left? It was precisely this experience that led us to the formula "unity—criticism—unity." Or, in other words, "learn from past mistakes to avoid future ones and cure the sickness to save the patient." We extended this method beyond our Party. We applied it with great success in the anti-Japanese base areas in dealing with the relations between the leadership and the masses, between the army and the people, between officers and men, between the different units of the army, and between the different groups of cadres. The use of this method can be traced back to still earlier times in our Party's history. Ever since 1927 when we built our revolutionary armed forces and base areas in the south, this method had been used to deal with the relations between the Party and the masses, between the army and the people, between officers and men, and with other relations among the people. The only difference was that during the anti-Japanese war we employed this method much more consciously. And since the liberation of the whole country, we have employed this same method of "unity—criticism—unity" in our relations with the democratic parties and with industrial and commercial circles. Our task now is to continue to extend and make still better use of this method throughout the ranks of the people; we want all our factories, co-operatives, shops, schools, offices and people's organizations, in a word, all our 600 million people, to use it in resolving contradictions among themselves.

In ordinary circumstances, contradictions among the people are not antagonistic. But if they are not handled properly, or if we relax our vigilance and lower our guard, antagonism may arise. In a socialist country, a development of this kind is usually only a localized and temporary phenomenon. The reason is that the system of exploitation of man by man has been abolished and the interests of the people are fundamentally identical. The antagonistic actions which took place on a fairly wide scale during the Hungarian incident were the result of the operations of both domestic and foreign counter-revolutionary elements. This was a particular as well as a temporary phenomenon. It was a case of the reactionaries inside a socialist country, in league with the imperialists, attempting to achieve their conspiratorial aims by taking advantage of contradictions among the people to foment dissension and stir up disorder. The lesson of the Hungarian incident merits attention.

Many people seem to think that the use of the democratic method to resolve contradictions among the people is something new. Actually it is not. Marxists have always held that the cause of the proletariat must depend on the masses of the people and that Communists must use the democratic method of persuasion and education when working among the labouring people and must on no account resort to commandism or coercion. The Chinese Communist Party faithfully adheres to this Marxist-Leninist principle. It has been our consistent view that under the people's democratic dictatorship two different methods, one dictatorial and the other democratic, should be used to resolve the two types of contradictions which differ in nature—those between ourselves and the enemy and those among the people. This idea has been explained again and again in many Party documents and in speeches by many leading comrades of our Party. In my article "On the People's Democratic Dictatorship," written in 1949, I said, "The combination of these two aspects, democracy for the people and dictatorship over the reactionaries, is the people's democratic dictatorship." I also pointed out that in order to settle problems within the ranks of the people "the method we employ is democratic, the method of persuasion, not of compulsion." Again, in addressing the Second Session of the First National Committee of the Political Consultative Conference in June two, I said:

The people's democratic dictatorship uses two methods. Towards the enemy, it uses the method of dictatorship, that is, for as long a period of time as is necessary it does not permit them to take part in political activity and compels them to obey the law of the People's Government, to engage in labour and, through such labour, be transformed into new men. Towards the people; on the contrary, it uses the method of democracy and not of compulsion, that is, it must necessarily let them take part in political activity and does not compel them to do this or that but uses the method of democracy to educate and persuade. Such education is self-education for the people, and its basic method is criticism and self-criticism.

Thus, on many occasions we have discussed the use of the democratic method for resolving contradictions among the people; furthermore, we have in the main applied it in our work, and many cadres and many other people are familiar with it in practice. Why then do some people now feel that it is a new issue? Because, in the past, the struggle between ourselves and the enemy, both internal and external, was most acute, and contradictions among the people therefore did not attract as much attention as they do today.

Quite a few people fail to make a clear distinction between these two different types of contradictions—those between ourselves and the enemy and those among the people—and are prone to confuse: the two. It must be admitted that it is sometimes quite easy to do so. We have had instances of such confusion in our work in the past; In the course of cleaning out counter-revolutionaries good people were sometimes mistaken for bad, and such things still happen today. We are able to keep mistakes within bounds because it has been our policy to draw a sharp line between ourselves and the enemy and to rectify mistakes whenever discovered.

Marxist philosophy holds that the law of the unity of opposites is the fundamental law of the universe. This law operates universally, whether in the natural world, in human society, or in man's thinking. Between the opposites in a contradiction there is at once unity and struggle, and it is this that impels things to move and change. Contradictions exist everywhere, but their nature differs in accordance with the different nature of different things. In any given thing, the unity of opposites is conditional, temporary and transitory, and hence relative, whereas the struggle of opposites is absolute. Lenin gave a very clear exposition of this law. It has come to be understood by a growing number of people in our country. But for many people it is one thing to accept this law and quite another to apply it in examining and dealing with problems. Many dare not openly admit that contradictions still exist among the people of our country, while it is precisely these contradictions that are pushing our society forward. Many do not admit that contradictions still exist in socialist society, with the result that they become irresolute and passive when confronted with social contradictions; they do not understand that socialist society grows more united and consolidated through the ceaseless process of correctly handling and resolving contradictions. For this reason, we need to explain things to our people, and to our cadres in the first place, in order to help them understand the contradictions in socialist society and learn to use correct methods for handling them.

Contradictions in socialist society are fundamentally different from those in the old societies, such as capitalist society. In capitalist society contradictions find expression in acute antagonisms and conflicts, in sharp class struggle; they cannot be resolved by the capitalist system itself and can only be resolved by socialist revolution. The case is quite different with contradictions in socialist society; on the contrary, they are not antagonistic and can be ceaselessly resolved by the socialist system itself.

In socialist society the basic contradictions are still those between the relations of production and the productive forces and between the superstructure and the economic base. However, they are fundamentally different in character and have different features from the contradictions between the relations of production and the productive forces and between the superstructure and the economic base in the old societies. The present social system of our country is far superior to that of the old days. If it were not so, the old system would not have been overthrown and the new system could not have been established. In saying that the socialist relations of production correspond better to the character of the productive forces than did the old relations of production, we mean that they allow the productive forces to develop at a speed unattainable in the old society, so that production can expand steadily and increasingly meet the constantly growing needs of the people. Under the rule of imperialism, feudalism and bureaucrat-capitalism, the productive forces of the old China grew very slowly. For more than fifty years before liberation, China produced only a few tens of thousands of tons of steel a year, not counting the output of the northeastern provinces. If these provinces are included, the peak annual steel output only amounted to a little over 900,000 tons. In 1949, the national steel output was a little over 100,000 tons. Yet now, a mere seven years after the liberation of our country, steel output already exceeds 4,000,000 tons. In the old China, there was hardly any machine-building industry, to say nothing of the automobile and aircraft industries; now we have all three. When the people overthrew the rule of imperialism, feudalism and bureaucrat-capitalism, many were not clear as to which way China should head—towards capitalism or towards socialism. Facts have now provided the answer: Only socialism can save China. The socialist system has promoted the rapid development of the productive forces of our country, a fact even our enemies abroad have had to acknowledge.

But our socialist system has only just been set up; it is not yet fully established or fully consolidated. In joint state-private industrial and commercial enterprises, capitalists still get a fixed rate of interest on their capital, that is to say, exploitation still exists. So far as ownership is concerned, these enterprises are not yet completely socialist in nature. A number of our agricultural and handicraft producers' co-operatives are still semi-socialist, while even in the fully socialist co-operatives certain specific problems of ownership remain to be solved. Relations between production and exchange in accordance with socialist principles are being gradually established within and between all branches of our economy, and more and more appropriate forms are being sought. The problem of the proper relation of accumulation to consumption within each of the two sectors of the socialist economy—the one where the means of production are owned by the whole people and the other where the means of production are owned by the collective—and the problem of the proper relation of accumulation to consumption between the two sectors themselves are complicated problems for which it is not easy to work out a perfectly rational solution all at once. To sum up, socialist relations of production have been established and are in correspondence with the growth of the productive forces, but these relations are still far from perfect, and this imperfection stands in contradiction to the growth of the productive forces. Apart from correspondence as well as contradiction between the relations of production and the growth of the productive forces, there is correspondence as well as contradiction between the superstructure and the economic base. The superstructure, comprising the state system and laws of the people's democratic dictatorship and the socialist ideology guided by Marxism-Leninism, plays a positive role in facilitating the victory of socialist transformation and the socialist way of organizing labour; it is in correspondence with the socialist economic base, that is, with socialist relations of production. But the existence of bourgeois ideology, a certain bureaucratic style of work in our state organs and defects in some of the links in our state institutions are in contradiction with the socialist economic base. We must continue to resolve all such contradictions in the light of our specific conditions. Of course, new problems will emerge as these contradictions are resolved. And further efforts will be required to resolve the new contradictions. For instance, a constant process of readjustment through state planning is needed to deal with the contradiction between production and the needs of society, which will long remain an objective reality. Every year our country draws up an economic plan in order to establish a proper ratio between accumulation and consumption and achieve an equilibrium between production and needs. Equilibrium is nothing but a temporary, relative, unity of opposites. By the end of each year, this equilibrium, taken as a whole, is upset by the struggle of opposites; the unity undergoes a change, equilibrium becomes disequilibrium, unity becomes disunity, and once again it is necessary to work out an equilibrium and unity for the next year. Herein lies the superiority of our planned economy. As a matter of fact, this equilibrium, this unity, is partially upset every month or every quarter, and partial readjustments are called for. Sometimes, contradictions arise and the equilibrium is upset because our subjective arrangements do not conform to objective reality; this is what we call making a mistake. The ceaseless emergence and ceaseless resolution of contradictions constitute the dialectical law of the development of things.

Today, matters stand as follows. The large-scale, turbulent class struggles of the masses characteristic of times of revolution have in the main come to an end, but class struggle is by no means entirely over. While welcoming the new system, the masses are not yet quite accustomed to it. Government personnel are not sufficiently experienced and have to undertake further study and investigation of specific policies. In other words, time is needed for our socialist system to become established and consolidated, for the masses to become accustomed to the new system, and for government personnel to learn and acquire experience. It is therefore imperative for us at this juncture to raise the question of distinguishing contradictions among the people from those between ourselves and the enemy, as well as the question of the correct handling of contradictions among the people, in order to unite the people of all nationalities in our country for the new battle, the battle against nature, develop our economy and culture, help the whole nation to traverse this period of transition relatively smoothly, consolidate our new system and build up our new state.

Document Themes and Analysis

Mao Zedong originally delivered this speech at an enlarged session of the Supreme State Conference in February 1957, but he revised the transcript before allowing it to be published in the *People's Daily* newspaper in June. In the revised transcript, Mao begins by proclaiming "the victories of the bourgeois-democratic revolution and of the socialist revolution" and the unity of the people of China. The people of China have emerged from a period of conflict and chaos, he claims, and are working together on "the great task of building socialism." However, he concedes that to say that there are no points of disagreement would be unrealistic.

In his speech, Mao addresses two primary types of conflict. Though the main body of the speech concerns internal issues, the first section lays out in detail the progression of entities and ideologies that Mao considers to be the enemy. The first and most obvious enemies are the Japanese and those who supported them in the occupation. Next are the "the bureaucrat-capitalists, the landlords and the Kuomintang reactionaries" who fought the Communists during the Chinese Civil War. Now that these enemies have been thoroughly defeated, the enemy of the people is "social forces and groups which resist the socialist revolution and are hostile to or sabotage socialist construction."

Mao describes the "contradictions" between the people and their external enemies as "antagonistic contradictions," in contrast to the contradictions among the people, which are "non-antagonistic," and those between "the exploited and the exploiting classes," which he sees as having aspects of both. It is inevitable, he notes, that conflicts should arise among people who are not working against socialism but who may be at odds with others engaged in the system. Mao also acknowledges that there are areas of conflict between the state, the community, and the individual. The group that Mao identifies as the "national bourgeoisie" can be antagonistic to "the working class and other sections of the working people," but conflicts can be resolved if they agree to work together in a nonexploitative way. Mao describes China as "a people's democratic dictatorship led by the working class and based on the worker-peasant alliance" and argues that this dictatorship is necessary in order to maintain order and "protect [the] people so that they can devote themselves to peaceful labor." Since this dictatorship is "led by the working class," it is a true democracy, but it needs strong leadership to keep it from devolving into anarchy.

Mao argues that the Hungarian Revolution, which he refers to as the "Hungarian incident," is a cautionary tale, not something to be emulated. He says it is an example of outsiders—"domestic and foreign counterrevolutionaries"—deceiving the people into believing that two-party systems and open elections would give them more freedom than socialism. Once proper government is in place and the people are protected from enemies both external and internal, he claims, the proper way to resolve differences among the people is the "unity-criticism-unity" method, in which consensus can be found through open conversation and persuasion.

The original version of this speech, given in February 1957, encouraged students and intellectuals to offer criticism of the government openly. Mao had assumed that this new open conversation would result in widespread praise for his leadership and that criticism would be directed at issues that Mao wished to reform and party members who had challenged him. When intellectuals finally began to criticize the government, however, they were unsparing and outspoken. Flyers and posters were widely distributed that criticized party members and policy. By June, when this revised version of the speech was published in the official newspaper, Mao was moving away from the open dialogue he had encouraged; within a month of its publication, he had begun a crackdown on dissenters, many of them identified during this Hundred Flowers Campaign.

—*Bethany Groff Dorau, MA*

Bibliography and Additional Reading

Mao Zedong. *The Secret Speeches of Chairman Mao: From the Hundred Flowers to the Great Leap Forward*. Ed. Roderick MacFarquhar et al. Cambridge: Council on East Asian Studies/Harvard University, 1989.

Schoenhals, Michael. "Original Contradictions: On the Unrevised Text of Mao Zedong's 'On the Correct Handling of Contradictions among the People.'" *Australian Journal of Chinese Affairs* 16 (1986): 99–112. JSTOR. 21 Dec. 2015.

Solomon, Richard H. *Mao's Revolution and the Chinese Political Culture*. Berkeley: University of California, 1971.

Letter from a Chinese "Rusticant"

Date: June 30, 1973
Author: Chang T'ieh Sheng (Zhang Tiesheng)
Genre: letter

Summary Overview

During the Cultural Revolution (1966-1976) Mao Zedong, communist leader of the People's Republic of China, wanted to establish a unique form of communism in in the county by ridding the nation of the complacency he saw developing in urban areas. By sending urban students into the countryside to live on collective farms with peasants, Mao believed the spirit that had propelled the communists to victory would be reborn. While many observers, even at that time, saw this program as a failure (most students were not able to adapt fully to rural life), this letter was published as a demonstration of the gains that were being made through this program. Initially published as "A Provocative Answer to an Examination," this letter seemed to confirm that at least some of the goals of the Cultural Revolution had been achieved.

Defining Moment

When the Chinese Communist Party was founded in Shanghai, in 1921, it was anticipated that as in Russia, the key to its ultimate victory would be in its urban roots. In 1945, after years of animosity and limited military conflict, a full-scale civil war erupted between the communist and the nationalist forces. Unexpectedly, the nationalists held all the major urban areas, and the communists' support was in the countryside. Winning the war in 1949, the communist government faced many economic as well as political challenges. A decade later, when some of Mao Zedong's policies failed, he believed that it was time for a renewal of the spirit that had carried the communists to power. This spirit, he believed, was to be found in the countryside, and so he initiated the Cultural Revolution. During the initial phase, the schools and universities were closed and most of the students were sent into rural areas to learn new "lessons" from the peasants by participating in agriculture as well as to help increase food production. (As had historically been the case, the educational system in China was oriented toward the urban population, with relatively few children of peasants able to attain any but the most basic level of education.) Some students were sent to the countryside for only a short time, while others ended up staying for years. At the same time, some students joined the newly created Red Guards, who were supposed to help purify the nation by imposing ideological consistency, but mainly they destroyed schools, factories, and people's lives through their rigid adherence to dogma and their reliance on harsh enforcement.

Mao Zedong shaking hands with a people's commune farmer. From 10th Anniversary Photo Collection of the People's Republic of China 1949–1959. Photo via Wikimedia Commons. [Public domain.]

In addition to learning from the peasants, the youths sent to the countryside were seen as not having been tainted by any anticommunist ideas, for they had been born after the 1949 communist victory in the civil war and knew only communism. In order to destroy the forces, real or imaginary, that opposed the communist programs for the nation, large groups of youth became Red Guards. They were sent out to destroy the remnants of bourgeois thought. Within a short time, however, many Red Guard units started going beyond their charge, causing wholesale destruction of schools, factories, and Chinese cultural traditions. Within a few years, in fact, the government had to call on the army to keep the Red Guards in check.

During the Cultural Revolution, there was great debate on many levels regarding those sent to the countryside. Basically, Chinese leaders were trying to decide if the resources of the nation were being strengthened by the addition of these youth to those working to provide food and other natural resources, or if the resources of the nation were being squandered as a result of so many students having had their educations suspended. The nation's leaders knew that at least some youths needed to complete their education, for the future of the nation. And so, as the schools and universities slowly reopened, many of the "rusticants" returned to their studies, whether officially or unofficially. Others, such as Chang T'ieh Sheng, remained in the countryside, continuing to work where they had been assigned. This resulted in ongoing debates at all levels, as indicated in this letter. Should the youth serve the nation by remaining on the collective farms, or by returning to the classroom (with the resulting emphasis on individual achievement)? This was a continuing issue until the death of Mao in 1976, which ended the Cultural Revolution.

Author Biography

Chang T'ieh Sheng (Zhang Tiesheng) was born in 1950 and lived in the province of Liaoning. He completed high school and sat to take an examination for university studies, but, in the heyday of the Cultural Revolution, chose the path of "rustication" instead. By handing in a blank exam and spending time in the countryside, he became something of a national hero, even winning a seat at the National People's Congress in 1975. After the Cultural Revolution, however, he was put on trial as part of a crackdown on leftists and sentenced to 15 years in prison. (This fate was common enough at the time.) After his release, Zhang, now living in Deng Xiaoping's capitalist-infused China, went in the direction of business, founding an animal-feed company called Wellhope Agri-Tech. The company went public in 2014, leaving Zhang a multimillionaire.

Historical Document

Letter from a Chinese "Rusticant"

Revered Leaders...

Since I was sent down to the countryside in 1968, I have always been enthusiastic about agricultural production, and spared no effort in my work. The strenuous manual labour and other work which last almost 18 hours ever day has prevented me from revising my professional studies. I only had time to hastily read over the mathematics teaching materials once after receiving notification on the 27th. As for the algebra questions, and the physics and chemistry on today's examination paper, I can only stare at them, feeling that although the spirit is willing, the flesh is weak. I do not want to write nonsense that bears no relation to what is in the books, lest the leadership waste time going over it.

I am willing to abide by the discipline and persist in carrying it out to the end, and therefore I conscientiously withdraw from the examination. To tell the truth, I am not prepared to accept and even have a strong aversion to those bookworms who neglect their proper duties, and are leisurely and carefree, because the examination is monopolized by this bunch of college-fetishists. In this busy summer hoeing and production season, I cannot bear to abandon the production work for the purpose of worming myself into a small house, because that would be too self-seeking. If I did that, I would stand condemned by the poor and lower-middle peasants' revolutionary devotion to their work as well as my own revolutionary conscience.

There is one thing that I can console myself with, and that is I have not held up at the work of the collective. I have overall and full responsibility for the [production] team. Since we have had a welcome fall of spring rain, everyone is indeed busy. In these circumstances where individual and collective interests are in direct conflict, it is a struggle (if I may say so)...

My political affiliations, family, social relations, etc. are all clean. To a boy like me, brought up in the city, the experience of the past few years has indeed had a great tempering effect, especially in reforming my ideology, emotions, and world outlook; you could call it a great leap. I do not feel ashamed about not answering the examination paper according to the requirements and rules (it has nothing to do with my fundamental knowledge and ability). I might have managed some of it, and glancing at the books could have got me a few dozen points (that's meaningless). If I had done so, I would not feel happy in myself. What I feel honored about is that under the new educational system, and with the wholehearted recommendation of the poor and lower-middle peasants and the leadership cadres, I have taken part in this study class.

Signed,

Chang T'ieh Sheng [Zhang Tiesheng]

Glossary

college-fetishists: individuals totally and excessively devoted to attending college

leadership: those "grading" the exam would include teachers and political operatives

small house: in collective farms, most people lived in dormitories; small houses were built by individuals who desired privacy or personal space and were contrary to the spirit of collectivism

Document Themes and Analysis

The Chinese rusticant (one who was moved to the country) who wrote this letter to those grading the entrance examinations choose an unusual manner in which to respond to the exam. Having decided not to take the test, he gave a fairly full explanation of why he had made that decision. Essentially, the call to serve the agricultural collective and the nation had taken precedence over his desire to further his education at the university. Although he had not volunteered to leave his studies in 1968, at the time he wrote this he had decided that his call to serve on the collective farm had been and would continue to be his focus.

Writing in an honorific manner, "Revered Leaders," he does seem to exaggerate as regards his level of enthusiasm. Being "sent down to the countryside" meant that he had been drafted to leave his home and academic pursuits to go to a collective farm. While he may have always "spared no effort," it was more likely that in the beginning he did this out of fear of punishment, or to gain favor, rather than because he was enthusiastic about working on the farm. However, Chang soon seemed to develop a sense of responsibility to the collective. Even when told that he would be able to take the exam in a few days (he was notified on the 27th), he did not take time away from his assigned tasks to study. If he had done so, he would have had to "abandon the production work" with the result that he would not have reflected the "revolutionary devotion" of a peasant, which by then had become his "own revolutionary conscience." The needs of the collective had become his, and he was now proud to eagerly serve it. Essentially, Chang writes that he had come to understand that in agriculture one's work is based on nature's schedule. If there was a "welcome fall" of rain, then one worked accordingly.

As Chang thought about the examination, he reflected how well he might have done on its various sections. Physics, chemistry, algebra, and other such subjects seem to have been the major components of the exam. Due to his work schedule, Chang states that he does not have time for any extensive review. Having been at the collective for three years, he understood that it would have taken more than a cursory look at the material for him to have worked up to his potential. He strongly criticizes those who avoided, or left, their assignments in the countryside. The "bookworms" who were only obsessed with attending college, rather than helping to build a strong society, were not to be emulated. The fact that he might have done "all right" on certain sections of the test was not acceptable, either. He needed to demonstrate his ability, in whatever area he worked.

In the closing paragraph, Chang makes it clear that he had not remained on the collective out of some fault of his own or his family. They were "clean." He states that he had been transformed by his experience in this new "educational system" of the collective farm. While not stating that he would not take the opportunity, he makes it clear that he had matured and was now facing the world on his own terms.

As various people have read this letter, they have proposed different reasons for its composition. Some accepted it at face value, and believed that Chang had changed during his time on the collective and was ready to stay indefinitely. Others have seen it as an attempt to get into the university, not by having high scores on math, physics, or chemistry sections, but by being the best in reflecting the Communist Party line. (Peasants were often held in high regard in theory, but not always in practice.) A third group believed that Chang wrote this sarcastically, not really meaning any of it, other than that people on a collective worked long hours. Finally, there had been a post-1976 view that the letter was a total fraud, with Chang having failed the exam. In this view, the letter was composed by supporters of the Cultural Revolution to justify it. All these positions have their merits. However, in the full text the third has come through as the least likely. (In the longer text, Chang states that with two full days to review he could have gotten acceptable scores.) If legitimate, which seems to be the case, the intent of the letter was to state clearly that the time on the collective had changed his outlook on life and given him a broader, more communal perspective. As much as the perspective tied in with the Cultural Revolution as a whole, ultimately it proved unsustainable. At Mao's death the Cultural Revolution ended, and a reverse trend of persecuting those who had so vigorously executed their duties took place. People like Chang/Zhang were imprisoned as leftist "counterrevolutionaries." Fifteen years later, Zhang emerged from prison and became a different kind of societal "hero," namely, a successful businessman.

—Donald A. Watt, PhD

Bibliography and Additional Reading

Buckley, Chris. "Zhang Tiesheng: From Hero under Mao to 'Hero of Wealth'." *New York Times*, August 18, 2014.

Dikötter, Frank. *The Cultural Revolution: A People's History 1962-1976.* New York: Bloomsbury Press, 2016.

Ji Xianlin with Chenxin Jiang (trans.) and Zha Jianying (intro.). *The Cowshed: Memories of the Chinese Cultural Revolution.* New York: New York Review Books, 2016.

Rene, Helena K. *China's Sent-Down Generation: Public Administration and the Legacies of Mao's Rustication Program.* Washington: Georgetown UP, 2013.

Unger, Jonathan. "China's Troubled Down-to-the-Countryside Campaign." *Contemporary China*, vol. 3, no. 2 (Summer 1979); pp. 79-92.

U.S. Embassy Cables Concerning the Crackdown in Tiananmen Square

Date: June 3–4, 1989
Author: James Lilley
Genre: report

Summary Overview

In early June 1989, the U.S. Ambassador to the People's Republic of China (PRC), James Lilley, sent a number of messages to prominent but unnamed State Department officials in Washington, D.C., about ongoing protests taking place in the capital city of Beijing. The messages sent on June 3 described a volatile situation in which thousands of the PRC's military troops had entered the city to confront demonstrators at Tiananmen Square, but they provided little hint of the violence that would dominate global headlines the following day. On June 4, however, Lilley reported that Embassy officials had received numerous accounts of the use of tear gas and live ammunition by the Chinese military against the demonstrators. Barricades had been erected by the demonstrators to slow the advance of the soldiers, but armed personnel carriers (APC) had broken through and reached the square. The American Embassy received conflicting reports of the number of people killed or injured, but, Lilley observed, "we expect the final count of dead and injured to be very high."

Defining Moment

The events that took place in Tiananmen Square on June 3-4 were rooted in the deep divisions in the PRC between reform-minded political leaders and their supporters, on the one hand, and the more powerful conservative members of the government who opposed even moderate changes to the Chinese political system, on the other. The reformist wing was led by Party Secretary Hu Yaobang, while the conservative wing was led by Deng Xiaoping, whose sole official position was chairman of the Central Military Commission but who nevertheless functioned as "Paramount Leader" of the nation. In 1987 Hu was dismissed from his position after he expressed support for a more open and transparent political system and refused to punish student protestors sufficiently. The decision to dismiss Hu angered many intellectuals and students, but it would be two years before they

A photo of Pu Zhiqiang, a student protester at Tiananmen, taken on 10 May 1989. The Chinese words written on the paper say: "We want the freedom of newspapers, freedom of associations, also to support the 'World Economic Herald', and support those just journalists." Photo by sfchoi8964, via Wikimedia Commons.

could transform their anger and frustration into a cohesive protest movement.

Growing anger and dissatisfaction with the Chinese government's unwillingness even to discuss political reform led Chinese students and intellectuals to organize a massive demonstration in Beijing. The protest was initially planned for May 4, 1989, the 70th anniversary of the founding of the Chinese Communist Party. However, when Hu died on April 15, it was decided to start the demonstrations early. Three days later, a large group of university students staged a sit-in at Tiananmen Square. The protestors demanded the full rehabilitation of Hu's reputation, an increase in funding for education, an end to government corruption, and fewer restrictions on speech and the press. The tenor of these demands indicated that the vast majority of protestors did not want to overthrow the government but merely to achieve modest reforms.

By the time of Hu's funeral on April 22, more than two hundred thousand people were participating in the demonstrations, and the number would grow to include as many as one million. Initially, Chinese officials stalled for time, hoping perhaps that the protests would fizzle out. However, when Mikhail Gorbachev, General Secretary of the Soviet Union, visited China in May, his presence and his reputation as a supporter of political reform emboldened the protestors, one of whom waved a banner that read "in the Soviet Union they have Gorbachev. In China we have whom?" The wording of the banner demonstrates that protestors were keenly aware of Gorbachev's efforts to reform Soviet society. In fact, the protests in Beijing happened at a time when similar movements were building in Eastern European countries (particularly in Poland, Hungary, and East Germany). But whereas in Europe, at this late stage in the Cold War, governments were unwilling to respond to protests with force, Chinese authorities felt no such hesitancy.

Author Biography

James Lilley was born on January 15, 1928 in Qingdao in Shandong Province, China, to American expatriate parents. In 1940 his family moved back to the United as the outbreak of World War II made it too dangerous for them to continue living there. After serving in the United States Army in 1945-46, Lilley earned a bachelor's degree from Yale and then a master's from George Washington University. In 1951 he joined the Central Intelligence Agency (CIA) where he specialized in East Asian affairs. In 1975 he was appointed national intelligence officer to China. In 1986 Lilley was chosen as U.S. Ambassador to South Korea. In 1989 he was appointed Ambassador to the PRC, a position that he would hold until 1991.

Historical Document

U.S. Embassy Cables Concerning the Crackdown in Tiananmen Square

FM AMEMBASSY BEIJING

TO SECSTATE WASHDC NIACT IMMEDIATE 0043 ...

SUBJECT: SITREP NO. 28: TEN TO FIFTEEN THOUSAND ARMED TROOPS STOPPED AT CITY PERIMETER BY HUMAN AND BUS BARRRICADES [3 June 1989]

REF: BEIJING 15383

CONFIDENTIAL ENTIRE TEXT.

TEN TO FIFTEEN THOUSAND HELMETED, ARMED TROOPS MOVED TOWARD BEIJING DURING THE LATE AFTERNOON/EARLY EVENING HOURS OF JUNE 3. AS OF 1930, LARGE CONVOYS HAVE BEEN STOPPED AS BEFORE BY BUS AND HUMAN BARRICADES. THE LARGEST CONCENTRATION OF TROOP TRUCKS IS ON THE WESTERN SIDE OF THE CITY IN FRONT OF THE NEW WORLD TRADE CENTER, ABOUT 5-6 KILOMETERS FROM TIANANMEN SQUARE. EMBOFFS SAW AT LEAST TWENTY TRUCKS THERE, BUT MORE THAN ONE HUNDRED HAD BEEN SEEN HEADING TOWARD THE CITY ON THAT ROUTE, SO WE ESTIMATE THAT THERE ARE ONE HUNDRED PLUS TROOP TRUCKS AT THAT LOCATION. THE TROOPS ARE HELMETED AND ARE CARRYING AUTOMATIC WEAPONS. MOST OF THEM SEEM TO BE STAYING IN THEIR TRUCKS FOR THE TIME BEING. MORE THAN 35 TRUCKS FILLED WITH HELMETED, ARMED TROOPS ARE STOPPED AT THE SECOND RING ROAD OVERPASS, DIRECTLY IN FRONT OF THE JIANGUOMENWAI DIPLOMATIC HOUSING COMPOUND. THERE ARE REPORTEDLY 82 TRUCKS BLOCKED BY FOUR LARGE DUMP TRUCKS ALONG THE ROAD TO CAPITAL AIRPORT. WE ALSO HAVE REPORTS OF TWENTY SIX TRUCKS STOPPED AND SURROUNDED BY CITY RESIDENTS BETWEEN THE LIDO HOTEL AND THE GREAT WALL HOTEL IN THE NORTHEASTERN SUBURBS. THERE ARE ABOUT TWO THOUSAND TROOPS JUST WEST OF THE GREAT HALL OF THE PEOPLE IN A STANDOFF WITH CITY RESIDENTS WHICH HAS BEEN GOING ON SINCE EARLY AFTERNOON. THE

POPULATION APPEARS HOSTILE TO PLA MOVEMENTS INTO THE CITY.

ELITE AIRBORNE TROOPS ARE MOVING FROM THE SOUTH AND TANK UNITS HAVE BEEN ALERTED TO MOVE. DAO OFFICERS ARE OUT CHECKING THE WESTERN SUBURBS. DAO IS REPORTING FURTHER DETAILS TO WASHINGTON. ALL EMBASSY INFORMATION SO FAR SUGGESTS THAT THE UNITS OTHER THAN THE AIRBORNE TROOPS ARE FROM THE 39TH ARMY.

THE TROOPS HAVE OBVIOUSLY NOT YET BEEN GIVEN ORDERS PERMITTING THEM TO USE FORCE. THEIR LARGE NUMBERS, THE FACT THAT THEY ARE HELMETED, AND THE AUTOMATIC WEAPONS THEY ARE CARRYING SUGGEST THAT THE FORCE OPTION IS REAL.

LILLEY

* * *

FM AMEMBASSY BEIJING

TO AMCONSUL CHENGDU POUCH...

SUBJECT: SITREP NO. 31: TIANANMEN AT 0145 ON - JUNE 4: GUNFIRE ON THE SQUARE, TWO APC'S - BURNING ON THE NORTH SIDE OF THE SQUARE

CONFIDENTIAL ENTIRE TEXT.

SUMMARY: AS OF 0145, ABC NEWS REPORTERS ON THE SQUARE REPORTED THE PRESENCE OF TROOPS AND RIOT POLICE ON THE SOUTHERN END OF TIANANMEN. TEAR GAS AND GUNFIRE WERE REPORTED ON THE SQUARE. EMBOFF SAW TRACERS BEING FIRED OVER THE SQUARE. ABC JOURNALISTS SAID THAT TWO ARMORED PERSONNEL CARRIERS WERE ON FIRE AT THE NORTHEAST AND NORTHWEST CORNERS OF THE SQUARE. A BARRICADE NEAR THE INTERSECTION OF FUXINGMEN AND THE SECOND RING ROAD WAS BREACHED AS TROOPS ADVANCED ON THE SQUARE FROM THE WEST. AS OF 0250, THE SITUATION IN THE CENTER OF THE CITY WAS VERY CONFUSED. TROOPS APPEAR TO BE ATTEMPTING TO CLEAR THE SQUARE FROM WEST TO EAST. WE HAVE NO ACCURATE COUNT OF DEAD AND WOUNDED, BUT CASUALTIES NO DOUBT WILL BE HIGH (##) DEMONSTRATOR WHO LAID DOWN IN FRONT OF AN ADVANCING APC AND WAS RUN OVER. UNCONFIRMED

ACCOUNTS CITE SEVENTY DEAD AND MANY WOUNDED. GIVEN THE AGGRESIVE PLA MOVES REPORTED BY ABC NEWS REPORTERS, WE EXPECT FINAL COUNTS OF DEAD AND INJURED TO BE VERY HIGH. END SUMMARY.

STUDENTS SET DEBRIS THROWN ATOP AT LEAST ONE ARMORED PERSONNEL CARRIER AND LIT THE DEBRIS, ACCORDING TO EMBOFF NEAR THE SCENE. ABC REPORTED THAT ONE OTHER ARMORED PERSONNEL CARRIER IS AFLAME. AT LEAST ONE BUS WAS ALSO BURNING, ACCORDING TO ABC NEWS REPORTERS ON THE SQUARE AT 0120. THE EYEWITNESSES REPORTED THAT TROOPS AND RIOT POLICE WERE ON THE SOUTHERN END OF THE SQUARE AND TROOPS WERE MOVING TO THE SQUARE FROM THE WESTERN SIDE OF THE CITY. THEY REPORTEDLY BROKE THROUGH A BARRICADE NEAR THE INTERSECTION OF FUXINGMEN AND THE SECOND RING ROAD. DEMONSTRATORS' BARRICADES HAVE SLOWED BUT NOT STOPPED THE TROOPS' ADVANCE. THERE HAS REPORTEDLY BEEN INDISCRIMINATE GUNFIRE BY THE TROOPS ON THE SQUARE. WE CAN HEAR GUNFIRE FROM THE EMBASSY AND JIANGUOMENWAI DIPLOMATIC COMPOUND. EYEWITNESSES REPORT TEAR GAS ON THE SQUARE, FLARES BEING FIRED ABOVE IT, AND TRACERS BEING FIRED OVER IT.

ACCORDING TO UNCONFIRMED REPORTS, SEVENTY HAVE BEEN KILLED AND LARGE NUMBERS WOUNDED. ANOTHER REPORT CITED NINE DEAD AND OVER ONE-HUNDRED WOUNDED AT THE FUXING HOSPITAL. THE CHILDRENS' HOSPITAL INDICATED THAT IT HAD 11 DEAD. WE HAVE A FIRM REPORT THAT AT LEAST ONE HAS DIED, HAVING BEEN RUN OVER BY AN APC. EYEWITNESSES SAID THAT AN APC MOVING TOWARD THE SQUARE FROM THE EAST CRASHED THROUGH A BARRICADE AND PLOWED RIGHT THROUGH A CROWD ON CHANGAN STREET. FINAL NUMBERS OF DEAD AND WOUNDED COULD BE VERY HIGH, BASED ON EYEWITNESS ACCOUNTS OF THE ARMY'S ACTION THUS FAR.

THE SITUATION IN THE CENTER OF THE CITY IS VERY CONFUSED. POLOFFS AT THE BEIJING HOTEL REPORTED THAT TROOPS ARE PUSHING A LARGE CROWD OF DEMONSTRATORS EAST ON CHANGANJIE. ALTHOUGH THESE TROOPS APPEAR NOT TO BE FIRING ON THE CROWD, POLOFFS REPORT FIRING BEHIND THE TROOPS COMING FROM THE SQUARE.

A LARGE CONVOY OF MILITARY VEHICLES IS COMING TOWARD THE CITY FROM THE WESTERN SIDE OF BEIJING.

SOME UNITS HAVE NOT ADOPTED SUCH AGGRESIVE MOVES. AT 0124, AN EMBASSY SPOUSE SAW TROOPS AT THE JIANGUOMENWAI OVERPASS NEXT TO THE DIPLOMATIC HOUSING COMPOUND TALKING CALMLY WITH THE CITY RESIDENTS BLOCKING THEIR PATH. CONVERSELY, PANIC REPORTEDLY SET IN AMONG PEOPLE ON THE WESTERN SIDE OF THE CITY WHERE THE VIOLENCE HAS BEEN WORST THUS FAR.

Document Themes and Analysis

Lilley's message of June 3 notes that ten to fifteen thousand Chinese troops had arrived in Beijing, with the largest concentration centered around the New World Trade Center, roughly 5 kilometers from Tiananmen Square. The troops, accompanied by 100 army trucks, are said to be helmeted and carrying automatic weapons. Some of the military trucks had reportedly been blocked from traveling around the city by civilian vehicles. Lilley reports that civilians remain generally hostile to the military presence. Noting that the Chinese military forces are helmeted, heavily armed, in combat-ready vehicles and including elite airborne units, the ambassador concludes that "the force option is real."

By 1:45 am the next day the first Chinese troops had reached Tiananmen Square where they were reported to have used tear gas and live ammunition on protestors to clear the area. Equally troubling, an APC reportedly had run over a protestor who attempted to block its advance. Other protestors lit cars and at least one bus on fire to block the military's advance into the square. These efforts, however, only worked in the short term because the APCs had pushed through the barricades. Lilley notes that there were numerous reports of Chinese troops firing indiscriminately at protestors.

Not surprisingly, given the chaotic nature of these events, numerous, conflicting reports circulated regarding the number of people killed. Lilley notes tersely that "final numbers of dead and wounded could be very high, based on eyewitness accounts of the Army's action."

In contrast to the behavior of soldiers around Tiananmen Square, troops stationed next to the diplomatic compound were observed talking calmly to protestors who blocked their way. The contrasting behavior may have occurred because the soldiers in Tiananmen Square were largely out of the view of foreign media, while those around the compound were not.

The June 3 messages sent by Lilley depict a tense and hostile situation, but not a violent one. When PRC forces entered Beijing on June 3, there were no reports of violence. However, this changed on the morning of June 4, when government forces, under orders from Deng, attacked demonstrators in Tiananmen Square and the surrounding area. While reports differ, it is estimated that the Chinese military killed between a few dozen and several hundred demonstrators that day. The military's actions in early June not only resulted in the deaths of many demonstrations, it also effectively destroyed any hope of political reform. Deng and his supporters had preserved the status quo for the foreseeable future. Large-scale protests demanding reform from the government would not be tolerated in China. Not surprisingly, in the aftermath of the protests the Chinese government targeted intellectuals and students who participated in or supported the protests. Untold numbers were arrested, and some were even executed for their role in the demonstrations. The crackdown on demonstrators at Tiananmen Square sent a clear message that those who demanded democratic political reform would be crushed.

The demonstrations in Tiananmen Square occurred at the same time as protests with similar demands were occurring in Eastern Europe. The communist governments of Eastern Europe were unwilling or unable to use violence to end the protests. As a result, much of Eastern Europe had moved away from totalitarian, communist rule by 1991. A similar situation emerged in Russia and the other states of the USSR. Such would not be the case in China, however, where the government remained willing to use force. The military crackdown on June 4 destroyed the reform movement. The PRC has seen little progress in the direction of democratic political reform since.

—Gerald F. Goodwin, PhD

Bibliography and Additional Reading

Baum, Richard. *Burying Mao: Chinese Politics in the Age of Deng Xiaoping*. Princeton, NJ: Princeton UP, 1996.

Cunningham, Philip J. *Tiananmen Moon: Inside the Chinese Student Uprising of 1989*. Lanham, MD: Rowman & Littlefield, 2008.

Gaddis, John Lewis. *The Cold War: A New History*. New York: Penguin Press, 2005.

Levine, Steven and Alexander Pantsov. *Deng Xiaoping: A Revolutionary Life*. New York: Oxford UP, 2015.

Mid-Century Rebels

A number of rebellions and revolutions took place in the mid-twentieth century, as the old colonial order and its legacy continued its downward slide. In Spain in the 1930s came the Spanish Civil War (1936–1939). In this conflict it was not leftist revolutionaries but rather forces on the right that overthrew a left-leaning republican government. It began when the elections of 1936 produced a Popular Front government consisting of liberals, democratic socialists, anarchists, and communists. Opposed to them were conservative forces made up of wealthy landowners, the Catholic clergy, most of the military, and members of the fascist Falange party. General Francisco Franco led this coalition of Nationalist forces against the Republicans, or Loyalists, in government. The Nationalists gained control of conservative areas in northwestern and southwestern Spain. They received aid, in the form of tanks and airplanes, from Nazi Germany and fascist Italy; this was to be a test of a new form of assault for these aggressive nations. The Loyalists, on the other hand, garnered aid from the Soviet Union and from volunteer International Brigades from democratic countries (most of them armed with rifles, grenades, and light canon). The war became a fierce and bloody one, with nearly a half million people killed in fighting or assassinated as enemy suspects. Ultimately, the Nationalists won control of Madrid, and many Loyalists were forced to flee to France to escape retribution. Spain remained a dictatorship under Franco until the 1970s, while the deep scars left by the war haunted the Spanish nation for decades afterward.

In British-controlled Kenya it was a different story. Militant Mau Mau nationalists (the name's origins are uncertain), chiefly of the Kikuyu tribe, rose up against Britons and other Europeans in Kenya in 1952. Labeled a secret terrorist organization, the Mau Mau advocated violent resistance to British domination in Kenya. In response, the colonial government in Nairobi launched a series of retributive military attacks against the Kikuyu and any other supporters they could identify. By 1956 the Mau Mau rebels had been dispersed to the hills. In the event, over 10,000 Kikuyu were killed and another 20,000 were placed in detention camps. Later the entire tribe was relocated. Despite the calamity faced by indigenous Africans, Mau Mau resistance led to a broader movement for independence in Kenya and elsewhere. One of the group's leaders, Jomo Kenyatta, went on to become the first prime minister of a sovereign Kenya in 1963.

Then there is the Cuban Revolution, well-known for its heroes Che Guevara and Fidel Castro. Cuba had been free of Spanish rule since 1898, and the United States had stepped in afterward to invest heavily in the sugar industry along with tourism and gambling. The country had prospered, though the distribution of wealth was highly unequal and two corrupt, repressive regimes—those of Gerardo Machado and Fulgencio Battista—had found little favor among the wider populace. This was the scene in 1958–1959 when the socialist militant Castro, aided by Guevara, gathered an armed antigovernment force to overthrow Battista. Declaring a socialist state and abolishing capitalism, Castro, as the nation's new leader, at first kept his distance from the Soviet Union and global communism. With U.S. hostility toward Cuba increasing, however, Castro drew closer to the Soviets and took up the mission to spread revolutionary Marxism (e.g., in Angola). Cuba remained under his increasingly dictatorial rule for decades. In 2008 he passed the reigns to his brother Raúl, who continued his policies.

■ ¡No Pasarán! ("They Shall Not Pass!")

Date: July 19, 1936
Author: Dolores Ibárruri
Genre: speech

Summary Overview

As the fascist Nationalist forces in the Spanish Civil War began their move to overthrow the (elected) government of the Second Republic, the leaders of the Republic called upon the people to fight the insurrection. Virtually all elite Spanish troops, most officers, and half the members of the military and para-military organizations had joined the Nationalist movement. The governing left-wing Popular Front coalition needed broad support if it was to survive. In a rousing speech, Dolores Ibárruri, one of the Front's members, called for broad support against the insurgent military slowly heading north toward the capital of Madrid. In this and other speeches, Ibárruri inspired not only non-rightwing Spaniards, but also anti-fascist foreigners, to join the fight against the Nationalist army. In part because of this speech, the quick victory the Nationalists had been expecting became a three-year civil war.

Defining Moment

In July, 1936, the latest in a series of crises had arisen in the governance of Spain. The duly elected left-wing government was being challenged by right-wing leaders of the military, with General Francisco Franco stepping forward to lead the insurrection. In 1923, a similar move had been made which established a military dictatorship, with the blessings of the then king, Alfonso XIII. (Ever since Alfonso XIII came to the throne, in 1902, a mixture of his interference and strong political divisions had made Spanish governance unstable, with thirty-three governments in just over twenty-one years.) In 1930, the military leader was forced from power, and in 1931, the monarchy was abolished, under threat of violence from the people. For the next five years centrists governed Spain, although from 1933 to 1936 these were propped up by an alliance with a right-wing party. When a strongly left oriented coalition, the Popular Front, won control of the Cortes (parliament) in the hotly contested election in February, 1936, the right-wing sought other means of change. Right-wing Nationalists used the pretext of the need for domestic stability, based on strikes related to the poor Spanish economy (in large part due to the global depression), and attacks on churches and other social institutions. Although the ultra-left-wing was re-

A banner reading ¡No pasarán! Madrid will be the graveyard of fascism *from the Siege of Madrid; photo taken by Soviet journalist Mikhail Koltsov. Photo courtesy of Nietzscheano66, via Wikimedia Commons.*

sponsible for some of these, many were initiated by right-wing provocateurs. This set the stage for the events of July, 1936.

With the best-trained Spanish troops stationed in Morocco, the Nationalist leaders made certain officers loyal to their cause were in charge of these units. With Franco going to Morocco from the Canary Islands, where he had been based, on July 17th, he announced the rebellion and called upon the people of Spain to support it in overthrowing the leftist government. He also called upon all Spanish troops to join the Nationalist movement. [The Nationalist movement had a fascist ideology and was supported by Germany and Italy, while the Republican cause (with Communists openly active in the government) was supported by the Soviet Union.] With the assistance of German and Italian ships and airplanes, the Nationalist forces quickly moved to the Spanish mainland, where they were joined by a sizeable number of less well trained Spanish mainland army and paramilitary troops. The Nationalist's hope was that, just as in 1923, their army could quickly take control of the capital, Madrid, and the coup d'état would be over.

Dolores Ibárruri, an elected member of the Spanish Cortes, went before the people two days after Franco's call to arms for the Nationalists, when the rebel forces were starting to move from Africa to Europe. She knew that the military forces in Spain were inferior to those that had been keeping the peace in the colony of Morocco, and that most of the military officers' political inclinations were toward the right, rather than the left. Thus, she called to the people to defend Madrid, with the pledge that the Nationalists "shall not pass" the entrance to the city. This plea and promise was heard around the world and thousands of people responded. The foreign supporters of the Republic became the International Brigade, which was organized in October, 1936. Because of this force, when the Nationalist troops came to Madrid, in November, 1936, they were beaten back, and the two-and-a-half year siege of Madrid began. Although the Nationalists ultimately prevailed, it was only after a bloody three-year civil war that devastated many parts of the country.

Author Biography

From a poor family, Dolores Ibárruri (1895-1989) at the age of fifteen left school and earned money as a seamstress. The difficult circumstances of her position led to her becoming politically active and, beginning in 1918, writing articles on politics using the name La Pasionaria. In 1920 she joined the Communist Party, remaining a member until her death. During the Second Spanish Republic, she was a well-known figure, and was elected, in 1936, to parliament on the Communist/Popular Front ticket. When the Spanish Civil War began in 1936, Ibárruri became a leading spokesperson for the Republic on the radio and at rallies, giving great inspiration to those supporting the Republic. When the war was in its final days, Ibárruri flew to the Soviet Union where she remained until 1977. Franco having died and a constitutional monarchy having been created, she then returned to Spain. She was again elected to parliament, but eventually age and ill health forced her to resign.

Historical Document

"They Shall Not Pass!"

¡No Pasarán!

Workers! Farmers! Anti-fascists! Spanish Patriots! Confronted with the fascist military uprising, all must rise to their feet, to defend the Republic, to defend the people's freedoms as well as their achievements towards democracy! Through the statements by the government and the Popular Front (parties), the people understand the graveness of the moment. In Morocco, as well as in the Canary Islands, the workers are battling, united with the forces still loyal to the Republic, against the uprising militants and fascists. Under the battle-cry 'Fascism shall not pass; the hangmen of October shall not pass!' workers and farmers from all Spanish provinces are joining in the struggle against the enemies of the Republic that have arisen in arms. Communists, Socialists, Anarchists, and Republican Democrats, soldiers and (other) forces remaining loyal to the Republic combined have inflicted the first defeats upon the fascist foe, who drag through the mud the very same honorable military tradition that they have boasted to possess so many times. The whole country cringes in indignation at these heartless barbarians that would hurl our democratic Spain back down into an abyss of terror and death. However, THEY SHALL NOT PASS! For all of Spain presents itself for battle. In Madrid, the people are out in the streets in support of the Government and encouraging its decision and fighting spirit so that it shall reach its conclusion in the smashing of the militant and fascist insurrection.

Young men, prepare for combat! Women, heroic women of the people! Recall the heroism of the women of Asturias of 1934 and struggle alongside the men in order to defend the lives and freedom of your sons, overshadowed by the fascist menace! Soldiers, sons of the nation! Stay true to the Republican State and fight side by side with the workers, with the forces of the Popular Front, with your parents, your siblings and comrades! Fight for the Spain of February the 16th, fight for the Republic and help them to victory! Workers of all stripes! The government supplies us with arms that we may save Spain and its people from the horror and shame that a victory for the bloody hangmen of October would mean. Let no one hesitate! All stand ready for action. All workers, all antifascists must now look upon each other as brothers in arms. Peoples of Catalonia, Basque Country, and Galicia! All Spaniards! Defend our democratic Republic and consolidate the victory achieved by our people on the 16th of February.

The Communist Party calls you to arms. We especially call upon you, workers, farmers, intellectuals to assume your positions in the fight to finally smash the enemies of the Republic and of the popular liberties. Long live the Popular Front! Long live the union of all anti-fascists! Long live the Republic of the people! The Fascists shall not pass! THEY SHALL NOT PASS!

Glossary

Hangman of October: Francisco Franco—In October, 1933, General Franco had forcefully put down leftist/nationalist anti-government movements in Asturias and Catalonia.

Popular Front: A coalition formed for the 1936 elections by the Socialist Workers' Party, Communist Party, Workers' Party of Marxist Unification, three leftist Republican parties and five other regional or trade groups.

Spain of February 16th: Date of last free election of the Second Republic, which was won by the Popular Front coalition.

Document Themes and Analysis

Although the Popular Front had defeated the National Front (a right-wing coalition) by only about 100,000 votes in the 1936 parliamentary elections, it was a legitimate victory. When nationalist sympathizers started fighting anyone loyal to the Popular Front government in Morocco, their spokesperson, and eventual leader, Francisco Franco called on members of the military, and the population at-large, to support the move to overthrow the National Front government. In response to this statement, the Popular Front, the Communist Party, and spokesperson Dorothy Ibárruri needed to make clear that they would not cave in. Ibárruri called for the unity of all anti-fascist groups. She sought to unite the various ethnic groups within Spain, by reminding them of Franco's past actions. She ended with an impassioned plea for victory with her well-known proclamation, "They shall not pass!" In her mind, if all non-fascists united, Franco and his forces would not only be unable to capture Madrid, but the Popular Front forces would hold other key areas blocking a fascist Nationalist victory.

Ibárruri began her plea by addressing those whom the Communist Party believed were their core supporters, workers and farmers. She did the same at the close of the speech, only adding intellectuals to the list. She and the Communist Party believed that their supporters would provide the foundation for the anti-fascist resistance. However, she was not naïve enough to believe that these groups would be able to do it on their own, even with the help of the members of the military that supported the government of the Republic. Thus, she expanded her call to "Spanish Patriots," later adding a list of the other groups that had participated in the Popular Front coalition: "Socialists, Anarchists, and Republican Democrats." She further tried to strengthen her message by reaching out to provincial ethnic groups that had suffered under past authoritarian regimes. Asturias, Galicia, Catalonia, and the Basque people were reminded of what they had at stake in the Nationalist uprising against the Republic. Although Ibárruri spoke confidently about the prospects of a united front against the fascist forces, it was clear from her call to arms that this was far from the truth. Group after group was named, as she sought greater inclusiveness in the fight.

Hope for any compromise, or peaceful coexistence, between the Popular Front and the National Front had disappeared two days earlier when fighting began in Africa. Heartened by the fact that not all the troops and officials in Morocco supported the Nationalist cause (although a vast majority of them did), Ibárruri called for total resistance to the revolt. In addition to naming and asking political parties and provincial/ethnic groups for support, Ibárruri cast her net even wider by making clear some of the right/freedoms that were at risk. The type of judicial system that Franco had supported in the past did not provide fair trials and procedures, as Ibárruri interpreted history. That civil rights and basic freedoms, especially among ethnic groups, would be lost if the Republic was defeated, was Ibárruri's correct assessment, as shown by the future actions of Franco's government. The issue, for Ibárruri, was greater than just a change in government. She believed there would be radical changes in the approach to government and in how people would be allowed to live. It was the "democratic Republic" versus the "fascist menace" that would "hurl our democratic Spain back down into an abyss of terror and death." As a result, Ibárruri took up a cry from several battles in World War I, "they shall not pass." Knowing that a coup d'état must result in taking control of the apparatus of the government in Madrid, it was there she made this statement and it was there that the Republican forces needed to take their stand. Although eventually the fascists did pass, it was a much greater struggle than many had believed would be the case. Since that time, the call "they shall not pass" has echoed down through the years, being used in a variety of settings and countries.

—Donald A. Watt, PhD

Bibliography and Additional Reading

Ibárruri, Dolores. *They Shall Not Pass: The Autobiography of La Pasionaria.* New York: International Publishers, 1976.

Morley, Imogen. "Anatomy of a Speech: ¡No Pasarán!—Dolores Ibárruri." *Language, Commu-*

nication and Collaboration. Berlin: Imogen Morley, 2017.

Nelson, Cary. "The Spanish Civil War: An Overview." *Modern American Poetry: About the Spanish Civil War*. Urbana-Champaign IL: University of Illinois, 2001.

Preston, Paul. *The Spanish Civil War: Reaction, Revolution, and Revenge* (revised and expanded edition). New York: W.W. Norton & Company, 2007.

Snyder, Timothy. "Savagery." *The New Republic*. New York: The New Republic, 2012.

■ Mau Mau Warrior Oath

Date: ca. 1952
Author: Anonymous
Genre: oath

Summary Overview

Mau Mau is the name given to a militant movement in colonial Kenya in the 1950s; the name is said to derive from an oath of unity called Mau Mau, as reproduced here. Following World War II, great political, economic, and social changes were present in Kenya as the country began to move toward independence from Britain. Throughout the continent, in fact, Africans employed legal methods along with nonlegal forms of resistance to extricate themselves from the legacy of European hegemony. Emerging from districts associated primarily with the Kikuyu people, the Mau Mau movement relied on secrecy and insurrection in an attempt to wrest power from the British colonials who ruled the country. In 1952 a state of emergency was declared as a means to bring the Mau Mau rebellion to an end. Most of the fighting ended four years later, although the emergency remained in place until 1959. Nearly 15,000 died during the rebellion, and almost 80,000 Kikuyu (and other Africans) were detained in crude prison camps.

Defining Moment

Following the construction of a major rail artery in Kenya in the 1920, settlement by Britons (and other Europeans) and East Indians expanded. Large European-owned farms or plantations formed the basis of the developing national economy and changed the social and political landscape in the process. South Asians operated many of the retail businesses. Africans served in the new economy primarily as laborers, or else they maintained their traditional agrarian way of life. As early as the 1940s European took steps to limit the political influence not only of Africans but of Asians as well, declaring a region known as the White Highlands the exclusive provenance of Europeans.

After World War II, African nationalism emerged across the continent, and Kenya was no exception. The first and foremost nationalist organization there was the Kenya African Union (KAU), founded in 1944 and headed, from 1947, by Jomo Kenyatta. Kenyatta, of Kikuyu background, had extensive experience with Westerners, having studied and lived in Europe for sixteen years. Under him, the KAU opposed the racist land policies of the colony and demanded representation in government.

In the predominantly Kikuya areas of central Kenya, the challenge to European control came in the form of an emerging resistance movement called Mau Mau, based on the oath of unity sworn by its members. By the early 1950s, perhaps tens of thousands had taken the oath, and the movement took a violent turn. After several settlers were killed in October 1952, the colonial government declared a state of emergency. Kenyatta was unjustly imprisoned by colonial authorities in 1953 on allegations of being the Mau Mau's leader; he spent the next nine years in detention.

Troops of the King's African Rifles on watch for Mau Mau rebels. Photo via Wikimedia Commons. [Public domain.]

Historical Document

Mau Mau Warrior Oath

I swear before God and before the people who are here that:

I have today become a soldier of Gikuyu and Mumbi and I will from now onwards fight the real fight for the land and freedom of our country till we get it or till my last drop of blood. Today I have set my first step (stepping over a line of a goat's small intestine) as a warrior and I will never retreat.

And if I ever retreat

May this soil and all its products be a curse upon me!

If ever I am called to accompany a raid or bring in the head of an enemy, I shall obey and never give lame excuses. ...

I will never spy or inform on my people, and if ever sent to spy on our enemies I will always report the truth. ...

I will never reveal a raid or crime committed to any person who has not taken the Ngero Oath (Oath of Violence or crime) and will steal firearms wherever possible. ...

I will never leave a member in difficulty without trying to help him. ...

I will obey the orders of my leaders at all times without any argument or complaint and will never fail to give them any money or goods taken in a raid and will never hide any pillages or take them for myself. ...

I will never sell land to any white man. And if I sell:

May this soil and all its products be a curse upon me!

[Source: Donald L. Barnett and Karari Njama, *Mau Mau from Within* (New York: Modern Reader, 1966), 131-32.]

Glossary

Gikuyu and Mumbi: the legendary father and mother of the Kikuyu people

Ngero Oath: oath of violence or crime

Document Themes and Analysis

The oath is an English translation of what was originally a Kikuyu-language pledge to the Mau Mau cause and its leaders and members. It is made sacrosanct by the invocation of God (the indigenous deity or otherwise) along with the Kikuyu mythological figures Gikuyu and Mumbi. The reference to having stepped over a "line of a goat's small intestine" suggests a ritual element to the verbal swearing-in ceremony and serves as a kind of inviolable boundary separating the Mau Mau participants from their enemy and the rest of the world. So too does the idea of fighting to one's "last drop of blood." Not once but twice a line is recited to indicate what will happen if a member violates his oath and fails to perform as expected of him: "May this soil and all its products be a curse upon me!" Given the traditional link to the land at the center of Kikuyu society, no worse fate could be imagined than to find oneself (and presumably one's family) severed from it. Such violent actions as raiding and killing ("bring[ing] in the head of an enemy"), pillaging, and stealing firearms are all explicitly sanctioned by the oath. Similarly, any actions that aid the enemy or harm the Mau Mau are prohibited. The enemy is specifically named the "white man," lest one forget. And the chief goal is to obtain "the land and freedom of our country" that rightfully belong to Indigenous Africans.

The rebellion was carried out both openly and surreptitiously. The colonial government arrested thousands of suspected Mau Mau rebels, on little or no evidence, and often sent them to shabby holding facilities. At one point an entire Kikuyu population was forcibly relocated, and act that won white authorities few friends domestically or internationally. At the same time, apartheid policies such as this were only beginning to be questioned by the world community; they formed the basis of government in South Africa and were widely practiced elsewhere on the continent wherever European colonials held power. By the end of the rebellion, the dead included about 12,000 Kikuyu and, on the side fighting to suppress the movement, some 2,000 Africans aligned with the colonial regime together with 100 Europeans and under fifty South Asians.

When the fighting was over, leaders of other Indigenous African populations in the country began to seek, and win, broader representation in the country and to support self-government. In the late 1950s, the legislature in the colony included more Africans and gained greater authority. By 1960 Britain was ready to concede that Kenya would become an African-led country, and in 1961 the first majority-African legislature was elected. However, because the renamed Kenya African National Union (KANU) party leader, Jomo Kenyatta, was still held in detention, KANU members voted not to participate in the forming of a government despite their clear majority. The major opposition party, the Kenya African Democratic Union (KADU), formed a government in collaboration with colonial representatives. After negotiations between the two parties, and an agreement by KANU to accept a more decentralized form of government, a new round of elections was held. In June 1963 Kenyatta became prime minister of a self-governing Kenya.

Initially, Kenya and neighboring Tanganyika (now Tanzania) and Uganda announced that they would create an East African federation, but this was quickly abandoned in favor of separate independence. Kenya became independent as a member of the British Commonwealth in December 1963, and declared itself a republic a year later. Kenyatta ruled the nation as its president until his death in 1978.

—*Michael Shally-Jensen, PhD*

Bibliography and Additional Reading

Edgerton, Robert B. *Mau Mau: An African Crucible*. New York: Free Press, 1989.

Githuku, Nicolas K. *Mau Mau Crucible of War: Statehood, National Identity, and Politics of Postcolonial Kenya*. Lanham, MD: Lexington Books, 2016.

Lovatt Smith, David. *Kenya, the Kikuyu, and Mau Mau*. Herstmonceux, UK: Mawenzi Books, 2005.

■ Fidel Castro's Speech at Twenty-One Nations Conference

Date: May 2, 1959
Author: Fidel Castro
Genre: speech

Summary Overview

In May 1959 Argentina's capital city, Buenos Aires, hosted the Twenty-One Nations Conference, a gathering of representatives from the nations making up the Organization of American States (founded 1948). This document is a translated excerpt from what was originally an hour-and-twenty-minute speech in Spanish by Fidel Castro to conference attendees. In his speech, Castro outlines the suffering occurring throughout much of the Americas, rails against dictatorships, and—because he was not yet a committed Communist—called for an increase in U.S. aid to the region. Castro had only recently risen to power in Cuba, following the revolution there that he had led. He had been sworn in as prime minister in February 1959 but had not yet consolidated his authority. Though he would go on to become one of United States' arch antagonists, he was not yet in open conflict with his northern neighbor at the time of the speech.

Defining Moment

From the end of World War II until Castro's 1959 speech, the United States poured tens of billions of dollars into the reconstruction of Western Europe. Giving a commencement speech at Harvard University on June 5, 1947, Secretary of State George C. Marshall called for the economic aid plan to help rebuild Europe. President Truman signed the European Recovery Program, dubbed the Marshall Plan, into law on April 3 of the next year. After injecting almost $13 billion (over $130 billion in 2016 dollars) into Western Europe, the Marshall Plan gave way to the Mutual Security Act, which authorized another $7.5 billion annually up through the time of Castro's speech. This aid stands as the impetus for Castro's call for more US aid within the Americas.

At the time he gave this speech, Castro had been prime minister of Cuba for less than eleven weeks, and former Cuban dictator Fulgencio Batista had been in exile for less than eighteen weeks. Shortly after being sworn into office, Castro began a tour of the Americas in order to stir up positive public relations for Cuba's change of government. He first went to the United States, where he met with Vice President

Fidel Castro, c. 1959. Photo via Wikimedia Commons. [Public domain.]

Richard Nixon, whom he immediately disdained; he continued to Canada, Trinidad, Brazil, and Uruguay; his tour ended in Argentina, where he gave this speech. According to eye witnesses, Castro spoke extemporaneously while standing, as opposed to the other speakers at the conference who sat and tended to use notes. The United States government was, no doubt, keeping a close eye on Castro and Cuba at this time, but this fiery address marks a time before Castro and the United States were in open conflict. Castro had not yet declared himself a Communist revolutionary, saying instead that he was a "humanist" revolutionary.

The aid proposal never met with any serious consideration in the United States, and in the following years, relations between the two nations became more troubled. In an environment of mutual anxiety, Cuba embraced a closer relationship with the United States' geopolitical nemesis, the Soviet Union. In October 1960, the United States initiated a trade embargo that persists to this day (despite some changes under the Obama administration). In January of 1961, the United States ended diplomatic relations with Cuba; these were reinstated only in July 2015. In April 1961, the CIA backed disaffected Cuban nationals in an attempted counterrevolution; Castro thwarted the attempt, which came to be known as the Bay of Pigs Invasion. In October 1962, Nikita Khrushchev and the USSR tried to install nuclear weapons in Cuba, but President John F. Kennedy pressured them to abandon their designs. Although the brinksmanship of the early 1960s was not replicated in the years after, US-Cuban relations remained virtually nonexistent until President Barack Obama announced a normalization on December 17, 2014.

Author Biography

Fidel Alejandro Castro Ruz was born on August 13, 1926 in Birán, Cuba. He became an ardent leftist and anti-imperialist activist while studying law at the University of Havana. After earning a law degree in 1950, Castro organized and led guerrilla fighters against Cuba's dictator Fulgencio Batista. He was imprisoned for his efforts in 1953. He was sentenced to fifteen years but released after less than two. He renewed his guerrilla campaign with increased vigor, and Batista was forced into exile in late 1958. Castro became prime minister of Cuba one and a half months later, in February 1959. He gave the Twenty-One Nations speech two months later. Domestically, Castro consolidated his authority. In the heyday of the Cold War, Castro's proclivities aligned Cuba with the USSR, and Cuban relations with the United States soon became strained. Two of the most notorious Cold War events, the 1961 Bay of Pigs Invasion and the 1962 Cuban Missile Crisis, placed Cuba in the epicenter of the Cold War. Through decades of US opposition and, ultimately, the fall of the Soviet Union, Castro remained in power in Cuba. Battling health issues in 2006, he ceded his authority to his brother and officially retired in 2008.

Historical Document

Fidel Castro's Speech At Twenty-One Nations Conference

We are all conscious of the sacrifices made by our peoples; we are all conscious of the hopes that have been prompting those sacrifices, and also of the expectant unrest caused in the conscience of America by the recent victories of democracy against dictatorial rulers. We have all cherished the illusion that tyrants are disappearing from the face of our Continent. Yet, the truth is that such disappearance is only an illusion, and nobody would dare to state here, honestly and frankly, how long will the constitutional governments of Latin America actually last; how long do they suppose this period of democratic awakening, which has cost so much suffering and so many sacrifices, will last; and also how long do they suppose those democratic governments, overrun with poverty and need, which create an unending series of troubles and conflicts will last, before those who are watching for the right moment to take power from those democratic rulers, through violence, of course. How is it possible for Democracy to hold its own under such circumstances? We have adopted the democratic ideal, which is the ideal of all the peoples of this hemisphere, because it is the ideal best fitting the idiosyncrasy and the ambitions of the peoples of this Continent, and yet economic and social conditions prevailing in Latin America make impracticable the actual realization of the democratic ideal in our countries, because regardless of who may be running the country, whether a right wing dictatorship or a left wing dictatorship, the fact is that it is a dictatorship which does not believe in the principles guiding the peoples of Latin America. And if we are sincerely concerned about whether our countries are going to fall in the hands of leftist dictatorship, it is just as logical and honest to show the same concern about the possibility that our countries might fall in the hands of right wing dictatorships. Because, after all, what Latin America wants and longs for, what Latin America is striving for, is just plain democracy. The truth is that we are showing just one of the ugly faces of evil to the people, but conceal the other equally ugly face, so that they won't see it.

Many speakers often discuss democracy with their listeners, and then refuse to grant democratic rights and privileges in their own backyards. They speak of democracy to the same peoples they are betraying, to the same peoples whose rights they are denying, but the people only see sacrifices. They have lost faith, the faith that is so necessary at this critical instant when we have to have our continent for democracy, but not for a theoretical democracy, not for a democracy with hunger and misery, not for a democracy under the reign of terror and oppression but for a true democracy, based on real respect for the dignity of men with all human liberties prevailing within a framework of social justice because the peoples of America want neither liberty without bread nor bread without liberty!

There is no more corrupt system of government than a dictatorship. (It is true that there are constitutional governments that are as corrupt as they are constitutional; but while the constitutional governments have to watch their step, have to take care of themselves, because they must hold elections and might lose them, or the people might refuse to vote, there are things which act as brakes to slow down and even stop corruption, aided by the freedom of speech: the elections held every two years.) On the other hand, in the case of a dictatorship, the men in power steal the people's money for ten, fifteen, twenty and even more years and make millions and millions of dollars. Nobody dares to accuse them, nobody complains, nobody protests, simply because nobody can do any such thing; nobody holds them back, nobody can replace them.... Consequently, simultaneously with the efforts toward our economic development, our peoples have to make special efforts of a moral character, and when such standards are definitely adopted, when the possibility to mobilize resources becomes more and more difficult to certain rulers because they do not represent the interests of their peoples, do not represent the will of their peoples, such handicaps will operate to improve the political standards of the nations of our Continent simultaneously with, and in the measure that we improve our economic status. On the other hand, we must not run the risk of strengthening dictatorships by cooperating with them. This is one of the risks to which we are all exposed. We do not agree with the theory to the effect that the ideal system of government for economic development is the dictatorship; and that, furthermore, corruption is a vice which tends to discredit us and conspires against economic development.... That's why the really democratic government like our own should not be satisfied with being considered democratic; we must be absolutely honest too. This is a considerable part of our cooperation, of the sacrifices we have to make. We must definitely be conscious of the fact that our duty is not to represent the interests of minorities. Because at these conventions, at these conferences and these meetings we ought to represent and further the interests of the majorities and, therefore, we ought to impose on ourselves the sacrifices required by our own countries, lest we might ask sacrifices from just one class, from the workers, for instance, and not to the other sectors of the country.

Because on an enterprise of this sort all sacrifices must be uniform for all the sectors of the nation, and this is something which the economic classes understand very clearly, as they have understood it in Cuba, where the government keeps on adopting its measures with the full support of the majority of the economic classes of the country, prompted by their desire to further the national interests.

I have gone over the speech of the United States delegation; I have read it carefully. It describes all the efforts made heretofore in the form of cooperation given through international credit agencies. It also mentions their recent contribution to the Interamerican Development Bank, the individual assistance given in certain cases to certain countries.... All of that is true. But the contribution given through that agency is utterly insufficient; I don't mean to say that the goodwill that prompted and led to those contributions was insufficient or that the desire to help and the sincerity of the offer was short in any way. The trouble is that the resources placed at the disposal of those international agencies have been utterly insufficient. Where it not so, why should Latin America be so pitifully underdeveloped? How could it be if our peoples had access to really sufficient credit agencies? Of the five hundred millions.... Of the billion dollars of basic capital, one half is our half, consisting of our own soft or weak currencies and affected by our inflationary problems; because if that money we are contributing is going to be worth anything it has to be backed by United States dollars, or by gold bullion. And I now ask you, where do you suppose we are going to get those dollars or that bullion? So there you are. The resources so nobly contributed, the resources we owe to international cooperation, are obviously and utterly insufficient. That's the truth. The references made by the United States delegation to the sacrifices made those contributions.... Well, there is no doubt that their contribution has been substantial and decisive. However, the United States can, thanks to their powerful economy, make sacrifices that are beyond the possibilities of our underdeveloped countries. That colossal economy of North America is perfectly capable of making that, and much greater sacrifices too. They have made them before, and that's is precisely why they are big and strong. However, they have not made them for the peoples of Latin America; their assistance money has not been channeled to our countries, to the peoples of the family of nations living in this hemisphere. Those sacrifices have been made in behalf of Europe, for its reconstruction after the war, and in behalf of remote countries and peoples of the Middle East; not in behalf of the peoples that are most closely linked by tradition and political and economic relations with the United States. Now, why should not we in Latin America expect the United States to give us the support, the help, the cooperation they have been giving right along to all those other countries of the world?

Document Analysis

Fidel Castro, Cuba's recently sworn-in prime minister at the time, covers much ground in this sprawling speech. The off-the-cuff style differs from most written documents and scripted speeches. That is not to say that the speech is not cogent or coherent; it is both, despite its ranging style.

Castro uses the word "dictatorship" nine times. Additionally, he employs the word "tyrants" and the phrase "dictatorial rulers" once each. With each usage, he rails against this concept as an evil that must be absolutely avoided. For example, he proclaims, "There is no more corrupt system of government than a dictatorship." This may be a bit surprising to read for modern-day students. Before Castro ceded power to his brother in 2006 due to health reasons, he had held singular power in Cuba for decades. Anti-Castro propaganda in the United States has amplified his reputation as a dictator. However, in May of 1959, no one would have labelled him such or considered his mention of the concept ironic. His comment would have applied instead to the recently deposed Cuban dictator Fulgencio Batista and others of his ilk.

Batista, who had been out of power for only a matter of months, is also key to understanding Castro's discussion of the right-left divide within his criticism of dictatorships. He proclaims, "And if we are sincerely concerned about whether our countries are going to fall in the hands of leftist dictatorship, it is just as logical and honest to show the same concern about the possibility that our countries might fall in the hands of right wing dictatorships." At this point in time, Castro was downplaying his socialist proclivities; however, given his leftist history and his quick ascendance to the world stage during the height of the Cold War, the United States was already concerned about his leftist leanings. Without admitting a preference for socialism, Castro reminds his audience that dictators come from every part of the political spectrum. In the person of Batista, Cuba had recently deposed a dictator from the far right.

Not until the final paragraph does Castro reference the United States directly. He calls for an increase in US aid to the Americas, citing the poverty of the region and US aid to other areas. Castro was still on relatively good terms with the United States at this point; US aid was still pouring into Europe. Castro praises democracy at length, something that will have been well received by an American audience. Finally, he makes sure to mention that the lack of aid from America does not spring from a lack of goodwill. Thus, his request seems genuine. On the other hand, one might argue that there is an element of cynicism, or antagonism, to it. Although the United States was expending money elsewhere, this speech in Argentina may have served as a kind of passive-aggressive means to elicit US aid. Castro had recently visited the United States and met with Vice President Richard Nixon, whom he did not like. Perhaps that experience enters into the tone or tenor of the speech when he talks about US aid.

Essential Themes

The sprawling style of Castro's speech might lead some to dismiss it altogether. However, a look at the carefully developed theme of "sacrifice" (or "sacrifices") may help to sway the reader to appreciate the speech. Castro uses the term "sacrifices" throughout. It begins as a synonym for sufferings. The first sentence states, "We are all conscious of the sacrifices made by our peoples." Specifically, Castro connects the term with collective suffering. However, in the final paragraph, the term takes on a new meaning. Sacrifices, here, refer to US aid to the Americas and elsewhere. Castro acknowledges that the United States has already contributed some aid to the Americas, but it has not been enough: "That colossal economy of North America is perfectly capable of making that, and much greater sacrifices to." The other three instances of "sacrifices" in the final paragraph take on much the same meaning. The development of this theme works to paint aid from the United States as representing a chance for the US to do its part for the other nations of the Americas, which have already been making sacrifices for long enough. Ultimately, though, Castro's plea failed to produce financial results, even as it presented him to a broad audience of Latin American leaders.

—*Anthony Vivian, MA*

Bibliography and Additional Reading

Castro, Fidel. *Capitalism in Crisis: Globalization and World Politics Today.* Minneapolis, MN: Ocean Press, 2000.

Quirk, Robert E. *Fidel Castro.* New York: Norton, 1995.

Ramonet, Ignacio, and Fidel Castro. *Fidel Castro: My Life: A Spoken Autobiography.* New York: Scribner, 2009.

Szulc, Tad. *Fidel: A Critical Portrait.* New York: Avon Books, 1986.

■ Second Declaration of Havana

Date: February 4, 1962
Author: Fidel Castro
Genre: speech

Summary Overview

When Cuban prime minister Fidel Castro delivered this speech in February 1962, relations between the United States and Cuba had deteriorated precipitously. The leader of Cuba since ousting the nation's former dictator, Fulgencio Batista, in 1959, Castro had first declared that he was not a Communist and had made overtures to the United States. These were not well received by the administration of President Dwight D. Eisenhower, which considered him a dangerous radical. After the botched Bay of Pigs episode in 1961, in which CIA-backed anti-Castro rebels failed to rally support against them, Castro moved rapidly toward Communism, declaring Cuba a socialist state in April 1961, and stating publicly that he was a Marxist-Leninist in December. Cuba was suspended from the Organization of American States in January 1962, and Castro delivered this speech shortly afterward, calling on Latin American states to overthrow the United States. In response, the United States imposed a full economic embargo on Cuba, driving Castro further into league with the Soviet Union.

Defining Moment

The island nation of Cuba has had a complex relationship with the United States throughout its history. First claimed by Christopher Columbus in 1492, Cuba was a Spanish colony until 1898, though Havana was briefly occupied by the British in 1762 and then exchanged for Florida. Throughout the nineteenth century, the United States invested heavily in sugar, tobacco, and mining interests in Cuba, whose position off the Florida coast made the country an ideal trade partner. In 1881, the US secretary of state James G. Blaine noted that Cuba was "part of the American commercial system." Primarily because of these economic interests, the United States was heavily involved in the Cuban War of Independence from 1895 to 1898. Cuban revolutionary leader José Martí gathered significant support for Cuban independence while living in the United States, and warships were sent to Havana in 1898 to end the subsequent civil war. The Spanish army left Cuba for the last time in December 1898, and the United States assumed control of Cuba on January 1, 1899.

Though the United States had been eager to assist Cuba in gaining independence, it also wanted to protect its economic interests. A temporary government was put in place, headed by Americans, and foreign investment in the nation reached an all-time high, while policies favorable to the United States were put in place. In 1902, with a friendly candidate in place, Tomás Estrada Palma, the United States handed over control of Cuba, with the stipulation that the United States had a right to intervene militarily in Cuba, a

The botched Bay of Pigs operation in 1961 marked a breakdown in US-Cuban relations: pictured here is a counter-attack by Cuban Revolutionary Armed Forces near Playa Girón, 19 April 1961. Photo by Rumlin, via Wikimedia Commons.

right that it exercised repeatedly to ensure that Cuba remained in reliably pro-American hands.

By the 1930s, Cuba had loosened its ties to the United States and initiated a series of reforms that gave greater autonomy to the island. In 1940, Fulgencio Batista won the presidency in a free election, but in 1952, after being out of office for eight years, he staged a coup, setting himself up as a dictator. Castro was involved in one of many revolts against Batista and was captured and sentenced to prison in 1953. He was released in 1955, and after exile in Mexico, he returned to Cuba and began guerrilla attacks on Batista's forces. Other rebel groups joined Castro, and by 1958, the nation was in full civil war. Batista fled Cuba in January 1959. After consolidating his power among the nation's rebel groups, Castro took control of Cuba. The United States, which had supported Batista during the revolution, was initially willing to work with Castro's government and sent a new ambassador to Havana. Relations quickly soured, however, as Castro nationalized land and industry, appropriating assets owned by US companies. In response, the United States severed diplomatic ties in January 1961, and engineered the ouster of Cuba from the Organization of American States in January 1962. On February 7, 1962, the United States banned all trade with Cuba, after the Second Declaration of Havana, in which Castro called on all Central and South American countries to revolt against the United States.

Author Biography

Fidel Alejandro Castro Ruz was born on August 13, 1926, near Biran, Cuba. He was the son of a wealthy Spanish sugar farmer. His father was married but had a second family with one of his servants, Castro's mother. The pair had seven children and later married when Castro was a teenager. Despite his illegitimate birth, Castro was educated at Jesuit boarding schools, reserved for the island's elites. Although intellectually bright, Castro was more interested in athletic pursuits in school. While attending El Colegio de Belén, he pitched for the school baseball team. In 1945, Castro entered the law school of the University of Havana, where he was first exposed to the ideas of Cuban nationalism and socialism. In 1947, he took part in a failed coup to oust Rafael Trujillo, the leader of the Dominican Republic. In 1950, Castro graduated from law school and opened a private law practice, pursuing a seat in the Cuban parliament. However, the 1952 election was canceled when General Batista's coup returned the onetime leader to power. Castro was involved in a failed insurrection against Batista in 1953 that made him a national hero. He was sentenced to fifteen years in prison but was released in 1955. After prolonged guerrilla warfare, the Batista government collapsed in 1959, and Castro was named prime minister. In 1976, he became the president. In 2008, he handed over power to his brother Raúl. He died in 2011.

Historical Document

Second Declaration of Havana

What is Cuba's history but that of Latin America? What is the history of Latin America but the history of Asia, Africa, and Oceania? And what is the history of all these peoples but the history of the cruelest exploitation of the world by imperialism?

At the end of the last century and the beginning of the present, a handful of economically developed nations had divided the world among themselves subjecting two thirds of humanity to their economic and political domination Humanity was forced to work for the dominating classes of the group of nations which had a developed capitalist economy.

The historic circumstances which permitted certain European countries and the United States of North America to attain a high industrial development level put them in a position which enabled them to subject and exploit the rest of the world.

What motives lay behind this expansion of the industrial powers? Were they moral, "civilizing" reasons, as they claimed? No. Their motives were economic.

The discovery of America sent the European conquerors across the seas to occupy and to exploit the lands and peoples of other continents; the lust for riches was the basic motivation for their conduct. America's discovery took place in the search for shorter ways to the Orient, whose products Europe valued highly.

A new social class, the merchants and the producers of articles manufactured for commerce, arose from the feudal society of lords and serfs in the latter part of the Middle Ages.

The lust for gold promoted the efforts of the new class. The lust for profit was the incentive of their behavior throughout its history. As industry and trade developed, the social influence of the new class grew. The new productive forces maturing in the midst of the feudal society increasingly clashed with feudalism and its serfdom, its laws, its institutions, its philosophy, its morals, its art, and its political ideology....

Since the end of the Second World War, the Latin American nations are becoming pauperized constantly. The value of their capita income falls. The dreadful percentages of child death rate do not decrease, the number of illiterates grows higher, the peoples lack employment, land, adequate housing, schools, hospitals, communication systems and the means of subsistence. On the other hand, North America investments exceed 10 billion dollars. Latin America, moreover, supplies cheap raw materials and pays high prices for manufactured articles. Like the first Spanish conquerors, who exchanged mirrors and trinkets with the Indians for silver and gold, so the United States trades with Latin America. To hold on to this torrent of wealth, to take greater possession of America's resources and to exploit its long-suffering peoples: this is what is hidden behind the military pacts, the military missions and Washington's diplomatic lobbying....

Wherever roads are closed to the peoples, where repression of workers and peasants is fierce, where the domination of Yankee monopolies is strongest, the first and most important lesson is to understand that it is neither just nor correct to divert the peoples with the vain and fanciful illusion that the dominant classes can be uprooted by legal means which do not and will not exist. The ruling classes are entrenched in all positions of state power. They monopolize the teaching field. They dominate all means of mass communication. They have infinite financial resources. Theirs is a power which the monopolies and the ruling few will defend by blood and fire with the strength of their police and their armies.

The duty of every revolutionary is to make revolution. We know that in America and throughout the world the revolution will be victorious. But revolutionaries cannot sit in the doorways of their homes to watch the corpse of imperialism pass by. The role of Job does not behoove a revolutionary. Each year by which America's liberation may be hastened will mean millions of children rescued from death, millions of minds, freed for learning, infinitudes of sorrow spared the peoples. Even though the Yankee imperialists are preparing a bloodbath for America they will not succeed in drowning the people's struggle. They will evoke universal hatred against themselves. This will be the last act of their rapacious and caveman system....

Document Analysis

Castro begins his speech by aligning Cuba with not only Latin America but also "Asia, Africa, and Oceania," parts of the world that he states have been subjected throughout history to imperial exploitation. He offers a brief historical perspective on how a "handful of economically developed nations" have been able to exploit two-thirds of the world's population for their own ruthless economic ends. The United States and a few European nations have been the offenders, he says, taking economic advantage of the rest of the world under the guise of "civilizing" it. Castro traces this development to Spanish conquest, when the "lust for riches" drove European nations across the world, bringing their feudal hierarchies with them. The feudal peasantry may have transformed over time into the exploited working class, but the motivation at the heart of the US relationship with Latin American is the same lust for profit, Castro explains.

Throughout his speech, Castro compares the brutal Spanish subjugation of indigenous people of the Americas with the contemporary relationship between the United States and Latin America. Just as the Spanish exchanged worthless "trinkets" for "silver and gold," the United States exploits Latin American countries, taking their natural resources and raw materials through unbalanced trade deals and defending their right to do so with military pacts that are only to the advantage of the United States. Meanwhile, Castro states, the citizens of these countries suffer from poor health care, high infant mortality, and crushing poverty.

Castro argues there is no point trying to combat this colossus through legal means. The "ruling class," supported by the United States, will never give up power. He states that the power must be taken from them by force and that doing so is not a passive process. When the United States is overthrown, it will mean "millions of children rescued from death." Castro ends his speech on an ominous note, as he warns that the United States is preparing a "bloodbath," which will be the last act of the "rapacious and caveman system."

Essential Themes

The inflamed rhetoric of the Second Declaration of Cuba was not lost on the United States, already convinced of the danger posed by its Cuban neighbor. On the other hand, Castro had good reason to be enraged. In 1961, the United States had supported a disastrous coup attempt launched at the Bay of Pigs, aimed at overthrowing Castro and justifying US military intervention in Cuba. Since relations with the United States were irretrievably damaged, Castro turned increasingly to the Soviet Union for economic support and defense. Castro believed, rightly, that the United States was prepared to use military force to unseat his government. The Soviet Union offered a deterrent to another Cuban invasion that also achieved the Soviets' goal of placing missiles within easy striking range of the United States. It would place missiles in Cuba, a move that Soviet premier Nikita Khrushchev felt was justified because of the Jupiter missiles the United States had placed in Turkey, near the Russian border. When a US spy plane identified and photographed the missile base in Cuba just before the missiles themselves arrived, President John F. Kennedy demanded their removal. After several days of international tension, an incident known as the Cuban Missile Crisis, the Soviet Union agreed to remove the missiles. For its part, the United States vowed not to invade Cuba and also offered a secret promise to remove its missiles in Turkey. After more than fifty years, the United and Cuba reestablished diplomatic relations in 2015.

—*Bethany Groff Dorau, MA*

Bibliography and Additional Reading

Erikson, Daniel P. *The Cuba Wars: Fidel Castro, the United States, and the Next Revolution.* New York: Bloomsbury, 2008.

Matthews, Herbert Lionel. *Fidel Castro.* New York: Simon, 1969.

Renwick, Danielle, and Brianna Lee. "US-Cuba Relations." *Council on Foreign Relations.* CFR, 4 Aug. 2015.

Schlesinger, Arthur M. *A Thousand Days: John F. Kennedy in the White House.* Boston: Houghton, 1965.

Staten, Clifford L. *The History of Cuba.* Westport: Greenwood, 2003.

Vietnam—and Cambodia

Most Americans know Vietnam as a place where a messy, bloody war was fought between U.S. forces and Vietnamese Communists in the 1960s and '70s. The United States, moreover, "lost" the war in the end, as the country ultimately was taken over by Communists.

But before there was any U.S. involvement in Vietnam—before there was a Vietnam War—there was the First Indochina War (1946–1954). That conflict pitted French colonial forces who had long governed the territory against Vietnamese anti-imperialist forces who sought to expel the Europeans and establish Vietnam as a self-governing nation. The result, after nearly a decade of bloodshed and hundreds of thousands of deaths, was an agreement, signed in Geneva, whereby the French would withdraw and Vietnam would be divided into northern and southern districts. Communist interests aligned under Ho Chi Minh were concentrated in the north, and noncommunist interests aligned under Emperor Bao Dai and his regime, as supported by the United States, were concentrated in the south. A section in the agreement specified that a general election was to be held in 1956, the idea being that through this process a unified national government would be created. Yet neither South Vietnam nor the United States signed onto the election, largely out of fear that they would not prevail, and so it never took place. Meanwhile, Bao Dai's chosen prime minister in South Vietnam, Ngo Dinh Diem, manipulated the power structure in order to eject the emperor and make himself head of state. In consequence, communist cadres (Viet Minh) already present in South Vietnam were activated, and southern-based anti-Diem guerilla forces and military units making up the National Liberation Front (NLF), or Viet Cong, also went into action. North Vietnam began supplying these groups with armaments and information.

Thus began a terrible war that lasted through three American administrations (Kennedy, Johnson, and Nixon), numerous South Vietnamese administrations (based in the capital Saigon), and left about 3.5 million dead (military and civilian). The United States invested so much in the conflict (losing about 55,000 of its soldiers) because it feared a "domino effect" if the Communists in North Vietnam won: other nations in the region, it was said, would then fall to communist revolutions in turn. The war did impact neighboring Laos and Cambodia, who suffered communist incursions and, in the case of Cambodia, U.S. bombing raids aimed at stopping them. After the war's end, moreover, Cambodia experienced a violent Maoist revolution under the Khmer Rouge; but that had less to do with any domino effect advanced by Vietnam—in fact, Vietnam and Cambodia fought a war against each other—than with internal Cambodian politics. In any case, over 1.3 million people met their deaths in the "Killing Fields" of Cambodia's murderous regime.

Geneva Accords on Indochina

Date: July 20, 1954
Genre: treaty

Summary Overview

Designed to address the outcome of a long-standing conflict between French forces and Vietnamese nationalists, who had been at war in Indochina since 1946, the Geneva Conference began on April 26, 1954. It included representatives from the Communist-backed Viet Minh, and its adversary, France, along with the United States, the Soviet Union, China, France, Great Britain, and others. The Geneva Conference dealt with a number of ongoing conflicts in Asia, but the impending defeat of French forces at Dien Bien Phu, and the French reluctance to continue their resistance to the Communist nationalist forces under Ho Chi Minh, pushed the topic of Vietnam to the forefront of the conversation.

During the conference, the French announced their intention to leave Vietnam within the year, so the delegates were compelled to structure a plan that would allow for a smooth transition to independence. The United States and the Soviet Union, allied with Communist China and the Viet Minh, were on opposite sides of these negotiations, refusing at times even to be in the same room with each other. The United States' policy of containment dictated that Communism must not be allowed to spread. The Soviet Union was deeply committed to the spread of its fundamental ideology. Both powers jockeyed for control of territory in Asia. The Geneva Convention agreed to divide Vietnam temporarily along the seventeenth parallel, while allowing for free elections, future independence, and reunification.

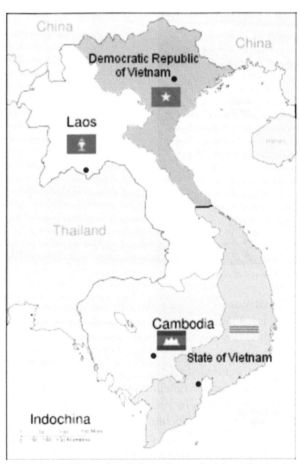

The partition of French Indochina that resulted from the Conference. Three successor states were created: the Kingdom of Cambodia; the Kingdom of Laos; and the Democratic Republic of Vietnam, the state led by Ho Chi Minh and the Viet Minh. The State of Vietnam was reduced to the southern part of Vietnam. The division of Vietnam was intended to be temporary, with elections planned for by 1956 to reunify the country. Image by SnowFire, via Wikimedia Commons.

Defining Moment

Indochina was a French colony that encompassed modern-day Vietnam, Laos, and Cambodia. The French established Catholic missions in the area as early as the 1600s and significant trade relations with regional monarchies throughout the nineteenth century. Between 1858, when the French first invaded Vietnam and set up the colony of Cochinchina, to 1893, when Laos was added as a French protectorate, the French established and consolidated control over the region. Indochina was governed by a French governor-general as the Indochinese Union, though tra-

The Geneva Conference. Photo via Wikimedia Commons. [Public domain.]

ditional monarchies were also allowed to continue. In southern Vietnam, where the original colony was established, French control was even more firmly entrenched, with a prefect as head of the government, which was entirely French.

Though sporadic rebellions took place, most notably in Cochinchina in 1919 and in the army in 1930, French control of Indochina was largely unchallenged until 1940, when Japan invaded and occupied the area. Even then, local French officials were allowed to remain in nominal control, though they answered to the occupied Vichy government in France, then under Nazi control. In 1945, Japan imprisoned the French officials and declared that Vietnam was an independent nation. After the defeat of Japan in World War II in August 1945, the French regained control over Laos, Cambodia, and southern Vietnam. In the north, however, the Viet Minh, led by the nationalist Ho Chi Minh, declared an independent Democratic Republic of Vietnam. Protracted negotiations between the French and the Viet Minh were unsuccessful, and the armies skirmished in November 1946. Hearing that their troops had been attacked, the French navy shelled the city of Haiphong, killing thousands of its residents. The Viet Minh retaliated by attacking Hanoi in December, and the conflict rapidly escalated into war.

Faced with a protracted war against guerrilla forces, France sought help from its traditional allies. The United States was officially neutral at first,

"Charles de Gaulle and Ho Chi Minh are hanged" in effigy by students demonstrating in Saigon, July 1964, on the 10th anniversary of the Geneva Accords. Photo via Wikimedia Commons. [Public domain.]

though it supported French involvement in Vietnam, fearing that Ho Chi Minh would allow Communism to spread across the country, if he were victorious. The United States and France set up an anti-Communist state in southern Vietnam under the former emperor, Bao Dai, seen in his own country as a puppet of the Western powers. The French, with increasing support from the United States under President Dwight D. Eisenhower, and the Viet Minh, with increasing support from the Soviet Union and China, continued to fight until 1954, when the Geneva Conference was called to address the matter, among other issues of international concern. In March, just before the conference began, French forces were surrounded at the village of Dien Bien Phu. They surrendered during the conference, on May 7. No longer able to sustain an armed resistance to the Viet Minh, the French asked the international community to broker a settlement.

Document Information

The Geneva Accords were agreed upon and announced on July 21, 1954, in Geneva, Switzerland. The Agreement on the Cessation of Hostilities in Viet-Nam, containing forty-seven articles, was agreed on the previous day. It was one of ten agreements produced at the conference.

Historical Document

Geneva Accords on Indochina

Chapter I

Provisional Military Demarcation Line and Demilitarized Zone

Article 1
A provisional military demarcation line shall be fixed, on either side of which the forces of the two parties shall be regrouped after their withdrawal, the forces of the People's Army of Viet-Nam to the north of the line and the forces of the French Union to the south.

The provisional military demarcation line is fixed as shown on the map attached (see Map No. 1).
It is also agreed that a demilitarized zone shall be established on either side of the demarcation line, to a width of not more than 5 Kms. from it, to act as a buffer zone and avoid any incidents which might result in the resumption of hostilities.

Article 2
The period within which the movement of all the forces of either party into its regrouping zone on either side of the provisional military demarcation line shall be completed shall not exceed three hundred (300) days from the date of the present Agreement's entry into force.

Article 3
When the provisional military demarcation line coincides with a waterway, the waters of such waterway shall be open to civil navigation by both parties wherever one bank is controlled by one party and the other bank by the other party. The Joint Commission shall establish rules of navigation for the stretch of waterway in question. The merchant shipping and other civilian craft of each party shall have unrestricted access to the land under its military control.

Article 4
The provisional military demarcation line between the two final regrouping zones is extended into the territorial waters by a line perpendicular to the general line of the coast.

All coastal islands north of this boundary shall be evacuated by the armed forces of the French Union, and all islands south of it shall be evacuated by the forces of the People's Army of Viet-Nam.

Article 5
To avoid any incidents which might result in the resumption of hostilities, all military forces, supplies and equipment shall be withdrawn from the demilitarized zone within twenty-five (25) days of the present Agreement's entry into force.

Article 6
No person, military or civilian, shall be permitted to cross the provisional military demarcation line unless specifically authorized to do so by the Joint Commission.

Article 7
No person, military or civilian, shall be permitted to enter the demilitarized zone except persons concerned with the conduct of civil administration and relief and persons specifically authorized to enter by the Joint Commission.

Article 8
Civil administration and relief in the demilitarized zone on either side of the provisional military demarcation line shall be the responsibility of the Commanders-in-Chief of the two parties in their respective zones. The number of persons, military or civilian, from each side who are permitted to enter the demilitarized zone for the conduct of civil administration and relief shall be determined by the respective Commanders, but in no case shall the total number authorized by either side exceed at any one time a figure to be determined by the Trung Gia military Commission or by the Joint Commission. The number of civil police and the arms to be carried by them shall be determined by the Joint Commission. No one else shall carry arms unless specifically authorized to do so by the Joint Commission.

Article 9
Nothing contained in this chapter shall be construed as limiting the complete freedom of movement, into, out of or within the demilitarized zone, of the Joint Commission, its joint groups, the International Commission to be set up as indicated below, its inspection teams and any other persons, supplies or equipment specifically authorized to enter the demilitarized zone by the Joint Commission. Freedom of movement shall be permitted across the territory under the military control of either side over any road or waterway which has to be taken between points within the demilitarized zone when such points are not connected by roads or waterways lying completely within the demilitarized zone.

Chapter II

Principles and Procedure Governing Implementation of the Present Agreement

Article 10
The Commanders of the Forces on each side, on the one side the Commander-in-Chief of the French Union forces in Indo-China and on the other side the Commander-in-Chief of the People's Army of Viet-Nam, shall order and enforce the complete cessation of all hostilities in Viet-Nam by all armed forces under their control, including all units and personnel of the ground, naval and air forces.

Article 11
In accordance with the principle of a simultaneous cease-fire throughout Indo-China, the cessation of hostilities shall be simultaneous throughout all parts of Viet-Nam, in all areas of hostilities and for all the forces of the two parties.

Taking into account the time effectively required to transmit the cease-fire order down to the lowest echelons of the combatant forces on both sides, the two parties are agreed that the cease-fire shall take effect completely and simultaneously for the different sectors of the country as follows:

Northern Viet-Nam at 8.00 a.m. (local time) on 27 July 1954

Central Viet-Nam at 8.00 a.m. (local time) on 1 August 1954

Southern Viet-Nam at 8.00 a.m. (local time) on 11 August 1954

It is agreed that Pekin mean time shall be taken as local time.

From such time as the cease-fire becomes effective in Northern Viet-Nam, both parties undertake not to engage in any large-scale offensive action in any part of the Indo-Chinese theatre of operations and not to commit the air forces based on Northern Viet-Nam outside that sector. The two parties also undertake to inform each other of their plans for movement from one regrouping zone to another within twenty-five (25) days of the present Agreement's entry into force.

Article 12
All the operations and movements entailed in the cessation of hostilities and regrouping must proceed in a safe and orderly fashion:

Within a certain number of days after the cease-fire Agreement shall have become effective, the number to be determined on the spot by the Trung Gia

Military Commission, each party shall be responsible for removing and neutralizing mines (including river- and sea-mines), booby traps, explosives and any other dangerous substances placed by it. In the event of its being impossible to complete the work of removal and neutralization in time, the party concerned shall mark the spot by placing visible signs there. All demolitions, mine fields, wire entanglements and other hazards to the free movement of the personnel of the Joint Commission and its joint groups, known to be present after the withdrawal of the military forces, shall be reported to the Joint Commission by the Commanders of the opposing forces;

From the time of the cease-fire until regrouping is completed on either side of the demarcation line:

The forces of either party shall be provisonally withdrawn from the provisional assembly areas assigned to the other party.

When one party's forces withdraw by a route (road, rail, waterway, sea route) which passes through the territory of the other party (see Article 24), the latter party's forces must provisionally withdraw three kilometres on each side of such route, but in such a manner as to avoid interfering with the movements of the civil population.

Article 13
From the time of the cease-fire until the completion of the movements from one regrouping zone into the other, civil and military transport aircraft shall follow air-corridors between the provisional assembly areas assigned to the French Union forces north of the demarcation line on the one hand and the Laotian frontier and the regrouping zone assigned to the French Union forces on the other hand.

The position of the air-corridors, their width, the safety route for single-engined military aircraft transferred to the south and the search and rescue procedure for aircraft in distress shall be determined on the spot by the Trung Gia Military Commission.

Article 14
Political and administrative measures in the two regrouping zones on either side of the provisional military demarcation line:

Pending the general elections which will bring about the unification of Viet-Nam, the conduct of civil administration in each regrouping zone shall be in the hands of the party whose forces are to be regrouped there in virtue of the present Agreement;

Any territory controlled by one party which is transferred to the other party by the regrouping plan shall continue to be administered by the former party until such date as all the troops who are to be transferred have completely left that territory so as to free the zone assigned to the party in question. From then on, such territory shall be regarded as transferred to the other party, who shall assume responsibility for it.

Steps shall be taken to ensure that there is no break in the transfer of responsibilities. For this purpose, adequate notice shall be given by the withdrawing party to the other party, which shall make the necessary arrangements, in particular by sending administrative and police detachments to prepare for the assumption of administrative responsibility. The length of such notice shall be determined by the Trung (lie Military Commission. The transfer shall be effected in successive stages for the various territorial sectors.

The transfer of the civil administration of Hanoi and Haiphong to the authorities of the Democratic Republic of Viet-Nam shall be completed within the respective time-limits laid down in Article 15 for military movements.

Each party undertakes to refrain from any reprisals or discrimination against persons or organizations on account of their activities during the hostilities and to guarantee their democratic liberties.

From the date of entry into force of the present Agreement until the movement of troops is completed, any civilians residing in a district controlled by one party who wish to go and live in the zone assigned to the other party shall be permitted and helped to do so by the authorities in that district.

Article 15

The disengagement of the combatants, and the withdrawals and transfers of military forces, equipment and supplies shall take place in accordance with the following principles:

The withdrawals and transfers of the military forces, equipment and supplies of the two parties shall be completed within three hundred (300) days, as laid down in Article 2 of the present Agreement;

Within either territory successive withdrawals shall be made by sectors, portions of sectors or provinces. Transfers from one regrouping zone to another shall be made in successive monthly instalments proportionate to the number of troops to be transferred;

The two parties shall undertake to carry out all troop withdrawals and transfers in accordance with the aims of the present Agreement, shall permit no hostile act and shall take no step whatsoever which might hamper such withdrawals and transfers. They shall assist one another as far as this is possible;

The two parties shall permit no destruction or sabotage of any public property and no injury to the life and property of the civil population. They shall permit no interference in local civil administration;

The Joint Commission and the International Commission shall ensure that steps are taken to safeguard the forces in the course of withdrawal and transfer

The Trung Gia Military Commission, and later the Joint Commission, shall determine by common agreement the exact procedure for the disengagement of the combatants and for troop withdrawals and transfers, on the basis of the principles mentioned above and within the framework laid down below:

The disengagement of the combatants, including the concentration of the armed forces of all kinds and also each party's movements into the provisional assembly areas assigned to it and the other party's provisional withdrawal from it, shall be completed within a period not exceeding fifteen (15) days after the date when the cease-fire becomes effective.

The general delineation of the provisional assembly areas is set out in the maps annexed to the present Agreement

In order to avoid any incidents, no troops shall be stationed less than 1,500 metros from the lines delimiting the provisional assembly areas.

During the period until the transfers are concluded, all the coastal islands west of the following lines shall be included in the Haiphong perimeter:

meridian of the southern point of Kebao Island

northern coast of Ile Rousse (excluding the island), extended as far as the meridian of Campha-Mines

meridian of Campha-Mines.

The withdrawals and transfers shall be effected in the following and within the following periods (from the date of the entry into force of the present Agreement):

Forces of the French Union

Hanoi perimeter-80 days

Haiduong perimeter-100 days

Haiphong perimeter-300 days

Forces of the People's Army of Viet-Nam

Ham Tan and Xuyenmoc provisional assembly area-80 days

Central Viet-Nam provisional assembly area-first instalment-80 days

Plaine des Jones provisional assembly area-100 days

Central Viet-Nam provisional assembly area-second instalment-100 days

Point Camau provisional assembly area-200 days

Central Viet-Nam provisions 1 assembly area-last instalment-300 days

Chapter III

Ban on the Introduction of Fresh Troops, Military Personnel, Arms, and Munitions. Military Bases

Article 16
With effect from the date of entry into force of the present Agreement, the introduction into Viet-Nam of any troop reinforcements and additional military personnel is prohibited.

It is understood, however, that the rotation of units and groups of personnel, the arrival in Viet-Nam of individual personnel onto temporary duty basis and the return to Viet-Nam of individual personnel after short periods of leave or temporary duty outside Viet-Nam shall be permitted under the conditions laid down below:

Rotation of units (defined in paragraph (c) of this Article) and groups of personnel shall not be permitted for French Union troops stationed north of the provisional military demarcation line laid down in Article 1 of the present Agreement, during the withdrawal period provided for in Article 2.

However, under the heading of individual personnel not more than fifty (50) men, including officers, shall during any one month be permitted to enter that part of the country north of the provisional military demarcation line on a temporary duty basis or to return there after short periods of leave or temporary duty outside Viet-Nam.

"Rotation" is defined as the replacement of units or groups of personnel by other units of the same echelon or by personnel who are arriving in Viet-Nam territory to do their overseas service there;

The units rotated shall never be larger than a battalion-or the corresponding echelon for air and naval forces;

Rotation shall be conducted on a man-for-man basis, provided, however, that in any one quarter neither party shall introduce more than fifteen thousand five hundred (15,500) members of its armed forces into Viet-Nam under the rotation policy.

Rotation units (defined in paragraph (c) of this Article) and groups of personnel, and the individual personnel mentioned in this Article, shall enter and leave Viet-Nam only through the entry points enumerated in Article 20 below;

Each party shall notify the Joint Commission and the International Commission at least two days in advance of any arrivals or departure of units, groups of personnel and individual personnel in or from Viet-Nam. Reports on the arrivals or departures of units, groups of personnel and individual personnel in or from Viet-Nam shall be submitted daily to the Joint Commission and the International Commission.

All the above-mentioned notifications and reports shall indicate the places and dates of arrival or departure and the number of persons arriving or departing;

The International Commission, through its Inspection Teams, shall supervise and inspect the rotation of units and groups of personnel and the arrival and departure of individual personnel as authorized above, at the points of entry enumerated in Article 20 below.

Article 17

With effect from the date of entry into force of the present Agreement, the introduction into Viet-Nam of any reinforcements in the form of all types of arms, munitions and other war material, such as combat aircraft, naval craft, pieces of ordnance, jet engines and jet weapons and armoured vehicles, is prohibited

It is understood, however, that war material, arms and munitions which have been destroyed, damaged, worn out or used up after the cessation of hostilities may be replaced on the basis of piece-for-piece of the same type and with similar characteristics. Such replacements of war material, arms and munitions shall not be permitted for French Union troops stationed north of the provisional military demarcation line laid down in Article 1 of the present Agreement, during the withdrawal period provided for in Article 2.

Naval craft may perform transport operations between the regrouping zones.

The war material, arms and munitions for replacement purposes provided for in paragraph(b) of this Article, shall be introduced into Viet-Nam only through the points of entry enumerated in Article 20 below. War material, arms and munitions to be replaced shall be shipped from Viet-Nam only through the points of entry enumerated in Article 20 below;

Apart from the replacements permitted within the limits laid down in paragraph (b) of this Article, the introduction of war material, arms and munitions of all types in the form of unassembled parts for subsequent assembly is prohibited;

Each party shall notify the Joint Commission and the International Commission at least two days in advance of any arrivals or departures which may take place of war material, arms and munitions of all types.

In order to justify the requests for the introduction into Viet-Nam of arms, munitions and other war material (as defined in paragraph (a) of this Article) for replacement purposes, a report concerning each incoming shipment shall be submitted to the Joint Commission and the International Commission. Such reports shall indicate the use made of the items so replaced;

The International Commission, through its Inspection Teams, shall supervise and inspect the replacements permitted in the circumstances laid down in this Article, at the points of entry enumerated in Article 20, below.

Article 18
With effect from the date of entry into force of the present Agreement, the establishment of new military bases is prohibited throughout Viet-Nam territory.

Article 19
With effect from the date of entry into force of the present Agreement, no military base under the control of a foreign State may be established in the re-grouping zone of either party; the two parties shall ensure that the zones assigned to them do not adhere to any military alliance and are not used for the resumption of hostilities or to further an aggressive policy.

Article 20
The points of entry into Viet-Nam for rotation personnel and replacements of material are fixed as follows:

Zones to the north of the provisional military demarcation line: Laokay, Langson, Tien-Yen, Haiphong, Vinh, Dong-Hoi, Muong-Sen;

Zone to the south of the provisional military demarcation line: Tourane, Quinhon, Nhatrang, Bangoi, Saigon, Cap St. Jacques, Tanchau.

Chapter IV

Prisoners of War and Civilian Internees

Article 21
The liberation and repatriation of all prisoners of war and civilian internees detained by each of the two parties at the coming into force of the present Agreement shall be carried out under the following conditions:

All prisoners of war and civilian internees of Viet-Nam, French and other nationalities captured since the beginning of hostilities in Viet-Nam during military operations or in any other circumstances of war and in any part of the territory of Viet-Nam shall be liberated within a period of thirty (30) days after the date when the cease-fire becomes effective in each theatre.

The term "civilian internees" is understood to mean all persons who, having in any way contributed to the political and armed struggle between the two parties, have been arrested for that reason and have been kept in detention by either party during the period of hostilities.

All prisoners of war and civilian internees held by either party shall be surrendered to the appropriate authorities of the other party, who shall give them all possible assistance in proceeding to their country of origin, place of habitual residence or the zone of their choice.

Chapter V

Miscellaneous

Article 22
The Commanders of the Forces of the two parties shall ensure that persons under their respective commands who violate any of the provisions of the present Agreement are suitably punished.

Article 21
In cases in which the place of burial is known and the existence of graves has been established, the Commander of the Forces of either party shall, within a specific period after the entry into force of the Armistice Agreement, permit the graves service personnel of the other party to enter the part of Viet-Nam territory under their military control for the purpose of finding and removing the bodies of deceased military personnel of that party, including the bodies of deceased prisoners of war. The Joint Commission shall determine the procedures and the time limit for the performance of this task. The Commanders of the Forces of the two parties shall communicate to each other all information in their possession as to the place of burial of military personnel of the other party.

Article 24
The present Agreement shall apply to all the armed forces of either party. The armed forces of each party shall respect the demilitarized zone and the territory under the military control of the other party, and shall commit no act and undertake no operation against the other party and shall not engage in blockade of any kind in Viet-Nam.

For the purposes of the present Article, the word "territory" includes territorial waters and air space.

Article 25
The Commanders of the Forces of the two parties shall afford full protection and all possible assistance and co-operation to the Joint Commission and its joint groups and to the International Commission and its inspection teams in the performance of the functions and tasks assigned to them by the present Agreement.

Article 26
The costs involved in the operations of the Joint Commission and joint groups and of the International Commission and its Inspection Teams shall be shared equally between the two parties.

Article 27
The signatories of the present Agreement and their successors in their functions shall be responsible for ensuring the observance and enforcement of the terms and provisions thereof. The Commanders of the Forces of the two parties shall, within their respective commands, take all steps and make all arrangements necessary to ensure full compliance with all the provisions of the present Agreement by all elements and military personnel under their command.

The procedures laid down in the present Agreement shall, whenever necessary, be studied by the Commanders of the two parties and, if necessary, defined more specifically by the Joint Commission.

Chapter VI

Joint Commission and International Commission for Supervision and Control in Viet-Nam

Responsibility for the execution of the agreement on the cessation of hostilities shall rest with the parties.

An International Commission shall ensure the control and supervision of this execution.

In order to facilitate, under the conditions shown below, the execution of provisions concerning joint actions by the two parties a Joint Commission shall be set up in Viet-Nam.

The Joint Commission shall be composed of an equal number of representatives of the Commanders of the two parties.

The Presidents of the delegations to the Joint Commission shall hold the rank of General,

The Joint Commission shall set up joint groups the number of which shall be determined by mutual agreement between the parties. The joint groups shall be composed of an equal number of officers from both parties. Their location on the demarcation line between the re-grouping zones shall be determined by the parties whilst taking into account the powers of the Joint Commission.

The Joint Commission shall ensure the execution of the following provisions of the Agreement on the cessation of hostilities:

A simultaneous and general cease-fire in Viet-Nam for all regular and irregular armed forces of the two parties.

A re-groupment of the armed forces of the two parties.

Observance of the demarcation lines between the re-grouping zones and of the demilitarized sectors.

Within the limits of its competence it shall help the parties to execute the said provisions, shall ensure liaison between them for the purpose of preparing and carrying out plans for the application of these provisions, and shall endeavour to solve such disputed questions as may arise between the parties in the course of executing these provisions.

An International Commission shall be set up for the control and supervision of the application of the provisions of the agreement on the cessation of hostilities in Viet-Nam. It shall be composed of representatives of the following States: Canada, India and Poland.

It shall be presided over by the Representative of India.

The International Commission shall set up fixed and mobile inspection teams, composed of an equal number of officers appointed by each of the above-mentioned States. The fixed teams shall be located at the following points: Laokay, Langson, Tien-Yen, Haiphong, Vinh, Dong-Hoi, Muong-Sen, Tourane, Quinhon, Nhatrang, Bangoi, Saigon, Cap St. Jacques, Tranchau. These points of location may, at a later date, be altered at the request of the

Joint Commission, or of one of the parties, or of the International Commission itself, by agreement between the International Commission and the command of the party concerned. The zones of action of the mobile teams shall be the regions bordering the land and sea frontiers of Viet-Nam, the demarcation lines between the re-grouping zones and the demilitarized zones. Within the limits of these zones they shall have the right to move freely and shall receive from the local civil and military authorities all facilities they may require for the fulfilment of their tasks (provision of personnel, placing at their disposal documents needed for supervision, summoning witnesses necessary for holding enquiries, ensuring the security and freedom of movement of the inspection teams, etc....). They shall have at their disposal such modern means of transport, observation and communication as they may require. Beyond the zones of action as defined above, the mobile teams may, by agreement with the command of the party concerned, carry out other movements within the limits of the tasks given them by the present agreement.

The International Commission shall be responsible for supervising the proper execution by the parties of the provisions of the agreement. For this purpose it shall fulfil the tasks of control, observation inspection and investigation connected with the application of the provisions of the agreement on the cessation of hostilities, and it shall in particular:

Control the movement of the armed forces of the two parties effected within the framework of the regroupment plan.

Supervise the demarcation lines between the regrouping areas, and also the demilitarized zones.

Control the operations of releasing prisoners of war and civilian Internees.

Supervise at ports and airfields as well as along all frontiers of Viet-Nam the execution of the provisions of the agreement on the cessation of hostilities, regulating the introduction into the country of armed forces, military personnel and of all kinds of arms, munitions and war material.

The International Commission shall, through the medium of the inspection teams mentioned above, and as soon as possible either on its own initiative, or at the request of the Joint Commission, or of one of the parties, undertake the necessary investigations both documentary and on the ground.

The inspection teams shall submit to the International Commission the results of their supervision, their investigation and their observations, furthermore they shall draw up such special reports as they may consider necessary or as may be requested from them by the Commission. In the case of a disagreement within the teams, the conclusions of each member shall be submitted to the Commission.

If any one inspection team is unable to settle an incident or considers that there is a violation or a threat of a serious violation the International Commission shall be informed; the latter shall study the reports and the conclusions of the inspection teams and shall inform the parties of the measures which should be taken for the settlement of the incident, ending of the violation or removal of the threat of violation.

When the Joint Commission is unable to reach an agreement on the interpretation to be given to some provision or on the appraisal of a fact, the International Commission shall be informed of the disputed question. Its recommendations shall be sent directly to the parties and shall be notified to the Joint Commission.

The recommendations of the International Commission shall be adopted by majority vote, subject to the provisions contained in article 42. If the votes are divided the chairman's vote shall be decisive.

The International Commission may formulate recommendations concerning amendments and additions which should be made to the provisions of the agreement on the cessation of hostilities in Viet-Nam, in order to ensure a more effective execution of that agreement. These recommendations shall be adopted unanimously.

When dealing with questions concerning violations, or threats of violations, which might lead to a resumption of hostilities, namely:

Refusal by the armed forces of one party to effect the movements provided for in the regroupment plan;

Violation by the armed forces of one of the parties of the regrouping zones, territorial waters, or air space of the other party;

the decisions of the International Commission must be unanimous.

If one of the parties refuses to put into effect a recommendation of the International Commission, the parties concerned or the Commission itself shall inform the members of the Geneva Conference.

If the International Commission does not reach unanimity in the cases provided for in article 42, it shall submit a majority report and one or more minority reports to the members of the Conference.

The International Commission shall inform the members of the Conference in all cases where its activity is being hindered.

The International Commission shall be set up at the time of the cessation of hostilities in Indo-China in order that it should be able to fulfil the tasks provided for in article 36.

The International Commission for Supervision and Control in Viet-Nam shall act in close co-operation with the International Commissions for Supervision and Control in Cambodia and Laos.

The Secretaries-General of these three Commissions shall be responsible for co-ordinating their work and for relations between them.

The International Commission for Supervision and Control in Viet-Nam may, after consultation with the International Commissions for Supervision and Control in Cambodia and Laos, and having regard to the development of the situation in Cambodia and Laos, progressively reduce its activities. Such a decision must be adopted unanimously.

All the provisions of the present Agreement, save the second sub-paragraph of Article 11, shall enter into force at 2400 hours (Geneva time) on 22 July 1954.

Done in Geneva at 2400 hours on the 20th of July 1954 in French and in Viet-Namese, both texts being equally authentic.

Document Analysis

The Agreement on the Cessation of Hostilities in Viet-Nam outlines a strategy for temporarily dividing Vietnam along the seventeenth parallel. Its forty-seven articles lay out the terms for this division, including both how the cease-fire and withdrawal are to be administered and the requirement that free elections be held within two years. The agreement begins with the establishment of the line of division and the maintenance of buffer zones on either side of the line, designed to prevent any incidents that could reignite hostilities. The withdrawal of troops from across this line is scheduled, with full separation no later than three hundred days. The barrier zone is to be cleared out completely within twenty-five days to avoid any conflict, and access to the demilitarized zone will be tightly controlled by a joint commission, comprising officers from both sides of the line, led by two generals, who will decide who can cross the zone. This internal joint commission is to be overseen by an international commission, with Canada, India, and Poland as its members. The representative of India is the head of this commission, whose mission is to be "responsible for supervising the proper execution by the parties of the provisions of the agreement" and whose decisions will be made by vote. This commission also has inspection authority and is to report any violations of the agreement to the members of the Geneva Convention.

The agreement contains numerous specific details for how the temporary separation of Vietnam is to be achieved. Significant "regrouping" needs to be done, as both French and Viet Minh forces are scattered throughout the country. In addition, personnel need to be able to go on leave and return without hostilities resuming; both sides need to be allowed to retrieve and rebury their dead; and prisoners of war and civilian prisoners need to be released, exchanged, and resettled. Very specific instructions are given for how both sides are to act toward each other during the withdrawal. For example, when troops need to pass on a roadway through hostile territory, the occupying army is required to withdraw by three kilometers (1.9 miles) to allow them through. Each force will withdraw to, and then control, their side of the demarcation line. This agreement makes clear that the intention is to separate Vietnam only until it can safely hold "general elections which will bring about the unification of Viet-Nam."

Essential Themes

Conflict over the partition of Vietnam began almost as soon as the document was signed. Ho Chi Minh was reluctant to give up the south of Vietnam, believing that it both should not be partitioned and had been won by the Viet Minh. The government of Bao Dai refused to sign the agreement, but the French agreed, thereby proving to all parties involved that he was just a puppet. The United States agreed to abide by the agreement, but would not sign it, believing that if the Geneva Accords were carried out, Ho Chi Minh would win a nationwide election and open up the nation to Communist control. France withdrew completely, leaving Ho Chi Minh firmly in control of the north and the United States supporting the south with military and economic aid. This involvement escalated slowly into the conflicts that eventually led to the Vietnam War, in which U.S. troops, seen as the colonial heirs of the French, fought Communist forces from the north, finally ceding all of the former French Indochina in 1973. The North Vietnamese captured the southern capital of Saigon in 1975.

—Bethany Groff Dorau, MA

Bibliography and Additional Reading

Maximin, Edward Francis. *Accommodation and Resistance: The French Left, Indochina, and the Cold War, 1944–1954.* New York: Greenwood Press, 1986.

Prados, John. *Vietnam: The History of an Unwinnable War, 1945–1975.* Lawrence: UP of Kansas, 2009.

Windrow, Martin. *The French Indochina War, 1946–1954.* Oxford: Osprey Military, 1998.

■ "The Path of Revolution in the South"

Date: 1956
Author: Le Duan
Genre: essay

Summary Overview

Le Duan was one of the top three leaders in the Vietnamese Communist Party and in North Vietnam. By the time he wrote this essay, it was clear that the election agreed to in the 1954 Geneva Accords to help unify North and South Vietnam, was not going to occur. Le Duan's essay had a two-fold purpose. While it was a call for a negotiated settlement, the author clearly saw the reluctance of the South to negotiate and thus placed the blame for the impending conflict on South Vietnam and the United States (which was propping up the South Vietnamese government). Secondly, this was a call by the North Vietnamese leaders for support of the cause of reunifying Vietnam, through armed conflict if necessary. Although it was still a few years until large-scale military action between North and South Vietnam would erupt, this document served as a foundation for the North's support of South Vietnamese insurgents as well as for the direct involvement of North Vietnamese forces.

Defining Moment

World War II brought about the end of colonization in many parts of the world, including Vietnam. Just as most of the French government cooperated with the Germans after the fall of Paris in 1940, so too most of the French colonial officers in Vietnam cooperated with the Japanese when the latter arrived in September of that same year. Once an Allied victory became all but assured in Europe, French nationalism began to increase among its colonial officials. Thus, in March 1945, the Japanese incarcerated the French and set up a puppet Vietnamese government. The Viet Minh, communist forces that had fought the Japanese throughout the war, were able to gain control of northern Vietnam by August and declared an independent state there. France returned after the conclusion of World War II and tried to re-establish a colony, ultimately losing in 1954 when the Geneva Accords were signed. In that agreement, two temporary states were established, a communist one in the North and a pro-Western one in the South.

When the provisions of the Geneva Accords fell apart in 1956, the communist leaders in the North had to decide whether to accept a divided country for the foreseeable future or to develop a new plan for Vietnam's unification as a communist state. There were moderates who were satisfied with the status quo, and others who wanted to try a new round of negotiations. Le Duan was the leader of the faction that wanted to reunify the country as soon as possible and by whatever means necessary. His "Path of Revolution" essay set forth the justification for military action because, to him, it was clear that peaceful negotiations were not going to occur. Having served the Communist Party in the South, Le Duan was certain that he understood the situation and what would be needed. As he lobbied other members of the Communist Party's Central Committee, he presented the idea that aggressive military action was the only alternative to negotiation.

At the 1956 meeting of North Vietnam's Central Committee, the discussions resulted in a decision as to which direction the committee would move to unify the country. As no negotiations were imminent, the committee chose the direction advocated by Le Duan. Le Duan was so successful in presenting his case, in fact, that he was elevated to membership in the secretariat at that meeting. In 1957, Le Duan was assigned the task of developing a full plan for the military struggle with the South, which was implemented in 1959. Although Ho Chi Minh was technically in charge until his death in 1969, Le Duan was the political leader of the military campaign in South Vietnam until the end of the war in 1975.

Author Biography

Le Duan (1907/08–1986) was born in the southern part of Vietnam while it was part of French Indochina. Having received a basic education, he worked as a clerk for the railroad system. While in this job, he became acquainted with Marxism. In 1928, he joined the Revolutionary Youth League and, two years later, was a founding member of the Indochina Communist Party. Within a few more years, he was a member of the Central Committee. As a result of this group's anti-French actions, Le Duan was twice imprisoned. Released from prison in 1945, he became an assistant to the communist leader Ho Chi Minh, focusing on activities in the south. In 1956, he was elevated to membership in the Secretariat of the Communist Party, becoming first secretary in 1959 and then head of the Communist Party in 1960. While officially sharing power with Ho Chi Minh, until Ho's death in 1969, when Ho's health declined in the mid-1960s Le Duan was clearly the party leader. Until his own death, he was first among equals in the political collective leadership of Vietnam.

Historical Document

"The Path of Revolution in the South"

The situation forces bellicose states such as the U.S. and Britain to recognize that if they adventurously start a world war, they themselves will be the first to be destroyed, and thus the movement to demand peace in those imperialist countries is also developing strongly. Recently, in the U.S. Presidential election, the present Republican administration, in order to buy the people's esteem, put forward the slogan "Peace and Prosperity," which showed that even the people of an imperialist warlike country like the U.S. want peace.

The general situation shows us that the forces of peace and democracy in the world have tipped the balance toward the camp of peace and democracy. Therefore we can conclude that the world at present can maintain long-term peace.

On the other hand, however, we can also conclude that as long as the capitalist economy survives, it will always scheme to provoke war, and there will still remain the danger of war.

Based on the above the world situation, the Twentieth Congress of the Communist Party of the Soviet Union produced two important judgments:

All conflicts in the world at present can be resolved by means of peaceful negotiations.

The revolutionary movement in many countries at present can develop peacefully.

Naturally in the countries in which the ruling class has a powerful military-police apparatus and is using fascist policies to repress the movement, the revolutionary parties in those countries must look clearly at their concrete situation to have the appropriate methods of struggle.

Based on the general situation and that judgment, we conclude that, if all conflicts can be resolved by means of peaceful negotiations, peace can be achieved.

Because the interest and aspiration of peaceful reunification of our country are the common interest and aspiration of all the people of the Northern and Southern zones, the people of the two zones did not have any reason to provoke war, nor to prolong the division of the country. On the contrary the people of the two zones are more and more determined to oppose the U.S.-Diem scheme of division and war provocation in order to create favorable conditions for negotiations between the two zones for peaceful unification of the country. The present situation of division is created solely by the arbitrary U.S.-Diem regime, so the fundamental problem is how to smash the U.S.-Diem scheme of division and war-provocation.

As observed above, if they want to oppose the U.S-Diem regime, there is no other path for the people of the South but the path of revolution. What, then, is the line and struggle method of the revolutionary movement in the South? If the world situation can maintain peace due to a change in the relationship of forces in the world in favor of the camp of peace and democracy, the revolutionary movement can develop following a peaceful line, and the revolutionary movement in the South can also develop following a peaceful line.

First of all, we must determine what it means for a revolutionary movement to struggle according to a peaceful line. A revolutionary movement struggling according to a peaceful line takes the political forces of the people as the base rather than using people's armed forces to struggle with the existing government to achieve their revolutionary objective. A revolutionary movement struggling according to a peaceful line is also different from a reformist movement in that a reformist movement relies fundamentally on the law and constitution to struggle, while a revolutionary movement relies on the revolutionary political forces of the masses as the base. And another difference is that a revolutionary movement struggles for revolutionary objectives, while a reformist movement struggles for reformist goals. With an imperialist, feudalist, dictatorial, fascist government like the U.S.-Diem, is it possible for a peaceful political struggle line to achieve its objectives?

We must recognize that all accomplishments in every country are due to the people. That is a definite law: it cannot be otherwise. Therefore the line of the revolutionary movement must be in accord with the inclinations and aspirations of the people. Only in that way can a revolutionary movement be mobilized and succeed.

The ardent aspiration of the Southern people is to maintain peace and achieve national unification. We must clearly recognize this longing for peace: the revolutionary movement in the South can mobilize and advance to success on the basis of grasping the flag of peace, in harmony with popular feelings. On the contrary, U.S.-Diem is using fascist violence to provoke war, contrary to the will of the people and therefore must certainly be defeated.

Can the U.S.-Diem regime, by using a clumsy policy of fascist violence, create a strong force to oppose and destroy the revolutionary movement? Definitely not, because the U.S.-Diem regime has no political strength in the country worth mentioning to rely on. On the contrary, nearly all strata of the people oppose them. Therefore the U.S.-Diem government is not a strong government it is only a vile and brutal government. Its vile and brutal character means that it not only has no mass base in the country but is on the way to being isolated internationally. Its cruelty definitely cannot shake the revolutionary movement, and it cannot survive for long.

The proof is that in the past two years, everywhere in the countryside, the sound of the gunfire of U.S.-Diem repression never ceased; not a day went by when they did not kill patriots, but the revolutionary spirit is still firm, and the revolutionary base of the people still has not been shaken.

Once the entire people have become determined to protect the revolution, there is no cruel force that can shake it. But why has the revolutionary movement not yet developed strongly? This is also due to certain objective and subjective factors.

Objectively, we see that, after nine years of waging strong armed struggle, the people's movement generally speaking now has a temporarily peaceful character that is a factor in the change of the movement for violent forms of struggle to peaceful forms. It has the correct character of rebuilding to advance later.

With the cruel repression and exploitation of the U.S.-Diem, the people's revolutionary movement definitely will rise up. The people of the South have known the blood and fire of nine years of resistance war, but the cruelty of the U.S.-Diem cannot extinguish the struggle spirit of the people.

On the other hand, subjectively, we must admit that a large number of cadres, those have responsibility for guiding the revolutionary movement, because of the change in the method of struggle and the work situation from public to secret, have not yet firmly grasped the political line of the party, have not yet firmly grasped the method of political struggle, and have not yet followed correctly the mass line, and therefore have greatly reduced the movement's possibilities for development.

At present, therefore, the political struggle movement has not yet developed equally among the people, and a primary reason is that a number of cadres and masses are not yet aware that the strength of political forces of the people can defeat the cruelty, oppression and exploitation of the U.S.-Diem, and therefore they have a halfway attitude and don't believe in the strength of their political forces.

We must admit that any revolutionary movement has times when it falls and times when it rises; any revolutionary movement has times that are favorable for development and times that are unfavorable. The basic thing is that the cadres must see clearly the character of the movement's development to lead the mass struggle to the correct degree, and find a way for the vast determined masses to participate in the movement. If they are determined to struggle from the bottom to the top, no force can resist the determination of the great masses.

In the past two years, the political struggle movement in the countryside and in the cities, either by one form or another, has shown that the masses have much capacity for political struggle with the U.S.-Diem. In those struggles, if we grasp more firmly the struggle line and method, the movement can develop further, to the advantage of the revolution. The cruel policy of U.S.-Diem clearly cannot break the movement, or the people's will to struggle.

There are those who think that the U.S.-Diem's use of violence is now aimed fundamentally at killing the leaders of the revolutionary movement to destroy the Communist Party, and that if the Communist Party is worn away to the point that it doesn't have the capacity to lead the revolution, the political struggle movement of the masses cannot develop.

This judgment is incorrect. Those who lead the revolutionary movement are determined to mingle with the masses, to protect and serve the interest of the masses and to pursue correctly the mass line. Between the masses and communists there is no distinction any more. So how can the U.S.-Diem destroy the leaders of the revolutionary movement, since they cannot destroy the masses? Therefore they cannot annihilate the cadres leading the mass movement.

In fact more than twenty years ago, the French imperialists were determined to destroy the Communists to destroy the revolutionary movement for national liberation, but the movement triumphed. It wasn't the Communist but the French imperialist themselves and their feudal lackeys who were destroyed on our soil.

Now twenty years later, U.S.-Diem are determined to destroy the Communists in the South, but the movement is still firm, and Communists are still determined to fulfill their duty. And the revolutionary movement will definitely advance and destroy the imperialist, feudalist government. U.S.-Diem will be destroyed, just as the French imperialists and their feudal lackeys were destroyed.

We believe that: the peaceful line is appropriate not only to the general situation in the world but also to the situation within the country, both nation-wide and in the South. We believe that the will for peace and the peace forces of the people throughout the country have smashed the U.S.-Diem schemes of war provocation and division.

We believe that the will for peace and Southern people's democratic and peace forces will defeat the cruel, dictatorial and fascist policy of U.S.-Diem and will advance to smash the imperialist, feudalist U.S.-Diem government. Using love and righteousness to triumph over force is a tradition of the Vietnamese nation. The aspiration for peace is an aspiration of the world's people in general and in our own country, including the people of the South, so our struggle line cannot be separated from the peaceful line.

Only the peaceful struggle line can create strong political forces to defeat the scheme of war provocation and the cruel policy of U.S.-Diem. We are determined to carry out our line correctly, and later the development of the situation will permit us to do so.

Imperialism and feudalism are on the road to disappearance. The victory belongs to our people's glorious task of unification and independence, to our glorious Communism we must pledge our lives. We shall win.

Glossary

Diem: Ngo Dinh Diem, president of South Vietnam

two zones: a means of referring to a divided Vietnam (north and south) without implying the legitimacy of South Vietnam

Document Themes and Analysis

Le Duan issues a call for peace in this essay, while outlining the reasons that war is justified. He maintains that most people want peace, but he also claims that the people in both North and South Vietnam desire, even more so, to be unified. This attitude, according to Le Duan, was the result of the "imperialist warlike country" of the United States and the "fascist" government of Diem joining forces in the South. Thus, in a paradoxical way, Le Duan argues that the communists and others seeking peace must work to overthrow Diem at all costs in order to foster peace and unification. As he saw it, the time was ripe for revolution against these twin oppressors of the people (the Diem regime and his US backers).

When Le Duan circulated this essay among the party and governmental leaders of North Vietnam, he understood that a weariness regarding war had arisen owing to the long recent struggle against the French. He included material from the Communist Party's Twentieth Congress in the Soviet Union to demonstrate that he understood the rationale for not wanting immediately to push for change in South Vietnam, when one could perhaps gain the desired ends through political negotiations. However, from his perspective, the latter route was not likely to advance the goal of unifying the nation under communist rule. Thus, even though frequently he invokes the terms "peace" and "peaceful" in his essay, the central message is to unleash all "appropriate methods of struggle"—up to and including armed conflict— against the oppressors. The "imperialist, feudalist, dictatorial, fascist" regime of Diem, supported by the United States, would never allow a peaceful transition and unification.

Although the oppression Le Duan refers to was, at this time, directed mainly against Buddhist opposition elements in the south rather than against communist groups, the author is correct to note that the "masses" have not been included in the governing system of the south and therefore might be ready to follow a communist push for change. Time and again, Le Duan refers to the violence of the Diem regime. He seems certain that while violence might stop the actions of a few, it was not going to stop broader change, particularly when virtually the entire population desired it. As part of his work to move the leadership of the Communist Party to his position, Le Duan intentionally sets the peaceful communists in opposition to the violent Diem regime. He places the blame for his proposed policy of aggressive military response on the leaders of the South and on the United States. The "half-way attitude" by which Le Duan characterizes leaders of various cadres refers not only to those in the South, but also to too-moderate leaders in the North. Through emphasizing the so-called "peaceful struggle line," the essayist attempts to justify "smashing" the Diem regime and obtaining the desired "unification and independence."

Although a communist from the inception of the party in Vietnam, Le Duan was often seen as a pragmatist who desired results rather than ideological purity. Thus, while he refers to the peaceful path toward

Le Duan. Photo via Wikimedia Commons. [Public domain.]

change put forward by Soviet communist leaders, Le Duan desires quicker results. He looks beyond using solely "strong political forces" to destroy the violent Di m regime. He talks up the notion of peace, yet in seeking the desired ends, he advocates an aggressive military stance toward the enemy. Because Di m, in 1955, had used a questionable election to displace the emperor who was put in place by the Japanese in 1945, and because he also refused to allow nationwide elections for unification, Le Duan did not regard negotiation as an option. For him, rather, aggression was justified. His use of President Eisenhower's 1956 campaign slogan, "Peace and Prosperity," demonstrates his belief that the desire for peace could eventually produce results beneficial to the people of Vietnam. While he incorrectly boasts that the conflict in Vietnam would destroy the United States, he is correct in his assessment that, in most nations, there is a point at which the people would rather realize peace than continue a conflict.

While his essay cannot be viewed as a blueprint for the North's reaching its desired goals, it is a call for the reactivation of the revolutionary struggle that had defeated the French. That message ultimately carried the day with the leaders of North Vietnam. In the next year, Le Duan was given the task of developing a plan for the political and military actions that would unfold in South Vietnam. The strategy began to be implemented in 1959, with the formation of the various oppositional organizations in the South in 1960. Although at first glance "The Path of Revolution in the South" might not seem relevant to the ensuing path of war, given that so much of its space is given over to pronouncements of peace, the essay proved key in pushing the people toward war. It also illustrates the approach that North Vietnam would take in its public pronouncements, picturing itself as desiring only peace and placing all the blame for the war squarely on the other side. Le Duan was able to win the necessary political support for the war in both North and South Vietnam, ultimately resulting in the communists' successfully reaching their goal of unifying the nation under their rule.

—Donald A. Watt, PhD

Bibliography and Additional Reading

Ang, Cheng Guan. *The Vietnam War from the Other Side: The Vietnamese Communists' Perspective.* London: Routledge, 2002.

Duiker, William. *Sacred War: Nationalism and Revolution in a Divided Vietnam.* New York: McGraw Hill, 1994.

Le, Quynh. "Vietnam Ambivalent on Le Duan's Legacy." *BBC News.* BBC, 14 Jul. 2006. news.bbc.co.uk/2/hi/asia-pacific/5180354.stm.

Nguyen, Lien-Hang T. *Hanoi's War: An International History of the War for Peace in Vietnam.* (The New Cold War History) Chapel Hill, NC: University of North Carolina Press, 2012.

Tucker, Spencer C. *The Encyclopedia of the Vietnam War: A Political, Social, and Military History.* 2nd ed. Santa Barbara: ABC-CLIO, 2011.

■ CIA Memo on National Liberation Front Methods

Date: November 29, 1963
Author: John A. McCone
Genre: memorandum

Summary Overview

One of the major blunders made by American war planners in the years leading up to the war in Vietnam, besides the near complete lack of understanding of Vietnamese culture, was not appreciating the depth of resentment harbored by residents of the south for the South Vietnamese government, led by Ngo Dinh Diem. By late 1963, southern Vietnamese revolutionaries had been working for years in towns and villages across the south to win popular support for their cause to put down the repressive regime of Diem. The United States, fearful of the spread of communism, took a position against the majority of the population in supporting Diem. In a memo commissioned by John A. McCone, then director of the Central Intelligence Agency (CIA), for delivery to Dean Rusk, the secretary of state under both presidents Kennedy and Johnson, American intelligence officers outlined the various methods used by the National Liberation Front (NLF) to ingratiate themselves to the South Vietnamese people. The document stands as a detailed analysis of what the NLF was doing to improve the lives of the people of the south, and serves to demonstrate the eagerness with which American officials sought to link southern revolutionaries to an international communist conspiracy.

Defining Moment

The strategy of "containment" as developed by American officials at the end of World War II, held that through the careful use of military force the spread of communism could be limited as not to overwhelm any single region. It was this idea that led to American intervention in the Korean Conflict, ultimately resulting in the creation of two distinct Koreas: a communist north and democratic south. After the French withdraw from Vietnam, the same approach was used in that country. Although neither north nor south wanted division, the Western powers meeting in Geneva separated the two along the seventeenth parallel. Vietnam, however, was very different from Korea. The weak, and often repressive regime of Ngo Dinh Diem in the south, standing in contrast to the popular and well-supported communist revolutionary movement of Ho Chi Minh in the north, instilled first resentment and then open revolt. What was in fact a civil and, in part, sectarian war in the south the West came to interpret as an attempted communist coup directed by the Soviet Union and China.

Ngo Dinh Diem. Photo via Wikimedia Commons. [Public domain.]

John McCone. Photo via Wikimedia Commons. [Public domain.]

As the violence escalated, southern activists consolidated the various communist and noncommunist anti-Diem forces operating in the south into a single paramilitary force that came to be known as the National Liberation Front, or Viet Cong. These various groups, having operated across the south since the 1940s, had pushed through massive land reforms, seizing farmland from wealthy landlords and redistributing it to the poor. In 1960, the Diem government, in a move it hoped would weaken the Viet Cong, brought back landlords to the farms and villages, often violently ejecting people from land that they had farmed for over a decade. To make matters worse, these landlords then demanded the poor, and now landless farmers, to pay back rent for the years of use. Seeing an opportunity, Ho Chi Minh began to support southern guerrilla fighters and sent North Vietnamese forces into Laos to create supply routes into the south.

With the election of John F. Kennedy, the United States, still badly misunderstanding the realities on the ground, further tied itself to the Diem regime. Vice President Lyndon Johnson even went so far as to declare Diem "the Winston Churchill of Asia." Among Diem's chief American supporters was John A. McCone, appointed director of the Central Intelligence Agency after the ousting of Allen W. Dulles following the Bay of Pigs. McCone believed, wrongly, that the Viet Cong had been agents of northern communists since the end of World War II and advocated for immediate American military involvement in support of the repressive Diem regime. When Diem was finally overthrown in early November of 1963, McCone bitterly objected to American support for the coup. He continued to advocate for greater American involvement, and although the information he and the CIA provided the Johnson administration did eventually lead to full American military intervention, McCone grew increasingly frustrated over what he considered a weak and feckless response to the communist takeover of Southeast Asia.

Author Biography

John Alexander McCone was born in California in 1902. Heir to an iron fortune, McCone attended the University of California at Berkeley, where he received a degree in mechanical engineering. Rising in private industry, he became an executive vice president at Consolidated Steel Corporation and, as a leading industrialist, served as an advisor for the Atomic Energy Commission. As his profile rose, McCone became ever more involved with the Central Intelligence Agency (CIA), until ultimately he was named as director following the resignation of Allen W. Dulles following the disastrous Bay of Pigs invasion of 1961. A proponent of the use of force during the Cuban Missile Crisis, McCone was the mastermind behind numerous covert plots while director of the CIA, including the overthrow of several democratically elected governments. Opposed to the 1963 plot to overthrow Ngo Dinh Diem, McCone became increasingly disillusioned by the Johnson administration's involvement in Vietnam, until he finally resigned as director in 1965. McCone died in 1991.

Historical Document

CIA Memo on National Liberation Front Methods

Memorandum Prepared for the Director of Central Intelligence
Washington, November 29, 1963.

SUBJECT: Viet Cong Quasi-Governmental Activities

In the "armed liberation" strategy of both Mao Tse-Tung and Ho Chi Minh, the establishment and gradual extension of "secure" base areas is a primary objective in the struggle. Within such secure areas, the Viet Cong have, since the beginning of resistance against the French in 1945–46, attempted to carry out quasi-governmental functions. Their purpose is two-fold and sometimes contradictory. They seek to win the voluntary support of the population by various activities of a welfare or civic-action nature. By example they try to show that they are more efficient, honest, and humane as administrators than the enemy regime. At the same time, they are concerned with exercising control and extracting support in the form of manpower, food and labor; these requirements frequently take priority and undo any favorable effects from their psychological operations.

In areas still not "secure" or not under strong Viet Cong influence, the guerrilla forces must live a hit-and-run existence and have little opportunity to act as the effective local administration. In these areas they must nonetheless rely upon support, shelter, and supply from the civilian populace, which is obtained not only by force but by positive steps to convince the population that its aspirations are those of the Viet Cong.

Much of our detailed knowledge with respect to Viet Cong activities in these directions comes from the period of Viet Minh resistance against the French. There is sufficient current reporting, however, to leave little doubt that the same pattern of activity is still being followed.

Viet Minh documents captured during the Indochina war frequently dealt with a program to raise rural living standards—the "new life" program. Such documents often contained statistics on the establishment of schools, numbers of children and adults in school, medical dispensaries, numbers of trained medical aides and midwives, sanitation efforts including numbers of wells and latrines dug, and food and livestock production. This effort and various other governmental activities were carried out under the authority of Administrative-Resistance Councils set up at the regional, provincial, district, and town levels.

A similar Viet Cong hierarchy of military, politico-administrative, and Liberation Front Committees now exists in South Vietnam, but Viet Cong troops themselves are frequently the agents of both governmental and civic-action tasks. While force and terrorism remain a major Viet Cong instrument against local officials of the South Vietnamese Government and recalcitrant villagers, recently captured Viet Cong documents clearly show that Viet Cong troops and agents are ordered to provide assistance to peasants and to avoid antagonisms and abuses, such as looting or violation of churches and pagodas.

A Communist land reform program in South Vietnam, begun by the Viet Minh, is still being carried out under the Viet Cong, but some difficulties have been encountered. This is reflected in the attitude of the Liberation Front, which watered down its initial emphasis on land reform, although free and unconditional distribution of land to poor peasants is still a part of its platform. Informants and Viet Cong prisoners indicate that early attempts by the Viet Cong to force "middle-class" peasants to give land to the poor were too harsh, caused peasant disputes and loss of production, and depleted the source of funds available for peasant loans and for support of Viet Cong troops. As a result, there appears to have been some modification of Viet Cong land reform activities to lessen pressure on "middle-class" peasants and encourage higher production. Although there are some references to communal farms, the Viet Cong do not appear to have stressed land collectivization in South Vietnam, where popular reaction to North Vietnam's brutal agrarian reform policies has been adverse.

Current reports also indicate that the Viet Cong provide assistance to peasants in land clearance, seed distribution, and harvesting, and in turn persuade or force peasants to store rice in excess of their own needs for the use of guerrilla troops. Controls are apparently imposed in Viet Cong zones to prevent shipments for commercial marketing in Saigon, or to collect taxes on such shipments. The Viet Cong themselves often pay cash or give promissory notes for the food they acquire.

Little detailed information is available on current Communist health and sanitation activities. Captured Viet Cong doctors or medical personnel indicate that dispensaries for treatment of Viet Cong wounded often are scattered inconspicuously among several peasant homes in a village, and that civilians are treated as facilities and supplies permit. Civilians as well as guerrilla forces are almost certainly instructed in methods of sanitation and disease prevention, but apparent shortages of medical personnel and medicines in some areas suggest that medical care for civilians in Viet Cong-dominated areas may be spotty.

There are also references to primary and adult education, much of it in the form of indoctrination, and to Viet Cong-run schools operating almost side by side with government schools, under the excuse that peasants lack the necessary documentation required to enter government schools. A Liberation Front broadcast of 19 November 1963 claimed that there were some 1,000 schools with 2 million pupils in "freed areas" of South Vietnam. These figures are doubtless exaggerated, but may be a gauge of a fairly extensive Communist educational effort.

A standard Viet Cong technique of gaining a foothold among tribal minorities in the highland areas of South Vietnam—where Communist encouragement of tribal autonomy gives them a political appeal—has been to select promising tribesmen, take them to North Vietnam for training in welfare activities as well as for political indoctrination, and return them to tribal villages where their new skills tend to assure them positions of prestige and leadership.

The Viet Cong also promote cultural activities-heavily flavored with propaganda—through press, radio and film media, as well as live drama and festivals. A student informant reported attending dramatic performances in a Viet Cong-held area, where plays, song, and dances provided entertainment and a dose of propaganda—often enthusiastically received.

There is little firm information about the Viet Cong effort to develop "combat hamlets." They appear to exist in areas where control by either side is missing or tenuous, and sometimes are located near government "strategic hamlets." Reports indicate that, like strategic hamlets, they are fortified externally, and their inhabitants are carefully trained in defensive procedures and escape routes, often interrelated with other nearby hamlets. Similar defensive systems have long prevailed in Viet Cong-controlled areas, although Viet Cong installations themselves may be innocent looking and easily evacuated buildings or huts.

A Viet Cong document discussing the successful construction of a "combat hamlet" indicates that primary stress is laid on determining the basic wants and needs of the inhabitants—frequently their concern for their own land. Propaganda is directed at convincing them that the government is threatening their interests, that defensive measures must be taken, and finally that offensive actions against government officials and troops are needed. The peasants presumably come to regard the Viet Cong as their protectors and to cooperate voluntarily with the Viet Cong military effort.

Glossary

propaganda: biased or misleading information used to promote a political point of view

Viet Cong: South Vietnamese communist guerrillas

Viet Minh: North Vietnamese communists

Document Analysis

The memo, titled "Viet Cong Quasi-Governmental Activities," is laid out into thirteen points, documenting the various ways in which forces of the National Liberation Front are trying to win the hearts and minds of the South Vietnamese people. From the beginning, the memo makes clear that the strategy of the NLF is one of "armed liberation," harking back to Mao Tse-Tung and Ho Chi Minh, the leaders of China and North Vietnam, respectively. These are communist tactics, at work since the 1940s, meant to win the support of South Vietnam's population, and take control of the region. The authority of the Viet Cong is limited, as in many regions where the NLF does not have complete control, communist forces can only conduct "hit and run" attacks.

Much of the intelligence, the memo continues, derives from captured Viet Minh documents, which outline efforts to improve the quality of life for the population, including education, medical care, and infrastructure. The Viet Cong are careful to treat the populace well in order to win them to their side. This is all done for propaganda purposes, by improving conditions for the peasantry of South Vietnam, the Viet Cong hope to turn the people against their government. As an example, the memo cites the NLF land reform program in which, the memo charges, middle-class farmers were forced to give their land to the poor. Perhaps aware that the evidence of such allegations is weak, the writer concedes that some modification to the policy must have occurred as many middle-class farmers have remained on their land and there appears to be little evidence of collectivization.

Food distribution, seed collecting, and sanitation improvements have all been implemented to turn the population. The Viet Cong has even set up schools to educate the poor, but, the writer assures their audience, the numbers of this programs success are surely exaggerated and used, it assumes, to spread communist propaganda. The writer does admit that many tribes in the region have been allowed autonomy, but this too, the writer assures their audience, is part of the same communist strategy. Most alarmingly, the Viet Cong appear to be setting up defenses and training the population in combat. The result is that the

Viet Cong soldier stands beneath a Viet Cong flag with an AK-47 rifle. Photo via Wikimedia Commons. [Public domain.]

population now, mistakenly, considers the Viet Cong their protectors and cooperates with them in their efforts.

Essential Themes

The November 1963 memo commissioned by John McCone on Viet Cong activities in South Vietnam, is a clear example of the colossal misalignment in American understanding of the situation in Vietnam. Contorting the facts to try and fit the narrative of a communist conspiracy to spread an insidious ideology across the globe, the memo paints a cynical picture of communist agents using medicine, education, and food to trick the people into resenting their government. Despite evidence of local autonomy, fair land distribution policies, and a lack of a strong NLF political-military establishment, the memo tells a tale of a south on the brink of hostile takeover, of a poor, naive population, being tricked into supporting an insidious enemy.

It is astounding to consider that at no point did American intelligence analysts stop to consider the repressive policies of the South Vietnamese government, that NLF forces could actually be working to better the lives of the South Vietnamese people, or that the general consensus of the population had swung wildly toward regime change. It was an attitude born out of a kind of colonial arrogance. Surely the United States, the most powerful, most sophisticated country in the world, knew what was best for Vietnam, even better than the Vietnamese. It was this lack of understanding—born out of notions of cultural superiority that propelled American strategy in Southeast Asia for two decades—that ultimately led to American military intervention in what was essentially a civil war.

As the conflict escalated, as more and more American soldiers lost their lives, military planners would continue to grow ever more frustrated by a lack of support from the local population. In time, the very people that the United States claimed it was fighting to liberate, would be come to be seen as the enemy. Atrocities committed by American troops and indiscriminate killing started to become more common, and the very nature of the war took on an ever-darker turn. Before long the entire region was destabilized as the American war against a nation's own people spread to Laos and Cambodia, and at every step, American political and military leaders viewed events not for what they were, but for what they in some sense wanted them to be.

—K. P. Dawes, MA

Bibliography and Additional Reading

Dedrick, Michael Robert. *Southern Voices: Biet Dong and the National Liberation Front.* Lexington: UP of Kentucky, 2022.

Herring, George. *America's Longest War.* New York: McGraw-Hill, 1996.

McNamara, Robert, and Brian VanDeMark. *In Retrospect: The Tragedy and Lessons of Vietnam.* New York: Random House, 1995.

VanDeMark, Brian. *Into the Quagmire: Lyndon Johnson and the Escalation of the Vietnam War.* New York: Oxford UP, 1995.

■ Message from Ho Chi Minh

Date: December 23, 1966
Author: Ho Chi Minh
Genre: address; letter

Summary Overview

By the end of 1966, hundreds of thousands of American soldiers were stationed in South Vietnam. Moreover, Rolling Thunder, the American bombing campaign, had been attacking targets in the North and the South for almost two years. On December 23, 1966, Ho Chi Minh, the president of the Democratic Republic of Vietnam (DRV, or North Vietnam), sent a short message to the American people to provide his interpretation of the ongoing conflict between his nation and its ally, the National Liberation Front (NLF), on the one hand, and the United States and its ally, the Republic of Vietnam (RVN, or South Vietnam), on the other.

Ho's message emphasized the cruel nature of the American war effort. He condemned the American use of napalm, toxic gas, and fragmentation bombs, all of which resulted in the destruction of many towns and the deaths of thousands of people. He made it clear, however, that he did not blame the American people for the devastation. In fact, he even noted that American soldiers were also victims of American foreign policy. He held President Lyndon Johnson as solely responsible for the continuation of the war. By differentiating between the American people and their government, Ho sought to divide Americans and encourage them to resist their president's aggressive policies.

Defining the Moment

At first glance, Ho Chi Minh's message to the American people seems odd, given that his nation was at war with the United States. However, Ho had some familiarity with the United States and had previously appealed to America for support. He had actually lived in Harlem in 1912–1913. As the Allied powers negotiated an end to World War I at the Paris Peace Conference in 1919, Ho hoped to meet President Woodrow Wilson and secure his support for national self-determination for Vietnam. He not only failed to secure a meeting, but was dismayed to learn that Wilson would not support Vietnamese independence.

Similarly, when Japan surrendered in August 1945 and World War II ended, Ho announced Vietnam's independence from French colonial rule in front of thousands of cheering supporters on September 2, 1945.

Ho Chi Minh portrait in c. 1946. Photo via Wikimedia Commons. [Public domain.]

In a blatant appeal for American support, Ho repeatedly referred to the American Declaration of Independence in hopes that the United States would endorse Vietnamese independence and prevent the return of the French. The United States, however, chose to support French political control of Vietnam. Ho's appeal in 1967 to the American people was not a novel tactic. The appeal in 1967 was different because North Vietnam and the United States were engaged in an ongoing war. Beginning in 1954, when the French lost control of their colonies in Southeast Asia, the United States supported several anticommunist regimes in South Vietnam with substantial aid. Between 1965 and 1966, the American role in the conflict escalated significantly. By the end of 1966, there were 385,000 American soldiers in the South. Additionally, as Ho noted, Rolling Thunder, the American bombing campaign, had bombed enemy targets in the North and the South for nearly two years, including 79,000 sorties in 1966 alone.

Ho was trying to communicate to the American people that the U.S. government was responsible for the escalation of the conflict, not North Vietnam. He emphasized the devastating effect which the war, especially Rolling Thunder, was having on all Vietnamese. As well, because of the American government's escalation, hundreds of thousands of American soldiers had been sent to Vietnam and might be killed. In a final attack on the Johnson administration, Ho charged it had shown no interest in peace negotiations.

Author Biography

Born Nguyen Sinh Cung in 1890 in the province of Nghe An in what was then French Indochina, Ho left Vietnam in 1911 seeking adventure aboard a French merchant steamboat. He ended up in France and joined the French Socialist Party at the beginning of World War I. In 1919, at the Paris Peace Conference, he failed to secure Woodrow Wilson's support for Vietnamese self-determination. Embittered by the rejection, Ho helped form the French Communist Party in 1920. During the 1920s and 1930s, Ho traveled back and forth between the Soviet Union, China, Thailand, and Vietnam.

When Japan occupied Vietnam in 1941, Ho secretly reentered Vietnam and formed the Viet Minh to resist Japanese control. When Japan surrendered, Ho, as the leader of the Viet Minh, announced Vietnam's independence to a throng of cheering supporters on September 2, 1945. However, with American support, France regained control of French Indochina. In 1946, the First Indochina War broke out, pitting the Viet Minh against France. In 1954, after the French defeat at Dien Bien Phu, France lost its colonies. The Geneva Accords established two separate states, with the northern state, the Democratic Republic of Vietnam, controlled by Ho Chi Minh. He would remain president of the DRV until his death in 1969.

Historical Document

Message from Ho Chi Minh

On the occasion of the New Year, I would like to convey to the American people cordial wishes for peace and happiness. The Vietnamese and American peoples should have lived in peace and friendship. But the U.S. Government has brazenly sent over 400,000 troops along with thousands of aircraft and hundreds of Warships to wage aggression on Vietnam. Night and day it has used napalm bombs, toxic gas, fragmentation bombs and other modern weapons to massacre our people, not sparing even old persons, women and children, it has burnt down or destroyed villages and towns and perpetrated extremely savage crimes. Of late, U.S. aircraft have repeatedly bombed Hanoi, our beloved capital.

It is because of the criminal war unleashed by the U.S. Government that hundreds of thousands of young Americans have been drafted and sent to a useless death for from then homeland, on the Vietnamese battlefield. In hundreds of thousands of American families, parents have lost their sons, and wives their husbands. Nevertheless, the U.S. Government has continually clamoured about "peace negotiations" in an attempt to deceive the American and world peoples. In fact, it is daily expanding the war. The U.S. Government wrongly believes that with brutal force it could compel our people to surrender. But the Vietnamese people will never submit. We love peace, but it must be genuine peace in independence and freedom. For independence and freedom, the Vietnamese people are determined to fight the U.S. aggressors through to complete victory, whatever the hardships and sacrifices may be.

Who has caused these sufferings and mournings to the Vietnamese and American people? It is the U.S. rulers. The American people have realized this truth. More and more Americans are valiantly standing up in a vigorous struggle, demanding that the American Government respect the Constitution and the honour of the United States, stop the war of aggression in Vietnam and bring home all U.S. troops. I warmly welcome your just struggle and thank you for your support to the Vietnamese people's patriotic fight. I sincerely wish the American people many big successes in their struggle for peace, democracy and happiness.

Document Themes and Analysis

Ho Chi Minh's message was an obvious attempt to influence American public opinion. He made it clear to his American readers that he bore no ill will for Americans and did not hold them responsible for the war. Instead, he placed blame solely on President Lyndon Johnson's administration, whose actions were neither in the best interest of the American people, nor the Vietnamese. Were it not for the actions of the American government, Vietnam and the United States would almost certainly have enjoyed a friendly and mutually beneficial relationship.

Ho denounced American military strategy during the war. He strongly condemned the use of "napalm bombs, toxic gas, fragmentation bombs and other modern weapons" which "massacre our people, not sparing even old persons, women and children, it has burnt down or destroyed villages and towns and perpetrated extremely savage crimes." This was intended to make Americans feel guilty about the harm their government had caused.

In a pointed appeal to the American people, he pointed out the potentially deadly effect that the war might have on young American men. Many of the young men sent to Vietnam would die a "useless death" causing considerable grief for their families.

He also addressed the claims of the Johnson administration that peace negotiations were forthcoming. The Johnson administration was not serious about negotiations and, in fact, was planning to escalate the war under the false premise that more troops and resources would force the DRV to surrender. Ho assured the American people that his government would never abandon its fight whatever the cost. If American officials claimed otherwise, they were lying.

To show that his assessment was not bizarre, Ho noted that many Americans had already begun "demanding that the American government respect the Constitution and the honour of the United States, stop the war of aggression in Vietnam and bring home all U.S. troops." He encouraged other Americans to join the movement to end the war in Vietnam.

In his December 23, 1966 message to the American people, Ho Chi Minh hoped to speak directly to them without interference from the Johnson administration.

At this point in the conflict, hundreds of thousands of American soldiers were fighting communist forces, and the Rolling Thunder bombing campaign was nearly two years old. The Johnson administration had fully committed itself to the war. Ho's message suggested that the American people were not fully aware of the American military effort and were certainly not in full support of American military intervention. Ho sought to give the impression that he was providing an accurate account of American actions in Vietnam, which the Johnson administration had not done.

Ho told the American people that there was no reason why the DRV and the United States could not live in peace and harmony. He and his people allegedly had no animosity for the American people. The American government was the primary impediment to peace. The American military strategy, notably the Rolling Thunder campaign, was killing innocent Vietnamese for no purpose. The war had led to the transport of American soldiers halfway across the world to die for no justifiable reason.

An obvious motivation for Ho's message was to destroy the Johnson administration's claims that it sought peace negotiations and that military victory was at hand. Ho made it clear that the DRV would fight until it unified the two Vietnams and achieved total national independence. Ho's depiction of the DRV's policy was accurate. The United States continued to bomb targets in the north and south, the number of American soldiers in Vietnam increased, and the war expanded beyond the borders of Vietnam. Yet the DRV remained resolute in its demand for reunification and complete independence even after Ho's death in 1969. The South Vietnamese government would collapse on April 30, 1975, and a unified and independent Vietnam would emerge under the direction of DRV leaders.

—Gerald F. Goodwin, PhD

Bibliography and Additional Reading

Brocheux, Pierre. *Ho Chi Minh: A Biography.* New York: Cambridge UP, 2007.

Duiker, William J. *Ho Chi Minh: A Life.* New York: Hachette Books, 2000.

Halberstam, David. *Ho.* Lanham, MD: Rowman & Littlefield Publishers, 2007.

Karnow, Stanley. *Vietnam: A History.* New York: Penguin Books, 1991.

The Paris Peace Accords

Date: January 27, 1973
Authors: Henry Kissinger, Le Duc Tho, et al.
Genre: treaty

Summary Overview

The signing of the Paris Accords in 1973 marked the end of almost a century of foreign intervention in Vietnam, going back to the beginning of French colonialism in the 1880s. It also marked an end to more than twenty-five years of intermittent warfare, both civil/sectarian and international, which began with the French re-entry into Vietnam in 1946 after losing the region to the Japanese in World War II. The growing antiwar segment of the American population was pleased that America's longest war to date was finally ending, and President Richard Nixon believed he was fulfilling his promises of exiting Indochina, while maintaining US global credibility.

The agreement itself deals with many of the usual issues involving the cessation of conflict between two belligerents, such as the end to bombing and the promise not to reintroduce troops. However, certain aspects of the document are unique to the American conflict in Vietnam. The latter includes issues pertaining to the continued presence of US military advisors, which had helped lead the United States into the conflict in the first place, and the very contentious issue of soldiers who had been captured or were missing in action. The document also relates, more generally, to the period's political debates over and later academic reflections on whether or not South Vietnam could have survived for long after the US exit in early 1973.

Defining Moment

Most centrally, and an issue that is somewhat debated by historians, the Paris Accords of 1973 represented the failure of the United States to solve the main dilemma faced by American presidents across three decades, from Dwight D. Eisenhower to Richard M. Nixon: how to create a viable, non-communist South Vietnam that could stand on its own. Technically, South Vietnam would survive for two more years, but the exit of the United States via the Paris Accords of 1973 signified the beginning of the end for a nation that had only officially existed for less than twenty years, since the Geneva Accords of 1954. For North Vietnam and communists in South Vietnam, the 1973 agreement was an enormous step toward final fulfillment of the 1954 Geneva Accords. The latter had provided for elections in 1956, but these never occurred because President Eisenhower and the South Vietnamese leader at that time, Ngo Dinh Diem, knew that the communists would triumph electorally and unite the country under a communist government. In fact, the first article of the Accords harkens back to the idea of a unified Vietnam as envisioned in the 1954 agreement.

For many in the United States, the final agreement to end American military involvement in Vietnam came as welcome news. The conflict was (and remains) one of the most contentious issues among Americans that occurred during the 1960s. It led to massive protests, especially during the 1968 Democratic Convention in Chicago; the 1969 antiwar demonstration in Washington, DC; and the protests in reaction to President Nixon's invasion of Cambodia in 1970, which led to the shootings of students at Kent State University in Ohio and Jackson State College in Mississippi. As for President Nixon himself, he was finally delivering on promises to get the United States out of Vietnam, which he had made during the 1968 presidential campaign. Still, exiting the conflict took him four years to accomplish, in part because he wanted to achieve, as he put it, "peace with honor," by which he generally meant preserving America's international credibility throughout the exit process by

"Agreement on Ending the War and Restoring Peace in Viet Nam"

This typed copy of the Paris Peace Accords was signed by several Hanoi Hilton POWs prior to their release, including the ranking officer, Col. Robbie Risner.

Gift of Lee Humiston, "NamPOW Friend and Keeper of the Flame"
A20060188000

The 1973 Treaty. Photo by Sanjay Acharya, via Wikimedia Commons.

Signing of the Peace Accords, January 1973. Photo via Wikimedia Commons. [Public domain.]

leaving in place what appeared to be a functioning South Vietnam. In reality, most observers, and most historians since, did not believe that South Vietnam would last long after American forces left.

Author Biography

The main American negotiator was Nixon's national security advisor Henry Kissinger, who would also be the US secretary of state starting later in 1973. Kissinger's diplomatic activities were wide-ranging, including "shuttle diplomacy" in the Middle East and in southern Africa during the early and mid-1970s. President Nixon often worked closely with Kissinger, even bypassing the State Department, to conduct American foreign policy. Kissinger would continue as secretary of state during the administration of President Gerald Ford.

Le Duc Tho was the primary negotiator on the Vietnamese side. He was a member of the highest ruling group in the communist structure of the North Vietnamese government, the Politburo. It took years of negotiations to reach an agreement that was satisfactory, even on a temporary basis, to all the parties involved—the United States, North Vietnam, the communists in South Vietnam, and the non-communist South Vietnamese government.

As a result of the 1973 Paris Accords, both men received a Nobel Peace Prize, although Le Duc Tho refused to accept his, and critics have said that Kissinger did not deserve his based on his involvement in the war and other military actions.

Historical Document

The Paris Peace Accords

Article 1
.... The United States and all other countries respect the independence, sovereignty, unity, and territorial integrity of Viet-Nam as recognized by the 1954 Geneva Agreements on Viet-Nam...

Article 2
A cease fire shall be observed throughout South Viet-Nam as of 2400 hours G.M.T., on January 27, 1973. At the same hour, the United States will stop all its military activities against the territory of the Democratic Republic of Viet-Nam by ground, air and naval forces, wherever they may be based, and end the mining of the territorial waters, ports, harbors, and waterways of the Democratic Republic of Viet-Nam. The United States will remove, permanently deactivate or destroy all the mines in the territorial waters, ports, harbors, and waterways of North Viet-Nam as soon as this Agreement goes into effect. The complete cessation of hostilities mentioned in this Article shall be durable and without limit of time....

Article 4
The United States will not continue its military involvement or intervene in the internal affairs of South Viet-Nam.

Article 5
Within sixty days of the signing of this Agreement, there will be a total withdrawal from South Viet-Nam of troops, military advisers, and military personnel including technical military personnel and military personnel associated with the pacification program, armaments, munitions, and war material of the United States and those of the other foreign countries mentioned in Article 3(a). Advisers from the above-mentioned countries to all paramilitary organizations and the police force will also be withdrawn within the same period of time.

Article 6
The dismantlement of all military bases in South Viet-Nam of the United States and of the other foreign countries mentioned in Article 3(a) shall be completed within sixty days of the signing of this Agreement.

Article 7
From the enforcement of the cease-fire to the formation of the government provided for in Article 9(b) and 14 of this Agreement, the two South Vietnam-

ese parties shall not accept the introduction of troops, military advisers, and military personnel including technical military personnel, armaments, munitions, and war material into South Viet-Nam....

Article 8
The return of captured military personnel and foreign civilians of the parties shall be carried out simultaneously with and completed not later than the same day as the troop withdrawal mentioned in Article 5. The parties shall exchange complete lists of the above-mentioned captured military personnel and foreign civilians on the day of the signing of this Agreement.

The Parties shall help each other to get information about those military personnel and foreign civilians of the parties missing in action, to determine the location and take care of the graves of the dead so as to facilitate the exhumation and repatriation of the remains, and to take any such other measures as may be required to get information about those still considered missing in action.

The question of the return of Vietnamese civilian personnel captured and detained in South Viet-Nam will be resolved by the two South Vietnamese parties on the basis of the principles of Article 21(b) of the Agreement on the Cessation of Hostilities in Viet-Nam of July 20, 1954. The two South Vietnamese parties will do so in a spirit of national reconciliation and concord, with a view to ending hatred and enmity, in order to ease suffering and to reunite families. The two South Vietnamese parties will do their utmost to resolve this question within ninety days after the cease-fire comes into effect....

Article 11
Immediately after the cease-fire, the two South Vietnamese parties will: achieve national reconciliation and concord, end hatred and enmity, prohibit all acts of reprisal and discrimination against individuals or organizations that have collaborated with one side or the other; ensure the democratic liberties of the people: personal freedom, freedom of speech, freedom of the press, freedom of meeting, freedom of organization, freedom of political activities, freedom of belief, freedom of movement, freedom of residence, freedom of work, right to property ownership, and right to free enterprise....

Chapter V
The Reunification of Viet-Nam and The Relationship Between North and South Viet-Nam

Article 15
The reunification of Viet-Nam shall be carried out step by step through peaceful means on the basis of discussions and agreements between North and South Viet-Nam, without coercion or annexation by either party, and without foreign interference. The time for reunification will be agreed upon by North and South Viet-Nam. Pending reunification:

The military demarcation line between the two zones at the 17th parallel is only provisional and not a political or territorial boundary, as provided for in paragraph 6 of the Final Declaration of the 1954 Geneva Conference.

North and South Viet-Nam shall respect the Demilitarized Zone on either side of the Provisional Military Demarcation Line.

North and South Viet-Nam shall promptly start negotiations with a view to re-establishing normal relations in various fields. Among the questions to be negotiated are the modalities of civilian movement across the Provisional Military Demarcation Line.

North and South Viet-Nam shall not join any military alliance or military bloc and shall not allow foreign powers to maintain military bases, troops, military advisers, and military personnel on their respective territories, as stipulated in the 1954 Geneva Agreements on Viet-Nam....

Article 21
The United States anticipates that this Agreement will usher in an era of reconciliation with the Democratic Republic of Viet-Nam as with all the peoples of Indochina. In pursuance of its traditional policy, the United States will contribute to healing the wounds of war and to postwar reconstruction of the Democratic Republic of Viet-Nam and throughout Indochina.

Article 22
The ending of the war, the restoration of peace in Viet-Nam, and the strict implementation of this Agreement will create conditions for establishing a new, equal and mutually beneficial relationship between the United States and the Democratic Republic of Viet-Nam on the basis of respect of each other's independence and sovereignty, and non-interference in each other's internal affairs. At the same time this will ensure stable peace in Viet-Nam and contribute to the preservation of lasting peace in Indochina and Southeast Asia....

The Return of Captured Military Personnel and Foreign Civilians

Article 1
The parties signatory to the Agreement shall return the captured military personnel of the parties mentioned in Article 8(a) of the Agreement as follows: all captured military personnel of the United States and those of the other foreign countries mentioned in Article 3(a) of the Agreement shall be returned to United States authorities; all captured Vietnamese military personnel, whether belonging to regular or irregular armed forces, shall be returned to the two South Vietnamese parties; they shall be returned to that South Vietnamese party under whose command they served.

Article 2
All captured civilians who are nationals of the United States or of any other foreign countries mentioned in Article 3(a) of the Agreement shall be returned to United States authorities. All other captured foreign civilians shall be returned to the authorities of their country of nationality by any one of the parties willing and able to do so.

Article 3
The parties shall today exchange complete lists of captured persons mentioned in Articles 1 and 2 of this Protocol.

Article 4
The return of all captured persons mentioned in Articles 1 and 2 of this Protocol shall be completed within sixty days of the signing of the Agreement at a rate no slower than the rate of withdrawal from South Viet-Nam of United States forces and those of the other foreign countries mentioned in Article 5 of the Agreement.

Persons who are seriously ill, wounded or maimed, old persons and women shall be returned first. The remainder shall be returned either by returning all from one detention place after another or in order of their dates of capture, beginning with those who have been held the longest....

With Regard to Dead and Missing Persons

Article 10
The Four-Party Joint Military Commission shall ensure joint action by the parties in implementing Article 8 (b) of the Agreement. When the Four-Party Joint Military Commission has ended its activities, a Four-Party Joint Military team shall be maintained to carry on this task.

With regard to Vietnamese civilian personnel dead or missing in South Viet-Nam, the two South Vietnamese parties shall help each other to obtain information about missing persons, determine the location and take care of the graves of the dead, in a spirit of national reconciliation and concord, in keeping with the people's aspirations....

People's Army of Vietnam (PAVN) prisoners released, Th?ch Hãn River, 24 February 1973. Photo via Wikimedia Commons. [Public domain.]

Document Analysis

While every treaty to end a conflict contains agreements to end the fighting in various ways, the Paris Accords of 1973 included many items specific to the American war in Vietnam. Even though the United States never invaded North Vietnam and fought exclusively in South Vietnam (with a brief invasion of Cambodia in 1970 and occasional bombing of both Laos and Cambodia), US President Lyndon Johnson, and especially Nixon, had bombed North Vietnam—heavily at times—in attempts to limit the capacity of the North to aid the communist rebels in South Vietnam and sometimes, as Nixon did in December 1972, to try to jumpstart stalled negotiations. American forces had also mined one of the main harbors of North Vietnam (officially called the Democratic Republic of Vietnam) earlier in 1972, and therefore Article 2 contained language that the United States would henceforth cease this activity in addition to ending military operations in South Vietnam itself.

In addition, both sides knew that it had been the presence of US military advisors in South Vietnam, first under Eisenhower in the late 1950s and then increasing in number under President John Kennedy in the early 1960s, that had helped to lead the United States toward higher levels of American involvement, up to and including Johnson's escalation in mid-1965. Therefore, Article 5 contained clear language that not only would regular American military personnel leave

Vietnam, but so too would "military advisers, and military personnel including technical military personnel and military personnel associated with the pacification program, armaments, munitions, and war material of the United States and those of the other foreign countries." Likewise, "advisors...to all paramilitary organizations and the police force" would leave forthwith. The Accords were trying to close all loopholes that would allow any reintroduction of outside armed forces.

The references to the return of prisoners, found in numerous places, were especially important for the United States, as public clamor had grown for the government to achieve the return of US troops captured by communist forces. By the end of the war in early 1973, around six hundred Americans remained in enemy hands, including more than thirty who had recently been imprisoned when shot down during Nixon's December 1972 bombing campaign of North Vietnam. All of these prisoners were returned to the United States as American forces left in early 1973, but a similar issue would linger for decades in the form of searching for Americans who were still missing in action (MIA) in the Indochina region. At the end of the war, almost 2,400 US servicemen remained unaccounted for; as of 2015, the number remains over 1,600, although the investigative work continues. As historian Gary Hess points out, while US MIA rates in earlier twentieth century wars were actually higher than in Vietnam, the issue remained influential for more than two decades in the relations between the two countries. Overall, while the Paris Accords was, in some respects, a standard treaty that included the removal of military forces, the specifics of future political developments, and language of reconciliation, the document also dealt with specifics of the American war in Vietnam, including aerial bombing of North Vietnam, the role of military advisors during the build-up to full-fledged war, and the thorny issue of prisoners of war (POWs) and MIAs.

Essential Themes

In addition to the themes already noted above, a central debate among Americans in the 1970s and among historians since then has been over whether or not the Paris Accords had contained the necessary stipulations for South Vietnam to survive on its own after American withdrawal. As historian Gary Hess notes, in early 1973, the South Vietnamese government "could claim control over 75 percent of the territory and 85 percent of the population of South Vietnam. Its army, including reserves, totaled about one million troops, nearly 10 times the estimated strength of Viet Cong and North Vietnamese units in the South" (Hess 132). In addition, most American bases and military hardware were simply turned over to South Vietnamese forces and, as historian George Herring indicates, "the United States kept a formidable armada of naval power and airpower" in the region (Herring 287–288). Nevertheless, with fighting resuming shortly after the exit of US forces, and after a final push in the first months of 1975 by communist forces in South Vietnam, that country ceased to exist by May 1, 1975. Some, including Nixon, Kissinger, and some of the final leaders of South Vietnam, later claimed that had Congress provided the funding for South Vietnam as requested in early 1975 by President Gerald Ford (who replaced Nixon in August 1974 in the wake of the Watergate scandal), the South would not have fallen. Still, most historians argue that no matter what the actions of the United States might have been, the ongoing unpopularity of various South Vietnamese governments, the unwillingness of most units in the South Vietnamese army to fight during the final campaigns between 1973 and 1975, and the decades-old determination by communist leaders and forces to unite the nation meant that South Vietnam was doomed after early 1973.

—Kevin Grimm, PhD

Bibliography and Additional Reading

Herring, George C. *America's Longest War: The United States and Vietnam, 1950–1975*, 3rd edition. New York: McGraw Hill, Inc., 1996.

Hess, Gary. *Vietnam and the United States: Origins and Legacy of War*, rev. ed. New York: Twayne Publishers, 1998.

Phillips, Jak. "Top 10 Nobel Prize Controversies: Nobel-Winner Wrangling, Henry Kissinger." *TIME*.

Time Inc., 7 Oct. 2011. content.time.com/time/specials/packages/article/ 0,28804,2096389_2096388_2096386,00.html.

US Department of Defense. "Soldier Missing from Vietnam War Accounted For (Newton)." *Defense POW/MIA Accounting Agency.* Department of Defense, 8 Jun. 2015. www.dpaa.mil/NewsStories/NewsReleases/tabid/10159/Article/598458/soldier-missing-from-vietnam-war-accounted-for-newton.aspx.

■ Story from the Khmer Rouge Killing Fields

Date: 1995 (concerning events c. 1975)
Author: Sisowath Doung Chanto; Digital Archive of Cambodian Holocaust Survivors
Genre: testimonial

Summary Overview

The Cambodian Genocide of 1975–1979 involved the systematic torture and killing of at least 2 million Cambodians, by Cambodians, during the rule of the communist Khmer Rouge regime. The Khmer Rouge, under the leadership of General Secretary Pol Pot, wanted to create a socialist, farming-based, racially pure utopia. To do so, they forced people to move from cities to rural areas and work the fields, imprisoned and tortured anyone considered an intellectual or enemy of the party, and killed members of minority ethnic and religious groups.

The Khmer Rouge caused the death of approximately a quarter of all those living in Cambodia during their short reign. Many starved or were worked to death in labor camps; since non-traditional medicine was forbidden, many also died of preventable diseases. In addition, over a million people were killed by the government because of suspected or alleged ties to anything seen as anti-revolutionary. Members of the previous government, anyone with an education or specialized skill, and anyone with even fleeting ties to foreign cultures were imprisoned. Prisoners were interrogated and tortured brutally and were eventually executed by stabbing or bludgeoning; their bodies were dumped in mass graves, which are now collectively known as the Killing Fields.

Defining Moment

Cambodia had declared independence from France in 1953. The new Kingdom of Cambodia tried to ensure peace during the transition to independence, but the war in neighboring Vietnam spilled over into Cambodian territory. Cambodians were forced to choose between the U.S.-backed South Vietnamese and the North Vietnamese Army. A civil war broke out between the established government and socialist rebels in 1968. In 1970, the ruling leader lost power and multiple new factions tried to take his place as head of government.

One of these factions, the Khmer Rouge, was composed mostly of Cambodians who had studied Marxist scholarship and respected the Maoist and Stalinist movements in China and Russia. Their leader was Pol Pot, a French-educated revolutionary who had spent several years developing a political movement while hiding in Vietnam. The Khmer Rouge party grew quickly and took control of most of rural Cambodia over the next few years. In 1975, they captured the capital city, Phnom Penh, and established a new state, which they called Democratic Kampuchea.

The Khmer Rouge set up a totalitarian government: they controlled every aspect of citizens' lives and eliminated their political opponents. The regime was opposed to all foreign influences and tried to establish a self-sufficient agrarian society. Its leaders believed that if all citizens were involved in manual labor and did not trade or interact with foreign governments, they would be able to establish a utopian communal society. Their disastrously romanticized idea of rural society was an extreme form of Maoism, which values the rural working class over urban industrial workers.

Author Biography

The damage wrought by the Khmer Rouge on Cambodian society was devastating. Even decades after the elimination of the professional classes, Cambodia struggles to regain the culture and stability that was lost under the regime. Many thousands of families were left with no knowledge of what happened to loved ones who disappeared without warning. As few records were kept of the killings, it is difficult to reconstruct the last days of many of the regime's victims.

The Digital Archive of Cambodian Holocaust Survivors (DACHS) publishes stories and images left from the regime online so that survivors can find information about their friends and families and so that the stories of the dead will not be forgotten. It was established by scholars who specialize in modern Cambodian history and photographers who work with images of the deceased. When many photographs of Khmer Rouge victims were discovered at the largest known prison site, they began cleaning, developing, and publishing them in an attempt to add names and stories to the anonymous faces of the dead. The work continues to this day.

Rooms of the Tuol Sleng Genocide Museum contain thousands of photos taken by the Khmer Rouge of their victims. Photo by Dudva, via Wikimedia Commons.

Historical Document

Story from the Khmer Rouge Killing Fields

Sisowath Doung Chanto
Birth Place: Phnom Penh, Cambodia
DOB: 02-13-70
Age: 25
Occupation: Graduate Student
Major: Political Science
Surviving Family Member(s):
Father deceased (executed by the Khmer Rouge)
Mother residing in Cambodia.
Three sisters. One is residing in Cambodia.

My father was one of the million victims who were killed by the Khmer Rouge genocide politics. Up to this today I cannot comprehend the reason for the execution of my father and other millions of my fellow country men. My father was not a man of politics nor was he a criminal by any means. As a far as I can remember, he was a family man like any other Cambodian men in the country. He was a loving and caring father. A great protector and provider for his family and for those worked in his shipping company. He was a patriotic man. He did not abandon Cambodia during the 1970-75 civil war because he wished to devoted his energy and resource for the reconstruction of the country after the war. Unfortunately, his patriotism was not greeted with gratitude but it was received by punishment then execution.

The brutality of his punishment was so extreme that even the executioner himself could not speak of it without shock. My mother got the chance to find the executioner in 1985 eight year after my father's execution. According to this Khmer Rouge cadre, named Met Chan, who was personally involved with the interrogation of my father described ways which he and his comrades punished my father.

From the time they took my father out of our hut, he was kicked, dragged and beaten all the way to the killing site. Before he was executed he was cuffed in chains along with three other men and was confined in a basement inside an abandoned temple. He went without food for several days because Khmer Rouge cadres knew that he was going to be killed anyway before they finally decided to take him to the grave. His face was swollen with bruises from the beating. His back and ribs were broken by the constant beating by the young Khmer Rouge Cadres. The beating was so severe that it paralyzed his speech and consciousness. By this time, he was just lying on the floor unable to move or ask for mercy. According to Met Chan, his last words were calling for his wife, son and daughter.

I guessed he was thinking about his family even though he was dying.

Two days after the interrogation, they took him to the killing ground. He was hit with a metal rod three times at the back of the head. Whether he died immediately from the blows was not mentioned by Met Chan. My Mother did not wish to know any more. My father Sisowath Doung Kara was executed on July 1978 just five months before the Vietnamese invaded Cambodia and liberated it from the Khmer Rouge.

I am one of the many voices speaking out atrocity of the Khmer Rouge's genocide politics.

There are millions of Cambodians who lost their immediate family members and loved ones. The Khmer Rouge regime not only traumatized millions of Cambodians' psychological function but it created a permanent scare in every Cambodian citizens. We lost so much. The greatest lost of all were those whose resources and capacities to advance our social development. A lot of talented individuals died because some defected semi-intellectuals such as Pol Pot and Ieng Sary were too incompetent to deal with social development. However, the essence of this testimony is not seeking sympathetic sentiments. It is a reminder of what happened to our society in the last 20 years. The Khmer Rouge legacy should not be neglected or overlooked because it was the past. It should be a monumental lesson for our future generation. Such an atrocity should never be allowed to reoccur. But it should never be forgotten.

In the memory of those who endured and survived the Cambodian Holocaust.

Glossary

cadre: a small group

Ieng Sary: one of the leading members of the Khmer Rouge and a driving force behind the mass killings; he was arrested in 2007 and put on trial, but died in 2013 before a verdict was issued

Document Themes and Analysis

In their attempt to bring about revolutionary change, the Khmer Rouge destroyed Cambodian society. They forcibly relocated people from cities to the countryside to work in the fields; thousands died during the forced marches from the cities to the country. Those who relocated and worked were seen as valuable to society, while anyone who resisted was arrested and killed.

In addition, the Khmer Rouge abolished currency—they imagined that an ideal society would have no money or class distinctions. They also abolished newspapers, private property, the education system, and western medicine. People who had no former experience farming were assigned quotas of crops to meet: if they did manage to send a certain amount of rice to the capital each month, for instance, they would be accused of sabotaging the revolution and killed. In trying to meet these quotas, hundreds of thousands of people in the countryside starved to death.

Many more deaths were caused when the regime outlawed western medicine. Though they had the knowledge and ability to save people from preventable diseases and illnesses, doctors were forbidden to use it, as non-traditional medicine had no place in the Khmer Rouge's new society. Under the regime, anyone who was considered an "intellectual" or had an education was suspected of opposing the revolution. People who could read, had travelled abroad, or had relatives who had participated in politics were taken away to be killed. The regime also persecuted ethnic minorities (mostly those of Vietnamese and Chinese descent), Muslims and Buddhist monks, and anyone who did not fit the regime's ideal of the uneducated, atheist, ethnically pure peasant class.

The regime stayed in power by terrorizing its citizens: people obeyed their commands because everyone knew they would be exterminated if they rebelled against the authorities. Many people were taken without warning from their homes or work sites and killed. Victims were often bludgeoned to death or strangled and their bodies were dumped in rural fields. No records were kept, and it was not until after the regime had been deposed that many mass graves were found. The anonymous burial sites are today collectively known as the Killing Fields. One of the most brutal killing sites was located in a former high school; it was known under the regime as S-21 and has now been turned into the Tuol Sleng Genocide Museum. Thousands were imprisoned, brutally tortured, and murdered at this site. Pictures were taken of many victims and a few notes of their interrogations and torture sessions remain.

When the Khmer Rouge were deposed by the Vietnamese in 1979, stories of the brutal killings began to come out. Most of those who had been murdered left no trace, so their families gathered what little information they could and told their stories. One survivor was Sisowath Doung Chanto, who was a child when his father was taken from their hut and tortured to death in an abandoned temple. He did not know anything about his father's last days until long after his death, and even today the reason for his execution (if there was one) is unknown. His story is a testament to the atrocities that the regime committed and an attempt to ensure that the world remembers the suffering of his father and the human effects of mass genocide and murder.

—Hannah Rich, MA

Bibliography and Additional Reading

Chandler, David P. *The Tragedy of Cambodian History: Politics War and Revolution Since 1945*. New Haven: Yale UP, 1991.

Ngor, Haing. *Survival in the Killing Fields*. New York: Basic Books, 2003.

Ung, Loung. *First They Killed My Father: A Daughter of Cambodia Remembers*. New York: Harper Perennial, 2000.

Mid-East Revolts and Revolutions in the Twentieth Century

The Middle East is both a cradle of civilizations and a central region linking three different continents: Africa, Europe, and Asia. It has been an area of strategic importance throughout history and continues to be so today, particularly as a global center of oil production. Ongoing hostilities between Muslim extremist groups operating in the region and various Middle Eastern and Western governments add to the political import of the area. For the past three-quarters of a century or more there has been enough turmoil in the region to threaten the peace of the world—more than once.

Beginning in 1908 the Young Turks, a reform and nationalist group, were increasingly important in Turkey. With the Ottoman Empire on its last legs, the Young Turks hoped to reestablish Turkish power in the region. During World War I they joined on the side of Germany and Austria-Hungary to fight against the Allied powers of the West. Their military efforts were admirable at times but unsustainable over the course of the war; the Ottoman state ceased to exist by 1922.

By the end of the next global conflict, World War II, most Middle Eastern nations had attained independence from their colonial overseers. The French gave up their mandates in Syria and Lebanon, for example, but fought to maintain control in Algeria in a long, ugly war (1954–1962) against the Algerian National Liberation Army. The British continued to maintain significant economic and political influence in a number of states, backed by a military presence. It was only with the start of native military coups led by populist figures such as Gamal Abdel Nasser of Egypt (ruled 1956–1970) that some of the older constitutional monarchies were overthrown and British influence in the region was lessened. Nasser became a hero in Egypt (and the bête noire of Britons) for, among other things, nationalizing the Suez Canal.

In Iran, meanwhile, the United States in 1953 carried out a British-sponsored plan to overthrow the left-leaning nationalist leader Mohammed Mossadegh in order to install the pro-Western Mohammad Reza Shah (son of long-reigning hero Reza Shah Pahlavi). However, the action would come back to haunt the Americans when, in 1979, Iran's Islamic revolution cast out Western influences and made the government there a sworn enemy of the United States. After the Iranian Revolution other forms of political Islam were taken up by nationalist leaders and non-state actors alike, all seeking to challenge the predominance of secular government in the Middle East.

The more recent series of revolts collectively labeled the Arab Spring (2010–2012) is addressed in a later section in this volume.

Proclamation of the Young Turks

Date: 1908
Author: Young Turks
Geographic region: Ottoman Empire (modern-day Turkey)
Genre: proclamation; political tract

Summary Overview

The Young Turk Revolution was a 1908 movement that removed the Ottoman Sultan Abdel Hamid II from absolute rule and instituted a constitution for the Ottoman Empire. The Ottoman Empire had been ruled by sultans for centuries and was in political and social decline by the mid-1800s. The Young Turk Revolution came thirty years after the First Constitutional Era, when activists had fought for the creation of a constitution that would give government representation to the people. In 1876, they were able to have this constitution implemented and establish a parliament, but it lasted for only two years before being removed by the Sultan. The 1908 Young Turk Revolution revived the constitution and re-opened the parliament, ushering in the Second Constitutional Era.

The Young Turk movement was a nationalist party that supported a strong Ottoman state. They wanted to create a nation-state that would be the equal of the European powers in diplomatic and economic influence. In their Proclamation of 1908, they announced their plans for the new government: they wanted to establish a strong central government that represented the people and respected the rights of all citizens. Other states had successfully replaced their absolute monarchies with constitutional governments, and the Young Turks hoped that their country could make a similar transition. The revolution did not bring about the intended effect, however, as the outbreak of World War I caused the collapse of the Ottoman Empire. During and after the war, the Young Turk government was largely responsible for the Armenian Genocide, in which over a million Armenians were killed by the state.

Defining Moment

The Ottoman Empire had been founded in the 1200s in what is now Turkey and expanded into the surrounding areas until the 1700s, when it reached the height of its power. Ottoman Sultans ruled much of the Middle East from their capital at Constantinople, establishing a vast bureaucratic and social network that tied the empire together. From the eighteenth century, however, the empire began to lose its diplomatic influence and was threatened by external warfare and internal weakness. Some sultans occasionally attempted social and political reform but were largely unsuccessful in causing any real change. In the 1870s, the Ottoman sultan Abdul Hamid II was facing a crisis: many intellectuals and bureaucrats wanted to reduce the role of the sultan and set up a constitutional monarchy similar to those in Europe.

The main social group pushing for constitutional reform was known as the Young Ottomans. The movement was begun by intellectuals who were dissatisfied with existing reforms and who wanted to preserve

Flag of the Young Turk Revolution. Image via Wikimedia Commons. [Public domain.]

the position of sultan but institute a constitution to reduce his power. Many of the Young Ottomans had studied in Europe and looked to European models for influence; at the same time, they wanted to keep Islam in a central role in government and to maintain continuity with the existing Ottoman empire.

Environmental disasters and wars abroad led to a tax increase in the early 1870s. This caused riots and social unrest throughout the empire, especially in the Balkan area, and the government put them down brutally. In addition, personal matters led to the abdication of two sultans before Abdul Hamid took the throne in 1876. Under pressure from his advisors and visiting Europeans, the new sultan agreed to give up some of his power and institute a constitutional monarchy.

The First Constitutional Era began on November 23, 1876. The constitution established a parliament of elected officials who would represent the views of the people. Political parties were not established by the constitution, nor did they have time to come into existence. The sultan retained legislative and executive power under the constitution, including the power to dissolve the constitution and parliament if he wanted. Still, this was a significant move away from autocracy and toward a representative government.

The First Constitutional Era lasted for only two years. Russia was threatening to invade Bulgaria,

Greek lithograph celebrating the Young Turk revolt in 1908 and the re-introduction of a constitutional regime in the Ottoman Empire. The angel holds a calico bearing the words "freedom, equality, brotherhood." Image via Wikimedia Commons. [Public domain.]

Young Turks flyer with the slogan Long live the fatherland, long live the nation, long live liberty written in Ottoman Turkish and French. Image via Wikimedia Commons. [Public domain.]

which was held by the Ottomans. War broke out in 1877 (the Russo-Turkish war, which would claim hundreds of thousands of lives in less than a year of fighting) and the sultan suspended the parliament. Using the pretense of social unrest, he banished the leader of parliament and took control of the empire back into his own hands in 1878. Many members of parliament and leaders of the Young Ottoman movement went underground or into exile as Abdul Hamid once again became the sole ruler of the Ottoman Empire. He would rule alone from Istanbul for the next thirty years.

Author Biography

At the end of the First Constitutional Era, the Young Ottoman politicians and activists who opposed the autocratic rule of Abdul Hamid were in a difficult situation. They had succeeded in passing a constitution and establishing a parliament, but the sultan had stripped this achievement from them with the excuse of quelling social unrest. They had pushed for modernization along European lines, but the sultan's conservative politics were once again directing the empire.

Over the next decades, members of the Young Ottoman movement regrouped and were joined by younger, more radical revolutionaries as well as members of the military. Drawing on the achievements of the earlier movement, they became known as the Young Turks. The group was bound together by their belief that the Ottoman constitution should be reinstated. In addition, they believed that the empire should be modernized along European lines. Though they recognized the important role of Islam in society, they planned to transition from a theocracy into a secular government. They were also influenced by the ideals of the Enlightenment, and many supported policies of respect and equality for ethnic groups within the empire.

The Young Turks hoped that their revolution would create a new society where citizens were linked by loyalty to the Ottoman nation rather than to the sultan. In this, they were influenced by the success of Meiji Japan, another autocratic power that had made a relatively successful transition from empire to republic. Japan had managed to adopt aspects of Western modernization without losing its cultural identity, and the Young Turks sought to replicate their transition.

The Young Turk movement was closely linked to the Committee of Union and Progress (CUP), a political party that advocated liberal reform and modernization. Many revolutionaries considered themselves both Young Turks and CUP members. After the successful Young Turk revolution, the CUP became the official political party of the revolutionary movement.

Beginning in the early 1900s, revolutionaries began to call more loudly for reform. Their voice was especially strong in the Balkan region, an area that was nominally Ottoman-controlled but where Russia and the European powers were also trying to exert influence. The crisis came in 1908 when a Russian-European alliance threatened to invade the Balkan area of Macedonia and take it from Ottoman control. Military leaders who were members of the Young Turk movement, motivated by Ottoman pride and the fear that the sultan would surrender the territory without a fight, rebelled against Abdul Hamid.

The rebels demanded the reinstatement of the constitution and Abdul Hamid conceded immediately. The Second Constitutional Era began when the parliament was convened in July of 1908. Some members of the original parliament, disbanded thirty years earlier, were in attendance. The institution of the parliament was seen as a significant victory for the revolutionary movement. Despite a few palace coups over the next few years, the Young Turks retained power, and the sultan was official deposed in 1909.

Though the future of the Ottoman Empire temporarily looked bright, events in Europe soon destroyed the Young Turks' hope for a new society. World War I began in 1914 and the empire joined the side of the Germans. The Young Turks tried to modernize the empire's military and infrastructure, but found this impossible without the support of the European powers. Germany and the Ottoman Empire lost the war and the empire was occupied. The parliament was dissolved in 1920.

The Young Turks' nationalist agenda was the driving force behind the Armenian Genocide, an ethnic cleansing that lasted from approximately 1915 to 1923 and resulted in the deaths of between 1 and 2 million Armenian men, women, and children. Ethnic Armenians, a historically persecuted minority in the empire, had originally hoped that they would be represented in parliament under the new Young Turk regime. Beginning in 1915, however, the new government used the excuse of conscription and national security to arrest, deport, and murder Armenians throughout the empire. Entire cities were destroyed as men were driven into forced labor and the remaining population was starved or marched to death. The exact number of dead is unknown today but is believed to number in the millions. A handful of Young Turk leaders were later put on trial, though their sentences were not carried out. Some of those who escaped justice were eventually assassinated by Armenian survivors of the genocide, who tracked them down and executed them in revenge.

Historical Document

Proclamation of the Young Turks

The basis for the Constitution will be respect for the predominance of the national will. One of the consequences of this principle will be to require without delay the responsibility of the minister before the Chamber, and, consequently, to consider the minister as having resigned, when he does not have a majority of the votes of the Chamber.

Provided that the number of senators does not exceed one-third the number of deputies, the Senate will be named as follows: one-third by the Sultan and two-thirds by the nation, and the term of senators will be of limited duration.

It will be demanded that all Ottoman subjects having completed their twentieth year, regardless of whether they possess property or fortune, shall have the right to vote. Those who have lost their civil rights will naturally be deprived of this right.

It will be demanded that the right freely to constitute political groups be inserted in a precise fashion in the constitutional charter, in order that article 1 of the Constitution of 1293 A.H. [Anno Hegira] be respected...

The Turkish tongue will remain the official state language. Official correspondence and discussion will take place in Turkish...

Every citizen will enjoy complete liberty and equality, regardless of nationality or religion, and be submitted to the same obligations. All Ottomans, being equal before the law as regards rights and duties relative to the State, are eligible for government posts, according to their individual capacity and their education. Non-Muslims will be equally liable to the military law.

The free exercise of the religious privileges which have been accorded to different nationalities will remain intact.

The reorganization and distribution of the State forces, on land as well as on sea, will be undertaken in accordance with the political and geographical situation of the country, taking into account the integrity of the other European powers...

Provided that the property rights of landholders are not infringed upon (for such rights must be respected and must remain intact, according to law), it will be proposed that peasants be permitted to acquire land, and they will be accorded means to borrow money at a moderate rate...

Education will be free. Every Ottoman citizen, within the limits of the prescriptions of the Constitution, may operate a private school in accordance with the special laws.

All schools will operate under the surveillance of the state. In order to obtain for Ottoman citizens an education of a homogenous and uniform character, the official schools will be open, their instruction will be free, and all nationalities will be admitted. Instruction in Turkish will be obligatory in public schools. In official schools, public instruction will be free. Secondary and higher education will be given in the public and official schools indicated above; it will use the Turkish tongue. Schools of commerce, agriculture, and industry will be opened with the goal of developing the resources of the country.

Steps shall also be taken for the formation of roads and railways and canals to increase the facilities of communication and increase the sources of the wealth of the country. Everything that can impede commerce or agriculture shall be abolished.

Glossary

anno hegira: an Islamic dating system that counts years starting from the pilgrimage of Muhammad in 622; 1293 A.H. is 1876 C.E. (the beginning of the First Constitutional Era)

Chamber: the assembly of parliament

predominance: supremacy, power

Document Analysis

In their 1908 Proclamation, the Young Turks lay out their vision of a society founded on Ottoman identity and respect for the constitution. The proclamation is influenced by European constitutional monarchies and values, but the authors still hope to retain Ottoman autonomy and cultural identity.

The central tenet of the Proclamation is the establishment of a representative government with "respect for the predominance of the national will." All citizens of the Ottoman empire will have the right to elect their own officials to parliament. The sultan will directly appoint a third of the parliament, thus retaining a significant amount of power but not the right to completely control the senate. In addition, the government is compelled to respect all its constituents equally. All Ottoman citizens, "being equal before the law as regards rights and duties," will have the right to vote, hold office, and participate in education.

In addition to creating a citizenry unified by Ottoman identity, the Young Turks value modernization. They plan to organize a state-run school system that will educate youth in Ottoman values. They also expect that the school system will be used to advance the country's industrial development: they will focus on "commerce, agriculture and industry" in order to bring the country's economic output to European levels. In addition to developing the country's material and intellectual resources, they plan to fund infrastructure ("roads and railways and canals") to carry the goods that the empire will produce. They optimistically foresee that a reorganization of society will put them in the same category as "the other European powers."

Essential Themes

The Young Turks wanted to maintain a separate identity from the European powers while competing with them in wealth and influence. Throughout their Proclamation, they discuss the shared rights that Ottoman citizens have: education, the right to vote and run for office, religious freedom, and state-sponsored education. Though they hope to move away from one-man rule by the sultan, they still favor a strong central government that will emphasize Ottoman values. They support Turkish as the national language and they hope to establish state-run schools that will teach children Ottoman values. The state will have the power to abolish anything that stands in the way of the march toward modernity.

Though the Proclamation claims to offer "complete liberty and equality, regardless of nationality" to all citizens, it was less than a decade before the Young Turk-led administration attempted to eliminate all of the Armenian citizens in the empire.

—Hannah Rich, MA

Bibliography and Additional Reading

Akcam, Tanar. *The Young Turks' Crime against Humanity: The Armenian Genocide and Ethnic Cleansing in the Ottoman Empire.* Princeton, NJ: Princeton UP, 2013.

Hanioglu, M. Sükrü. *Preparation for a Revolution: The Young Turks, 1902–1908.* New York: Oxford UP, 2001.

———. *A Brief History of the Late Ottoman Empire.* Princeton, NJ: Princeton UP, 2010.

Proclamation of the Algerian National Liberation Front

Date: November 1, 1954
Author: National Liberation Front
Geographic region: Algeria
Genre: proclamation; political tract; speech

Summary Overview

The Algerian National Liberation Front (FLN), made up of Algerian militants opposed to French rule, fought a war of independence against the French government in Algeria from 1954 to 1962. The French had occupied Algeria since the 1840s. The Algerian War ended when the French withdrew from Algeria and handed over rule of the country to an Algerian-led government.

The war is famous for the use of guerrilla tactics by the FLN and for the brutal retaliations against Algerians carried out by the French. The FLN realized the importance of having public opinion on their side, and they attempted throughout the war to gain the support of Algerians and of the international community. The French, on the other hand, quickly lost the moral high ground with their indiscriminate violence and publicized killings of civilians. After nearly eight years of war, the French government negotiated a truce with Algeria that led to the cessation of hostilities and the establishment of an independent Algerian government.

The FLN was founded by Algerians who had been active in revolutionary groups prior to the outbreak of war. The group announced its existence and the beginning of the War of Independence on November 1, 1954, by releasing a Proclamation that lays out their objectives, demands for independence, and plans for war if the French do not withdraw.

Defining Moment

The French had established a colonial government in Algeria in 1840. French colonists controlled political and social policies, and they held much of the fertile and developed land in the country after having seized it from native Algerians in the first wave of colonialism. By 1900, France had a colonial empire that reached as far as the Pacific Ocean, but the Algerian colony was their longest-held possession and a defining part of France's identity as an imperialist power.

Islamic and nationalist movements were founded in Algeria in the early twentieth century to oppose France, but they made little progress under the colonist-dominated system. One early voice in favor of Algerian independence was Messali Hadj (1898-1974), who founded one of the first nationalist parties. As anti-French activism had been banned in Algeria, he travelled Europe promoting the Algerian cause, spending time in jail and under house arrest. Despite these early efforts, it was not until World War II that the first major anti-French resistance movements gained traction. When France had been invaded by Nazi Germany and the pro-Nazi Vichy government ruled France and the colonies, an Allied force invaded Algeria to free it from German rule. The Allies repealed many of the repressive Vichy laws that had been unpopular with native Algerians, but they also demanded that Algeria supply soldiers to fight against the Germans. Muslim leaders were unwilling to encourage their people to fight on behalf of the French without having a say in their own government.

The French government ignored Algerian calls for self-government. Dissatisfaction with the status quo, intensified by famine and unemployment, continued to grow in Algeria until 1945; riots and police violence broke out even at celebrations to mark the end of the European war. In retaliation, the French government attacked suspected revolutionaries as well as civilian areas.

National Liberation Army soldiers next to the Algerian flag. Photo by Zdravko Pe?ar, via Wikimedia Commons.

Despite the violence and Algerian calls for self-government, French public opinion was very much in favor of preserving Algeria as a French colony. Messali Hadj, who had been under house arrest for much of the war, founded another independence movement (called the Movement for the Triumph of Democratic Liberties, or MTDL), this time with a military branch. The movement was wildly successful in the 1947 elections despite electoral interference by French colonists.

In response to their political defeat, the French government developed an assembly consisting of two groups: one to represent the Muslim majority and the other to represent the colonists, a small minority of the general population. In addition, the 1948 assembly elections were once again rigged in favor of the colonists.

The obvious interference with the political system spurred widespread political activism. Anti-French demonstrations broke out across the country. Older party leaders who had fought to be treated equally by the French began to be pushed aside in favor of younger revolutionaries who advocated pushing the French out of Algerian society altogether. At the same time, French colonists who saw these movements as a threat to their political and social power began to fear the loss of privilege that a more egalitarian society would bring. Algerian society became even more polarized than it already had been, and violence frequently broke out at protests.

After one such protest in 1952, Messali Hadj was arrested and deported to France. His MTDL was soon dissolved, with many of its members going underground and founding new committees with a stronger focus on the military arm. By 1954, several anticolonial revolutionary groups were ready to take aim at the French government by organized military means. The most successful of these groups was to be a small group known as the National Liberation Front.

Author Biography

The *Fronte de Libération Nationale* (abbreviated as the FLN; anglicized as the National Liberation Front) was founded by members of the MTLD who were committed to an armed revolution against French colonial rule of Algeria. They planned to continue their predecessors' opposition to French rule by political means, but they added an organized strategy of military resistance. The FLN sprang into the fight against France on November 1, 1954 with the issuance a proclamation urging all Algerians to join their cause against the French. With the FLN's call to arms, the Algerian War of Independence officially began.

The eight-year war was a bloody and complicated revolution that led to hundreds of thousands of deaths, millions of refugees, and the eventual collapse of France's overseas empire. Both sides used guerilla tactics, targeted civilians, and tortured their opponents. Throughout the war, members of the FLN directed military actions against the French while attempting to get the support of the international community, including the United Nations. At the same time, the French quickly alienated the world by using brutal tactics against the Algerian people, militants, and civilians alike.

The FLN slowly shifted the war from rural areas into the cities. Beginning in 1956, the main theater of action was the capital city of Algiers. The rebels bombed several popular French cafes in 1956 and increased acts violence in the city, including shootings and bombings. They also agitated for a nationwide general strike. The French responded by instituting total martial law over the city: they used soldiers to break the strike, imposed a curfew, and tortured detainees. Their brutal methods caused a near-universal shift in Algerian opinion to the side of the rebels and increased global support for the FLN. In their attempt to regain control of the colony, the French made their rule intolerable to its inhabitants.

The war intensified until 1958. In that year, voters in France expressed their dissatisfaction with the politicians who had been unable to quell the violence and ensure the safety of the French colonists in Algeria. Charles de Gaulle, who had himself been a guerrilla leader during World War II and was the most respected man in French politics, reentered government. He toured Algeria in an attempt to appeal to both colonists and native Algerians, promising safety to the former and reform to the latter. He called for suffrage for all Algerians (including women) and set up a committee to draft a new constitution that would treat the colony more equally. When pressed, however, he revealed that Algerians would always be second-class citizens in a French-run society. His lack of commitment to total equality alienated Algerians and his attempt to compromise alienated French colonists.

Seizing the moment, the FLN established their own government-in-exile in Tunisia. Their public relations campaign was beginning to take hold in France and abroad: intellectuals and private citizens wrote and provided financial aid to the revolution, and the United Nations began to take an interest. By 1961, negotiations for a peace had begun.

In a February referendum, Algerians voted by a large majority for independence. Violence continued until a ceasefire was decreed in March 1962. The negotiations that followed led to a truce in June and then the decree on July 3, 1962 of Algerian independence from France. After 132 years of colonization and a traumatic eight-year war, Algeria was free to determine its own government.

The FLN immediately seized political control of Algeria, established itself as the ruling party, and outlawed opposition. Despite some internal conflicts, the party reigned for over 25 years under the control of various long-term leaders; no multi-party elections were held. It was not until 1990 that the FLN, pressured by strikes and protests, allowed other parties to participate in elections. They were defeated in the first open local elections, but political and religious divisions soon led to the Algerian Civil War, another brutally bloody war marked by drawn-out conflict and atrocities. At the end of the war, which lasted from 1991 to 2002, the FLN reestablished itself as a major political party, and FLN politicians currently hold about a third of the elected seats in Algeria's national government.

Historical Document

Proclamation of the Algerian National Liberation Front

To the Algerian people

To the Militants of the National Cause

To you who are called upon to judge us, the Algerian people in a general way, the militants more particularly, our purpose in distributing this proclamation is to enlighten you concerning the profound reasons which have impelled us to act by revealing to you our program, the meaning of our action, and the cogency of our views the, goal of which remains National Independence within the North African framework. Our wish as well is to help you avoid the confusion maintained by imperialism and its corrupt political and administrative agents.

Before all else, we consider that after decades of struggle the National Movement has reached its final stage of realization. In fact, as the goal of the revolutionary movement is to create all the favorable conditions needed for the launching of operations for liberation, we believe that internally the people are united behind the sign of independence and action; and externally the climate of détente is favorable for the settling of minor problems (among them ours) with the support of our Arab and Muslim brothers above all. The events in Morocco and Tunisia are significant in this regard, and profoundly mark the process of the liberation struggle in North Africa. It is worth noting that for quite some time we have been, in this regard, precursors in the unity of action, unfortunately never realized among the three countries.

Today, many are resolutely engaged on this path and we, relegated to the rear, suffer the fate of those who events have passed by. It is thus that our national movement, overwhelmed by years of immobilisme and routine, poorly oriented, deprived of the indispensable support of public opinion, and overtaken by events, has progressively disintegrated, to the great satisfaction of colonialism, which thinks it has carried off its greatest victory in its struggle against the Algerian vanguard. The hour is serious.

Facing this situation, which risks becoming irreparable, a group of young leaders and conscious activists, rallying around it the majority of the healthy and decisive elements, has judged that the moment has arrived to move the National Movement out of the impasse into which it was backed by personal struggles and fights over influence, in order to launch it, at the side of the Moroccan and Tunisian brothers, into the true revolutionary struggle.

To this end, we insist on specifying that we are independent of the two clans that are fighting over power. Placing national interest above all petty and erroneous considerations of personality and prestige, in conformity with revolutionary principles, our action is directly solely against colonialism, our only blind and obstinate enemy, which has always refused to grant the least freedom by peaceful means.

These are, we think, sufficient, reasons for a movement of renewal to present itself under the name of National Liberation Front, releasing itself in this way from all possible compromises, and offering the possibility to all Algerian patriots of all social classes, of all the purely Algerian parties and movements, to integrate themselves into the struggle for liberation, without any other consideration.

In summary, we spell out below the major elements of our political program:

Goal: National Independence by:
The restoration of the sovereign, democratic and social Algerian state, within the framework of Islamic principles.

The respect of all fundamental liberties without distinction of race or religion.

Internal Objectives:
Political reform by the returning of the National Revolutionary Movement to its true path and by the wiping-out of the vestiges of corruption and reformism, the causes of our current regression.

The gathering together and organization of all the healthy energies of the Algerian people for the liquidation of the colonial system.

External Objectives:
The internalization of the Algerian problem.

The realization of North African unity within its natural Arabo-Islamic framework.

Within the framework of the U.N. Charter, the affirmation of our active sympathy with regard to all nations who support our operations for liberation.

Means of Struggle:
In conformity with revolutionary principles, and taking into account the internal and external situations, the continuation of the struggle by all possible means until the realization of our goal.

In order to reach these objectives, the National Liberation front will have two essential tasks to carry out simultaneously: an internal action, on the fronts of politics and action, and an external action, with the goal of the making of the Algerian problem a reality for the entire world, with the support of all our natural allies.

This is a heavy task which necessitates the mobilization of all national energy and resources. It is true that the struggle will be long, but the result is certain.

In the last place, in order to avoid all false interpretations and subterfuges, in order to prove our real desire for peace, to limit the number of human lives lost and the amount of blood spilled, we propose to French authorities an honorable platform of discussion, if these latter are animated by good faith and recognize once and for all in the people they subjugate the right to dispose of themselves:

The opening of negotiations with the authorized spokesmen of the Algerian people on the basis of the recognition of sovereignty through Algerian liberation, one and indivisible.

The creation of a climate of confidence through the liberation of all political prisoners, the lifting of all measures of exception, and the ceasing of all pursuit of the fighting forces.

The recognition of Algerian nationality by an official declaration abrogating the edicts, decrees and laws making Algeria a "French land," which is a denial of the History, the geography, the language, the religion, and the mores of the Algerian people.

In Return:
French cultural and economic interests, honestly acquired, will be respected, as will persons and families.

All Frenchmen wishing to remain in Algeria will have the choice between their nationality of origin, in which case they will be considered foreigners vis à vis the laws in place, or they will opt for Algerian nationality, in which case they will be considered such in rights and obligations.

The bonds between France and Algeria will be defined and will be the object of an agreement between the two powers on the basis of equality and mutual respect.

Algerians! We invite you to think over our above Charter. Your obligation is to join with it in order to save our country and restore to it its freedom. The National Liberation Front is your front. Its victory is yours.

As for us, resolved to pursue the struggle, sure of your anti-imperialist sentiments, we give the best of ourselves to the Fatherland.

The Secretariat

Glossary

abrogating: repealing, removing, denying

cogency: coherence, clearness

détente: lessening of hostilities

mores: customs, habits

sovereign: self-governing, self-determining

vestiges: traces

vis a vis: with respect to, in regard to

Document Analysis

The FLN's issuance of this Proclamation is today considered the first action of the Algerian War of Independence. The authors are prepared for a long-term, all-out, radical revolution that would completely overturn the existing society. They are aware that they will be fighting against the full power of the French establishment and French society, which has exploited Algerians and considered them second-class citizens for over a hundred years. They also realize the importance of international opinion and of winning not only battles but the respect and loyalty of the Algerian people. To that end, they use this proclamation to lay out their objectives, acknowledge the magnitude of their undertaking, and win public opinion to their side.

The first part of the speech also addresses the issue of public opinion. Creation of "favorable conditions" for the liberation movement depends on the support of the people being liberated, and the authors state that the unity of the Arab and Muslim societies is of primary importance. "Placing national interest above all," the FLN states that their aim is to support all those who support the revolution. They appeal to shared values and virtues—"independence and action," "freedom by peaceful means," patriotism, and liberation—in addressing an audience unified by opposition to imperialism.

The next part of the speech lays out the goal of the revolution: the establishment of Algerian self-government, free of external influences. The inclusion of both internal and external objectives is an important part of the FLN's strategy. For the duration of the war, they fought the French at home while also trying to get support for their cause abroad. As the war went on, their appeals to the United Nations were especially important in gaining international sympathy.

In the final section of the proclamation, the FLN offers an ultimatum and warns their opponents that they are willing to fight to the death for freedom. They speak directly to the French to request "recognition of Algerian nationality" and the elimination of French claims. The FLN states openly that the labeling of Algeria as French is a harmful construct invented to support French interests at the expense of Algerian. They offer an olive branch—if the French cooperate, Algeria will support a peaceful transition for the French colonists still in Algeria. Though they do not explicitly state what will happen if their demands are not met, they state their desire to limit—but not eliminate—"the number of human lives lost and the amount of blood spilled." If the French continue their colonization, the FLN will "give the best of ourselves" to the struggle.

Essential Themes and Impact

The Proclamation was published on November 1, 1954. On that day, the FLN attacked several police and military locations around Algeria, killing seven people total. The day became known as *Toussaint Rouge* ("Red All Saints' Day", after the Catholic holiday on which it took place). French authorities increased the number of troops stationed in Algeria, but the French government did not acknowledge the demands of the revolutionaries. In a speech addressing the attacks, the French president continued to state that Algeria was a French land and would remain French forever.

It took a few years for the revolutionary movement to gain traction abroad, but the FLN worked on all fronts to gain support in Algeria. Their military arm launched attacks against French bases and their intellectuals wrote and spoke in favor of liberation. At first, the French viewed the revolution as a problem to suppress by military action, but the FLN worked on both military and social fronts to gain support. As the war went on, the French realized that they would not be able to win by violence alone. After eight years of terror and bloodshed in Algeria and (to a lesser extent) France, the revolution led to the liberation of Algeria and the creation of the modern Algerian state.

—*Hannah Rich, MA*

Bibliography and Additional Reading

McDougall, James. *A History of Algeria*. New York: Cambridge UP, 2017.

Shepard, Todd. *The Invention of Decolonization: The Algerian War and the Remaking of France*. Ithaca, NY: Cornell UP, 2008.

Stone, Martin. *The Agony of Algeria*. New York: Columbia UP, 1997.

CIA Summary of the Overthrow of Premier Mossadeq of Iran

Date: March 1954
Author: Donald N. Wilber
Genre: government document

Summary Overview

In the late summer of 1953, British and American intelligence services worked together to orchestrate a coup to overthrow the democratically elected prime minister of Iran, Mohammad Mossadeq (also spelled Mosaddegh or Mosaddiq). The British relied heavily on Iranian oil, which they had controlled since 1909, and Mossadeq led a popular movement to nationalize the oil fields. The British responded to nationalization with a boycott, removing trained personnel from Iranian refineries and refusing to purchase or transport Iranian oil. This led to an economic crisis, and fears in the West that the Soviet Union would exploit this instability to gain influence in Iran through the Tudeh Party, Iran's Communist party. The shah, or monarch, of Iran was reluctant to support the coup plot, which hinged on a royal decree that would remove Mossadeq and install a pro-Western prime minister, Fazlollah Zahedi. After significant pressure from the CIA, the shah agreed to support the coup, which replaced Mossadeq with Zahedi and reopened Iranian oil to Western investment. The following year, one of the main CIA organizers of the coup, Donald N. Wilber, wrote a classified history of the event that was not made public until the year 2000.

Defining Moment

Great Britain's interest in Iranian oil began in earnest on May 28, 1901, when the shah granted the petroleum rights over vast areas of territory to a British citizen, William Knox D'Arcy. When oil was not immediately discovered, D'Arcy was forced to accept other investors. Significant quantities of oil were discovered in 1908, and in 1909, the Anglo-Persian Oil Company (APOC) which would later become British Petroleum, was formed. By 1913, a massive refinery in Abadan was pumping oil destined for the British Empire. Under the agreement with D'Arcy, the Iranian government's share of the oil profits was just 16 percent, and the company declined to open its books for inspection.

Just before World War I, the British navy upgraded their ships from coal to oil, and the British government gained a controlling interest in the APOC. The British economy and military were dependent on a steady flow of inexpensive Iranian oil. During the war, the British stationed troops in Iran to

Premier Mossadeq. Photo via Wikimedia Commons. [Public domain.]

Coup supporters celebrate victory in Tehran. Photo via Wikimedia Commons. [Public domain.]

protect their pipelines and proposed in 1919 that Iran become a British protectorate. Though this was not accepted by Iran, the British continued to control the vast majority of Iranian territory, but not without opposition. In the 1920s and 1930s, the Iranian government fought to renegotiate the D'Arcy agreement and regain greater control of the nation's resources. In 1933, a new sixty-year agreement was reached, which increased payments to the Iranian government and reduced the amount of land under direct APOC control.

Britain's relationship with Iran became even more complicated during World War II. The Soviet Union was a key British ally and was holding the Axis armies at bay on the Eastern Front, and this two-front war was key to Britain's survival. The Soviet Union depended on Iranian oil to resupply its army, and though Iran was neutral, the shah was suspected of Nazi sympathies. British and Soviet forces therefore invaded Iran in 1941. The ruler, Reza Shah, was deposed and replaced by his son, Mohammad Reza Pahlavi, who remained in power until 1979.

After the war, the Iranian parliament wanted greater control over the country's oil reserves. Mossadeq was the leader of the nationalization movement and was elected prime minister of Iran in 1951. On May 2, Mossadeq declared the oil fields to be the property of Iran alone. The response from Britain was to remove all trained personnel from the refineries and organize and international boycott of Iranian oil. Production and sales dropped precipitously, leading to an economic crisis and internal unrest. By 1952, British and American intelligence officers had begun to develop a plan to oust Mossadeq. Dwight D. Eisenhower, the newly elected president of the United States, was afraid that the Soviet Union would be able to take advantage of the instability in Iran and decided to support the coup.

Author Biography

Donald Newton Wilber was born in Wisconsin on November 14, 1907. He attended New Trier High School and then went to Princeton University, where he graduated with a BA in 1929, as well as an MFA and PhD in architecture in 1949. Wilber's area of scholarly expertise was the Middle East, and he traveled and wrote extensively in Iran, Afghanistan, and Sri Lanka. Wilber's book Iran, Past and Present was published in 1948, establishing him as an expert on Iranian history. These scholarly endeavors gave Wilbur cover for his activities with the CIA, which he joined in 1948. He was a primary planner of the overthrow of Mossadeq in favor of a government friendlier to Western interests. Wilber served in the CIA until 1970, while working with various prestigious universities. He died on February 2, 1997, in Princeton, New Jersey, survived by his wife and two daughters.

HISTORICAL DOCUMENT

SECRET

Summary

By the end of 1952, it had become clear that the Mossadeq government in Iran was incapable of reaching an oil settlement with interested Western countries; was reaching a dangerous and advanced stage of illegal, deficit financing; was disregarding the Iranian constitution in prolonging Premier Mohammed Mossadeq's tenure of office; was motivated mainly by Mossadeq's desire for personal power; was governed by irresponsible policies based on emotion; had weakened the Shah and the Iranian Army to a dangerous degree; and had cooperated closely with the Tudeh (Communist) Party of Iran. In View of these factors, it was estimated that Iran was in real danger of falling behind the Iron Curtain; if that happened it would mean a victory for the Soviets in the Cold War and a major setback for the West in the Middle East. No remedial action other than the covert action plan set forth below could be found to improve the existing state of affairs.

It was the aim of the TPAJAX project to cause the fall of the Mossadeq government; to reestablish the prestige and power of the Shah; and to replace the Mossadeq government with one which would govern Iran according to constructive policies. Specifically, the aim was to bring power to a government which would reach equitable oil settlement, enabling Iran to become economically sound and financially solvent, and which would vigorously prosecute the dangerously strong Communist Party.

Once it had been determined definitely that it was not in American interests for the Mossadeq government to remain in power and CIA had been so informed by the Secretary of State in March 1953, CIA began drafting a plan whereby the aims state above could be realized through covert action. An estimate entitled "Factors Involved in the Overthrow of Mossadeq" was completed on 16 April 1953. It was here determined that an overthrow of Mossadeq was possible through covert operations. In April it was determined that CIA should conduct the envisioned operation jointly with the British Secret Intelligence Service (SIS). By the end of April, it was decided that CIA and SIS officers would draw up a plan on Cyprus which would be submitted to CIA and SIS Headquarters, and to the Department of State and the Foreign Office for final approval. On 3 June 1953, US ambassador Loy Wesley Henderson arrived in the United States where he was fully consulted with regard to the objective and aims, as stated above, as well as CIA's intentions to design covert means of achieving the objective and aims.

The plan was completed by 10 June 1953 at which time Mr. Kermit Roosevelt, Chief of the Near East and Africa Division, CIA (who carried with him the views of the Department of State, CIA, and Ambassador Henderson); Mr. Roger Goiran, CIA Chief of Station, Iran; and two CIA planning officers met in Beirut to consider the plan. With minor changes the operational proposal was submitted to the SIS in London on 14 June 1953.

On 19 June 1953, the final operational plan, agreed upon by Mr. Roosevelt for the CIA and by British Intelligence in London, was submitted in Washington to the Department of State; to Mr. Allen W. Dulles, Director of CIA; and to Ambassador Henderson for approval. Simultaneously, it was submitted to the British Foreign Office by SIS for approval. The Department of State wanted to be assured of two things before it would grant approval of the plan:

That the United States Government could provide adequate grant aid to a successor Iranian Government so that such a government could be sustained until an oil settlement was reached.

That the British Government would signify in writing, to the satisfaction of the Department of State, its intentions to reach an early oil settlement with a successor Iranian Government in a spirit of good will and equity.

The Department of State satisfied itself on both of these scores.

In mid-July 1953, the Department of State and the British Foreign Office granted authorization for the implementation of the TPAJAX project, and the Director of CIA obtained the approval of the President of the United States. The SIS, with the concurrence of the CIA Director and Ambassador Henderson, proposed that Mr. Roosevelt assume field command in Tehran of the final phases of the operation. It was determined by the Department of State that it would be advisable for Ambassador Henderson to postpone his return to Iran, from Washington consultation, until the operation had been concluded. Arrangements were made jointly with SIS whereby operational liaison would be conducted on Cyprus where a CIA officer would be temporarily stationed, and support liaison would be conducted in Washington. Rapid three-way communications were arranged through CIA facilities between Tehran, Cyprus, and Washington. The time set for the operation was mid-August.

In Iran, CIA and SIS propaganda assets were to conduct an increasingly intensified propaganda effort through the press, handbills, and the Tehran clergy in a campaign designed to weaken the Mossadeq government in any way possible. In the United States, high-ranking US officials were to make official statements which would shatter any hopes held by Premier Mossadeq that American economic aid would be forthcoming, and disabuse the Iranian public of the Mossadeq myth that the United States supported his regime.

General Fazlollah Zahedi, a former member of Mossadeq's cabinet, was chosen as the most suitable successor to the Premier since he stood out as the only person of stature who had consistently been openly in opposition to Mossadeq and who claimed any significant following. Zahedi was to be approached by CIA and be told of our operation and its aim of installing him as the new prime minister. He was to name a military secretariat with which CIA would conclude a detailed staff plan of action.

From the outset, the cooperation of the Shah was considered to be an essential part of the plan. His cooperation was necessary to assure the action required of the Tehran militart garrisons, and to legalize the succession of a new prime minister. Since the Shah had shown himself to be a man of indecision, it was determined that pressure on him to cooperate would take the following forms:

The Shah's dynamic and forceful twin sister, Princess Ashraf Pahlavi, was to come from Europe to urge the Shah to dismiss Mossadeq. She would say she had been in contact with US and UK officials who had requested her to do so.

Arrangements were made for a visit to Iran by General H. Norman Schwarzkopf, former head of the US Gendarme Mission, who the Shah liked and respected. Schwarzkopf was to explain the proposed project and get from the Shah signed firmans (royal decrees) dismissing Mossadeq, appointing Zahedi, and calling on the Army to remain loyal to the crown.

The principal indigenous British agent, who bona fides had been established with the Shah, was to reinforce the Shah that this was a joint US-UK action.

Failing results from the above, Mr. Roosevelt, representing the President of the United States, would urge the Shah to sign the above-mentioned firmans. When received, the firmans would be released by CIA to Zahedi on the day called for in the plan. On D-Day, the Shah was to be at some location outside of Tehran so that Zahedi, armed with the royal firmans and with military support, could take over the government without danger of the Sha's reversing his stand, and to avoid any attempt on the Shah's life.

Through agents in the Tehran military, CIA was to ensure, to the degree possible, Tehran Army cooperation in support of the Shah-appointed new prime minister.

The following public statements made in the United States had tremendous impact on Iran and Mossadeq, and contributed greatly to Mossadeq's downfall:

The publication, on 9 June 1953, of President Eisenhower's 29 June 1953 letter to Premier Mossadeq made it clear that increased aid would not be forthcoming to Iran.

The Secretary of State's press conferences of 28 July 1953 stated that ". ... The growing activities of the illegal Communist Party in Iran and the toleration fo them by the Iranian Government has caused our government concern. These developments make it more difficult to grant aid to Iran."

The President's Seattle speech at the Governors' convention, in which he stated that the United States would not sit by and see Asian countries fall behind the Iron Curtain, had definite effect.

In cooperation with the Department of State, CIA had several articles planted in major American newspapers and magazines which, when reproduced in Iran, had the desired psychological effect in Iran and contributed to the war of nerves against Mossadeq.

After considerable pressure from Princess Ashraf and General Schwarzkopf, and after several meetings with Mr. Roosevelt, the Shah finally signed the required firmans on 15 August 1953. Action was set for 16 August. However, owing to a security leak in the Iranian military, the chief of the Shah's bodyguard, assigned to seize Mossadeq qith the help of two truckloads of pro-Shah soldiers, was overwhelmed by superior armed forces still loyal to Mossadeq. The balance of the military plan was thus frustrated for that day. Upon hearing that the plan has misfired, the Shah flew to Baghdad. This was an act of prudence and had been at least partially foreseen in the plan. Zahedi remained in hiding in CIA custody. With his key officers, he eluded Mossadeq's security forces which were seeking to apprehend the major opposition elements.

Early in the afternoon of 17 August 1953 Ambassador Henderson returned to Tehran. General Zahedi, through a CIA-arranged secret press conferences and through CIA covert printing facilities, announced to Iran that he was legally prime minister and that Mossadeq had staged an illegal coup against him. CIA agents disseminated a large quantity of photographs of the firmans, appointing Zahedi prime minister and dismissing Mosssadeq. This had tremendous impact on the people of Tehran who had already been shocked and angered when they realized that the Shah had been forced to leave Iran because of Mossadeq's actions. US Ambassador Burton Y. Berry, in Baghdad, contacted the Shah and stated that he had confidence that the Shah would return soon to Iran despite the apparent adverse situation at the time. Contact was also established with the Shah in Rome after he had flown there from Baghdad. Mr. Roosevelt and the station consistently reported that Mossadeq's apparent victory was misleading; that there were very concrete signs that the Army was still loyal to the Shah; and that a favorable reversal of the situation was possible. The station further urged both the British Foreign Office and the Department of State to make a maximum effort to persuade the Shah to make public statements encouraging the Army and populace to reject Mossadeq and to accept Zahedi as prime minister.

On 19 August 1953, a pro-Shah demonstration, originating in the bazaar area, took on overwhelming proportions. The demonstration appeared to start partially spontaneously, revealing the fundamental prestige of the Shah and the public alarm at the undisguised republican move being started by the Communists as well as by certain National Frontists. Station political action assets also contributed to the beginnings of the Pro-Shah demonstrations. The Army very soon joined the pro-Shah movement and by noon of that day it was clear that Tehran, as well as certain provincial areas, were controlled by pro-Shah street groups and Army units. The situation was such that the above-mentioned military plan could then be implemented. At the station's signal, Zahedi came out of hiding to lead the movement. He first broadcast over Radio Tehran and announced that the government was his. The General Staff offices were then seized, Mossadeq's home was gutted, and pro-Mossadeq politicians and officers arrested. By the end of 19 August, the country was in the hands of the new Premier, Zahedi, and members of the Mossadeq government were either in hiding or were incarcerated.

The Shah returned shortly to Iran where he was given a rousing popular reception. The Shah was deeply moved by the fact that his people and Army had revolted in the face of adversity against a vindictive Mossadeq and a Communist Party riding the crest of a temporary victory and clearly planning to declare Iran a republic. The Shah felt for the first time that he had the mandate of his people, and he returned determined to regain firm control of the Army.

In order to give Zahedi badly needed immediate financial assistance so that the month-end payrolls could be met before the United States could provide large scale grant aid, CIA covertly made available $5,000,000 within two days of Zahedi's assumption of power.

[The C.I.A.'s secret history of the 1953 coup in Iran was a nearly 200-page document, comprising the author's own account of the operation and a set of planning documents he attached. The New York Times on the Web is publishing the introduction and many of the planning documents. But the Times decided not to publish the main body of text after consulting prominent historians who believed there might be serious risk that some of those named as foreign agents would face retribution in Iran.

Because the introductory summary and the main body of the document are inconsistent on a few dates and facts, readers may note discrepancies between accounts. In its reporting, the Times as relied upon details in the C.I.A. document not published here. In addition, certain names and identifying descriptions have been removed from the documents available on the Web.]

Document Analysis

This selection is the introduction and summary of Wilber's CIA history of the coup. It begins with a brief recap of the reasons that the CIA and British intelligence had decided to remove Mossadeq from power. The first sentence outlines perhaps the principal British concern: "By the end of 1952, it had become clear that the Mossadeq government in Iran was incapable of reaching an oil settlement with interested Western countries." They believed furthermore that Mossadeq was acting recklessly, contrary to the constitution of Iran, and was in danger of leading the nation "behind the Iron Curtain," or into Soviet-style Communism —perhaps the principal American concern. If Iran turned to Communism, it would advance Soviet interests in the Middle East at the expense of the West, and so the decision was made to replace the Mossadeq government with one that would "govern Iran according to constructive policies." By April 1953, a coup was agreed upon as the best course of action, and plans were drawn up for a joint operation between the CIA and British Secret Intelligence Services. By mid-July 1953, the plan was approved by both governments; in the United States, the operation was named TPAJAX, or Operation Ajax.

The lead-up to the coup involved a propaganda war, with US officials making clear in public statements that economic aid would not be offered to Mossadeq's Iran. At the same time, opposition to Mossadeq was fomented inside the country, particularly through the media. A top army general, Fazlollah Zahedi, was picked to replace Mossadeq as prime minister. However, the plot also hinged on the cooperation of the shah, Mohammad Reza Pahlavi, who was extremely reluctant to involve himself in a plot by foreign powers and is described by Wilber as "a man of indecision." The report lays out the ways that pressure was brought to bear on the shah, from bringing his sister and US Army general H. Norman Schwarzkopf Sr. to negotiate with him, to readying the orders for him to sign and promising to spirit him away while the coup was taking place. On August 15, under considerable pressure, the shah signed the decrees needed to oust Mossadeq.

The plot seemed doomed from the beginning. A security leak meant that the element of surprise was lost, and Mossadeq initially escaped capture. The shah fled to Iraq, and the CIA worked to gather support for the newly appointed Zahedi by disseminating copies of the decrees replacing Mossadeq. On August 19, with the help of some CIA agents, a pro-shah demonstration in the streets of Tehran gathered momentum. By the end of the day, the capital was in the hands of supporters of Zahedi and the shah, and Mossadeq and his supporters were arrested.

The report ends by noting that the CIA secretly transferred five million dollars to Zahedi's government within two days in order to keep the government running until promised US grant aid was forthcoming.

Essential Themes

The Iranian coup of 1953 was the first of several CIA operations that sought to encourage rivals of obstreperous or Communist-leaning leaders during the Cold War; for example, the following year, in 1954, the CIA engineered a coup in Guatemala to overthrow the democratically elected government of Jacobo Árbenz, and in 1961, the CIA backed the ill-fated Bay of Pigs Invasion intended to oust Fidel Castro, the Communist leader of Cuba. When the extent of US intervention in these countries was suspected, or confirmed, it led to long-term resentment and distrust of US policy in these regions. The overthrow of Mossadeq was no exception. The shah continued to rule until 1979 in close association with the United States and Britain. When he was overthrown by militants led by Ayatollah Khomeini in 1979, the depth of animosity toward the United States in Iran was made clear. The American Embassy was attacked and the staff taken hostage, accused of spying and manipulating the Iranian people. Tensions with Iran remain high in part because of the historical distrust sewn during the 1953 coup.

—*Bethany Groff Dorau, MA*

Bibliography and Additional Reading

Abrahamian, Ervand. *The Coup: 1953, the CIA, and the Roots of Modern US-Iranian Relations.* New York: New, 2013.

Bowie, Robert R. & Richard H. Immerman. *Waging Peace: How Eisenhower Shaped an Enduring Cold War Strategy*. New York: Oxford UP, 1998.

Gasiorowski, Mark J. *Mohammad Mosaddeq and the 1953 Coup in Iran*. Syracuse, NY: Syracuse UP, 2004.

Gamal Abdel Nasser on the Nationalization of the Suez Canal

Date: July 26, 1956
Author: Gamal Abdel Nasser
Genre: speech

Summary Overview

In July 1956 the new Egyptian president, Gamal Abdel Nasser, sent shockwaves through the world of commerce and politics when he announced his government's takeover of the Suez Canal. From its opening in 1869, the Suez Canal was a vital link for European trade with Asia and many parts of the Middle East. Anything that might upset the flow of ships, and the goods they transported, would precipitate a major crisis. Thus, when Nasser announced the nationalization of the Suez Canal Company, many members of the global community reacted strongly. While the speech Nasser gave on July 26, 1956, dealt with the economic matter of the purchase of shares of the Universal Company of the Suez Maritime Canal by the government of Egypt, and the continuation of operations, it also represented a political slap in the face to the British and the French, who had been running the canal. The turmoil that developed among members of the international community resulted in the political and military conflict known as the Suez Crisis. Within months, British, French, and Israeli forces invaded Egypt to try to force Egypt to relinquish control of the canal and return it to its previous owners (mainly British and French); they also hoped to overthrow Nasser. Egypt, however, by obtaining the backing of the United States and the Soviet Union, not only successfully weathered these events and kept control of the canal, but also strengthened its position in the Middle East and brought the country into a leadership role within the global non-aligned movement.

Defining Moment

The Suez Canal Company was originally developed in 1858 as a joint venture between French entrepreneurs and the Ottoman Empire's regional governor in Egypt. However, under political pressure, the Ottoman Empire gave Egypt partial independence in 1867, and then financial problems forced the Egyptian viceroy (khedive) to sell Egypt's 44 percent of the company's stock to the British government in 1875. From that point forward the British, which controlled trade going around the horn of Africa, sought to control trade going through the canal as well. Invited in to help the Egyptian government put down a revolt, British troops took control not only of that situation but of the canal as well. Thus, from 1882 the Suez Canal was both owned by European interests and managed

Nasser, c. 1962. Photo by Stevan Kragujevic, via Wikimedia Commons.

Damaged Egyptian tank and vehicles, Suez Crisis, 1956. Photo via Wikimedia Commons. [Public domain.]

on a day-to-day basis by them. Several times in the decades prior to 1956 the British had been asked to leave, and Egyptian leaders had sought a larger role in canal operations. The British had been slowly removing their troops and had agreed to the transfer of leadership in canal operations in the future. The final withdrawal of British troops (negotiated with Nasser in 1954) occurred on July 18, 1956.

Nasser had come into power after a 1952 coup against King Farouk, who had lost popular support owing to his lavish lifestyle. Nasser sought to develop Egypt economically, through the construction of a dam on the Nile River at Aswan. As a former military leader, he also wanted to strengthen the military for possible use against Israel. Trying to be neutral in the Cold War, Nasser traded with, and accepted assistance from, both Western and Communist nations. While the United States and the United Kingdom had initially pledged funds to build the dam, when Nasser bought weapons from a Communist source, both nations pulled out of the project. Nasser had previously pressed for greater Egyptian control of the Suez Canal, and the end of U.S. support for the dam gave him one excuse to take over the operations of the canal. The money earned from its operations would, according to Nasser's plan, be used to build the Aswan Dam. With the last foreign troops (British) having been withdrawn from Egypt eight days prior to this speech, Nasser felt secure in making the move. His dramatic step not only resulted in Egypt gaining control of canal operations (technically, it had always owned the land on which the canal was built) but helped Egypt and Nasser become leaders within the Arab and non-aligned communities.

Author Biography

Gamal Abdel Nasser (January 15, 1918—September 28, 1970) was born into what might be considered a middle-class family, with his father working as a postal supervisor in a variety of offices. While in school, Nasser became active in anti-British, anti-colonial demonstrations that ended up with him being wounded and acquiring a criminal record. Although he remained a strong nationalist, when demonstrations died out after a new British-Egyptian treaty was signed, Nasser completed school and began to study law. Dropping out, he sought entrance into the military but was denied owing to his criminal record. Gaining support from a high government official, he was admitted to the military college and was commissioned in 1938. At his first posting (Mankabad) he met other young officers with a similar nationalist orientation and they began discussing how to rid the nation of the British and to advance a modern political/economic agenda. During the 1948 Arab-Israeli War, Nasser became a national hero as commander of a small Egyptian force surrounded by Israeli troops, which held its position until negotiations for that territory were concluded between the leaders of the respective governments. Later, He was among those sent to negotiate the final agreement ending hostilities.

After the war, Nasser expanded the group that had formed in Mankabad, with it becoming the Association of Free Officers. Slowly developing his network of allies, Colonel Nasser finally led a coup in 1952, although politically he remained in the background and pushed General Naguib to be the head of the government. Nasser was more radical in the economic reforms he desired, and by 1954 he had pushed Naguib out of power, although he did not himself become president until June 1956. The nationalization of the canal made Nasser very popular among Egyptians. During his reign he pushed through many economic changes and major construction projects. He was a leader in the Arab world and a major player on the world stage. However, his strong leadership also meant that many human right violations occurred during his rule. He ruled until his death in 1970.

Historical Document

Gamal Abdel Nasser on the Nationalization of the Suez Canal

In the Name of the Nation

The President of the Republic,

Considering the two firmans issued on November 30, 1854 and January 5, 1856 (respectively) concerning the preferential rights relating to the administration of the Suez Canal Transit Service and the establishment of an Egyptian joint-stock company to operate it; and Law No. 129 of 1947 concerning public utility concessions; and Law No. 317 of 1952 concerning individual labor contracts; and Law No. 26 of 1954 concerning joint-stock companies, limited partnerships by shares and limited liability companies; with the advice of the State Council; has issued the following law:

Article I

The Universal Company of the Suez Maritime Canal (Egyptian joint-stock company) is hereby nationalized. All its assets, rights and obligations are transferred to the Nation and all the organizations and committees that now operate its management are hereby dissolved.

Stockholders and holders of founders' shares shall be compensated for the ordinary or founders shares they own in accordance with the value of the shares shown in the closing quotations of the Paris Stock Exchange on the day preceding the effective date of the present law.

The payment of said indemnity shall be effected after the Nation has taken delivery of all the assets and properties of the nationalized company.

Article II

An independent organization endowed with juristic personality and annexed to the Ministry of Commerce, shall take over the management of the Suez Canal Transit Service. The composition of the organization and the remuneration of its members shall be fixed in an order of the President of the Republic. In so far as managing the Transit Service is concerned the organization shall have all the necessary powers required for the purpose without being restricted by Government regulations and procedures.

Without prejudice to the auditing of its final accounts by the State Audit Department, the organization shall have an independent budget prepared in accordance with the rules in force for commercial concerns. Its financial year shall begin on July 1 and end on June 30 each year. The budget and final accounts shall be approved by an order of the President of the Republic. The first financial year shall begin on the effective date of the present law and end with June 30, 1957.

The organization may delegate one or several of its members to implement its decisions or to discharge any duty assigned to these members.

It may also set up from among its own members or from among other people, a technical committee to assist it in its own research work and studies.

The chairman of the organization shall represent it before the courts, government agencies, and other places, and in its dealings with third parties.

Article III

The assets and rights of the nationalized company in the Republic of Egypt and abroad are hereby frozen. Without specific permission obtained in advance from the organization provided for in Article II above, banks, organizations and private persons are hereby prohibited from disposing of those assets or making any payment requested them or due by them.

Article IV

The organization shall retain all the present officials, employees and laborers of the nationalized company at their posts; they shall have to continue with the discharge of their duties; no one will be allowed to leave his work or vacate his post in any manner and for any reason whatsoever except with the permission of the organization provided for in Article II above.

Article V

All violations of the provisions of Article III above shall be punished by imprisonment and a fine equal to three times the value of the amount involved in the offense. All violations of the provisions of Article IV shall be punished by imprisonment in addition to the forfeiture by the offender of all rights to compensation, pension or indemnity.

Article VI

The present order shall be published in the Official Gazette and shall have the force of law. It shall come into force on the date of its publication. The

Minister of Commerce shall issue the necessary administrative orders for its implementation.

It shall bear the Seal of the State and be implemented as one of the State laws.

Given this 18th day of Zull Heggah, 1375 A.H. [July 26, 1956]

Gamal Abdel Nasser

Glossary

firman: a ruler's administrative order or edict; the term originated during the Ottoman Empire

juristic personality: a legal entity capable of making all forms of legal agreements and undertaking corporate operations

Document Analysis

On July 26 Nasser spoke to a large crowd for more than two and a half hours, with the central point of his speech being the nationalization of the Suez Canal. Nasser had been studying politics, especially the politics of revolution, for more than twenty years when he made the decision to take control of canal operations. He understood the repercussions of taking control from the Europeans, and sought to mitigate these by paying the previous owners a fair price for their asset. In addition, he made it clear that the canal would continue to function and that Egypt was totally committed to this move. Contemporaneous records indicated that Nasser only fully developed this plan a few days prior to its announcement; he was seeking to give his action a basic legal foundation and a means to domestically enforce the decision.

Egyptian leaders since the time of the pharaohs had desired, and some attempted, to build a canal connecting the Red Sea and the Nile River or Mediterranean Sea. A few attempts had been successful in temporarily connecting the Nile and the Red Sea, but none were lasting. Thus, when Europeans entrepreneurs proposed the creation of a canal in the 1850s, they were following in the footsteps of previous generations. As part of his speech, Nasser pointed out that most of the canal had been dug by Egyptians, and used this as part of the underlying reason why Egypt should have control of the canal operations. (He conveniently ignored the fact that Egypt had originally owned part of the company operating the canal.) In the introduction to this official document, Nasser outlined the executive orders that had created the "joint-stock company" operating the canal. Thus, he made certain there could be no legal action based on a lack of clarity as to what was being nationalized.

Articles I and III stated that all assets of the operating company were being nationalized, not just those within Egypt. Nasser understood that it would be harder to nationalize things outside of Egypt, but their clear inclusion in Article III gave a legal foundation for any legal actions necessary in other countries. In Article I, the Universal Company of the Suez Maritime Canal was told that what might be termed a hostile takeover had occurred, with the assets of this company being merged into Egypt's Ministry of Commerce. As in normal mergers/takeovers, the stockholders of the company would be paid for their stock, based on the last price of the previous day's trading on, in this case, the Paris Stock Exchange. Nasser was trying to smooth the takeover of the canal, by doing away with what would have been a major obstacle, if no payment had been made. Nasser anticipated that some shareholders, and European politicians, would object to his action. He believed that this compensation would weaken these objections substantially. Paying for the stock was a key step—the carrot—in the eventual acceptance of his action by the global community. Conversely, the stick that he wielded was contained in Article V, which allowed for "imprisonment and a fine" for those who failed to follow the orders dictated by Article III.

Articles II, IV, and V outlined how the continuing operation of the canal would be implemented. The second article specified the relationship between the new "Suez Canal Transit Service" and the government of Egypt. It also made provision for replacing the private corporation's board of directors with "an independent organization endowed with juristic personality" that would oversee the operations of the canal. The fourth and fifth articles insured that those handling the day to day operations of the canal would remain in their positions, until the new management decided to replace them. Article IV mandated that these individuals remain in place, while Article V outlined the types of punishments that could be imposed upon individuals who failed to follow the regulations outlined in Article IV. The scope of possible punishment ranged from "forfeiture" of monetary items to actual incarceration. While virtually all Egyptians working for the canal would have no reason to quit their jobs because of the nationalization, Nasser hoped that this would keep the foreign workers in place until an orderly transition could be established to replace those who might desire to leave.

The last article, Article VI, was included to follow a common legal formulation in which a new law, or executive order, had to be announced publically through an established process. While Nasser's speech in Alexandria told people what was happening, and it did happen on the day of the speech, the written publication of the edict "in the Official Gazette" made it clearly a law under the established procedures of the Egyptian government. Nasser wanted to ensure that this dramatic act, which would transform the international shipping industry and global commerce, was not thwarted by a legal technicality. (By following the technicalities in the process for the implementation of a new law, Nasser hoped it would quiet some international and domestic objections.) Whether or not under Egyptian law Nasser had the power to nationalize the canal operations and abrogate an international agreement, he did have the backing of the military and Egyptian people when he nationalized the canal. Domestically, this was all that was needed for the nationalization to be successful.

Essential Themes

When Nasser stepped forward in Alexandria to speak to the audience gathered to hear him, his primary message was simple: The operation of the Suez Canal was being taken over by the Egyptian government. However, he added two auxiliary messages that he hoped would insure a tranquil transition, in canal operations and in Egypt's relationships with other nations. Nasser's statement that the company running canal operations "is hereby nationalized" gave the essential point of this speech. Even though the agreement that had established the company running the canal had another twelve years on its lease, and the owners of the company had expected another twelve years of income from this concession, Nasser put an end to this arrangement. While he went on to clarify how the canal company was being brought into the government (via the Ministry of Commerce), this was secondary to the fact that canal operations were being nationalized.

Nasser understood that there would be resistance to this dramatic action. In order to try to keep friendly relations with the United Kingdom and France and various influential individuals, Nasser clearly stated that the current owners of company stock would be paid for their shares, based on the value from the preceding day's transactions. By making this secondary point a part of the speech, he hoped to undercut any negative reaction from stock owners or the European governments. Obviously, the invasion by British and French forces three months later showed that this was a false hope in terms of the governments. However, for the individuals who owned the stock, his decision to pay market value for their shares reduced many complications that might have arisen had he seized the assets of the company without payment.

The other secondary message was that canal operations would continue without interruption, by his proclamation that anyone working for the canal had to remain working for the canal administration, unless the Egyptian government gave permission for a worker to leave. This was a multi-purpose point, assuring workers that they still had jobs, assuring the shipping industry that competent individuals would still be running the canal, and ensuring that the operations could not be sabotaged by certain key individuals leaving their posts. Although foreign workers had less to fear, by holding their pensions hostage Nasser made sure that they would remain during the transition.

As Nasser announced this bold step, undertaken to make Egypt more self-sufficient, he was establishing himself, and his nation, as a role model for others seeking to move from colonial status to true independence. Although the move did not go as smoothly as he had hoped—for example, the Sinai was temporarily lost to invading forces—Nasser was ultimately successful in nationalizing the canal's operations and, except in times of warfare, it has operated efficiently under Egyptian control. While there were at first some serious obstacles to overcome, in the long run the nationalization of the canal has worked out well for Egypt.

—Donald A. Watt, PhD

Bibliography and Additional Reading

Aburish, Said K. *Nasser: The Last Arab*. New York: Thomas Dunne Books, 2004.

Adel, Ezzat. "The Day Nasser Nationalised the Canal." *BBC News*. London: The British Broadcasting Corporation, 2006.

Doran, Michael. *Ike's Gamble: American's Rise to Dominance in the Middle East*. New York: Free Press, 2016.

Kyle, Keith. *Suez.* New York: St. Martin's Press, 1991.

Milner, Laurie. "History: The Suez Crisis." *BBC.* London: The British Broadcasting Corporation, 2014.

Slany, William Z. "Foreign Relations of the United States, 1955-1957, Suez Crisis, July 26-December 31, 1956, Volume XVI." *Office of the Historian: Department of State.* Washington: United States Department of State, 2018.

Ayatollah Khomeini on "The Great Satan"

Date: November 5, 1979
Author: Ruhollah Khomeini
Genre: speech

Summary Overview

The Iranian Revolution of 1979 saw the overthrow of the shah, whom the United States supported, by leaders of a fundamentalist religious movement that had gained in popularity in the months and years leading up to the revolution. On November 4, 1979, a mob of Iranian militants, many of them university students, seized the United States Embassy in Tehran, Iran, taking more than sixty people hostage. The following day, Ayatollah Ruhollah Khomeini, a cleric and leader of the Iranian Revolution, gave a speech praising the actions of the revolutionaries and denouncing the United States and its influence in Iran. He famously called the United States the Great Satan for its alleged role in manipulating Iran, including supporting the unpopular, authoritarian shah (king). The shah had been ousted in January 1979 amid widespread rioting, and the ayatollah installed a regime governed by Islamic law in his place. The ayatollah's anti-Western speech would set the tone for Iran's relations with the United States for decades to come.

Defining Moment

American involvement in Iran can be traced to Iran's ties to Great Britain and the discovery of significant quantities of oil in Iran in the early 1900s. In 1909 the Anglo-Persian Oil Company (APOC) which would later become British Petroleum (BP), was formed. The British economy and military were dependant on a steady flow of inexpensive Iranian oil, and during World War I the British stationed troops in Iran to protect their pipelines. Though Iran was technically an independent nation, the British controlled large amounts of its territory.

The United States became involved in Iran as an ally of Great Britain during World War II. Though Iran was neutral, the shah was suspected of Nazi sympathies. Combined British and other Allied forces invaded Iran and the shah, Reza Shah Pahlavi, was deposed and replaced by his son, Mohammad Reza Shah Pahlavi.

In 1951 the popular nationalist Mohammad Mossadeq was elected prime minister of Iran and announced that he would nationalize the nation's oil production. Fearing the loss of these strategic oil reserves, British and US intelligence orchestrated a

Ayatollah Khomeini, 1970s. Photo via Wikimedia Commons. [Public domain.]

coup that replaced Mossadeq with a pro-Western leader and restored the power of the shah. The shah returned most of Iran's oil wealth to the United States and Britain and headed a secular government that attempted to modernize and westernize the nation. He received vast amounts of foreign aid in return for his loyalty, but was seen by many Iranians as a puppet of the United States who brutally suppressed his own people.

In 1963 the shah clashed with a group of conservative Islamic clerics led by Ayatollah Ruhollah Khomeini, who preached a return to a religious state that would throw off Western oppression. The uprising was suppressed, and Khomeini imprisoned and then exiled to Iraq, but discontent with the shah's autocratic regime continued to grow. Protests erupted throughout Iran during the 1970s, and government crackdowns could not prevent the growing instability. On January 6, 1979, the shah fled to Egypt, and on February 1, 1979, Khomeini returned to cheering crowds. Under his leadership an Islamic state was established, with the ayatollah declared its supreme leader for life. He reinstated Islamic law and purged the government and civil service of opposition to his new regime, killing thousands.

Anti-American fervor swept the country as Khomeini gave impassioned speeches about purging the nation of Western influence. On November 4, 1979, a group of militant protestors scaled the walls of the United States Embassy in Tehran and took more than sixty hostages, demanding the extradition of the shah, who was in the United States for cancer treatment. The next day Khomeini gave a memorable speech in support of their efforts against what he viewed as Iran's greatest enemy.

Author Biography

Ruhollah Khomeini was born on September 24, 1902 in Khomeyn, Iran. He was from a family of Shia Islamic mullahs and was educated in a series of Islamic schools. After World War I he studied at a seminary until he moved with his religious teacher to the city of Qom in 1922. He studied history, philosophy, and religion, and was a lecturer and noted scholar of Shia Islam in Qom. He wrote prodigiously on Islamic law and philosophy, and was an outspoken critic of the shah. He was made an ayatollah, or religious leader, in the 1950s, and a supreme religious leader or grand ayatollah, in 1963.

Khomeini was imprisoned for antigovernment protests in 1963 and then exiled, first to Iraq and then to France, where he continued to communicate with his followers in Iran and call for an Islamic republic. When the shah was overthrown in 1979, Khomeini returned to Iran as the leader of the revolution and installed a strict Islamic regime while suppressing opposition. He was the political and religious ruler of Iran until his death on June 3, 1989.

Historical Document

Ayatollah Khomeini on "The Great Satan"

In the name of God, the merciful, the compassionate

[America, the Great Satan]

I have in mind a story in which on the day the Prophet attained prophethood, that Great Satan shouted and gathered all the devils around himself to say that we are facing some difficulties. In this revolution, the Great Satan, which is the United States, is gathering the devils around himself with a shout. And he has gathered both the baby devils who are in Iran, and the devils outside of Iran, and has started a ruckus.

You all know that during the reign of these two evil men [reference to the two Shahs of the Pahalavi dynasty]—whose reign was also against the law—Iran was at one period captive to Britain, and at another, to the United States. I mean, mostly, the US. The British brought Reza Khan and made him an officer over us, and Mohammad Reza, when the Allied Forces came to Iran—as they said—it was best that Mohammad Reza remains. Of course, they did not see what is best for the nation, they meant what is best for themselves. During this time extensive problems affected our nation—whether women or men—you all know. Many of you don't remember much of it, which I do remember, that they, during the time of Reza Khan, in the name of unity in form, in the name of lifting the veil, the things they did, what calamities they bestowed on this country. What bullying, what children were aborted as a result of their attacks on women to pull off their veils. That period passed in bitterness, and those same Allied Forces that had brought him—meaning the British—those same people took him from here. And they announced it, too. On the Dehli Radio, which at that time was in their hands, they announced that we brought him and after he betrayed us, we took him. And later, he gathered up his jewelry and packed his bags and placed them in the ship to take with him, on the way—as told by one of his companions—they approached his ship with a special ship for carrying animals, and they took Reza Khan to that place where he belonged. And he said "the luggage?" and they said "that will come later". He was taken to that island and they took the luggage for themselves.

Then it was this second one's turn for plundering, which most of you remember. I mean, all of you remember the end. Also the beginning, many of you remember what they did, and what crimes they committed in this country, and with what deceptive names. Unfortunately, some people believed their extensive propaganda, and some who are partners in their crimes and are still active. These are those same devils who now, with the shouts of the US, have become active, who are busy with deviousness. And our nation must neutralize these conspiracies with vigilance and astuteness.

[Deception and gossip of the enemy]

It is important, these conspiracies... these deceptions, this gossipmongering that is now common. Many rumors for weakening the spirits of the nation. Imagine several thieves kill some people in a place. Then we see that the news arrives that they've killed 100 people somewhere, they've beheaded 25 people. The second time, 400 people were killed, although none of this happened. They want to create rumors to weaken. "All the destroyed checkpoints, all that happened"; it's all to create some mischief and weaken your spirits, our spirits.

Including things that keep being said, and keep being promulgated from around that "a revolution has taken place, but nothing really happened, it's just a revolution and things went from a monarchy form to a mullah form. But nothing's changed." This is something that I also said yesterday. And again I submit to you: that what the nation wanted, all of that has taken place. What did the nation want? When the nation roared, what was it saying? Wasn't it saying "freedom and independence and Islamic Republic?" Which one hasn't happened? Right now there is freedom, such that you and I can sit here and talk. Could we do this five years ago? Independence is there. Right now, this ruckus that the US has created and all this noise that this Great Satan screams and gathers the other devils around itself, this is because its hands have been tied. Its hands from taking our resources; they've been tied from its interest here. And it is afraid that its hands will be tied until the end; that's why it is conspiring.

[Occupying the American nest of spies (e.g. US embassy)]

And that center that our youngsters went and took over—as they informed us—was the center of spying and conspiracy. America expects that it can take the Shah over there, to be busy with conspiracies, and also create a base here for conspiracies, and that our youngsters [will] just sit and watch. Again the rotten roots became active to get us to intervene and tell the youth that "you should come out of the place" where they went. The youth did something because they saw, because they upset these youngsters. A Shah that plundered this country for fifty years and looted it and gave it away, given others to take, and taken himself, and more important than this, has killed so much, has killed civilians—the 15th of *Khordad*—the way it became infamous—fifteen thousand people were murdered. On the day of the 15th of *Khordad* and from that time until now, maybe we have had one hundred thousand dead and several hundred thousand wounded, who we are everyday faced with these injured ones. Just now they told me that there are some injured here who, on the day of the *aid-e Qadir,* the injured are one segment of them. Many of them are the same ones injured during the revolution, at their hands. They said that on the day of *aid-e Qadir,* "they're having a meeting, you should come, too." Of course I will also go there. They expect that a person who, for fifty years, has done that to this nation, and now the US, with a silly excuse, has taken him and is safeguarding him, and has provided his comfort, and in the name of being sick, or in reality being sick—it makes no difference—has taken him over there and is keeping him, and our youth that protested there, they dispersed them or jailed them. In these two or three days that on that Statue of Liberty—which is a bald-faced lie in the US, "liberty"—our young people went there and chained themselves there and placed a banner there that you must return the Shah. The police went and dispersed them and apprehended several of them. They expect to take our firstrate criminal and keep him there and support him, and also create a center of conspiracy here, and create a center for distributing things that are conspiracy, I don't know, do all the things they want to do, and our nation, and our youth, and our young people from the university, and our devout young people sit and watch so that the blood of this one hundred thousand people, approximately—more or less —is wasted, in order to show respect for Mr. Carter and others like him. There must be no conspiracies. But of course if there were no conspiracies, if these sabotages did not exist, if that corrupt act didn't exist, all the people are free to be present here. But when there is a conspiracy at play, when those kinds of corrupt acts take place, it upsets our youth. Young people expect that in this world where their country—for which they have made so much effort—is in their own hands. When they see a conspiracy where they want to return to the previous situation and again all their things are lost to the wind, they cannot sit still. There must not be an expectation that they sit still and watch. And they plundered, now carry out their conspiracies, and this conspiracy grows and whatnot. Our young people must destroy these conspiracies with all their focus and with strength.

[Underground and hidden conspiracies]

Today is not a day for us to sit and watch. Today, the situation is a little deeper, a little worse, than the time when Mohammad Reza was there. At that time, it was clear that this traitor was standing up against the nation. And the nation knew him and was standing up against him. Today, there are underground betrayals. Specifically, underground betrayals are being fomented in the very embassies that exist, the most important and the majority of which belong to the Great Satan, which is the US. And you cannot sit still and they carry out their conspiracy. One day we realize that a country was destroyed, and with irrelevant talk like 'democracy' and the like, deceives us that the country is a democracy, and anybody has the right to stay here; has the right to foment a conspiracy. This irrelevant talk has to be set aside. And our nation, just as it has happened up to now, must continue the same way from now on and cut off the hands of these people. And if these people don't get it, and don't return the Shah who has taken our treasures and placed large sums in banks—that we may be aware of some of them—has placed them in banks, and it all belongs to the nation, unless they return him, and if they don't return him, we will deal with them in a different way. We will deal with Britain in a different way, as well. They shouldn't imagine that we are just sitting still and listening and they can do whatever they damn please. No, it's not like this. The issue is, again, the revolution. A larger revolution than the first one will take place. They must sit in their place and return this traitor. And that other traitor; the traitor Bakhtiar, they must return him. Not that they take that traitor Bakhtiar there and he can sit down and foment a conspiracy and gather people around himself and—I submit to you—write a newspaper and create information, and the British government to arrest and incarcerate our young people for protesting against the Shah or against Bakhtiar. If they don't let go of them and deliver these criminals, or at least expel them from their countries, we have another duty and will act on that duty.

[Not showing weakness in front of conspiracies]

We must go forward with power. If we show weakness, if they sense that we have become weak, if these diminutions that our unfair writers make of our nation, if they feel that these writings have affected us, if they feel this, they will be emboldened and will attack. They will do worse things. Don't feel weakness in yourselves. The more these writers write that "Nothing's happened and this country is in the same place as before," and, like it's written in a piece that I saw the day before yesterday, that "in the previous regime, political activists were jailed, were imprisoned, and now too political activists are imprisoned, this has not changed with them, in the previous regime, there was suffocation and the like, now is the same way." Well, this is to weaken our spirits. Now we will take this under consideration.

[The difference between prisoners during the monarchy and the Islamic Republic]

In the previous regime, some people were imprisoned. Some people were captive. Now, too, some people are imprisoned. No doubt. But who are they? In the previous regime, who was imprisoned, and in the current regime, who are imprisoned? Which groups were executed in the previous regime? Let's look at who was executed in the previous regime and who is executed in the current regime? They don't look at that. They just say all this and think that our youth will be tricked by these words. In the previous regime, the ones they killed, [were] the best of our young people, committed, religious, because they said don't violate, they said don't ruin our country. They were Islamic scholars. This Mr. Montazeri was in jail for ages. That late Mr. Taleghani was in jail, and many like them. The ones who were executed, who were they? The late Sa'eidi was executed, and people like him. These same clerics that they took from around these people and sometimes, they were in jail. This, Mr. Lahouti who is now in the *Sepah*, he was imprisoned for a long time. And what calamities has this man witnessed, and what insults he has endured. In exile, scholars from this *howzeh*, the learned men of this *howzeh*, the scientists of this *howzeh*, were in exile. Here, there, they took them and exiled them. Those who were jailed back then, were these kinds of people. And the ones who were executed were these kinds of people. And the ones exiled were these kinds of people. Now let's look at this side of the story, that there is no difference between now and then. Has been executed: Hoveyda, Nasiri. They are tearing their hearts out for him. These who are writing that there has been no change; these are the same people who in the US, they speak of that why? Why? Why? And those unjust advocates of human rights are calling out, why is he executed? Those same people who when he is writing "why are there executions in Iran?" do not write about many places where there are genocides by this corrupt US, and they don't say a word about that. But here, that they executed Hovayda, or executed Nasiri, or these corrupt individuals, they are making a lot of noise. And the ones here who are of their kind, they write that there is no difference; now there are executions, back then there were executions, too. Who are the ones imprisoned? Who were they back then? Do you find one imprisoned individual today who is a decent person and is in prison? Do you find a person who is a religious person, a nationalistic person, a person? Back then when they were imprisoned, all the nationalists were imprisoned. And all, I submit to you, like that. And now, who is imprisoned? Those who have committed many crimes and all those crimes, these are in prison. Now see the situation of the imprisonment of these criminals, with the situation of presents back then with those criminals, with these devout people. The situation of then was such that you have to hear from the people who were in prison how things were. These things, as much as we have information, the most important of which is Tehran, the people who are there, and we have constantly instructed, will never abuse anyone. Prison terms are not the kinds that create dissatisfaction. It's prison, but these unfair [writers] write that the prisons are worse than that time, at that place, in those prisons. In one of those prisons, they sawed off the leg of one of our scholars—as has been said. Now these prisons are worse than those? These are all the same devils that Carter has gathered around himself by a great shout, because, in the same way that that Great Satan is scared of the Quran and Islam, now they, too, are afraid of this movement, which is an Islamic movement. And, following that Great Satan, are busy with treachery to weaken the spirit of our people. Our nation, our valorous youth, must go forward with complete strength and not fear these conspiracies. These are not humans that humans should be afraid of.

[Hands behind the veil in Kurdistan unrest]

And these disturbances that sometimes these same devils cause, and the followers of these depraved causes, resolving these, too, is not a problem. They imagine that the situation of Kurdistan is a situation that cannot be resolved. The situation in Kurdistan, if they were not mixed with the Kurdish people, and were not amongst the young and the women and children, we don't want even one innocent person to get killed, if they weren't there, then it would be nothing to mow them down and annihilate them. But unfortunately, it's like this, right now. You have heard, for sure, that these unfair [people] use women and children as shields, and by using them as shields, killed our young people. And those brave young men, so as not to kill the innocent, did not resist. Well, if they were not mixed with them, it would be no effort to destroy them. They are not much of a force. They are a bunch of hoodlums. These hoodlums, we were faced with them in the past, too. These are a bunch of hooligans that are thieves. Sometimes they kidnap, or kill people, too. They are not a force now against the force of the government, or against the force of the nation. We, whenever we want, all the people may go up to Kurdistan and destroy them, but we want the situation to be fixed in peace. These unfair [people] won't let us. Now a group has gone to resolve the problem in peace, to see "what do you want?" The things that they want, we gave to them. Will give. But they want America. They, if you ask them directly, what they want in their hearts, the Democrat Party [*Hezb-e democrat*] will say that we "want the interests of the masses." Meaning, they express a tendency for the Left, but all of them are rightwing, the dishonest right.

Be strong brothers, sisters, be strong with strength. Islam is behind you. The elevated and sublime God is behind you. Go forth with power and strength and build this country yourselves. The country must be build by your hands. May God bless you all.

Document Analysis

Khomeini begins his speech with a traditional Islamic invocation, known as the Basmala, which calls on the name of God. He relates a story from the Qur'an about the Prophet Mohammed, who challenged evil so much that Satan summoned his demons for assistance. He draws a parallel to Iran's challenge to the United States: the Iranian revolution has caused the United States, which he directly calls "the Great Satan," to attempt to gather support among "devils" both inside and outside of Iran. In this way he immediately positions the United States and Iran as mortal enemies grounded in religious conflict.

Khomeini then gives a brief overview of the history of Western involvement in Iran. He describes the last two shahs as "evil men" and pawns of the United States and Britain, who have only their own interests at heart. He describes the "calamities bestowed on this country" by the pro-Western shahs, focusing on the literal and symbolic "lifting of the veil," or traditional Islamic dress for women, as the destruction of moral and cultural values. Khomeini notes that there were some Iranians who cooperated with the shahs and now sympathize with the United States. He claims that these forces are still at work, and they must be found and destroyed.

Khomeini warns his audience not to listen to rumors and Western propaganda, particularly suggestions that the ayatollah's supporters are committing crimes or that the revolution has simply replaced the monarchy with religious authority. These are only the murmurs of a desperate United States, he claims, and proof that the Great Satan is worried. He asserts that the fact that he is able to make this speech, which surely would not have been allowed by the shah, is evidence that the revolution is succeeding in throwing off Western control and providing freedom.

The ayatollah then addresses the seizure of the US Embassy—which he calls a "center of spying and conspiracy"—by revolutionaries as a noble act by young people who could not sit idly by and watch the shah escape punishment and continue to conspire with the United States against the Iranian people. Khomeini announces that he will not intervene to release the hostages or make the revolutionaries leave the embassy. The United States is defending a murderer, he argues, who for fifty years has executed his own countrymen. Western powers must return the shah and other figures from the pro-Western Iranian government for trial. Khomeini also warns that the enemies of the state are harder to identify but even more dangerous now that they are not in power and are trying to bring down the righteous government through spying and intrigue disseminated through embassies.

Khomeini also addresses the issue of the mass imprisonments and executions in Iran, drawing a distinction between those before and after the revolution. He argues that good people, especially religious leaders and scholars, were imprisoned and executed by the shah, but that the revolutionaries have only imprisoned and executed corrupt thieves and spies. He claims that Western onlookers and human rights activists criticizing his regime are hypocritical both for ignoring this difference and for failing to condemn atrocities committed by the United States.

He closes his speech with a description of the Kurdish rebellion, which he claims is incited by Western disruption. Khomeini says the rebellion is little threat and could be put down easily, except they use women and children as shields. The speech ends, as it began, with an Islamic invocation and the assurance that "Islam is behind you."

Essential Themes

The Iran hostage crisis and Khomeini's hostile rhetoric led to great tension between Iran and the United States and consequences on both sides, including American economic sanctions against Iran and the failure of US President Jimmy Carter's reelection bid when he was unable to resolve the hostage situation. Of the sixty-six hostages taken, thirteen were quickly released and another was freed later. The remaining fifty-two hostages were held for 444 days and released soon after President Carter left office in 1981. Khomeini continued to lead an anti-Western theocracy and refer to the United States as Iran's greatest enemy, the Great Satan. He was also hostile to the world's other superpower, the Soviet Union, calling it the Lesser Satan, while Israel was termed the Little

Satan. The ayatollah further encouraged militant Islamic revolution in neighboring countries, and Iran was at war with Iraq for eight years.

Khomeini dismantled many of the economic drivers that had supported Iran's prosperity under the shah. Trade with the West was virtually eliminated and oil production plummeted. During the war with Iraq, Khomeini liquidated much of the nation's gold reserves and inflation skyrocketed. Despite bread lines and war, Khomeini was the undisputed leader of Iran for the remainder of his life, and he embodied the principal of rule by those who carried out Islamic law. The term "Great Satan" would become a lasting symbol of Islamic resistance to Western power.

—*Bethany Groff Dorau, MA*

Bibliography and Additional Reading

Axworthy, Michael. *Revolutionary Iran: A History of the Islamic Republic.* New York: Oxford UP, 2016.

Kinzer, Stephen. *All the Shah's Men: An American Coup and the Roots of Middle East Terror.* Hoboken, NJ: Wiley, 2003.

Lesch, David W. *1979: The Year That Shaped the Modern Middle East.* Boulder, CO: Westview, 2001.

Diary Excerpts of an American Hostage in Iran

Dates: November 4, 12, 14, 1979; February 6, 22, 1980
Author: Robert C. Ode
Genre: diary

Summary Overview

On November 4, 1979, militant Muslim Iranian students seized the US Embassy compound in Tehran and took sixty-three Americans hostage. Images of American embassy personnel being paraded blindfolded, and angry crowds burning American flags, galvanized rage at Iran and passionate support for the hostages in the United States. American news programs broadcast daily the number of days the hostages were held, and American citizens tied yellow ribbons around trees and poles in support of the hostages. The hostages' captivity lasted 444 days. The national humiliation at the hands of militant Islamic students, combined with the Soviet invasion of Afghanistan in December 1979, seemed to underscore declining American power since its defeat in Vietnam and set the stage for resurgent patriotism and a more aggressive US foreign policy during the 1980s.

Defining Moment

In 1953, the reformist Iranian Prime Minister Mohammed Mossadegh nationalized the Anglo-Iranian Oil Company. The Central Intelligence Agency (CIA) and British intelligence ousted Mossadegh and installed the Shah of Iran, Mohammed Reza Pahlavi, as the political head of state. For the next twenty-five years, the shah imposed control over Iran through his brutal secret police, the Savak.

Iran became a pillar of US power in the Middle East. The shah used Iran's oil wealth to build the region's most powerful military with US weaponry. Although President Jimmy Carter proclaimed Iran "an island of stability," the veneer of calm belied deep discontent across Iranian society. The CIA assured Carter that the shah was in no danger of falling, even as anti-shah protests grew larger in 1977 and 1978.

The protests were led by a diverse coalition of secular nationalists, leftists, and conservative Shiite clerics, but soon coalesced behind the leadership of the Ayatollah Ruhollah Khomeini, who guided the movement from exile in Paris.

In January 1979 the shah fled Iran for Egypt before settling in Panama and later returning to Egypt. In February, Khomeini made a triumphant return to Iran greeted by delirious crowds. Iran's revolutionary government was led by secular nationalists, and the nation was swept by revolutionary ferment as different factions contended for influence. Increasingly, Khomeini's power grew as he guided events from his residence in the holy city of Qom.

In February leftists seized the US Embassy but were cleared out by the government. As the embassy became a focal point for daily anti-American protests, the Carter administration reduced the number of employees at the 27-acre compound from over 1,000 to under 100.

The Embassy seizure on November 4 was sparked by President Carter's decision to admit the shah to New York City for cancer treatment. Hundreds of militants calling themselves Muslim Students Following the Imam's [Khomeini's] Line, stormed the Embassy, planning to hold the Americans hostage for a week while they broadcasted their grievances with the United States and demanded the return of the shah to stand trial. Soon, however, their occupation became enmeshed in Iran's internal power struggles, and Khomeini used the hostage taking to discredit his secular rivals and advance his own goal of a theocratic Iran.

The Americans scrambled to hold off the militants until they could destroy as many top secret documents as possible. (The students painstakingly taped together volumes of shredded documents.) Six embassy personnel were able to slip away and after being secretly sheltered in the Canadian Embassy were later snuck safely out of the country. US Charge d'affaires Bruce Laingen and two others were at Iran's Foreign Ministry and taken hostage and held there. Twelve African American and women hostages were soon released.

The students declared the Embassy a "Den of Spies" and interrogated the hostages to determine which were with the CIA and what conspiracies the United States was hatching. No conspiracy was discovered, and as time went on the students used information they unearthed to discredit rivals of Khomeini for having met with the Americans.

Carter came under countervailing pressure from two advisors. National Security Advisor Zbigniew Brzezinski urged him to prioritize America's reputation abroad; he counseled the mining of ports, the imposition of a naval blockade, and the launching of bombing raids. Secretary of State Cyrus Vance, on the other hand, advised patience and the prioritizing of the hostages' lives. (Vance later resigned to protest Carter's decision to authorize an ill-fated rescue mission). Carter generally followed Vance's approach. He met early with the hostages' families, some of whom became media celebrities over the ensuing months.

During the initial seizure, several Americans were filmed blindfolded and jeered at by an angry crowd. As their captivity lengthened, hostages would be seen only sporadically, such as when American leftist sympathizers with Iranian grievances like the Rev. William Sloane Coffin and other ministers visited and were permitted to conduct a public Christmas ceremony with some of the hostages. Other hostages were intermittently allowed to be interviewed by international media, especially if they were critical of Carter's refusal to turn over the shah.

After the failed US rescue effort, the hostages were dispersed outside of Tehran, but were returned by late summer. A few events impacted the negotiations, notably the death of the shah in July 1980 and the invasion of Iran by Saddam Hussein's Iraq two months later. When an agreement was finally reached through Swiss and Algerian intermediaries, the hostages departed just after the swearing in of Ronald Reagan as president on January 20, 1981.

Author Biography

Robert C. Ode was born on December 10, 1915, in Piano, Illinois, and grew up in Manistee, Michigan. After high school he joined the Navy and saw action in the Pacific during World War II. In 1947 he joined the Foreign Service. In 1957 he married his wife Rita, a fellow foreign service officer. Although retired at sixty, he returned to temporary duty and was called to Iran for a forty-five-day term when he was seized at the American Embassy, becoming, at sixty-five, the oldest of the hostages. Ode died in Sun City West, Arizona, on September 8, 1995.

Historical Document

Diary Excerpts of an American Hostage in Iran

Nov.4 1979: Since I wasn't sure whether we were expected to work at the Consular Section, in view of what the Charge' had told me last evening, I went to the office just the same at 7:30 as I had quite a bit of work to do anyway. When I got there, however, I found that everyone was coming to work as usual but we were not open to the general public. About 9:00 I was in my office when a young American woman, apparently the wife of an Iranian, was shown into my office as she wanted to obtain her mother-in-law's Iranian passport that had been left at the Consular Section a day or so before for a non-immigrant visa. Just as I was talking to her in an attempt to find out to whom the passport had been issued, when it was left with us, etc., we were told by the Consul General to drop everything and get up to the second floor of the Consular Section. I really didn't know what was happening but was told that a mob had managed to get into the Embassy Compound and, for our own protection, everyone had to go upstairs immediately.

I noticed that the Consul General was removing the visa plates and locking the visa stamping machines. I went upstairs with the American woman and could see a number of young men in the area between the rear of the Consular Section and the Embassy CO-OP store. We were told to sit on the floor in the outer hallway offices. A Marine Security Guard was present and was in contact with the main Embassy building (Chancery) by walkie-talkie. After an hour or so we could hear that the mob, which turned out to be student revolutionaries, were also on the walkie-talkie. The Marine Guard then advised that we were going to evacuate the Consular Section.

There were some visitors on the second floor in the Immigrant Visa Unit and the American Services Unit. I was asked to assist an elderly gentleman, either an American of Iranian origin or an Iranian citizen, I don't know, since he was almost blind and was completely terrified, and to be the first one out of the building. When we got outside he was met by a relative who took him away in his car. The students outside the Consular Section appeared to be somewhat confused at that point and the Consul General and about four other American members of the Consular Section, of which I was one, started up the street with the intention of going to his residence. When we were about I h blocks from the Consular Section we were surrounded by a group of the students, who were armed, and told to return to the Compound.

When we protested a shot was fired into the air above our heads.

It was raining moderately at the time. We were taken back to the Compound, being pushed and hurried along the way and forced to put our hands above our heads and then marched to the Embassy residence. After arriving at the residence I had my hands tied behind my back so tightly with nylon cord that circulation was cut off. I was taken upstairs and put alone in a rear bedroom and after a short time was blindfolded. After protesting strongly that the cord was too tight the cord was removed and the blindfold taken off when they tried to feed me some dates and I refused to eat anything I couldn't see. I strongly protested the violation of my diplomatic immunity, but these protests were ignored. I then was required to sit in a chair facing the bedroom wall. Then another older student came in and when I again protested the violation of my diplomatic immunity he confiscated my U.S. Mission Tehran I.D. card. My hands were again tied and I was taken to the Embassy living room on the ground floor where a number of other hostages were gathered. Some students attempted to talk with us, stating how they didn't hate Americans—only our U.S. Government, President Carter, etc. We were given sandwiches and that night I slept on the living room floor. We were not permitted to talk to our fellow hostages and from then on our hands were tied day and night and only removed while we were eating or had to go to the bathroom.

December 12 and 14 (approximately): On December 14 I was taken out doors for the first time for exercise—my 41st day of captivity! Although I had been exercising in my rooms by pacing back and forth as much as possible, being out in the fresh air for the first time made me feel almost as though I had just gotten up from a hospital bed for the first time after a long period in the hospital! I actually felt rather weak and wobbly! One of the guards asked me why I didn't jump around and exercised more vigorously, rather than just walk around in the yard, but I actually couldn't—just felt too weak! Either on December 12 or 14 I was given two letters that had arrived from Rita, as well as one from Grandma Bode! I was delighted to receive them—the first that I had heard from anyone and noted that the address was the "Iran Working Group, Wash. D.C." However, I had to return the letters to my captors after having read them, and was not allowed to retain them in my possession, even though I protested that they were personal letters from my wife and a friend. I immediately answered them and was told that I could now write as often as I wished. I had to request paper, envelopes and a ball-point pen from the guard on duty each time and had to return the pen and any unused paper as I wasn't permitted to retain them. At that moment, I was the only one in my room to receive mail. I felt badly about this as I knew that, Bruce German in particular, was very worried about his wife and children.

February 6, 1980: At 2:00 a.m. the door to our room was flung open. All four of us in our room were suddenly awakened and told to "stand-up" by masked men in camouflage fatigue uniforms, bearing machine guns and automatic rifles. Naturally, we had no idea what was happening and were terrified! When one man pointed his rifle at me and I asked him not to do so, I was told "Don't speak!" We then had to put on our trousers and shoes, were blindfolded and taken into the corridor where we had to lean against the wall in police search fashion. A rifle butt knocked my feet further apart as they apparently were too close together to suit the uniformed guards. After several minutes standing against the wall I was taken into another room, required to strip and each item of clothing inspected, including my underwear briefs which I also had to remove; pockets were emptied in my trousers, belt removed, etc. Then I was told I could dress but belt was not returned at that time; was again blindfolded and returned to my room. The room was a shambles—thoroughly ransacked, sheet and blankets torn off the bed, mattress askew, etc. All personal possessions had been examined, my medical ointment for my spine taken, plus my safety razor, etc. Fortunately, my letters from home and friends were still there. My belt was then returned. Others in my room had family photos taken—Bany Rosen never had his belt returned: everything was in chaos. One of the guards who took me to the bathroom afterward said that the men were from a special security force and that they were "very angry"! Our drinking glasses and porcelain dishes were removed and plastic dishes were substituted. We never did learn the reason for the "Gestapo" type raid. I had a delayed reaction from this frightening experience as about an hour after I had finally fallen asleep again I woke up with my heart pounding so heard I thought it was going to leap out of my chest! [note: Ode had a heart murmur.]

April 22. 1980: Another noisy demonstration today. Lasted about 3 to 4 hours. This time was not directly in front of the Embassy but close enough so that we had a diet of the usual amplified chants of "Allah—is greater"; "Khomeini—is great", etc. Then in the afternoon Hamid I, our supervisor, dropped in for no apparent reason and started in on the usual harangue. Seems he must have listened to a Press Conference given by President Carter and began to tell us, in a rambling, almost incoherent manner, about how Carter had lied about Iran; how the press asked him many questions about the hostages that he refused to answer... said "We are working on it", etc.; how Carter must return the Shah; tried to impress on us how good the students were to the hostages, etc., etc. which I told him was a lot of B.S. and reminded him about our treatment, especially during the first four months. The usual pointless discussion!

Document Themes and Analysis

The hostages were moved to different buildings and rooms on the Embassy grounds. Most were held in the Chancery building, many in the basement of a warehouse the hostages called "the Mushroom," since fungi grew in the dank environment and others in the ambassador's residence. The hostages were forbidden to speak to each other, were usually blindfolded with hands tied, were fed three times a day, and could use the toilet as needed. Those held in basements could go months without seeing sunlight.

Each found their own unique way to survive the ordeal, which consisted of long periods of boredom punctuated by moments of terror. Some were passive, others looked for opportunities to push back, and at least one collaborated with the hostage takers. These excerpts from the diary of Robert Ode, which he maintained throughout his captivity, highlight many of the various types of experiences the hostages endured.

Ode's entry for November 4 captures the confusion when a routine day of processing visas turned chaotic as the students invaded the Embassy grounds. He notes that even many of the "students outside... appeared to be somewhat confused..." Like other Embassy personnel, Ode "protested the violation of my diplomatic immunity." The student radicals saw themselves as defenders of the oppressed and exemplars of Islamic virtue and portrayed themselves in idealistic terms. A few sought to justify their action to Ode: "Some students attempted to talk to us, stating they didn't hate Americans—only our U.S. government, President Carter, etc."

The hostage takers sometimes allowed the hostages to write and receive letters, although this was erratic, and many letters were never sent or received. In his entry for December 12 and 14, Ode describes his joy at receiving letters from his wife and "Grandma Bode." On rare occasions hostages would be allowed to walk outside or to watch movies. But for the most part they were left to entertain themselves by reading or exercising in place in their small, designated areas. Ode describes his exhilaration at being allowed outdoors for the first time in forty-one days.

Terror could erupt as it did on February 6 when masked guards stormed the hostages' rooms and herded them out and spread-eagled them along a wall. Other hostages described this as a mock execution in which they were certain they were about to die by firing squad. In fact, as Ode notes, when they returned to their rooms they found the spaces ransacked. The mock execution turned out to be a ruse to get all the hostages outside in order to search their premises (for what is not known).

Another daily part of the hostages' lives was the anti-American street protests that occurred outside the Embassy. The protests ebbed and flowed in size and intensity. They could become part of the daily tedium, or, on some occasions, their ferocity could become sources of dread. The images of these angry crowds burning US flags and chanting anti-American slogans became daily fare on American television and fueled Americans' rage at Iran. Ode describes these demonstrations, writing, "Another demonstration today. Lasted 3 to 4 hours. This time was not directly in front of the Embassy, but close enough so that we had a diet of the usual amplified chants of 'Allah—is greater'; 'Khomeini is great,'" etc.

—*Robert Surbrug, PhD*

Bibliography and Additional Reading

Bowden, Mark. *Guests of the Ayatollah: the Iran Hostage Crisis: The First Battle in America's War with Militant Islam*. New York: Grove Press, 2006.

Eizenstat, Stuart E. *President Carter: The White House Years*. New York: St. Martin's Press, 2018.

Wells, Tim. *444 Days: The Hostages Remember*. New York: Harcourt, 1985.

The Revolt against Communism in Europe

As early as 1946, in the aftermath of World War II, Winston Churchill warned of an "Iron Curtain" descending in Central and Eastern Europe as the Soviet Union exerted its control in the region. Member states were expected to follow the party line (i.e., the policies set by the Communist Party of the Soviet Union, based in Moscow). Deviations were not abided, although Yugoslavia under Josip Tito managed to forge something of a separate path. Both Hungary in 1956 and Czechoslovakia in 1968 sought to go the same route, with revolts against hardline governments erupting in each; but the Communist authorities suppressed these uprisings using violent means. Nevertheless, in most European countries under Communist control three emerged thriving underground movements; they circulated antigovernment literature, sought contacts with the West, and recruited new members—often at the risk of imprisonment or death. Charter 77 in Czechoslovakia was one such movement, but there were others as well.

In Poland, for example, although there was a diffuse anticommunist network operating since the 1960s, it turned out to be the Polish trade union Solidarity, founded in 1980, that had the most impact. After a protest against the Polish Communist regime in Gdansk in 1981, the head of state, General Wojciech Jaruzelski, declared martial law and arrested the thirty-eight regional delegates of Solidarity. Although this was an alarming development, the event is pointed to by some historians as the start of the decline and breakup of the Communist bloc, as regimes throughout the Soviet sphere became increasingly unpopular and, ultimately, unsustainable. Moscow struggled to maintain an impression of unfazed authority after the Chernobyl nuclear disaster in 1986, but by 1989 popular demands for reform led to the of the opening of the Berlin Wall and the subsequent collapse of communist dominance throughout Europe and other Soviet-controlled areas in Central Asia.

Resolution of Hungarian Student Protestors

Date: October 22, 1956
Genre: political tract

Summary Overview

With the death of Soviet leader Joseph Stalin in 1953, an era of uncertainty made itself known, if only briefly. It was marked by conflict and internal struggles within the Communist governments of the Soviet Union and its satellite states in Eastern Europe. By 1956, Nikita Khrushchev established his leadership in the Soviet Union and denounced Stalin's brutal, totalitarian regime in the so-called Secret Speech. Shortly after this speech was leaked, protesters in Poland and Hungary felt that the time was right to demand political and economic reforms from their Soviet-backed governments. Hungarian journalists and students called for the removal of hard-line Communist leader Mátyás Rákosi, and he resigned in July. His replacement, Ernõ Gerõ, allowed the body of László Rajk, a Communist official who had been executed in 1949, to be reinterred in Budapest in early October. His burial quickly became a mass protest against Soviet repression in Hungary, and university students revived the Union of Hungarian University and Academy Students (abbreviated MEFESZ in Hungarian), which had been banned by the government. On October 22, student union members at the Technical University of Budapest drew up a list of sixteen demands, including the withdrawal of Soviet troops, and planned a protest for the following day. For the next twelve days, their movement gained widespread popular support, eventually overthrowing the national government, but was eventually crushed by Soviet troops.

Defining Moment

Hungary was a key ally of Nazi Germany during World War II, lured by the promise of the return of territory lost in World War I. In March 1944, the German army occupied Hungary, replacing its regent with a fascist dictator. After a bloody siege, the Soviet army captured Budapest on February 13, 1945, and began an occupation that would last for decades. After the war, harsh reparation payments were imposed on Hungary by the Soviet Union and the currency collapsed. Hungarian Communists were sent back from exile in the Soviet Union to play key roles in the government. Many, like Rákosi, had spent years away from their compatriots, and had deep loyalties to the Soviet totalitarian leader, Joseph Stalin.

Despite Soviet occupation and strong-arm diplomacy bent on crushing opposition to the chosen candidates of the Hungarian Communist Party, a true multiparty democracy briefly emerged in Hungary after the war. By May of 1949, however, the Soviet-backed Communist Party had taken control of

Mátyás Rákosi. Photo by BERKÓ PÁL, via Wikimedia Commons.

the government through threats and coercion. In August, the National Assembly approved a new constitution based on the Soviet model, renaming the country the People's Republic of Hungary, with Mátyás Rákosi as its leader. The nation was firmly under the control of the Soviet Union. Rákosi arrested and imprisoned anyone he perceived as a threat, including Foreign Secretary László Rajk. Rajk made a confession under torture and was executed on October 15, 1949.

Rákosi closely followed Stalin's example, purging thousands of members of the Communist faithful, fearing any challenge to his authority. He instigated sweeping social and economic reforms as well, expanding the educational system to promote Communist ideology, weakening the church, and collectivizing farms. He encouraged the development of unprofitable heavy industry to support the Soviet Union, and allowed Hungary's uranium resources to be stripped. The economy sank, and the standard of living fell precipitously. He gave the secret police wide latitude to arrest, detain, and torture Hungarian citizens. Rákosi was powerful but increasingly unpopular, and pockets of resistance continued in Hungary, despite harsh reprisals. After Stalin's death in 1953, he was briefly replaced as prime minister by reformer Imre Nagy. Nagy liberalized Hungarian media, began discussions on how the economy could be improved, and even considered withdrawing Hungary from the Warsaw Pact, a mutual defense treaty made up of the Soviet Union and its satellite states in Eastern Europe. Nagy's tenure was short-lived, however, and he was replaced by a Rákosi supporter in 1955. In February 1956, Nikita Khrushchev's "Secret Speech," which was actually widely circulated, denounced Stalin and his followers. By July, Rákosi, who was widely hated, had come to be seen as a liability by the Soviet Union and was replaced as general secretary of the Communist Party—a position he had held since 1945—by Ernõ Gerõ. In October, the party's Central Committee declared that Rajk had been falsely accused and wrongly executed, and Imre Nagy was al-

Nikita Khrushchev. Photo by Bundesarchiv/ Heinz Junge, via Wikimedia Commons.

lowed to assume party membership, though not leadership. Also in October, university students began reforming student unions, which had been banned. On October 22, a group of students at Budapest Technical University compiled a list of sixteen demands, including the reinstatement of Nagy as prime minister.

Document Information

The sixteen demands made by the students of the Budapest Technical University were released on October 22, 1956, with a call for a protest the following day. The October 23 action is considered the start of the Hungarian Revolution of 1956.

Historical Document

Students of Budapest!

The following resolution was born on 22 October 1956, at the dawn of a new period in Hungarian history, in the Hall of the Building Industry Technological University as a result of the spontaneous movement of several thousand of the Hungarian youth who love their Fatherland:

1. We demand the immediate withdrawal of all Soviet troops in accordance with the provisions of the Peace Treaty.

2. We demand the election of new leaders in the Hungarian Workers' Party on the low, medium and high levels by secret ballot from the ranks upwards. These leaders should convene the Party Congress within the shortest possible time and should elect a new central body of leaders.

3. The Government should be reconstituted under the leadership of Comrade Imre Nagy; all criminal leaders of the Stalinist Rákosi era should be relieved of their posts at once.

4. We demand a public trial in the criminal case of Mihaly Farkas and his accomplices. Matyas Rakosi, who is primarily responsible for all the crimes of the recent past and for the ruin of this country, should be brought home and brought before a People's Court of Judgment.

5. We demand general elections in this country, with universal suffrage, secret ballot and the participation of several Parties for the purpose of electing a new National Assembly. We demand that the workers should have the right to strike.

6. We demand a re-examination and re-adjustment of Hungarian - Soviet and Hungarian - Yugoslav political, economic and intellectual relations on the basis of complete political and economic equality and of non-intervention in each other's internal affairs.

7. We demand the re-organization of the entire economic life of Hungary, with the assistance of specialists. Our whole economic system based on planned economy should be re-examined with an eye to Hungarian conditions and to the vital interests of the Hungarian people.

8. Our foreign trade agreements and the real figures in respect of reparations that can never be paid should be made public. We demand frank and sincere

information concerning the country's uranium deposits, their exploitation and the Russian concession. We demand that Hungary should have the right to sell the uranium ore freely at world market prices in exchange for hard currency.

9. We demand the complete revision of norms in industry and an urgent and radical adjustment of wages to meet the demands of workers and intellectuals. We demand that minimum living wages for workers should be fixed.

10. We demand that the delivery system should be placed on a new basis and that produce should be used rationally. We demand equal treatment of peasants farming individually.

11. We demand the re-examination of all political and economic trials by independent courts and the release and rehabilitation of innocent persons. We demand the immediate repatriation of prisoners of war and of civilians deported to the Soviet Union, including prisoners who have been condemned beyond the frontiers of Hungary.

12. We demand complete freedom of opinion and expression, freedom of the Press and a free Radio, as well as a new daily newspaper of large circulation for the MEFESZ [League of Hungarian University and College Student Associations] organization. We demand that the existing 'screening material' should be made public and destroyed.

13. We demand that the Stalin statue, the symbol of Stalinist tyranny and political oppression should be removed as quickly as possible and that a memorial worthy of the freedom fighters and martyrs of 1848-49 should be erected on its site.

14. In place of the existing coat of arms, which is foreign to the Hungarian people, we wish the re-introduction of the old Hungarian Kossuth arms. We demand for the Hungarian Army new uniforms worthy of our national traditions. We demand that 15 March should he a national holiday and a non-working day and that 6 October should be a day of national mourning and a school holiday.

15. The youth of the Technological University of Budapest unanimously express their complete solidarity with the Polish and Warsaw workers and youth in connection with the Polish national independence movement.

16. The students of the Building Industry Technological University will organize local units of MEFESZ as quickly as possible, and have resolved to convene a Youth Parliament in Budapest for the 27th of this month (Saturday) at which the entire youth of this country will be represented by their delegates. The students of the Technological University and of the various other Univer-

sities will gather in the Gorkij Fasor before the Writers' Union Headquarters tomorrow, the 23rd of this month, at 2.30 p.m., whence they will proceed to the Palffy Ter (Bem Ter) to the Bem statue, on which they will lay wreaths in sign of their sympathy with the Polish freedom movement. The workers of the factories are invited to join in this procession.

Document Analysis

The statement of demands of the Hungarian students begins with a telling statement of the significance they ascribe to their actions. They are at "the dawn of a new period in Hungarian history," and their demands are "a result of the spontaneous movement of several thousand of the Hungarian youth who love their Fatherland."

First and foremost, the students demand the end of the postwar Soviet military occupation. They also demand that new elections by secret ballot be held at all levels of the Communist Party, and that new open elections be held for the National Assembly as well. They demand that Nagy return to lead the government and that Rákosi, who is "primarily responsible for all the crimes of the recent past and for the ruin of this country," and who had left for the Soviet Union, be returned to Hungary to stand trial.

Concerned with the economic crisis in Hungary, the student demands deal with the economy in some detail. The details of postwar reparations payments, as well as exclusive uranium sales to the Soviets, are to be revisited, and political and economic ties between Hungary, the Soviet Union, and Yugoslavia to be made more equitable and based on nonintervention. The collectivization of agriculture had caused particular hardship for the Hungarian people, so the students demand "equality of treatment for individual farms," as well as a living wage for industrial workers, and the right of workers to organize and strike. The entire planned economy of Hungary is to be reexamined and adjusted.

Freedom of speech and a removal of hated symbols of oppression make up the final section of the student's demands. They call for the formerly banned student union, MEFESZ, to have its own newspaper, and for guarantees of freedom of the press. The statue of Stalin that dominated the central city park of Budapest is to be taken down "as quickly as possible." National symbols and emblems are to be returned to those that had meaning to Hungarians. March 15, the day that the Hungarian Revolution of 1848 had begun a century before, and October 6, the day that Rejk was reburied, were to be nationally recognized holidays. The students also expressed solidarity with the

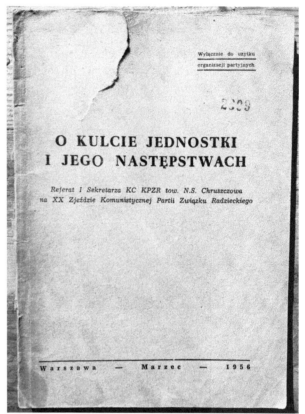

First edition of Krushchev's "Secret Speech." Photo by Wikiwlh, via Wikimedia Commons.

Polish people, who were struggling to regain greater control over their national affairs as well. A march of students and workers in Budapest is announced for the following day, and a national Youth Parliament is proposed to convene in Budapest on October 27. This document is, in short, a demand for reform in nearly every aspect of Hungarian cultural, social, and political life.

Essential Themes

The students' demands for reform were the spark that set off the Hungarian Revolution of 1956. They were read to a gathering crowd on the following afternoon, and then the crowd made its way to the Parliament buildings, growing as it marched. The demonstrators also pulled down the hated statue of Stalin and gathered at the headquarters of the national radio station to air their demands. During skirmishes with police

Imre Nagy, 1945. Photo by Jánosi Katalin, via Wikimedia Commons.

outside the Radio Budapest building, tear gas was thrown from the building, and police shot into the crowd. Hungarian soldiers sent to support the police switched sides instead, joining the protesters. The following day, as Soviet tanks rolled into Budapest, Nagy was returned to power as prime minister, and protests continued, with sporadic street fighting between protestors, police, and Soviet forces. Nagy quickly agreed to many of the demands of the protesters, calling for independence from the Soviet Union, the withdrawal of troops, free elections, freedom of the press, and the end of Hungary's involvement with the Warsaw Pact. There was a brief lull in the fighting, but the Soviet Union was not willing to release control over Hungary, and on the night of November 3, Soviet tanks and troops surrounded Budapest. Despite significant resistance, and even a late-night petition to the United Nations Security Council by the protesters, the following day, Soviet tanks entered the city and crushed the revolution. Thousands of Hungarians were killed and many more fled Soviet reprisals. Nagy was arrested on November 22 in Yugoslavia and executed on June 16, 1958. Though the Soviet stranglehold on Hungary was stronger than ever, the uprising both exposed weaknesses in the Soviet bloc in Eastern Europe and encouraged Khrushchev to consider economic and social reforms.

—*Bethany Groff Dorau, MA*

Bibliography and Additional Reading

Fowkes, Ben. *Eastern Europe 1945–1969: From Stalinism to Stagnation*. Harlow: Longman, 2000.

Jones, Christopher D. *Soviet Influence in Eastern Europe: Political Autonomy and the Warsaw Pact*. Brooklyn: Praeger, 1981.

Lendvai, Paul. *One Day That Shook the Communist World: The 1956 Hungarian Uprising and Its Legacy*. Princeton: Princeton UP, 2008.

Sebestyen, Victor. *Twelve Days: The Story of the 1956 Hungarian Revolution*. New York: Pantheon, 2006.

■ The "Two Thousand Words" Manifesto

Date: July 27, 1968
Author: Ludvík Vaculík
Country: Czechoslovakia
Genre: essay; political tract

Summary Overview

In this 1968 manifesto, Czech writer Ludvík Vaculík denounces the repressive rule of the Communist Party of Czechoslovakia and calls for reform. He describes the situation in Czechoslovakia in terms of the failure of the Communist leadership, though without challenging Communism itself or the Czechoslovak government's dependency on the Soviet Union. He sees the rule of the Communist Party as authoritarian and corrupting to Czech society. However, he also sees reform-minded Communists as potential allies. Vaculík calls for popular activism. He also recognizes the possibility of foreign (meaning Soviet) intervention to suppress the reform movement, saying that the people will fight for a government that represents them.

Defining Moment

In the aftermath of World War II, the Soviet Union occupied many Eastern European countries, including Czechoslovakia, and placed Communist governments in power there. (Not all Eastern European Communist governments were Soviet allies; Yugoslavia and later Albania were exceptions.) Like the Soviet Union itself, Eastern European Communist governments operated on the Leninist model of the one-party state, in which every aspect of state power was controlled by the Communist Party. Secret police forces modeled on the Soviet KGB were essential instruments of rule, and Soviet troops continued to maintain bases in many countries. The Eastern European countries controlled by the Soviet Union were bound in an economic agreement, the Council for Mutual Economic Assistance (COMECON), founded in 1949, and a military alliance, the Warsaw Pact, founded in 1955.

Eastern European Communist governments faced a series of challenges over the following decades, particularly after Soviet leader Nikita Khrushchev's "de-Stalinization" speech in 1956. At first, these challenges were usually precipitated by divisions within the ruling Communist parties. Czechoslovakia's "Prague Spring" in 1968 was one of the most dramatic and influential challenges to Communism in the period of Communist domination of Eastern Europe. Like the earlier Hungarian uprising

Author Ludvík Vaculík, 2010. Photo by Mercy, via Wikimedia Commons.

of 1956, it began with dissension within the Communist Party itself. In January 1968, the reformist Communist Alexander Dubèek took over leadership of Czechoslovakia from the more authoritarian Antonín Novotný. Dubèek began some cautious steps toward liberalization, including the limited legitimization of political activity outside the Communist Party and the end of censorship. Dubèek's reforms encouraged Czechoslovaks to press for more changes, possibly even democratization, but it also caused concern among Communist hard-liners in and out of Czechoslovakia, and particularly in the Soviet regime of Leonid Brezhnev.

Author Biography

Ludvík Vaculík was a member of the Czechslovak Communist Party and the Writers Union, the official organization of Czechoslovak writers. In July 1967, he gave a speech at the Writers Union Congress attacking the leadership of the party and the concept of the party's leading role in society, a fundamental tenet of orthodox, Soviet-style Communism. The next year, with the encouragement of reform-minded members of the Czechoslovak Academy of Sciences, and cosigned by dozens of other writers and intellectuals, Vaculík published this essay, under the full title "The Two Thousand Words That Belong to Workers, Farmers, Officials, Scientists, Artists, and Everybody." It initially appeared in three Czech newspapers and one literary weekly, in June 1968, a day after the abolition of censorship.

Following the end of the Prague Spring and the reestablishment of an authoritarian Communist regime, Vaculík, along with many other dissidents, was expelled from the Communist Party and faced harsh censorship and repression. He became active in the circulation of illegal manuscripts known as *samizdat*, and was one of the signatories of the 1977 democratic manifesto Charter 77. He survived to see the fall of Communist rule in Czechoslovakia in 1989, the dissolution of the country into the Czech Republic and Slovakia, and died in 2015.

HISTORICAL DOCUMENT

Two Thousand Words that Belong to Workers, Farmers, Officials, Scientists, Artists, and Everybody

The first threat to our national life was from war. Than came other evil days and events that endangered the nation's spiritual well-being and character. Most of the nation welcomed the socialist program with high hopes. But it fell into the hands of the wrong people. It would not have mattered so much that they lacked adequate experience in affairs of state, factual knowledge, or philosophical education, if only they had had enough common prudence and decency to listen to the opinion of others and agree to being gradually replaced by more able people.

After enjoying great popular confidence immediately after the war, the communist party by degrees bartered this confidence away for office, until it had all the offices and nothing else. We feel we must say this, it is familiar to those of us who are communists and who are as disappointed as the rest at the way things turned out. The leaders' mistaken policies transformed a political party and an alliance based on ideas into an organization for exerting power, one that proved highly attractive to power-hungry individuals eager to wield authority, to cowards who took the safe and easy route, and to people with bad conscience. The influx of members such as these affected the character and behavior of the party, whose internal arrangements made it impossible, short of scandalous incidents, for honest members to gain influence and adapt it continuously to modern conditions. Many communists fought against this decline, but they did not manage to prevent what ensued.

Conditions inside the communist party served as both a pattern for and a cause of the identical conditions in the state. The party's association with the state deprived it of the asset of separation from executive power. No one criticized the activities of the state and of economic organs. Parliament forgot how to hold proper debates, the government forgot how to govern properly, and managers forgot how to manage properly. Elections lost their significance, and the law carried no weight. We could not trust our representatives on any committee or, if we could, there was no point in asking them for anything because they were powerless. Worse still, we could scarcely trust one another. Personal and collective honor decayed. Honesty was a useless virtue, assessment by merit unheard of. Most people accordingly lost interest in public affairs, worrying only about themselves and about money, a further blot on the system being the impossibility today of relying even on the value of money. Personal relations were ruined, there was no more joy in work, and the nation, in short, entered a period that endangered its spiritual well-being and its character....

* * *

Since the beginning of this year we have been experiencing a regenerative process of democratization. It started inside the communist party, that much we must admit, even those communists among us who no longer had hopes that anything good could emerge from that quarter know this. It must also be added, of course, that the process could have started nowhere else. For after twenty years the communists were the only ones able to conduct some sort of political activity. It was only the opposition inside the communist party that had the privilege to voice antagonistic views. The effort and initiative now displayed by democratically-minded communists are only then a partial repayment of the debt owned by the entire party to the non-communists whom it had kept down in an inequal position. Accordingly, thanks are due to the communist party, though perhaps it should be granted that the party is making an honest effort at the eleventh hour to save its own honor and the nation's. The regenerative process has introduced nothing particularly new into our lives. It revives ideas and topics, many of which are older than the errors of our socialism, while others, having emerged from below the surface of visible history, should long ago have found expression but were instead repressed. Let us not foster the illusion that it is the power of truth which now makes such ideas victorious. Their victory has been due rather to the weakness of the old leaders, evidently already debilitated by twenty years of unchallenged rule. All the defects hidden in the foundations and ideology of the system have clearly reached their peak. So let us not overestimate the effects of the writers' and students' criticisms. The source of social change is the economy. A true word makes its mark only when it is spoken under conditions that have been properly prepared—conditions that, in our context, unfortunately include the impoverishment of our whole society and the complete collapse of the old system of government, which had enabled certain types of politicians to get rich, calmly and quietly, at our expense. Truth, then, is not prevailing. Truth is merely what remains when everything else has been frittered away. So there is no reason for national jubilation, simply for fresh hope.

In this moment of hope, albeit hope still threatened, we appeal to you. It took several months before many of us believed it was safe to speak up; many of us still do not think it is safe. But speak up we did exposing ourselves to the extent that we have no choice but to complete our plan to humanize the regime. If we did not, the old forces would exact cruel revenge. We appeal about all to those who so far have waited on the sidelines. The time now approaching will decide events for years to come....

* * *

There has been great alarm recently over the possibility that foreign forces will intervene in our development. Whatever superior forces may face us, all we can do is stick to our own positions, behave decently, and initiate nothing ourselves. We can show our government that we will stand by it, with weapons if need be, if it will do what we give it a mandate to do. And we can assure our allies that we will observe our treaties of alliance, friendship, and trade. Irritable reproaches and ill-argued suspicions on our part can only make things harder for our government, and bring no benefit to ourselves. In any case, the only way we can achieve equality is to improve our domestic situation and carry the process of renewal far enough to some day elect statesmen with sufficient courage, honor, and political acumen to create such equality and keep it that way. But this is a problem that faces all governments of small countries everywhere.

* * *

This spring a great opportunity was given to us once again, as it was after the end of the war. Again we have the chance to take into our own hands our common cause, which for working purposes we call socialism, and give it a form more appropriate to our once-good reputation and to be fairly good opinion we used to have ourselves. The spring is over and will never return. By winter we will know all....

Document Analysis

Vaculík lays out a denunciation of the Czechoslovak regime and a brief narrative of how things arrived at their present state. The troubles begin with World War II, in which Czechoslovakia lost its national independence and even its existence to Nazi Germany. The socialist program of the Soviet-backed Communists may have raised people's hopes momentarily, but it had become a disaster both materially and spiritually. The merger of party and state institutions, key to the Leninist program, was corrupting to both, in Vaculík's telling. As the Communist Party became more oriented toward simply holding power, it attracted people into its leadership who were interested in power and not ideas or policy. Governmental institutions had lost any accountability to society, as elections became meaningless forms. The government's corruption reached into private life and society, as citizens lost the ability to trust each other. Even Czech money was becoming worthless.

Vaculík says that as the Communist Party expanded its control and the space for public political debate shrank, the only place where debate still continued came to be within the party itself. He credits "democratically-minded communists" in the party with attempting an "eleventh hour" program of reform—presumably visible in Dubèek's rise to power. Although Vaculík's denunciation of the regime overall is bitter, it is reformist rather than revolutionary. Vaculík does not attack Communism per se or the regime's dependency on the Soviet Union by name, although the threat from "foreign forces" he refers to are clearly the Soviets and their Warsaw Pact allies. Vaculík claims that many Communists had fought against the corruption of the Communist leadership and were equally victims with non-Communist Czechoslovaks. He does not invoke Western states as models, and he closes with an invocation of "our common cause, which for working purposes we call socialism." Vaculík calls for civic action involving the people who have not yet involved themselves in reform efforts, who have "waited on the sidelines"; their help is needed to complete "our plan to humanize the regime."

Vaculík does not envision Czechoslovakia leaving the Soviet bloc, as can be seen by his claim that it should not change any of its existing relationships. He does however leave open the possibility that the Czech people would defend a reformist Czech government from foreign (i.e. Soviet) forces "with weapons if need be," although he does not emphasize this. His words make clear that neither the return of hard-line Communism nor the victory of democratization is inevitable, and that much depends on the coming months.

Essential Themes

Both the content of this document and the fact that it was published without any official authorization or prior consultation with the Communist authorities energized Czechoslovaks who believed that reform of the system was possible. However, it also raised the concern of the Soviet leadership over the dangers of the Czechoslovak opposition and the weakening of Communism in that country. Dubèek, like Vaculík, hoped that Czechoslovakia's remaining in the Warsaw Pact would be enough for the Soviets to tolerate the Prague Spring reforms, but this hoped proved vain.

The Prague Spring ended the night of August 20 with the invasion of Czechoslovakia by the Soviets and allied Warsaw Pact forces. Despite mostly nonviolent resistance, the Soviets reestablished strongly authoritarian Communist rule through superior force. (The Czechoslovak invasion is sometimes considered the first expression of the Brezhnev Doctrine, the Soviet belief in intervening in situations where an existing Communist government of a Soviet ally was threatened.) Although Dubèek clung to power until the following April, he was then replaced by the hard-line Communist Gustav Husák, who reversed Dubèek's reforms. The new regime was even more repressive than the Czechoslovak Communist Party had been before the Prague Spring.

The type of opposition that "The Two Thousand Words" showed to Communist leadership, without attacking Communism itself, quickly became obsolete as dissidents took a more forthrightly anti-Communist and anti-Soviet approach. They also began to identify more openly with the capitalist and democratic West and to seek alliances there. Vaculík's book recounting his experiences as a dissenter, *A Cup of Coffee with My Interrogator* (1987), was published in the West, as were the works of other Czechoslovak dissenters. This was true throughout the Soviet bloc as well as in Czechoslovakia—the next major reformist movement, Poland's Solidarity movement, emerged outside the Communist Party and was uninterested in Communist reform.

The struggle against the Czechoslovak Communist regime ended in 1989 with the Velvet Revolution, when the Communists were peaceably overthrown following the liberalization of the Soviet Union under Mikhail Gorbachev and his renunciation of the Brezhnev Doctrine. The Velvet Revolution was followed by the dissolution of Czechoslovakia along ethnic lines into the Czech Republic and Slovakia in 1991.

—William E. Burns, PhD

Bibliography and Additional Reading

Bilefsky, Dan. "Ludvik Vaculik, Influential Czech Writer and Dissident, Dies at 88." *New York Times*. New York Times, 10 June 2015.

Bischof, Gu"nter, Stefan Karner, and Peter Ruggenthaler, eds. *The Prague Spring and the Warsaw Pact Invasion of Czechoslovakia in 1968*. Lanham: Lexington, 2010.

Navrátil, Jaromír, ed. *The Prague Spring 1968: A National Security Archive Documents Reader*. New York: Central European UP, 1998.

Vaculík, Ludvik. *A Cup of Coffee with My Interrogator: The Prague Chronicles of Ludvík Vaculík*. Trans. George Theiner. London: Readers Intl., 1987.

Williams, Kieran. *The Prague Spring and Its Aftermath: Czechoslovak Politics, 1968–1970*. Cambridge: Cambridge UP, 1997.

Charter 77

Date: January 6, 1977
Country: Czechoslovakia
Genre: charter; political tract

Summary Overview

Before it was an organized movement, Charter 77 was a statement by a group of Czechoslovak intellectuals ("Chartists") about the poor state of human rights in Communist-ruled Czechoslovakia. The document listed the many areas in which the government actively denied people their human rights and pointed out that these were all violations of international agreements the government had made. The Charter 77 statement announced the formation of a loose association also called Charter 77 to work for the improvement of Czechoslovak society. Among its more prominent members was the playwright Václav Havel, who would later become president of the independent Czech Republic.

Defining Moment

After the suppression of the 1968 Prague Spring reform movement, Czechoslovakia went from being one of the more tolerant of the Communist regimes of Eastern Europe to being one of the more repressive. The conservative regime of Gustáv Husák, put into power by the Soviets after crushing the Prague Spring, particularly targeted liberal intellectuals, who were regarded as troublemakers and agents of the West.

The 1975 Helsinki Accords, which Czechoslovakia—like all the other European countries except Albania—agreed to, contained an extensive series of commitments to basic human rights and freedoms such as those of travel and information. In early 1976, the government also ratified two United Nations covenants on human rights, the International Covenant on Civil and Political Rights and the International Covenant on Economic, Social and Cultural Rights. It printed these covenants in government newspapers which sold out quickly, giving readers a convenient way to measure the government's performance against its commitments. Although most people were not optimistic that Communist countries would actually adhere to these commitments, the Helsinki Accords and the UN covenants served as a focus for dissidents in Czechoslovakia and elsewhere to condemn the hypocrisy, dishonesty, and repressiveness of their governments, as well as attract international attention by charging their governments with having violated international agreements.

One of the events that triggered the formation of Charter 77 was the arrest of members of a dissident rock band, the Plastic People of the Universe, after they had participated in an impromptu rock festival in Bojanovice, a small community outside Prague. (Since they did not hold a musician's license granted by the government, the Plastic People of the Universe could not appear in regular venues.)

Author Biography and Document Information

The charter is the product of a loosely affiliated group of Czechoslovak dissident intellectuals. No single figure is credited with writing the document or founding the group, but the document designates three of its leading signatories as spokesmen for the movement: playwright Václav Havel, academic philosopher Jan Patoèka, and the lawyer and former Communist official Jiøí Hájek. Patoèka died shortly after, on March 13, 1977, of exhaustion and illness, and his death was treated as a martyrdom to the movement.

On the document's first appearance, it had 242 signatories, although many more were added in the subsequent weeks and months. Signatories were predominantly male, about 80 percent of the total. Signatories were also heavily concentrated in the region of Prague, the capital city, and disproportionately Czech, with only a handful of signatories from Czechoslovakia's other major ethnic group, the Slovaks. (The Slovaks who did sign were mostly people who resided in predominantly Czech Prague.) The Chartists included a range of political positions, from those with roots in the Communist Party and the Communist reform movement of the late 1960s to Protestant and Catholic activists. Some of those with a party background had broken from Communism entirely, while others still held out hope for a reformed Communism different from that of Husák. Not all those who sympathized with the document were signatories. The organizers discouraged some people from signing, such as university students who could lose their scholarships.

Historical Document

Charter 77

In the Czechoslovak Register of Laws No. 120 of October 13, 1976, texts were published of the International Covenant on Civil and Political Rights, and of the International Covenant on Economic, Social and Cultural Rights, which were signed on behalf of our republic in 1968, reiterated at Helsinki in 1975 and came into force in our country on March 23, 1976. From that date our citizens have enjoyed the rights, and our state the duties, ensuing from them. The human rights and freedoms underwritten by these covenants constitute features of civilized life for which many progressive movements have striven throughout history and whose codification could greatly assist humane developments in our society. We accordingly welcome the Czechoslovak Socialist Republic's accession to those agreements. Their publication, however, serves as a powerful reminder of the extent to which basic human rights in our country exist, regrettably, on paper alone.

The right to freedom of expression, for example, guaranteed by Article 19 of the first-mentioned covenant, is in our case purely illusory. Tens of thousands of our citizens are prevented from working in their own fields for the sole reason that they hold views differing from official ones, and are discriminated against and harassed in all kinds of ways by the authorities and public organizations. Deprived as they are of any means to defend themselves, they become victims of a virtual apartheid.

Hundreds of thousands of other citizens are denied that "freedom from fear" mentioned in the preamble to the first covenant, being condemned to the constant risk of unemployment or other penalties if they voice their own opinions.

In violation of Article 13 of the second-mentioned covenant, guaranteeing everyone the right to education, countless young people are prevented from studying because of their own views or even their parents'. Innumerable citizens live in fear of their own or their children's right to education being withdrawn if they should ever speak up in accordance with their convictions.

Any exercise of the right to "seek, receive and impart information and ideas of all kinds, regardless of frontiers, either orally, in writing or in print" or "in the form of art" specified in Article 19, Clause 2 of the first covenant is followed by extra-judicial and even judicial sanctions, often in the form of criminal charges, as in the recent trial of young musicians [referring to the trial of the band Plastic People of the Universe].

Freedom of public expression is inhibited by the centralized control of all the communication media and of publishing and cultural institutions. No philosophical, political or scientific view or artistic activity that departs ever so slightly from the narrow bounds of official ideology or aesthetics is allowed to be published; no open criticism can be made of abnormal social phenomena; no public defense is possible against false and insulting charges made in official propaganda.

The legal protection against "attacks on honor and reputation" clearly guaranteed by Article 17 of the first covenant is in practice non-existent: false accusations cannot be rebutted, and any attempt to secure compensation or correction through the courts is futile; no open debate is allowed in the domain of thought and art. Many scholars, writers, artists and others are penalized for having legally published or expressed, years ago, opinions which are condemned by those who hold political power today.

Freedom of religious confession, emphatically guaranteed by Article 18 of the first covenant, is continually curtailed by arbitrary official action; by interference with the activity of churchmen, who are constantly threatened by the refusal of the state to permit them the exercise of their functions, or by the withdrawal of such permission; by financial or other transactions against those who express their religious faith in word or action; by constraints on religious training and so forth.

One instrument for the curtailment or in many cases complete elimination of many civic rights is the system by which all national institutions and organizations are in effect subject to political directives from the machinery of the ruling party and to decisions made by powerful individuals. The constitution of the republic, its laws and legal norms do not regulate the form or content, the issuing or application of such decisions; they are often only given out verbally, unknown to the public at large and beyond its powers to check; their originators are responsible to no one but themselves and their own hierarchy; yet they have a decisive impact on the decision-making and executive organs of government, justice, trade unions, interest groups and all other organizations, of the other political parties, enterprises, factories, institutions, offices and so on, for whom these instructions have precedence even before the law.

Where organizations or individuals, in the interpretation of their rights and duties, come into conflict with such directives, they cannot have recourse to any non-party authority, since none such exists. This constitutes, of course, a serious limitation of the right ensuing from Articles 21 and 22 of the first-mentioned covenant, which provides for freedom of association and forbids any restriction on its exercise, from Article 25 on the right to take part in the conduct of public affairs, and from Article 26 stipulating equal protection by the law without discrimination.

This state of affairs likewise prevents workers and others from exercising the unrestricted right to establish trade unions and other organizations to protect their economic and social interests, and from freely enjoying the right to strike provided for in Clause 1 of Article 8 in the second-mentioned covenant.

Further civic rights, including the explicit prohibition of "arbitrary interference with privacy, family, home or correspondence" (Article 17 of the first covenant), are seriously vitiated by the various forms of interference in the private life of citizens exercised by the Ministry of the Interior, for example by bugging telephones and houses, opening mail, following personal movements, searching homes, setting up networks of neighborhood informers (often recruited by illicit threats or promises) and in other ways.

This Ministry frequently interferes in employers' decisions, instigates acts of discrimination by authorities and organizations, brings weight to bear on the organs of justice and even orchestrates propaganda campaigns in the media. This activity is governed by no law and, being clandestine, affords the citizen no chance to defend himself. In cases of prosecution on political grounds the investigative and judicial organs violate the rights of those charged and those defending them, as guaranteed by Article 14 of the first covenant and indeed by Czechoslovak law.

The prison treatment of those sentenced in such cases is an affront to their human dignity and a menace to their health, being aimed at breaking their morale. Clause 2, Article 12 of the first covenant, guaranteeing every citizen the right to leave the country, is consistently violated, or under the pretense of "defense of national security" is subjected to various unjustifiable conditions (Clause 3).

The granting of entry visas to foreigners is also treated arbitrarily, and many are unable to visit Czechoslovakia merely because of professional or personal contacts with those of our citizens who are subject to discrimination.

Some of our people—either in private, at their places of work or by the only feasible public channel, the foreign media—have drawn attention to the systematic violation of human rights and democratic freedoms and demanded amends in specific cases. But their pleas have remained largely ignored or been made grounds for police investigation.

Responsibility for the maintenance of rights in our country naturally devolves in the first place on the political and state authorities. Yet not only on them: everyone bears his share of responsibility for the conditions that prevail and accordingly also for the observance of legally enshrined agreements, binding upon all individuals as well as upon governments. It is this sense of co-responsibility, our belief in the importance of its conscious public acceptance and the general need to give it new and more effective expression that led us to the idea of creating Charter 77, whose inception we today publicly announce.

Charter 77 is a loose, informal and open association of people of various shades of opinion, faiths and professions united by the will to strive individually and collectively for the respecting of civic and human rights in our own country and throughout the world—rights accorded to all men by the two mentioned international covenants, by the Final Act of the Helsinki conference and by numerous other international documents opposing war, violence and social or spiritual oppression, and which are comprehensively laid down in the U.N. Universal Charter of Human Rights.

Charter 77 springs from a background of friendship and solidarity among people who share our concern for those ideals that have inspired, and continue to inspire, their lives and their work. Charter 77 is not an organization; it has no rules, permanent bodies or formal membership. It embraces everyone who agrees with its ideas and participates in its work. It does not form the basis for any oppositional political activity. Like many similar citizen initiatives in various countries, West and East, it seeks to promote the general public interest. Charter 77 does not aim, then, to set out its own platform of political or social reform or change, but within its own field of impact to conduct a constructive dialogue with the political and state authorities, particularly by drawing attention to individual cases where human and civic frights are violated, to document such grievances and suggest remedies, to make proposals of a more general character calculated to reinforce such rights and machinery for protecting them, to act as an intermediary in situations of conflict which may lead to violations of rights, and so forth.

By its symbolic name Charter 77 denotes that it has come into being at the start of a year proclaimed as Political Prisoners' Year—a year in which a conference in Belgrade is due to review the implementation of the obligations assumed at Helsinki.

As signatories, we hereby authorize Professor Dr. Jan Patocka, Dr. Vaclav Havel and Professor Dr. Jiri Hajek to act as the spokesmen for the Charter. These spokesmen are endowed with full authority to represent it vis-a-vis state and other bodies, and the public at home and abroad, and their signatures attest to the authenticity of documents issued by the Charter. They will have us and others who join us as their colleagues taking part in any needful negotiations, shouldering particular tasks and sharing every responsibility. We believe that Charter 77 will help to enable all citizens of Czechoslovakia to work and live as free human beings.

Prague,

1 January 1977

Document Analysis

Charter 77 opens with an appeal to the international agreements protecting human rights to which Czechoslovakia was a signatory, including the two UN covenants and the recently signed Helsinki Accords. The document does not call for regime change or democratization, but for the regime to observe the human-rights agreements that it has already made. The fundamental rhetorical device is the contrast of the lofty agreements that the Czechoslovak government has signed regarding human rights and the dismal reality of Czechoslovakia. Czechoslovaks lack freedom of expression, as citizens who express themselves fearlessly can be barred from work in their chosen professions as well as subjected to other kinds of penalties. Those who disagree with the regime may lose their or even their children's right to education.

The government's secret police can ceaselessly interfere with the private lives of Czechoslovak citizens through opening mail, wiretaps and bugging, and even house searches. Networks of informers both violate privacy and make it difficult for Czechoslovaks to trust each other. Citizens arrested on political charges have no due process or right of appeal. They are subject to harsh conditions in prison, intended to break their spirit. Those who wish to leave the country are not allowed to, in violation of the regime's public commitment to freedom of movement.

There is also no room in Czechoslovak public life for art or personal expression that deviates from "the narrow bounds of official ideology or aesthetics," because it cannot be published or promoted. This makes it impossible to identify or work to solve social problems. Czechoslovaks also lack freedom of religion. Even complaining about the injustice of Czechoslovak society can bring harsh punishment.

The issues identified by the charter are principally those that affect intellectuals. The document does not call for changes in the economy, except for the formation of independent trade unions. By not taking an economic stance, the charter could remain acceptable to everyone from reform Communists and socialists to those interested in moving toward a more open market. However, ignoring economic issues also limited the document's appeal at a time when Czechoslovaks were aware that, despite the growth of the economy, their material lives were not as good as those in the non-Communist West. Czechoslovaks primarily interested in "bread-and-butter" issues would find little in the charter to address their concerns.

Underlying the numerous restrictions on individual freedom in Czechoslovakia is the Communist Party's monopoly on power, meaning there is no institution to check or counterbalance the party. The constitution of the Czechoslovak state, like the international human rights agreements to which the regime is a party, is essentially meaningless in the face of the party's dominance.

The charter concludes by announcing the formation of an informal group, also called Charter 77, to open a civic discussion about the conditions of Czechoslovak society. The document is careful to establish that the group is not a hierarchy or a political party competing for power, but a loose group "united by the will to strive individually and collectively for the respecting of civic and human rights in our own country and throughout the world." The members are described as coming from various backgrounds, political and religious. Finally, the document expresses a wish to open "a constructive dialogue with the political and state authorities" about ways to move toward a greater respect for human and civil rights in Czechoslovakia.

Essential Themes

The government responded fiercely to Charter 77, denouncing it and its signatories and mobilizing regime intellectuals in an "anti-Charter" group. Several signers were imprisoned or otherwise punished, although none were executed. Ironically, since the charter could not be legally published or circulated in Czechoslovakia, many Czechoslovaks knew of it primarily from the regime's campaign against it. The document was published in Western newspapers and circulated in underground copies in Czechoslovakia. It generated a large secondary samizdat literature (banned literature that was reproduced and passed from person to person), including commentaries on the charter and defenses of its signers against the attacks of the government. Charter 77 attracted a great deal of attention in the West, the group received the first Andrei Sakharov Freedom Award (named after the famous Soviet dissident) from the Norwegian Helsinki Committee in 1984. An International Committee for the Support of Charter 77 in Czechoslovakia was formed in Paris and attracted leading Western intellectuals and writers, including the American novelist Saul Bellow and the West German writer Heinrich Böll.

Many of the Charter 77 activists became leaders in Czechoslovakia's peaceful transition from Communism in 1989—the "Velvet Revolution"—and in the independent Czech and Slovak states. Václav Havel became president of the Czech Republic. With the end of the Communist regime, however, the charter became a document primarily of historical interest. An attempt to form a political party based on the charter's principles, the Civic Forum, failed completely, and the Charter 77 group itself was dissolved after the overthrow of Communism. Groups outside Czechoslovakia placed themselves in the tradition of Charter 77, including a British constitutional reform group, Charter 88; a Hungarian opposition group, Charter 92; a Belarusian human rights group, Charter 97; and a Chinese human rights group, Charter 08.

—William E. Burns, PhD

Bibliography and Additional Reading

Bolton, Jonathan. *Worlds of Dissent: Charter 77, the Plastic People of the Universe, and Czech Culture under Communism.* Cambridge, MA: Harvard UP, 2012.

Havel, Václav. *Letter to Olga: June 1979–September 1982.* Trans. Paul Wilson. New York: Holt, 1989.

McRae, Robert. *Resistance and Revolution: Vaclav Havel's Czechoslovakia.* Ottawa: Carleton UP, 1997.

Skilling, H. Gordon. *Charter 77 and Human Rights in Czechoslovakia.* London: Allen, 1981.

CIA Cable on the Situation in Poland

Date: December 24, 1981
Author: Central Intelligence Agency (CIA)
Genre: report

Summary Overview

Events in Poland in the 1980s proved key in setting the stage for the end of the Cold War. At the time this cable was written, forces for change had been under way in the nation for more than two years. Outside of Poland, yet central to the nation's view of itself, was the selection of Cardinal Karol Wojtyla as pope (John Paul II) in October 1978. Traditionally a strong Catholic nation, Poland under the sway of a Polish pope strengthened its ties to the one institution—the church—that could confront the Communist government. Internally, the Solidarity Trade Union, the first union in a Communist country not controlled by the Communist Party, was formally established in September 1980, and in addition to its economic agenda, Solidarity maintained close ties with the Catholic Church. Inspired by both the pope and Solidarity, the Polish people expressed their dissatisfaction with the Communist government through strikes and protests, resulting in martial law being declared on December 13, 1981. The CIA and other US governmental bodies monitored the situation closely.

Defining Moment

As World War II drew to a close, the armies of the Soviet Union pushed west, crossing Poland, as they moved toward and into Germany. The Allies' joint forces of the western European nations and the United States pushed into Germany from the west. An agreement had been reached to the effect that whichever Allied country was in control of an area would be allowed to establish national governments in the area. This tacitly gave the Soviet Union permission to create Communist governments throughout Eastern Europe, including Poland. Thus, beginning in 1945, Polish governments were controlled by the Communist Party. In 1980, therefore, when the Solidarity trade union began to agitate against the Communist government in Poland, it was taking actions that many considered unthinkable. It was widely assumed that if the Polish leaders did not quickly step in to control the situation, the Soviet Union would send in troops, as it had done previously in other Eastern European countries. Over a period of fifteen months, however, Polish leaders permitted Solidarity to carry on. Finally, on December 13, 1981, General Wojciech Jaruzelski declared a state of martial law and suspended all activities by Solidarity.

In consequence, thousands of individuals were arrested and all major mining and manufacturing facilities found themselves with Polish army troops assigned to them in order to quash any labor activism. The CIA report reprinted here was issued less than two weeks after the imposition of martial law. While not supporting the Communist government, church leaders did not want large numbers of people killed, or the lives of average citizens made unbearable. Similarly, the government knew that the Catholic Church, under Pope John Paul II, was the only organization that could challenge the status quo sufficiently as to cause the Soviets to impose control from the outside. In order to preclude that prospect, the Polish government did not initially act against the church in issuing its martial law proclamation; and the church, in turn, was careful not to take any action that might make the situation worse and invite intervention. As illustrated in the accompanying CIA cable, then, there were three sides to this situation, each with its own reasons for not desiring to disrupt the delicate balance.

Author Biography

Unnamed individuals from the Directorate of Operations division of the Central Intelligence Agency wrote this report for use by officials in the United States. The unnamed source mentioned in the document is most likely Ryszard Kuklinski, a colonel in the Polish Army with access to many secret Polish documents and someone who spied for the United States. (He may also have spied for the Soviet Union.)

The Central Intelligence Agency was created in 1947 as an heir to the Office of Strategic Services, which operated during World War II. In between, these duties were handled by the Central Intelligence Group. The Directorate of Operations is the section of the CIA that undertakes covert operations to secure the information requested by the president or those acting on behalf of the president. This office was previously called the Clandestine Service.

Historical Document

CIA Cable on the Situation in Poland

Intelligence Information Cable

THIS IS AN INFORMATION REPORT, NOT FINALLY EVALUATED INTELLIGENCE

CITE TDFIRDB-315/23025

DIST 24 DECEMBER

COUNTRY POLAND/ USSR

SUBJECT: SOVIET PRESSURE ON POLISH GOVERNMENT TO ACT AGAINST THE POLISH CHURCH

D O I: LATE DECEMBER 1981

SOURCE: A FORMER POLISH GENERAL STAFF OFFICER WHO MADE THE FOLLOWING COMMENTS BASED ON HIS PAST EXPERIENCE AND CONTACTS.

WHILE THERE ARE NO POLISH PLANS PER SE TO ACT AGAINST THE CHURCH VERY STRONG PRESSURE WAS EXERTED BY THE SOVIETS TO COMPEL THE POLES TO SEVERELY CURTAIL THE ACTIVITIES OF THE CATHOLIC CHURCH. SOME SOVIET MILITARY OFFICERS HAVE ARGUED THAT THE MAIN CAUSE: FOR THE CUIRRENT POLISH SITUATION IS THE CHURCH'S INFLUENCE IN POLAND AND THE ELECTION OF A POLISH POPE. THE SOVIETS CONDEMNED THE POLISH DECISION TO ALLOW THE POPE TO VISIT POLAND IN JUNE 1979, AND DEMANDED THAT CHURCH INFLUENCE BE RADICALLY LIMITED. ACTIONS SUBSEQUENTLY TAKEN BY THE POLISH SECURITY SERVICE AGAINST THE CHURCH INCLUDED RECORDING ALL [SIC] SERMONS BY PRIESTS, REPORTING INFORMATION ON CHURCH ACTIVITIES AND THE POLITICAL LEANINGS OF BISHOPS AND PRIESTS. MINISTRY OF INTERNAL AFFAIRS DAILY SITUATION REPORTS GIVEN TO TOP POLISH LEADERS, INCLUDE A SECTION ON THE CHURCH.

IF IT HAS NOT BEEN DONE YET, THE CURTAILMENT OF CHURCH ACTIVITIES DEMANDED BY THE SOVIETS WILL BE ACCOMPLISHED IN THE NEAR FUTURE. WITHIN THE MILITARY COUNCIL, THE LIMITATION OF THE CHURCH IS THE SECOND GOAL TO BE PURSUED AS SOON AS THE RESISTANCE OF THE WORKERS IS BROKEN. CURTAILMENT OF CHURCH ACTIVITIES WOULD INCLUDE LIMITING THE FREEDOM OF PREISTS AND BISHOPS AND OTHER CLERGY, CANCELLING RELIGIOUS EDUCATION IN SCHOOLS, CANCELLING THE CONSTRUCTION OF NEW CHURCHES AND CONFINING ALL CHURCH ACTIVITIES TO EXISTING CHURCHES ONLY. PRIESTS, BISHOPS, NUNS, ALL OTHER CLERICS WHO SPEAK OUT AGAINST THE REGIME WILL BE ISOLATED AND ARRESTED. AT PRESENT, EFFORTS ARE BEING MADE TO ISOLATE ONLY THOSE WHO ARE PARTICULARLY VOCAL IN CONDEMNING THE GOVERNMENT AND SUPPORTING SOLIDARITY. LATER MORE HARSH MEASURES WILL BE TAKEN. HIGH LEVEL SOVIET MILITARY PRESSURE ON THE POLES IN THIS REGARD INCLUDES SOME SUGGESTIONS FOR MEASURES AGAINST THE CLERGY. THESE HAVE INCLUDED GETTING PRIESTS DRUNK, PATERNITY SUITS AGAINST PRIESTS, AND A SMEAR CAMPAIGN TO COMPROMISE THE CLERGY. A TYPICAL EXAMPLE OF THE SOVIET ATTITUDE TOWARDS THE POLISH CHURCH OCCURRED LAST SUMMER, WHEN WARSAW PACT COMMANDER-IN-CHIEF V. I. KULIKOV VISITED POLAND. HE ASKED TO SEE A FILM OF THE POPE'S VISIT, THROUGHOUT WHICH HE RAILED ABOUT HOW UNTHINKABLE IT WAS THAT A CHURCH LEADER COULD GET SUCH A RECEPTION IN A COMMUNIST COUNTRY.

3.[SOURCE COMMENT: IN ONE CONVERSATION AMONG KULIKOV, POLISH LEADER WOJCIECH JARUZELSKI, AND SEVERAL OTHER GENERALS, THE HATRED FOR THE POPE AND THE DEMAND THAT THE POLES ACCEPT SOCIALISM AND REJECT GOD WAS CLEARLY EVIDENT. IT IS NOT EXCLUDED THAT THE SOVIETS WOULD TRY TO ASSASSINATE THE POPE. AT A JULY 1981 MEETING WITHIN THE GENERAL STAFF, GENERAL WLADYSLAW HERMASZEWSKI, WHO IS CLOSE TO THE SOVIETS, REPEATED THE SOVIET LINE THAT ALL THE PROBLEMS BEGAN WITH THE ELECTION OF THE POPE. HE SAID THAT AT THAT TIME THERE WERE MANY POLES WHO WOULD DO "THE SAME THING AS THE TURK," THAT IS TRY TO ASSASSINATE THE POPE. SOURCE BELIEVES THAT THE SOVIETS OBVIOUSLY HAD A HAND IN THE ASSASSINATION ATTEMPT OF THE POPE AS THEY ARE THE ONLY ONES WHO WOULD BENEFIT FROM SUCH AN ACTION. THE SOVIETS HAVE STATED AND STRONGLY BELIEVE

THAT SO LONG AS THERE IS A POLISH POPE, COMMUNISM WILL NOT TAKE ROOT IN POLAND.]

4. THROUGHOUT THE PAST YEAR, THERE HAVE BEEN VERY STRONG PRESSURES ON JARUZELSKI TO LIMIT THE INFLUENCE OF THE CHURCH IN POLISH SOCIETY. THE POLES HAVE ARGUED THAT THE TIME IS NOT RIGHT TO DO SO AND AT PRESENT CONDITIONS ARE NOT RIPE FOR IT. THEY TRIED TO SHOW THE 'POSITIVE ASPECTS OF CHURCH INFLUENCE', FOR EXAMPLE, THE CHURCH AND CARDINAL STEFAN WYSZYNSKI, NOW DECEASED, AS BEING A FORCE FOR MODERATION AND FOR CALM. THE SOVIETS, HOWEVER, DISREGARD THIS LINE OF REASONING.

Document Analysis

During most of the one thousand years that Poland had been a predominately Christian nation, the Catholic Church had supported the state and the state had supported the Church. However, with the imposition of a Communist government after World War II, a government that was officially atheistic, this all changed. When, 30 years later, native son Karol Wojtyla was elected pope, the situation changed again. Pope John Paul II desired to make a visit to his homeland in 1979, and, much to the dismay of the Soviet leaders, the Polish government permitted it. The millions of people who attended the thirty-two services the pope held during his nine-day visit, became more unified in both their faith and their Polish nationalism. The potential strength of the Church became clear to the Communist leaders, and how such influence could be kept in check became their top priority. Nonviolent ways in which to blunt the Church's message and discredit its leaders were considered, on the grounds that use of direct force was too dangerous (in terms of world perceptions). The symbol of John Paul II was too strong to combat, however.

Thus, when Solidarity, with the assent of the Church, organized unrest against the government in 1980, the Communist government had to decide whether or not to directly confront the Church. Most believed that Solidarity would not have arisen without the symbol of John Paul II and the support of the Church. The various plans described in the cable were discussed by Communist authorities but never fully implemented. Although some individual church leaders were harassed or arrested, the government decided that the highest priority was the "resistance of the workers" rather than the activities of the church. The differences between Polish Communist leaders and Soviet leaders are clearly illustrated in the text. A visiting Soviet official, reviewing the Pope's 1979 visit, states that it was unimaginable that the Pope could be invited and given a positive "reception in a Communist country." In response to Soviet pressure, the Polish leader's response is that "the time is not right" to come down on the Church.

As can be seen from some of the points in this document, the church had a much closer relationship with the Communist government of Poland than it had with many other Communist states. Allowing religion classes in schools and the construction of (some) new churches were things that would never be permitted in most other countries of the Eastern Bloc. While not explicitly mentioned in the text, yet understood by the writer and his intended readers, prior to the breakup of Yugoslavia, Poland was the only country in Eastern Europe to be predominately Roman Catholic. This gave it strong ties with Western Europe. Any strong acts against the Church would have international repercussions. Thus, the Polish leaders never pushed the Church too hard.

Essential Themes

There are two basic thoughts expressed in the text: 1) that the Church needs to be controlled by the (Communist) state, and 2) that if the Polish government does not accomplish this, then the Soviet Union may take it upon itself to do so. The United States opposed the Communist government in Poland and needed this information in order to better understand the imposition of martial law. In the slightly more than two years since Pope John Paul II's visit, it had become clear to the Polish leaders that allowing that visit had been a monumental mistake. Speaking a decade later, General Jaruzelski stated that John Paul II's visit had been the "detonator" that led to the eventual fall of the Communist government. Within this document, arguments are given as to why the Catholic Church needed to be brought under control, but it also illustrates the fact that the government did not have the resolve to do this. While several types of surveillance are mentioned, as well as some small steps to take against individual clergy, no mention is made of any plans for large-scale confrontations with the Church.

What seems to have been the reason behind that decision is the threat of Soviet intervention in Polish affairs. Prior incidents such as the Soviet invasion of Hungary in 1956 and the Warsaw Pact invasion of Czechoslovakia in 1968, were likely in the Polish leaders' minds. They knew that if the Soviets invaded, other leaders would be in place when the Soviets left. Thus, the Polish leaders had to take steps, or at least consider steps, that would satisfy the Soviet leaders without incurring the ire of the Church or the world at large. Many people then and now believe that the declaration of martial law was prompted more by fears of the Soviet Union than by fears of either Solidarity or the Church. Some of the former Polish leaders have claimed that a Soviet invasion was imminent, although that has yet to be conclusively documented. Whatever prompted Jaruzelski to declare martial law, the government was successful in virtually destroying the influence of the Solidarity movement for the next several years. At the same time, a lack of resolve to forcefully confront the Catholic Church, even while making an enemy of it, eventually cost the government the stability it desired. Leaders's fears about the Church came true. With the continued influence of the pope, the Church solidified its strong position within Polish society, supporting causes that eventually allowed for the revival of Solidarity. Meanwhile, the Communist regime was sidelined. Regime leaders seemed to have understood the situation yet did nothing to change it dramatically, ultimately watching the Communist state collapse in Poland in 1989.

—Donald A. Watt, PhD

Bibliography and Additional Reading

Ash, Timothy Garton. *The Polish Revolution: Solidarity*. New Haven: Yale UP, 2002.

Barnes, Jane and Helen Whitney. "John Paul II & the Fall of Communism." *Frontline*. Boston: WGBH Educational Foundation, 2014. Documentary.

Kemp-Welch, A. *Poland under Communism: A Cold War History*. Cambridge: Cambridge UP, 2008.

Kramer, Mark. "The Kuklinski Files and the Polish Crisis of 1980-1981: An Analysis of the Newly Released CIA Documents on Ryszard Kuklinski." *Cold War International History Project: Working Paper #59*. Washington: Woodrow Wilson International Center for Scholars, 2009.

MacEachin, Dougland J. *US Intelligence and the Polish Crisis: 1980-1981*. Washington: Center for the Study of Intelligence, 2000.

Weigel, George. *The End and the Beginning: Pope John Paul II—The Victory of Freedom, the Last Years, the Legacy*. New York: Doubleday, 2010.

Egon Krenz Letter to Mikhail Gorbachev

Date: November 10, 1989
Author: Egon Krenz
Genre: letter

Summary Overview

The final collapse of state communism in Europe began in East Berlin in late 1989, with the breaching of the Berlin Wall. On November 10 of that year, Egon Krenz, the leader of the German Democratic Republic (GDR, or communist East Germany), informed Mikhail Gorbachev, head of the Union of Soviet Socialist Republics (USSR) that East German officials had opened the Bornholmer Strasse border crossing the previous night. Krenz explained that the border had been opened after thousands of East Germans showed up at the crossing, demanding entry into West Berlin (part of the democratic Federal Republic of Germany).

According to Krenz, had the guards not opened the gates, the consequences—violence and numerous fatalities—would have been far worse. Sixty thousand East Germans had crossed into West Berlin, but the majority returned the following day. East German authorities once again closed the border, allowing only those with proper authorization to cross, and Krenz asked Gorbachev to contact western governments to ensure that they would not encourage further disruptions at the border. The letter revealed the weaknesses of the communist East German government and presaged its collapse.

Defining Moment

The city of Berlin had been a point of contention since the end of World War II. After its surrender Germany was divided into four zones of occupation with the United States, Great Britain, France, and the Soviet Union each occupying a zone. Berlin was located inside the Soviet zone, but because of its symbolic importance as the capital of Germany it was also divided into four zones. In May 1948 President Harry Truman convinced Great Britain and France to merge their zones with the American zone, including those in Berlin. A new German state known as the Federal Republic of Germany (FRG), better known as West Germany, was formed. Angered over what he interpreted as an aggressive act, Joseph Stalin, General Secretary of the Soviet Union, ordered a blockade around the western sectors of Berlin to force the United States and its allies to abandon the city. Truman did not back down and ordered a massive airlift to feed the Germans in West Berlin. Stalin abandoned the blockade. However, tensions over Berlin did not end. On August 13, 1961 the

Egon Krenz, 1984. Photo courtesy of Bundesarchiv, via Wikimedia Commons.

East German government, at the direction of the USSR and to prevent its citizens from fleeing to West Berlin and then West Germany, constructed a wall separating East and West Berlin. For nearly three decades the Berlin Wall would serve not only as a barrier between East and West Berlin but also as a powerful symbol of the Cold War between the communist and noncommunist nations.

Like other countries aligned with the USSR, East Germany experienced monumental changes in 1989. By year's end, the Berlin Wall would be torn down and East Germany would exist as a country in name only.

These changes began in May, 1989 when Hungary opened its border with Austria. In August alone, tens of thousands of East Germans traveled to Hungary and then crossed the border into Austria and then into West Germany where they received automatic citizenship. When the East German government banned travel to Hungary, East Germans began clandestinely escaping through Czechoslovakia. By late October 200,000 East Germans had fled the country.

That same month massive protests broke out in Leipzig and East Berlin demanding that the government of General Secretary Erich Honecker institute reforms similar to those previously introduced by Mikhail Gorbachev in the USSR. Some groups leading these protests, most notably New Forum, called for moderate reforms which didn't directly challenge the fundamentals of a communist society, while others, the Social Democratic Party and Democracy Now, boldly pushed for revolutionary political and economic changes.

These protests eventually led Honecker to resign on October 18. However, organized protests demanding significant reform continued under his successor, the more moderate Egon Krenz. On November 9 Krenz's government announced that it would support free elections and the easing of travel restrictions. However, during the press conference announcing these decisions, Gunter Schabowski, a Politburo official, mistakenly stated that East Germans were permitted to cross into West Germany immediately and without restriction. The news spread quickly and tens of thousands of East Germans gathered at the Berlin Wall and other border

Mikhail Gorbachev. Photo by Vladimir Vyatkin /RIA Novosti Archive, via Wikimedia Commons.

crossings. Border guards at the Bornholmer Strasse crossing point opened the gates and thousands of East Germans flooded into West Berlin.

Author Biography

Born on March 19, 1937 in modern day Kolobrzeg, Poland, Egon Krenz served in the East Germany military before joining the Socialist Unity Party of Germany in 1955. After serving in the East German parliament for most of the 1970s, Krenz became a member of the Politburo, the governing body of East Germany, in 1983. Protests in the fall of 1989 led to the resignation of General Secretary of the GDR Erich Honecker, and Krenz succeeded him. Facing a crisis over the Berlin Wall, Krenz stumbled and the wall was torn down. He was out of office by December 1989. In 1997, he was sentenced to six and a half years in prison for the murder of four East Germans who had been killed trying to cross the border into West Berlin.

Historical Document

Egon Krenz Letter to Mikhail Gorbachev

[November 10, 1989]

[LETTER, GENERAL SECRETARY OF THE GDR SED (Socialist Union Party) EGON KRENZ TO GENERAL SECRETARY OF THE CC CPSU MIKHAIL GORBACHEV]

General Secretary
CC CPSU [Central Committee, Communist Party of the Soviet Union]
comrade Mikhail Sergeevich Gorbachev
Moscow

Dear comrade Mikhail Sergeevich Gorbachev!

In connection with the developments of the situation in GDR, tonight it became necessary to make a decision to permit the exit of citizens of the German Democratic Republic to West Berlin as well. A large gathering of people at the KPP [Kontrollpassierpunkt checkpoint] to West Berlin demanded a quick decision from us. Denying passage to West Berlin could have led to serious consequences whose scale would become unforeseeable. The articles of the Quadripartite agreement on West Berlin does not bear on this decision, since permissions for exit into West Berlin to visit relatives have been given out up until now as well.

Last night, about 60 thousand citizens of the GDR crossed the KPP into West Berlin. Of these, about 45 thousand returned back to the GDR.

From 6 o'clock in the morning today, only persons having the appropriate visa from the GDR can go into West Berlin. The same also applies for permanent exit from the GDR.

I request, dear comrade Mikhail Sergeevich Gorbachev that you instruct the USSR ambassador in the GDR to get in touch without delay with the representatives of the Western powers with the aim of ensuring normal order in the city and of averting provocations on the state border from West Berlin.

With communist greetings

Egon Krenz
General Secretary of the SED

East German border guard at Berlin Wall, July 1988. Photo by Neptuul, via Wikimedia Commons.

Document Analysis

On November 10, 1989 General Secretary Egon Krenz wrote a detailed letter to Mikhail Gorbachev, General Secretary of the USSR, informing him about the developing situation in East Germany and explaining the decision to allow East German citizens to cross into West Berlin the day before. Krenz explained that in response to ongoing protests in East Germany, authorities had decided to "permit the exit of citizens of the German Democratic Republic to West Berlin." The magnitude of these protests had required a quick decision. He argued strongly that denying passage to those who had congregated along the Bornholmer border crossing would have had serious consequences. While Krenz did not say so explicitly, he clearly feared a violent reaction were East Germans not allowed temporary passage to West Berlin.

Krenz reported that sixty thousand East Germans had crossed the border into West Berlin, but forty-five thousand returned the following day. These numbers suggested that the majority of the people who crossed into West Berlin had no intention of leaving East Germany permanently. However, at the same time a significant number, fifteen thousand, had not yet returned. Many East Germans clearly wanted to leave their country.

Fearing that more people would flee if he did not intervene, Krenz informed Gorbachev that as of six a.m., only people with appropriate government visas would be allowed to cross into West Berlin. This signaled a return to the original policy.

Krenz's letter concludes with a request that Gorbachev instruct the Soviet Foreign Minister to contact representatives of the Western powers to ensure that they do not encourage further disorder around the crossings. However, at that point there was really nothing Krenz, Gorbachev, or anyone else could do to prevent East Germans from continuing to cross into West Berlin.

Essential Themes

In his letter Krenz seeks to explain and defend the decision to temporarily open the border with West Berlin on the previous night. He also wants to assure Gorbachev that future disruptions at the border could be prevented and that the widespread desire of East Germans to cross into West Germany was likely temporary. However, in reality the border then was no more secure than the night before. If anything the situation was worsening as Germans had begun dismantling the wall. There was little Krenz, Gorbachev, or anyone else could have done to control or alter the situation. Over the next few days thousands of East Germans not only crossed into West Berlin but, along with West Germans, stood and danced on the Berlin Wall. Others began to demolish it using hammers and chisels. Unwilling to use force to stop these actions, East German officials could do little but watch. Krenz's letter reveals the imminent collapse of his government and a communist East Germany aligned with the USSR.

The question remained at the time: what would happen to East Germany? Most western leaders, with the exception of West German Chancellor Helmut Kohl, initially opposed the reunification of East and West Germany, fearing that a united Germany would threaten the post–World War II political order in Europe. However, as the weeks passed it became clear that reunification was all but inevitable. By January, 1990 even Hans Modrow, Krenz's replacement, admitted to Gorbachev that the majority of East Germans wanted a unified state. Gorbachev eventually came to agree that this was the best course of action, and on October 3, 1990 the two German states, which had been divided since the end of World War II, became one.

The events of November 9-10, 1989 had a dramatic impact not only on the future of Germany but also on communism in Europe. For many Europeans living under Communist rule, the quick destruction of the Berlin Wall signaled that anything was possible. By December 1989 communist governments had been overthrown in Bulgaria, Czechoslovakia, and Romania. During the next year most countries making up the Soviet Bloc in Europe replaced their governments.

—*Gerald F. Goodwin, PhD*

Bibliography and Additional Reading

Gaddis, John Lewis. *The Cold War: A New History.* New York: Penguin, 2005.

Herring, George C. *From Colony to Superpower: U.S. Foreign Relations Since 1776.* Oxford: Oxford UP, 2008.

Leffler, Melvyn P. *For the Soul of Mankind: The United States, the Soviet Union, and the Cold War.* New York: Hill & Wang, 2007.

Turner, Henry Ashby. *Germany from Partition to Reunification.* New Haven: Yale UP, 1992.

Gorbachev's Farewell Address

Date: December 25, 1991
Author: Mikhail Gorbachev
Genre: speech

Summary Overview

On December 25, 1991 Mikhail Gorbachev, President of the Union of Soviet Socialist Republics (USSR), announced his resignation and, more importantly, the dissolution of the Soviet Union. He noted that when he assumed leadership of the USSR, the Soviet empire was threatened by previous governments' unwillingness to adapt the communist economic system to a changing world and the decades' long arms race with the United States. Through Gorbachev's efforts the nation had achieved significant reforms guaranteeing a more prosperous future. However, Gorbachev recognized that his attempts to achieve democratic reform had provoked opponents to try to overthrow his government, in August 1991. He therefore warned Russian citizens that anti-democratic forces would continue to try to reverse the changes his government had accomplished unless the people remained steadfast in their defense of democratic goals.

Defining Moment

Gorbachev's final address to the Russian people represented the culmination of years of upheaval in the Soviet Empire. Since 1985 Gorbachev had pushed through a reformist agenda centered on democratic political change and the end of rigid control of the economy as demanded by Marxist ideology. Unintentionally, the Soviet leader had encouraged demands for wholesale immediate reform and the desires of various ethnic and nationalist groups inside the Soviet bloc for freedom.

The first signs of cracks in the Soviet empire appeared in Poland in April 1989, when the Solidarity Movement's protests against martial law and economic stagnation led General Wojciech Jaruzelski, Gorbachev's close ally in the state, to legalize pro-Solidarity political parties and announce free elections. When the Soviet Union did not intervene, anti-communists won a resounding victory during the June elections, and Lech Walesa, a pro-Solidarity candidate, was elected to the presidency.

In October of the same year, in the German Democratic Republic (GDR), better known as East Germany, massive protests erupted against the communist government. In less than a month, a new

Gorbachev's farewell announcement came on December 25, 1991. Photo by John Matthew Smith, via Wikimedia Commons.

government in East Germany eased travel restrictions, a decision that would lead to the destruction of the Berlin Wall within a few months and the reunification of the two Germanys in 1990. Protests in neighboring Czechoslovakia led to the resignation of the Communist government and the election of dissident poet Vaclav Havel in late 1989. By the summer of 1990, Ukraine, Latvia, and Hungary, among others, had thrown off the yoke of communism. Equally significant, on March 15, 1990, Russian citizens voted to create the position of President of the Soviet Union. Previously the head of the Russian state had always been the General Secretary of the Communist Party. When Boris Yeltsin was elected President of Russia on June 12, 1991, Gorbachev remained the leader of a crumbling empire but was no longer the highest ranking official in his country.

This visible disintegration of the Soviet Union dramatically impacted Gorbachev's political status. On August 18, 1991, Soviet hardliners staged a coup, placing Gorbachev under house arrest and trying to seize control of the government. The hardliners sought to preserve the Communist party and what was left of the Soviet Union, but their efforts only hastened its collapse. Yeltsin quickly rallied anti-coup demonstrators, and the coup fell apart after a few days. These events weakened Gorbachev's prestige and power and raised Yeltsin's profile. In early December 1991, under Yeltsin's leadership, Russia, Belarus, Ukraine and other countries replaced the Soviet mantle with a loose confederation of states known as the Commonwealth of Independent States.

On December 25, 1991, Gorbachev accepted reality and announced his resignation as well as the official dissolution of the Soviet Union.

Author Biography

Mikhail Gorbachev was born in 1931 in the village of Privolnoe in the Stavropal region of Southern Russia. Like many of his generation, his early life was marked by World War II and the German invasion of the Soviet Union. In the summer of 1942, the Germany army occupied Gorbachev's small village, causing considerable hardship for the women and children who remained there. After the war, Gorbachev earned a law degree at Moscow State University. He returned to Stavropal where for the next two decades he steadily advanced through the ranks of the Communist Party. In 1978 he was appointed Secretary of Agriculture, joining the Politburo a short time later. On March 12, 1985, he was unanimously elected General Secretary of the Communist Party of the Soviet Union, the top leadership post. Under his leadership, the Soviet Union experimented with political liberalization (*glasnost*) and economic restructuring (*perestroika*). His foreign policies were characterized by cuts in Soviet military forces and negotiated arms-control agreements with the United States. Gorbachev held the position of General Secretary until the office was abolished on March 15, 1990, and he was appointed president. He resigned from the presidency on December 25, 1991. He continued to speak and write, including about the authoritarian turn of Russia under Vladimir Putin. He died in 2022.

Historical Document

Gorbachev's Farewell Address

Addressing you for the last time as president of the USSR, I find it necessary to state my position with regard to the path we have embarked on since 1985—especially since controversial, superficial, and biased judgments abound.

Fate has decided that, when I became head of state, it was already obvious there was something wrong in this country. We had plenty of everything; land, oil, gas, and other natural resources, and God has also endowed us with intellect and talent—yet we lived much worse than people in other industrialized countries, and the gap was constantly widening. The reason was apparent even then—our society was stifled in the grip of a bureaucratic command system. Doomed to serve ideology, and bear the heavy burden of the arms race, it was strained to the utmost. All attempts at implementing half hearted reforms—and there have been many—failed one after another. The country was losing hope.

We could not go on living like this. We had to change everything radically.

For this reason I never regretted that I did not use my position as general secretary merely to reign for a few years. This would have been irresponsible and immoral. I understood that initiating reforms on such a large scale in a society like ours was a most difficult and risky undertaking. But even now, I am convinced that the democratic reforms started in the spring of 1985 were historically justified. The process of renovating the country and bringing about fundamental change in the international community proved to be much more complex than originally anticipated. However, let us acknowledge what has been achieved so far.

Society has acquired freedom; it has been freed politically and spiritually. And this is the most important achievement, which we have not fully come to grips with, in part because we still have not learned how to use our freedom. However, a historic task has been accomplished.

The totalitarian system, which prevented this country from becoming wealthy and prosperous a long time ago, has been dismantled.

A breakthrough has been made on the road to democratic reforms. Free elections, freedom of the press, freedom of worship, representative legislatures, and a multiparty system have all become realities.

We have set out to introduce a pluralistic economy, and the equality of all forms of ownership is being established. In the course of the land reform, peasantry is reviving, individual farmers have appeared, and millions of hectares of land have been allocated to the urban and rural population. Laws were passed on the economic freedom of producers, and free enterprise, shareholding, and privatization are under way.

Shifting the course of our economy towards a free market, we must not forget that this is being done for the benefit of the individual. In these times of hardship, everything must be done to ensure the social protection of the individual—particularly old people and children.

We live in a new world. An end has been put to the Cold War, the arms race, and the insane militarization of our country, which crippled our economy, distorted our thinking, and undermined our morals. The threat of a world war is no more.

Once again, I should like to stress I have done everything in my power during the transitional period to ensure safe control over nuclear weapons.

We opened ourselves up to the rest of the world, renounced interference in the affairs of others, and the use of troops beyond our borders, and we have gained trust, solidarity, and respect.

We have become a major stronghold for the reorganization of modern civilization on the basis of peaceful, democratic principles.

The peoples and nations of this country have acquired genuine freedom to choose their own way towards self-determination. The quest for a democratic reform of our multinational state had led us to the point where we were about to sign a new union treaty.

All these changes demanded utmost exertion and were carried through under conditions of an unrelenting struggle against the growing resistance from the old, obsolete, and reactionary forces—the former party and state structures and the economic management apparatus—as well as our patterns, our ideological prejudices, our egalitarian and parasitic psychology. The changes ran up against our intolerance, a low level of political culture, and a fear of change. That is why we have wasted so much time. The old system tumbled down even before the new one could begin functioning. And our society slid into even deeper crisis.

I am aware of the dissatisfaction with today's grave situation, the harsh criticism of authority at all levels, and of my personal role. But I would like to stress once again: In so vast a country, given its heritage, fundamental changes cannot be carried out without difficulties and pain.

The August coup brought the overall crisis to a breaking point. The most disastrous aspect of this crisis is the collapse of statehood. And today I watch apprehensively the loss of the citizenship of a great country by our citizens—he consequences of this could be grave for all of us.

I consider it vitally important to sustain the democratic achievements of the last few years. We have earned them through the suffering of our entire history and our tragic experience. We must not abandon them under any circumstances, under any pretext. Otherwise, all our hopes for a better future will be buried.

I am speaking of this frankly and honestly. It is my moral duty.

Today I want to express my gratitude to all those citizens who have given their support to the policy of renovating this country and who participated in the democratic reform. I am thankful to statesmen, political and public leaders, and millions of ordinary people in other countries—to all those who understood our objectives and gave us their support, meeting us halfway and offering genuine cooperation.

I leave my post with concern—but also with hope, with faith in you, your wisdom and spiritual strength. We are the heirs of a great civilization, and its revival and transformation to a modern and dignified life depend on all and everyone.

I would like to express my heartfelt thanks to those who stood by my side, defending the right and good cause over all these years. We certainly could have avoided certain errors and done better in many ways. But I am convinced that, sooner or later, our common efforts will bear fruit and our peoples will live in a prosperous and democratic society.

Document Analysis

On December 25, 1991 Mikhail Gorbachev delivered his final address as president of the USSR announcing both his resignation and the dissolution of the Soviet Union. He acknowledged that his leadership of the USSR, which began in 1985, had given rise not only to significant controversy but also to major challenges. This was not surprising because when he became leader, "it was already obvious there was something wrong in this country." The nation was blessed with an abundance of land, natural resources like oil and gas, and many intelligent people, but the Russian people had a far lower standard of living than citizens of other industrialized nations, a gap that was continuing to grow. Gorbachev argued that previous governments' refusal to develop policies outside the framework of communist ideology and the arms race with the United States had placed heavy strains on the Soviet economy.

On taking office Gorbachev stated his view about the need to "change everything radically." He recognized that change, especially radical change, would be difficult and risky, but it was necessary to improve the lives of the nation's citizens. As a result of democratic reforms, which began in 1985, "the totalitarian system, which prevented this country from being wealthy and prosperous a long time ago," had been thoroughly dismantled to the great benefit of the Russian people.

As well, efforts to achieve democratic reforms had transformed the dream of free elections, a representative legislature, freedom of the press, and tolerance of religious beliefs into reality. Reforms related to property ownership and economic production were proceeding in a similar direction. These reforms were initiated to improve the lives of all Russians, but especially the most vulnerable, children and the elderly. These reforms were possible because of the changing nature of the world—the end of the Cold War, the lessening of the arms race, and, with it, the threat of a global conflict.

Gorbachev reminded the Russian people that despite the necessity of reform, "old, obsolete, and reactionary forces" opposed and complicated his efforts at every turn. Such obstructionist forces were behind the attempt to overthrow his government in August. Despite this resistance by some, Gorbachev argued that the democratic accomplishments of the last few years must not be eroded, "otherwise, all our hopes for a better future will be buried."

Gorbachev thanked all Russians who supported his government's attempts to achieve democratic reform as well as political leaders and private citizens of other countries who supported Russia during this transitional period. He concluded by expressing hope and optimism that Russia would continue to move toward democracy and freedom.

Essential Themes

Gorbachev's final address to the Russian people marked the end of both his political career and the existence of the Soviet Union. When he was appointed General Secretary of the Communist Party and the official leader of the USSR in March 1985, he took office intending to reform Soviet society to ensure the survival of the Soviet Union and the international communist movement. In many respects, Gorbachev successfully implemented his reformist agenda. He liberalized the Soviet economy and passed significant democratic reforms. Despite these efforts, he was unable to prevent the collapse of the USSR. Beginning in Poland in 1989, large scale protests against Communist rule broke out throughout the Soviet Bloc. Although Gorbachev wanted to ensure the survival of the Soviet Union, he did not want bloodshed. Unwilling and perhaps unable to put down the protests with force, Gorbachev accepted their success.

As the Soviet Union crumbled, Gorbachev's grip on power in Russia was significantly weakened with the election of Boris Yeltsin to the presidency in June 1991. Unlike Gorbachev, Yeltsin had no desire to preserve the Soviet Union. Gorbachev's grip on power was further weakened when Soviet hardliners seized him and attempted to gain control of the government in August 1991.

By the time Gorbachev delivered his final address, his power and authority had all but evaporated. He was essentially the leader of a country that no longer existed. The day after his speech, the hammer and sickle flag of the Soviet Union was taken off the Kremlin for the last time and replaced with the Russian flag. Both the Soviet Union and Gorbachev's attempt to strengthen it through reform had ultimately met with failure.

—Gerald F. Goodwin, PhD

Bibliography and Additional Reading

Gaddis, John Lewis. *The Cold War: A New History*. New York: Penguin, 2005.

Gorbachev, Mikhail. *Memoirs*. New York: Doubleday, 1996.

Kantowicz, Edward R. *Coming Apart, Coming Together: The World in the 20th Century*. Grand Rapids, MI: Wm. B. Eerdmans Pub. Co., 2000.

Leffler, Melvyn P. *For the Soul of Mankind: The United States, the Soviet Union, and the Cold War*. New York: Hill & Wang, 2007.

Other Modern Revolutionary Changes

Having been occupied by Japan during World War II, then liberated by U.S.-led Allied forces near the end of the war, the Philippines remained a U.S. ally and strategic partner in the Western Pacific region for decades afterward. Between 1965 and 1986 the country was ruled by the dictator Ferdinand Marcos, whom the U.S. government tolerated. To quell increasing unrest in the Philippines, including a simmering communist insurgency, Marcos maintained martial law during the 1970s and continued to rule with a firm grip in later years. Political opponents had little recourse, and domestic critics were dealt with harshly. In elections in 1986 Marcos claimed victory, but the election was widely regarded as fraudulent. In the capital city of Manila, a massive protest broke out called the People Power Revolution. The city was overrun by protestors for several days, and opposition figures gave speeches. Under pressure from Filipinos as well as foreign governments (including the United States), Marcos finally abdicated and fled to Hawaii. This was a relatively rare case of a largely bloodless, peaceful revolution, though many had suffered or died beforehand to bring it to fruition.

Less peaceful, but nonetheless remarkable, was the steady unwinding of the policy of apartheid—racial separation—and its government backers in South Africa. Since the 1950s the all-white government running the country had hardened its policies mandating racial separateness. Even though 75 percent of the population was black, the white minority (14 percent) required black South Africans to live in separate "homelands" and follow strict rules when traveling or working outside them. The oldest black political organization in the country, the African National Congress (ANC), was banned in 1960 and its leader, Nelson Mandela, was sentenced to life in prison in 1964. Guerrilla attacks against the government and other targets took place off and on over the years, as did public protests—which were violently put down by officials. By the late 1970s the ANC had gained a broad popular following among black residents and others opposed to apartheid. The international community became more active as well, with many foreign entities divesting themselves of holdings in South Africa in the 1980s to protest the country's racist policies. Under such pressure, South African president F. W. de Klerk, who had replaced the hardliner P. W. Botha in 1989, removed the ban on the ANC and released Mandela from prison. In 1991 apartheid was officially abandoned, and two years later a constitution transitioning to a multiracial government was completed. In free elections in 1994, Mandela became South Africa's first black president.

On the opposite side of the globe, in Venezuela, a revolution of a different sort took place beginning in 1998. That was the year the popular leader of the United Socialist Party of Venezuela, Hugo Chávez, was elected president. He set about transforming Venezuelan government and society to align with what he termed his Bolivarian revolution (referring to the revered early nineteenth century South American liberator Simón Bolívar). Under Chávez, Venezuela produced a new legislature, a new constitution, a new supreme court, and a new electoral body. The state-owned oil industries and Venezuela's military were purged of perceived opponents. Chavez's approach was that of a populist authoritarian: he focused on using the state's resources to serve the poor—the president's main constituency. Aligning himself with Cuba's Fidel Castro, along with the Marxist guerrillas (known as the FARC (Fuerzas Armadas Revolucionarias de Colombia)) fighting in Colombia, Chávez angered many of Venezuela's longtime foreign partners, including the United States. He faced a domestic coup attempt in 2002, after which he further consolidated his grip on power and won reelection in 2006. After Chávez's death in 2013, the government fell under his number two, Nicolás Maduro, whose ruinous policies and patently dictatorial approach further alienated democratic governments around the world.

Corazon Aquino on Achieving Peace through Peaceful Means

Date: November 12, 1986
Author: Corazon Aquino
Genre: speech

Summary Overview

Throughout much of the 1970s and 1980s, the political situation in the Philippines was tumultuous. By 1973, President Ferdinand Marcos had served two terms in office, and the 1935 Constitution of the Philippines barred him from seeking a third term. Rather than holding the open elections required by the constitution, however, Marcos declared martial law and abolished the constitution. He remained in office as a dictator. One of the leading members of the opposition to Marcos, Senator Benigno Aquino, was arrested, imprisoned, and eventually assassinated. At that point, Aquino's wife, Corazon Aquino, emerged as a major political figure in her own right. The daughter of two powerful political families, and an advisor to her husband for many years, Corazon Aquino became the leader of the People Power Revolution. This was a largely nonviolent protest movement marked by demonstrations and speeches against the Marcos regime. In 1985, with his grip on the country beginning to slip, Marcos called for a "snap election" (an election held earlier than the normal schedule) to take place in February 1986; he believed he could use it to solidify his leadership. The various opposition parties soon all unified around the candidacy of Corazon Aquino, and most election observers (including impartial outside bodies) expected her to win. When the election results were announced, however, Marcos claimed victory, which caused unrest among the Filipino population.

Aquino spoke out, claiming that the results had been falsified and she was the true winner. It was only after several days of massive civil demonstrations and protests during February, and complaints from foreign countries (including the United States) against the Marcos regime, that Marcos gave in and fled the country. Aquino became the accepted leader of the Philippines. She immediately reinstated a constitution and reestablished a democratically elected congress and normal political processes.

Ferdinand Marcos, 1982. Photo by Bluemask, via Wikimedia Commons.

Defining Moment

When Marcos originally took control over the Philippine state, he was much more popular than he was at the end of his reign. The early 1980s took a deep toll on his country, though both the nation as a whole and the Marcos regime in particular continued to enjoy U.S. support. When the United States experienced a recession in 1981, the Philippines found itself in a great deal of debt, which caused serious economic hardship for the Filipino people. In addition, Marcos began to show signs of illness (he was eventually diagnosed with a fatal type of lupus), which caused people to begin to lose faith in him. His support from the United States had been in place for two main reasons: he allowed a large U.S. military presence in the Philippines (in the form of naval and air bases), and he was a staunch fighter against communism in the island nation (where a number of communist groups were active).

U.S. support for Marcos began to be withheld in the early 1980s, as the Philippines experienced a major economic recession due, in part, to the debt Marcos incurred in propping up his government. The electoral fraud he routinely relied on to keep him and his allies in office became increasingly anathema to American legislators. Pressure from the United States was one reason why Marcos called for the snap election in 1986. Yet, while many observers from around the world declared the results of that election to be fraudulent, U.S. president Ronald Reagan suggested that there likely had been fraud on both sides. Thus, when Marcos was finally forced to flee the Philippines, he received U.S. military transportation and other assistance and went to a city not in a third-party country but rather to Honolulu, Hawaii.

Author Biography

Corazon Aquino, universally known as Cory, was born in the Philippines on January 25, 1933. Both her mother's and her father's families were politically influential, including political officials and activists. Aquino attended high school in the United States after the end of World War II, then returned to the Philippines to attend law school. During law school, she met Benigno Aquino, known as Ninoy, who served as both a senator and governor in the Philippines. Due to his political opposition to Ferdinand Marcos, Ninoy was arrested and confined for seven years. During that time, Corazon Aquino became more politically active, and when Ninoy decided to run for president from his prison cell, she made appearances at rallies and gave speeches on his behalf. When Ninoy needed treatment for a heart problem in 1980, Aquino and

Corazon Aquino in 1986. Photo via Wikimedia Commons. [Public domain.]

her family went to the United States with him. After his assassination, she became leader of the opposition to Marcos and a major figure in the People Power Revolution. Upon becoming the first female president of the Philippines in 1986, Aquino had not previously held any political office.

Her administration weathered several political storms, natural disasters, and coup attempts during her presidency, but Aquino was ultimately able to guide her country to a more respected place in world affairs. She was succeeded as president in 1992, and while she did not hold public office again, she remained politically active. She was named *Time* magazine's "Woman of the Year" in 1986 and received the J. William Fulbright Prize for International Understanding in 1996. After receiving a diagnosis of colorectal cancer in 2008, she died in 2009 at the age of seventy-eight. Since her death, many public landmarks and institutions have been named in her honor.

Historical Document

Corazon Aquino on Achieving Peace through Peaceful Means

[Delivered in Waseda, Japan, November 12, 1986]

In Japan, I understand, it is contrary to custom for women to take the leading role, especially in the realm of politics. For much of my life, in fact until three years ago, I had much in common with the Japanese woman and wife. I had chosen to marry a very dominant man; one who was to become the focus and center of my life, and the vortex of Philippine politics. Ninoy was the kind of man who had to be No. 1 not only in politics but in the home as well. And so my life around his. I was the dutiful wife, silent and supportive; the woman remembered by his friends as the one who served coffee, much as the Japanese woman serves tea. Some of these friends of his are now my ministers. They do not talk about the times when I served them coffee. But all in all I was happy in my role, for I loved him greatly.

Today I am No. 1. Not only at home but over our entire country. Ninoy would have been amazed, but also proud. For he would not fail to say that it is thanks to the many things I learned at his side. And it is true – up to a point.

Ninoy no longer influences the specific directions or decisions I must make as President of the Philippines. But I must say that the reason I am where I am today is because, as was usual between us, Ninoy took the lead and I followed.

It was Ninoy who conceptualized, embraced and promoted the philosophy of reconciliation and nonviolence that became the moving force of our bloodless February revolution. It was also Ninoy who was the first rallying point of People's Power that propelled me to the Presidency, keeps me there, and determines the course our nation is taking today.

Most people believe that People Power was born after Ninoy's death. It was really born in 1978, when he was still in prison.

In 1978, Marcos called for elections in another attempt to legitimize the naked power grab he made when he declared martial law in 1972. He wanted to prove that he and his friends had the mandate of the people. Everyone knew that the elections would be fraudulent, that the results were already prepared. Marcos controlled the Commission on Elections, the media, and the national mint. The opposition, which had none of these things, and whose leaders were either in jail, like Ninoy, or under surveillance or city arrest, clearly did not stand a chance. But Ninoy decided to take up the challenge and ran as the figurehead of the opposition slate from his prison cell. He could not campaign, of course, but our daughter Kris, then seven years old, took her father's place at the platform and appealed to the people during rallies. On the eve of elections, Ninoy was given one concession. He would be questioned on television by a government panel regarding his political views and the accusations that the government had made against him. He was taken straight from solitary confinement and thrust in front of the television cameras. I don't know how he did it, but he bested them all. He answered all the accusations and went on to accuse the government in turn. Right after the broadcast, the city of Manila exploded in a noise barrage of people beating pots and pans, car drivers honking their horns, and people shouting in the streets. It was as if they wanted to tell Ninoy, swiftly thrown back in his cell, that he was not alone. The government was helpless to stop the non-violent, if hardly peaceful, demonstration. This was the germ of People Power that would hibernate through the rest of the winter of our oppression until Ninoy's willing sacrifice of his life brought the spring of our liberation.

Ninoy would remember this night and ponder its meaning in his cell and later on in exile. This demonstration had shown the limits of tyranny, that could reach everywhere except the hearts of brave men and women. He went on to read the works of men who had also experienced the peaceful but irresistible power of ordinary people to say, No more, and demand a change. He read Gandhi and Martin Luther King. From Gandhi, he drew his arrival statement when he had decided to return to his homeland for one last desperate effort to bring peace and reconciliation to his divided land.

"I have returned of my own free will," his statement read, "to join the ranks of those struggling to restore our rights of freedom through nonviolence. According to Gandhi, the willing sacrifice of the innocent is the most powerful answer to insolent tyranny that has yet been conceived by God and Man." But as you saw on Japanese television, he never read that statement. He was dead before his feet touched the land he loved.

It was after his death that People Power blossomed in all its glory. Two million people accompanied his coffin to the grave, under the hot sun and the pouring rain. Again, the government was powerless. It had issued threats against any who joined the funeral march. It grounded public transport so that people would be inconvenienced. It held a grand ball so that the people would see its indifference to their protest. But the funeral march went on, mournful and silent. Thousands of candles lit the way to his gravesite. As his coffin slipped into the ground, Ninoy's spirit entered his race. But Ninoy dead was more to be feared than when he was alive. For now his spirit was free to animate his people with the courage that had allowed him to face death. Courage, he said, is infectious. That night began the epidemic of bravery, from which the government learned there was no immunity.

The burden of Ninoy's mission to liberate his people in peace fell on my shoulders. I was reluctant to take it on. I was not a politician. And now that he was dead, I had once more to take on myself the role of father and mother to our children. And so I stipulated two conditions before I would take on the leadership of the struggle for freedom. Two conditions I believe could not be fulfilled. One was that Marcos would commit the folly of calling for a snap election. And the other was the impossible demand that one million people would sign a petition asking me to run for President. And that is exactly what happened. In an excess of arrogance, Marcos called for elections to prove once and for all that the opposition was nothing. And over a million people signed a petition to prove he was wrong.

Again, in this election as in the previous one, Marcos had the guns, the goons, and the national mint. With these things, he believed he could buy the people's mandate or, at least, thwart their will by fabricating a victory for himself at the polls. He was wrong. I and my running mate, with hardly any funds and barely any organization, nonetheless got the people. Or rather, the people got us in the grip of their determination to be rid once and for all of the tyranny that had abused and degraded them. Neither his tricks nor his thuggery could stem the irresistible tide of People Power that swept us to victory. Against his corruption, the people pitted their integrity by refusing to be bought. Against his threats, the people pitted their courage as they wrapped their arms around the ballot boxes to protect them from his thugs. Even his computer technicians, who were tasked with fabricating a fraudulent vote count walked out in protest. And against his debased parliament that proclaimed him the victor in the face of my overwhelming victory at the polls, they launched their nonviolent revolution. One million Filipinos gathered in Luneta Park to proclaim me and Doy Laurel as the victors of the election, the President and Vice-President of the People.

From that spot I proclaimed the strategy to vindicate the people's will, to implement their decision to make me President. I outlined a program of passive resistance and civil disobedience that called, as a starter, for a boycott of Marcos enterprises. I could not predict when we would succeed, but we were certain that the end of Marcos was near. Marcos could stay in the Palace but he had already lost the rest of the country. This was so clear to everyone that no one was afraid to join the nonviolent campaign and in the end, even the army stood down. A military revolt called by a brave handful of soldiers under Minister Enrile and General Ramos, who declared themselves for my Presidency was immediately surrounded by a protective wall of People Power summoned by the Cardinal. That wall stood up to the tanks of the dictator. Marcos had lost every shred of legitimacy and, on the fourth day of the revolt, slipped away into exile.

As I came to power peacefully, so shall I keep it. This is my contract with my people and my commitment to God. The way of nonviolence had not exhausted itself in the struggle for Filipino freedom. It has the potential to give our nation a lasting and honorable peace as well. In that belief, I have called for negotiations with the communist rebels. Some people say I am naive to have done this. I can only say that I owe it to our people, who have lived in fear of the gun for so long, to exhaust every means within reason to give them the peace they so much deserve.

I do not know if I will succeed. I know I must try if only to show that before I take up the sword of war, I shall have stripped the olive branch of peace of every leaf of offering. I am confident of the power of government to deal forcefully with the insurgency in the last resort. The courage and skills of the new Filipino soldier assure us that we shall never lose our dearly bought freedoms. The real challenge is to achieve peace by the ways of peace. This is the best assurance that it will last and serve as the foundation for the national cooperation that is needed to restore my country's wasted fortunes. You have seen this in your own history. You never achieved so much in war, as you did in peace. It is that experience of your country that inspires me to go on trying. I ask you to share with me the hope and prayers that I will succeed.

[*Source*: Aquino, C. C. (1986). *Speeches of President Corazon C. Aquino: August 8–December 31, 1986.* (Manila: Office of the President of the Philippines).]

Document Themes and Analysis

The first section of Aquino's speech is carefully designed to address the fact that she was both the first woman to hold such a high public office in the Philippines, and had never held political office in any capacity before. She identifies herself with Ninoy, her husband, who was one of the most powerful symbols of opposition to Marcos, and suggests that he would have been proud of her. She highlights Ninoy's contributions to the movement, even when he was imprisoned, and suggests that his mission must be carried on. She says that she had been reluctant to fill his shoes, knowing that she already had responsibilities as the principal parent to her children, but notes that the people—1 million of them—asked her to take on the role.

Establishing the public demand for her presidency is particularly important given the circumstances of the last years of Marcos's dictatorship. In this speech, she seeks to show that she was a candidate duly elected by the people and to reassure the Filipino population that the electoral corruption and fraud they had experienced over the past decade were now behind them.

One of the major foci of Aquino's speech is the nonviolent nature of the People Power Movement. Marcos, like many dictators, had relied on martial law, unjust imprisonment, and assassinations to maintain his grip on power. The People Power Movement engaged in civil protest and disobedience that was essentially nonviolent, and Aquino reassures her people in this speech that she will not use violent means to retain power now that she has it.

It should be noted that "nonviolent" does not mean inactive or passive. While a great deal of the popular protest focused on demonstrations in the streets of Manila (especially Epifanio de los Santos Avenue), there were also sympathetic military forces working to occupy strategic locations and arrest Marcos. At one point, the Philippine Marine Corps refused direct orders to kill a member of the opposition leadership; this defection was critical to preventing the kind of mass bloodshed against protestors that could otherwise have occurred. The protestors also showed a great deal of courage as they faced down armed police and military units deployed by the regime.

Aquino's own government was not without its faults. Among other things, she supported leaders who later turned out to be corrupt. And yet she represented a successful, peaceful revolutionary movement that forced a change in government and left its mark on Philippine history and politics.

—*Michael Shally-Jensen, PhD*

Bibliography and Additional Reading

Aquino, Corazon. *To Love Another Day: The Memoirs of Cory Aquino.* Edited by Lopa Rapa. Independent, 2020.

Espiritu, Talitha. *Passionate Revolutions: The Media and the Rise and the Fall of the Marcos Regime.* Athens: Ohio University Press, 2017.

Komisar, Lucy. *Corazon Aquino: The Story of a Revolution.* New York: George Braziller, 1987.

■ Nelson Mandela—Nobel Peace Prize Acceptance Speech

Date: December 10, 1993
Author: Nelson Mandela
Genre: speech; address

Summary Overview

Nelson Mandela's speech to the Nobel Committee is an optimistic and admirable outlining of his goals for the future of South Africa, after the crushing structural inequality and debasement of human life that took place there under the system of apartheid. In this speech, Mandela not only speaks about his goals and South Africa's place in the global community, but he also draws attention to social justice activists and revolutionaries around the world. He honors not only the struggles that his own people have faced and continue to face, but the struggles faced by so many people across the globe. It was here that Mandela spoke the immortal words "an injury to one is an injury to all."

Defining Moment

South Africa was unique in its codification of racism into a governmental system. Apartheid, translated from the Afrikaans word for "apartness," was a more extreme version of the American policy of "separate, but equal," which also contributed to severe inequality and racism in the United States. From 1948, when the Afrikaner Nationalist Party came into power, apartheid segregated people, legally and socially, based on skin color. White Africans were at the top of the hierarchy, while black Africans were at the very bottom even though the black African population accounted for 68.6 percent of the total population in 1946 (and 76 percent of the population in 1990).

In 1950, the Group Areas Act was introduced which physically separated different racial groups, and the Population Registration Act required people to be registered with the government according to their race. In 1959, the Promotion of Bantu Self-Government Act made land ownership a right of white Africans only, and black Africans were often forcibly removed from their homes, no longer allowed to live in cities; they could only rent property from white Africans. Marriage between races was also outlawed, as was voting by black Africans.

Resistance to these laws and governmental system existed from the very beginning, but were largely unable to stop the deterioration of conditions, get help from other nations, or make changes to the point of view of governmental leaders, through peaceful or violent means. Nelson Mandela was arrested and tried four times and spent over twenty-seven years in prison trying to affect change. It was not until police opened fire on protesters and killed several dozen in 1960 that the international community began to take notice. For the next several decades, international pressure mounted as grassroots organizations grew in strength and internal protests continued. Then, in 1989, South African President P. W. Botha resigned and F. W. de Klerk came to power. His very first act as president was to lift the ban on protest groups, such as Mandela's African National Congress (ANC). He followed this by allowing freedom of the press and releasing political prisoners, including Mandela. This was the first true step toward governmental shift and the revolution orchestrated by protestors and Nelson Mandela. This document shows the culmination of these changes: the creation of a democratic governmental system, the free election of Nelson Mandela, and the international acknowledgement of the architects of this revolution.

Author Biography

Nelson Mandela, born Rolihlahla Mandela, is part of the Madiba clan and was born in the village of Mvezo, in the Eastern Cape of South Africa. A promising student, his academic studies warred with his desire to help his people and make an impact on injustice in South Africa. This resulted in his expulsion from University College of Fort Hare due to his role in student protests. He would eventually earn his bachelor's degree, but from this time his interests were much more tuned toward politics. After joining the ANC and becoming an important member, he was arrested and tried multiple times for inciting workers to strike and treason. He was sentenced to life in prison.

From prison Mandela was able to organize talks between the government and the now-banned ANC to try to end apartheid. He was successful and eventually released from prison on February 11, 1990. He had served 26 years. He became ANC President in 1991, won the Nobel Peace prize alongside South African President F. W. de Klerk, and voted for the first time in 1994 – in an election which resulted in his presidency. He spent his term as president working to heal the incredibly deep divides in his society and spent the rest of his life pursing this same goal. He died at home in Johannesburg in 2013.

Nelson Mandela in 1994. Photo by John Mathew Smith, via Wikimedia Commons.

Historical Document

Your Majesty the King,

Your Royal Highness,

Esteemed Members of the Norwegian Nobel Committee,

Honourable Prime Minister, Madame Gro Harlem Brundtland, Ministers, Members of Parliament and Ambassadors, Fellow Laureate, Mr. F.W. de Klerk, Distinguished Guests,

Friends, Ladies and Gentlemen,

I extend my heartfelt thanks to the Norwegian Nobel Committee for elevating us to the status of a Nobel Peace Prize winner.

I would also like to take this opportunity to congratulate my compatriot and fellow laureate, State President F.W. de Klerk, on his receipt of this high honour.

Together, we join two distinguished South Africans, the late Chief Albert Lutuli and His Grace Archbishop Desmond Tutu, to whose seminal contributions to the peaceful struggle against the evil system of apartheid you paid well-deserved tribute by awarding them the Nobel Peace Prize.

It will not be presumptuous of us if we also add, among our predecessors, the name of another outstanding Nobel Peace Prize winner, the late Rev Martin Luther King Jr.

He, too, grappled with and died in the effort to make a contribution to the just solution of the same great issues of the day which we have had to face as South Africans.

We speak here of the challenge of the dichotomies of war and peace, violence and non-violence, racism and human dignity, oppression and repression and liberty and human rights, poverty and freedom from want.

We stand here today as nothing more than a representative of the millions of our people who dared to rise up against a social system whose very essence is war, violence, racism, oppression, repression and the impoverishment of an entire people.

I am also here today as a representative of the millions of people across the globe, the anti-apartheid movement, the governments and organisations that joined with us, not to fight against South Africa as a country or any of its peoples, but to oppose an inhuman system and sue for a speedy end to the apartheid crime against humanity.

These countless human beings, both inside and outside our country, had the nobility of spirit to stand in the path of tyranny and injustice, without seeking selfish gain. They recognised that an injury to one is an injury to all and therefore acted together in defense of justice and a common human decency.

Because of their courage and persistence for many years, we can, today, even set the dates when all humanity will join together to celebrate one of the outstanding human victories of our century.

When that moment comes, we shall, together, rejoice in a common victory over racism, apartheid and white minority rule.

That triumph will finally bring to a close a history of five hundred years of African colonisation that began with the establishment of the Portuguese empire.

Thus, it will mark a great step forward in history and also serve as a common pledge of the peoples of the world to fight racism, wherever it occurs and whatever guise it assumes.

At the southern tip of the continent of Africa, a rich reward in the making, an invaluable gift is in the preparation for those who suffered in the name of all humanity when they sacrifi[c]ed everything—for liberty, peace, human dignity and human fulfillment.

This reward will not be measured in money. Nor can it be reckoned in the collective price of the rare metals and precious stones that rest in the bowels of the African soil we tread in the footsteps of our ancestors.

It will and must be measured by the happiness and welfare of the children, at once the most vulnerable citizens in any society and the greatest of our treasures.

The children must, at last, play in the open veld, no longer tortured by the pangs of hunger or ravaged by disease or threatened with the scourge of ignorance, molestation and abuse, and no longer required to engage in deeds whose gravity exceeds the demands of their tender years.

In front of this distinguished audience, we commit the new South Africa to the relentless pursuit of the purposes defined in the World Declaration on the Survival, Protection and Development of Children.[1]

The reward of which we have spoken will and must also be measured by the happiness and welfare of the mothers and fathers of these children, who must walk the earth without fear of being robbed, killed for political or material profit, or spat upon because they are beggars.

They too must be relieved of the heavy burden of despair which they carry in their hearts, born of hunger, homelessness and unemployment.

The value of that gift to all who have suffered will and must be measured by the happiness and welfare of all the people of our country, who will have torn down the inhuman walls that divide them.

These great masses will have turned their backs on the grave insult to human dignity which described some as masters and others as servants, and transformed each into a predator whose survival depended on the destruction of the other.

The value of our shared reward will and must be measured by the joyful peace which will triumph, because the common humanity that bonds both black and white into one human race, will have said to each one of us that we shall all live like the children of paradise.

Thus shall we live, because we will have created a society which recognises that all people are born equal, with each entitled in equal measure to life, liberty, prosperity, human rights and good governance.

Such a society should never allow again that there should be prisoners of conscience nor that any person's human right should be violated.

Neither should it ever happen that once more the avenues to peaceful change are blocked by usurpers who seek to take power away from the people, in pursuit of their own, ignoble purposes.

In relation to these matters, we appeal to those who govern Burma that they release our fellow Nobel Peace Prize laureate, Aung San Suu Kyi, and engage her and those she represents in serious dialogue, for the benefit of all the people of Burma.[2]

We pray that those who have the power to do so will, without further delay, permit that she uses her talents and energies for the greater good of the people of her country and humanity as a whole.

Far from the rough and tumble of the politics of our own country. I would like to take this opportunity to join the Norwegian Nobel Committee and pay tribute to my joint laureate. Mr. F.W. de Klerk.

He had the courage to admit that a terrible wrong had been done to our country and people through the imposition of the system of apartheid.

He had the foresight to understand and accept that all the people of South Africa must through negotiations and as equal participants in the process, together determine what they want to make of their future.

But there are still some within our country who wrongly believe they can make a contribution to the cause of justice and peace by clinging to the shibboleths that have been proved to spell nothing but disaster.

It remains our hope that these, too, will be blessed with sufficient reason to realise that history will not be denied and that the new society cannot be created by reproducing the repugnant past, however refined or enticingly repackaged.

We would also like to take advantage of this occasion to pay tribute to the many formations of the democratic movement of our country, including the members of our Patriotic Front, who have themselves played a central role in bringing our country as close to the democratic transformation as it is today.

We are happy that many representatives of these formations, including people who have served or are serving in the "homeland" structures, came with us to Oslo. They too must share the accolade which the Nobel Peace Prize confers.

We live with the hope that as she battles to remake herself, South Africa, will be like a microcosm of the new world that is striving to be born.

This must be a world of democracy and respect for human rights, a world freed from the horrors of poverty, hunger, deprivation and ignorance, relieved of the threat and the scourge of civil wars and external aggression and unburdened of the great tragedy of millions forced to become refugees.

The processes in which South Africa and Southern Africa as a whole are engaged, beckon and urge us all that we take this tide at the flood and make of this region as a living example of what all people of conscience would like the world to be.

We do not believe that this Nobel Peace Prize is intended as a commendation for matters that have happened and passed.

We hear the voices which say that it is an appeal from all those, throughout the universe, who sought an end to the system of apartheid.

We understand their call, that we devote what remains of our lives to the use of our country's unique and painful experience to demonstrate, in practice, that the normal condition for human existence is democracy, justice, peace, non-racism, non-sexism, prosperity for everybody, a healthy environment and equality and solidarity among the peoples.

Moved by that appeal and inspired by the eminence you have thrust upon us, we undertake that we too will do what we can to contribute to the renewal of our world so that none should, in future, be described as the "wretched of the earth."[3]

Let it never be said by future generations that indifference, cynicism or selfishness made us fail to live up to the ideals of humanism which the Nobel Peace Prize encapsulates.

Let the strivings of us all, prove Martin Luther King Jr. to have been correct, when he said that humanity can no longer be tragically bound to the starless midnight of racism and war.

Let the efforts of us all, prove that he was not a mere dreamer when he spoke of the beauty of genuine brotherhood and peace being more precious than diamonds or silver or gold.

Let a new age dawn!

Thank you.

---

1. The Declaration of the Rights of the Child, approved unanimously by the United Nations General Assembly on 20 November 1959, proclaimed ten fundamental rights, including those Mandela mentions.
2. Aung San Suu Kyi was granted the 1991 Nobel Peace Prize. See pp. 1–21.
3. "Arise, ye wretched of the earth" is a line in the English version of the Internationale, a revolutionary socialist hymn written in Paris in 1871 and sung thereafter by socialists and communists.

From Nobel Lectures, Peace 1991–1995, Editor Irwin Abrams, World Scientific Publishing Co., Singapore, 1999. Copyright © The Nobel Foundation 1993

Glossary

dichotomies: division or contrast between two things that are opposed or entirely different

microcosm: a miniature version of the characteristics or features of something much larger

scourge: a person or thing that causes great trouble or suffering

shibboleths: customs, principles, or beliefs distinguishing a particular class or group of people (often seen as outdated or no longer important)

veld: uncultivated land or grassland in southern Africa

Document Analysis

Perhaps one of the most striking aspects of Nelson Mandela's revolutionary actions were the inclusive nature of them. Never did he press for the fortunes of black Africans to improve at the expense of white Africans. He wanted equality for all people—and he showed this far more in his actions than simply in his words. In the opening seconds of his speech, he draws attention to his fellow Nobel recipient, earlier activists, and contemporary activists from around the world. He was not a man alone, but part of a greater body of humanity, all of whom deserve respect, honor, and a chance for a quality life. His words promoted a "common human decency" and the ideal of justice that "an injury to one is an injury to all." In Mandela's vision, no one, no matter their position in society, suffered.

This was an inspiring position to take, because he had faced such crushing inequity throughout his life. Moreover, the people of South Africa had faced these struggles due to the passive acceptance and indifference of countries that did nothing to help through the history of apartheid. Mandela pushes people to be better and to do more when he states "indifference, cynicism or selfishness" will not be how he and his people are remembered in the future. That good thoughts and hopes are not enough, but that action, continuous, difficult action, is necessary to make change.

Mandela's "brotherhood" of man reverberates throughout this speech. He never speaks of his individual actions, nor choices he alone made, or even his particular role in the changes in South Africa. Rather, he focuses on how people can and should work together for a common goal—the improvement of each life by improving all lives.

Essential Themes

Nelson Mandela had a dream similar to that of Martin Luther King Jr. whom he honors in this speech. They dreamed of a world where the inequalities and hatred they had faced in their lives would be overturned and overcome. These are exceptional dreams; but incredibly difficult to make reality. Changing the quality of life for South Africans was not a simple mission, for it required more than changing the opinions of the people about race and equality. It required a complete change in the systems which ran the government, organized the physical space of the city and countryside, and regulated economics at all levels of society. In comparison, changing laws is easy.

Because of the great challenges of overhauling a whole society, South Africa still faces great inequality today. The goals of Mandela (and de Klerk) have not been met—but they are still inspiring people to strive for a brighter future for themselves and their children, to eventually escape the "starless midnight." Perhaps one of the most important lessons of Mandela's speech and of his life is that change is not a single action, but an investment in working as hard as you can towards a goal and hoping that one day someone might achieve it for the benefit of everyone.

—*Anna Accettola, PhD*

Bibliography and Additional Reading

"A History of Apartheid in South Africa." *South African History Online: Towards a People's History*. Available at www.sahistory.org.za/article/history-apartheid-south-africa

"Biography of Nelson Mandela." *Nelson Mandela Foundation: Living the Legacy*. www.nelsonmandela.org/content/page/biography.

Mandela, Nelson. *Long Walk to Freedom: The Autobiography of Nelson Mandela*. New York: Little Brown & Co., 1994.

Spence, Jack, and David Welsh. *Ending Apartheid*. New York: Taylor & Francis, 2014.

■ Hugo Chávez Speech in Havana

Date: September 1, 2003
Author: Hugo Chávez
Genre: speech

Summary Overview

Hugo Chávez, the president of Venezuela, spoke at the 2003 United Nations Convention Against Desertification, which grew out of a conference in Rio de Janeiro in 1992. It addressed the need for sustainable development and to combat the impact of land degradation leading to desertification, or the transformation of green habitat to desert. In 1994, Agenda 21 was adopted as a plan to address these issues, and entered into force in 1996. Yearly United Nations (UN) meetings, in Rome, Dakar, Recife, Bonn, and Geneva, created a Committee on Science and Technology and a Group of Experts. At the 2003 UN meeting in Havana, Chávez recognized the dangers facing countries of the Global South. He talked about his policies in Venezuela to create a new model for development.

The perspective Chávez brought to the conference was that of a developing country often at the mercy of policies imposed by wealthier nations. He quoted the phrase that underdeveloped countries are in reality overrun countries. Chávez bragged about the laws adopted by Venezuela to improve agriculture and water quality. He called for the countries faced with soil degradation to band together to demand greater resources and even create their own institutions to provide money rather than depending on the great powers, a rather revolutionary concept.

Defining Moment

The depletion of soil and land degradation are threats to the earth, the food supply, and humanity. This was recognized at the United Nations (UN) conference in Rio de Janeiro and reaffirmed in yearly meetings. Within the framework of the UN, the program called Agenda 21 had four areas: combating poverty; protecting the environment; strengthening the role of underrepresented groups; and implementing programs through financial and educational policies. It called on every signing nation to develop its own plans and assumed the major powers that provided financial backing to world and UN programs would provide leadership.

Agenda 21 was supposed to be nonpolitical and focus on technical aspects of sustainable development. However, at the 2003 meeting in Havana, Hugo Chávez, a socialist, called for radical changes throughout the program. His Bolivarian revolution in

Hugo Chavez in 2011. Photo courtesy of the Office of the President of Brazil, via Wikimedia Commons.

Venezuela, beginning with his election in 1998 (and named after the nineteenth-century hero Simón Bolívar), promoted a participatory democracy that included urban poor and rural populations and sought to reduce the power of Venezuela's political and financial elites. This was not an easy transformation, and Chávez was temporarily removed from power in 2002 in a coup d'état that was supported by the United States. The strong negative reaction to the coup by Venezuelans brought Chávez back to office, and emboldened him to call for the nations of the Global South to form a bloc to demand a greater share of resources and power in order to address the problems of poverty and land degradation. He was not willing to sit and talk about programs when he felt that the people of developing nations were suffering from policies that benefited richer nations. Chávez's proposals did not get widespread approval, but he demonstrated that an alternative to the global power structure was possible.

Author Biography

Hugo Rafael Chávez Frías, known as Hugo Chávez, was a Venezuelan military officer and politician who was elected to four terms as president between 1998 and 2012. He replaced a corrupt political leadership and initiated economic and social reforms to help Venezuela's poor. His policies were controversial and generated opposition, resulting in a coup that briefly ousted him from office. He returned to power and governed until he died of cancer at age fifty-eight in 2013.

Hugo Chávez was born in 1954 and grew up in a modest home. After finishing high school, he studied at the Academy of Military Sciences in Caracas. Chávez served in the Venezuelan military, rising to the rank of lieutenant colonel. He admired the Peruvian leftist military president, Juan Velasco Alvarado and the Panamanian military president Omar Torrijos, and formed a group of officers that became the Revolutionary Bolivarian Movement-200 (MBR-200). In 1992 Chávez attempted a coup against President Carlos Andrés Pérez. The coup failed, and Chávez spent two years in jail before being freed.

Chávez gained a political following from groups that regarded Venezuelan politics as corrupt, and he was elected president in 1998 in a leftist coalition. Quickly, Chávez began to implement social and economic reforms, and proposed a new constitution. While critics claimed Chávez was becoming authoritarian, he countered that his reforms were necessary to stamp out corruption and address the needs of the poor. Chávez used the profits from the state-run oil company to fund many of his programs.

The Republic of Venezuela became the Bolivarian Republic of Venezuela under Chávez, harkening to the great Venezuelan independence hero, Simón Bolívar, who tried to unite the continent into one great nation in the early 1800s. Chávez coordinated his policies with those of other left-leaning Latin American countries, forming a regional bank to counter the power of the International Monetary Fund, and creating a regional bloc, the Bolivarian Alliance for the Peoples of our America, or ALBA.

Chávez became friends of Fidel Castro and supported Cuba. When diagnosed with cancer, Chávez went to Cuba for treatment. However, the cancer spread and shortly after he was elected for a fourth term, he died (2013).

Historical Document

[Sixth Session of the United Nations Convention to Combat Desertification September 1, 2003]

Thanks Fidel [Castro] for your support, thanks Fidel for your comments.

In Venezuela we adopted a set of laws for the water, the fishery, the lands, in order to initiate the transformation of the model.

And what happened? That was on November 2001.

On December of that year 2001 started the conspiracy framed by the elite, the oligarchy, the great forces that had governed Venezuela for decades, or centuries, together with their hegemonic international allies, then came the terrorist, oligarchic, national and transnational coup d'état on April 11, 2002, intended to stop this project and to derogate all these laws which are already having a positive impact on the real transformation of a savage system which has ravaged a large portion of our country and has contributed to the devastation of the planet.

Of course the leaders of this coup in Venezuela and their international allies had not foreseen the reaction of the people and the unexpected happened, the tyrannical and despotic government that had overthrown our government and imprisoned me, massacring the population, was in turn overthrown by the people before the rooster sang three times.

The dictatorship did not last 72 hours and the Constitution was restored, and our people is fighting for this flag, this cause and this project.

Well then, as I was saying a while ago, this view point is not exposed to make you feel pessimistic, but to recognize the scope of the problem, and as Fidel said a minute ago, we cannot be begging from the powerful of this world, we must uphold our dignity, not our individual dignity but the dignity of the peoples that have been oppressed, exploited and massacred for such a long time, the dignity of the heroes who fought and died for the freedom of our countries during the last five hundred years.

We cannot become beggars, we cannot preach in the desert. We in Venezuela what we do is to demand, regardless of the size or power of the others, we demand respect.

Eduardo Galeano, one of our greatest [writers], in reference to this has said that we are not underdeveloped countries, what we are is overrun countries, we have been overrun for centuries, but we have to uplift our dignity, our moral force to make our claim to the world, particularly to the northern developed countries, whose dignified representatives are also here and we express our respect to their heads of states and government and our best regards to their peoples, but since we have been overrode, invaded, and vexed over the centuries, and nobody should take offense at these words because they are true, and as José Gervasio Artigas, the leader from Uruguay said: " My truth causes no offense and gives me no fears," and this is the truth, at least our truth.

As the world changes, very strong winds of change are blowing through South America, not only in Venezuela, but also in Brazil, Argentina and many other countries that are witnessing the rise of new leaders. I come from that South America which is right here, next to the Caribbean.

In South America, let me tell you, only three years ago maybe less, we felt lonely at the summits in adopting a stand, in making proposals, in criticizing Neoliberalism, in suggesting debates on topics such as the foreign debt or the FTAA [Free Trade Agreement for the Americas].

In fact, only when Fidel attends a summit, sometimes he cannot attend because he is democratically excluded, but in some occasions, for example, the first time Fidel and I coincided in a summit and started to argue with the other presidents, we were left alone, the two of us. I remember Fidel wrote a note on a small piece of paper:

—I no longer feel as the only devil in these summits.

However, nowadays in most of the meetings held by South American presidents the criticism of Neoliberalism, the debate on the foreign debt, the FTAA [see below], the World Trade Organization (WTO), poverty and peoples have become common topics. I must tell you that in South America there are strong winds of change, as in other parts of the world, the world is changing.

Can we do anything to accelerate this change? Yes, we can.

How?

In the first place, telling the truth. Secondly, joining our wills, devising a strategic plan, walking together. It is essential to unite the South, because the North is united, they get together and make decisions.

But every time it is more difficult for them to do so. According to the last news I heard, one of these northern summits will be held on board a transatlantic ship, in the middle of the ocean, in order to escape from the harassment of the opponents of globalization and the poor of the world.

The union of the south is a most, but a union to free ourselves, not to continue enslaved.

At what cost?

At whatever it takes.

At the cost of life?

Yes, it does not matter, how important can the life of a man, or a woman, or a group of us be if the aim is to save from this threat millions of persons, even those yet unborn or who are being born right now.

In South America, for example, we are proposing the establishment of such unity, but not the unity suggested by Washington, the FTAA, the Free Trade Agreement for the Americas, because to sign this agreement as it is would be to sign the death sentence for our grandchildren. From Venezuela we are suggesting an alternative to the FTAA, because we are certain that it is not the right way, well, maybe only the right way to hell. We are suggesting the Bolivarian Alternative for the Americas, the ALBA, based on the ideals of Bolivar, who fought two hundred years ago and shaped only a portion of his dream which was later shattered, but Bolivar's ideal was to unify all the Caribbean, he said so in Jamaica, Percival Patterson knows what I am saying because he is a Bolivarian.

I dream, he said in Kingston in the year one thousand [eight hundred] and sixteen, of making this part of the world into only one great nation, greater for its freedom and glory than for the huge wealth lying in its womb. The integration of our peoples.

And this is valid for Africa and for Asia, we have to walk the southern ways, with more strength than in the past, the same banners, but more strength.

For example I tell the South American peoples that with political will and a little courage we could create a monetary fund for Latin American, and the Caribbean of course.

Who says we cannot do it?

A different monetary fund, ruled by us. I tell the South Americans that we have oil and state-owned oil companies. We could create a Petroamerica integrated by Brazil, Venezuela, Colombia, Ecuador, Peru, Bolivia, Cuba which also has oil, Fidel told me recently that by the year two thousand and eight they will be ready to join the OPEC, it seems that there is an oil field under the island.

Trinidad and Tobago is one of the first producers of gas in the continent. I recently paid a visit, dear friends of the Caribbean, to our comrade Prime Minister Mannin, there in Port of Spain, and he proposed a project to me and I immediately told him he can count on Venezuela's support, because we have joined the gas fields in the Trinitarian and Venezuelan Atlantic area which contains important gas reserves. The project is to build a gas pipeline until Guadalupe, I think. I told him Venezuela is ready to cooperate in the construction of this pipeline to take the gas, which is a clean and cheap source of energy, to the peoples of the Caribbean. This pipeline could reach all the islands of the eastern Caribbean and even Cuba, this is a viable project, a study has been made, it will depend on the amount of the resources we are able to pump form the Atlantic waters in Venezuela, Trinidad and Tobago and the Caribbean itself.

This would provide enough energy to improve the living standards of the peoples of these southern countries in the first place.

These are some ideas of what we can do, instead of begging or preaching in the desert.

In the last 5 years— for example, I have heard many voices, mine included, saying:

—The international economic structure needs to be reformed.

We have repeated that assertion over and over again, I myself have repeated it throughout 2 years, but I no longer will, now I say:

We in the South must create our own financial structures. And they must be strong ones, because I am certain that the International Monetary Fund is not willing to change, not at all!

They believe they own the Olympus and they have the right to impose their criteria on the world, even if that brings about the world's destruction.

These are some of the ideas that we are discussing in Venezuela and other South American countries, and these ideas are gaining strength among the people, the intellectuals, the workers, the women, the social movements, political parties, parliaments.

Only then we will be able to promote these ideas with the required power and consistency, so that the world really starts to change.

If we leave the change of the world in the hands of the powerful, when Mars returns he will look at the Earth as if he were looking into a mirror. And we cannot let it happen.

Two years ago in Geneva I ended my speech with an expression that came to my mind during the Millennium Summit, I will repeat it because I believe it is possible, with WILL, UNITY, BOLDNESS and COURAGE, now at the beginning of the new millennium, in spite of all the signs to the contrary, I believe a better, different, beautiful world is possible. I hope the Earth never resembles Mars, though Mars is very handsome, the red planet!, but I hope our planet will never be like the Martian deserts, but like the little roads surrounded by trees and bushes.

I repeat once more, Mr. President, dear friends, now from Havana, with all my heart and affection: LET'S SAVE THIS OUR WORLD!

Thank you very much.

Document Analysis

At the United Nations Convention Against Desertification held in Havana in 2003, Hugo Chávez responded warmly to the speech by the host, Fidel Castro. Chávez rose to speak, thanking Fidel for his comments, and then spoke on the theme of world nations' vulnerability not only to climate change and soil degradation but to the political and economic threat of domination by wealthy nations. After commenting on laws passed by his administration in Venezuela to address soil and water issues, Chávez immediately delves into the political opposition that attempted to unseat him in a "terrorist, oligarchic, national and transnational coup." Chávez claims that this opposition was sponsored and supported by his opponents' international allies, including the United States, who wanted to halt his policies. He maintains that the people of Venezuela refused to accept the coup and returned him to power. Chávez points out that several Latin American countries in the early 2000s were headed by left-wing presidents, and believes that this solidarity should allow them to demand their rightful place among nations, rather than beg for money.

Chávez calls on the Global South of developing nations to unite against the power of Northern countries that control the World Trade Organization and other international monetary programs. As an alternative, he cites ALBA, the Bolivarian Alliance for the Peoples of our America, an organization that included many Latin American nations dedicated to providing support for development projects, as a way to replace dependence on money from the United States and Europe. As Simón Bolívar wanted to unite all the lands of Latin America, Chávez wanted to unite the Global South to fight for its rights.

Chávez advocates for a powerful petroleum consortium of Latin American and Caribbean countries, with pipelines supplying the region. He refers to the topic under consideration, desertification and soil degradation, only at the very end of his speech. He hopes that Earth will never resemble Mars, with its mostly dry soil, and ends with a call to save the planet.

Essential Themes

Hugo Chávez was an advocate for the Global South and a staunch opponent of the powerful nations that controlled many of the world's resources and much of the world's wealth. His Bolivarian Revolution transformed Venezuela from a corrupt liberal democracy into a participatory system under authoritarian leadership. He changed the country's constitution, opened channels for ordinary citizens to participate, and focused the country's resources on the poor. These policies earned him the hatred of the elites who had dominated the government and the economy in the past, and they tried (but failed) to remove him. Chávez's spirit of confrontation and challenge extended to the United States and other countries that supported his domestic opponents, and he brought this attitude to the UN meeting in Havana in 2003, nominally to discuss methods of halting soil degradation and ways to support sustainable development.

Chávez subsumes the goal of reducing soil degradation within a broader fight to advance the ability of developing countries to control their own destinies. He presents a broad socialist framework that clashes with the capitalist economies of the world's most advanced nations. Since these same countries supplied the majority funding for the UN and the international programs, like the desertification Agenda 21 program, Chávez spars with these powers in his speech. He recognizes that such a stance will bring opposition and recounts his own experience with a coup attempt against him. Hugo Chávez was a combative presence on the world stage, partnering with Cuba, Iran, and other countries to challenge the supremacy of the United States. He urged a united stance, not just in combating soil degradation but in energy and finance.

—*James A. Baer, PhD*

Bibliography and Additional Reading

CarbonBrief. "Explainer: 'Desertification' and the Role of Climate Change." August 6, 2019. www.carbonbrief.org/explainer-desertification-and-the-role-of-climate-change.

Carroll, Rory. *Comandante: Hugo Chávez's Venezuela*. New York: Penguin, 2014.

Glantz, Michael H. *Desertification: Environmental Degradation in and around Arid Lands,* Boca Raton, FL: CRC Press, 2020.

Gott, Richard. *Hugo Chávez and the Bolivarian Revolution.* New York: Verso, 2011.

Slayikoya, Sara Popescu. "Causes and Effects of Desertification on People and the Environment." *Greentumble,* April 29, 2019. greentumble.com/causes-and-effects-of-desertification.

United Nations. "United Nations Conference on Environment & Development, Rio de Janeiro, 3 to 14 June 1992: Agenda 21." sustainabledevelopment.un.org/content/documents/Agenda21.pdf.

Ukraine—the Orange Revolution

The Orange Revolution was a large-scale protest by Ukrainian citizens sparked by the results of the 2004 presidential election. In what was widely regarded as a rigged process, the official results showed that the pro-Russia candidate and current prime minister, Viktor Yanukovych, had beaten the opposition candidate, Viktor Yushchenko. Large protests in Kyiv and elsewhere in the election's wake came to be named after the color used by supporters of Yushchenko and his party, Our Ukraine.

Starting from November 21, supporters of the Our Ukraine party began to erect a tent city on the Maidan, or Independence Square, in Kyiv. Over the next few days the number of protesters grew to over 100,000. Despite the Election Commission's approval of the results, the protest continued. Then, on November 27, the Ukrainian Parliament entered a vote of no-confidence in the Election Commission. As protestors remained on-site, the Supreme Court of Ukraine called for a new election. And on December 26, as a result of the redone election, Viktor Yushchenko of Our Ukraine was elected president.

The Orange Revolution achieved a temporary balance in public opinion. In addition, the political elite began to listen to voters. However, this gave rise to the development of populism, which did not promote reforms. Further disenchantment of citizens with Viktor Yushchenko's policies over time brought the previous president, Viktor Yanukovych, back to power in 2010.

Yanukovych made promises to pivot the country away from Russia and toward the European Union, starting with energy resources. In 2013, however, he reneged on that promise, causing a gathering of protesters once again. After early protests were crudely broken up by the police, on December 1 hundreds of thousands of people came to the center of Kyiv. This time the protest was labeled the Euromaidan, to invoke both the desired turn to Europe and the city square in which it took place. Ultimately, Yanukovych was forced from power and fled the country—for Russia—in February 2014.

Later that year, in a show of disapproval, Russia's authoritarian leader Vladimir Putin, in addition to "annexing" the Ukrainian territory of Crimea, launched a low-grade war of occupation in the largely Russian-speaking Donbas region of eastern Ukraine. Even more alarming, in 2022 Putin launched a full-scale war against Ukraine to try to "return" it to Russian control. His war plans quickly fell apart, however, and today Ukrainians continue to fight the foreign aggressor.

Inaugural Speech by Ukrainian President Viktor Yushchenko

Date: January 23, 2005
Author: Viktor Yushchenko
Genre: speech

Summary Overview

As the newly elected president of Ukraine, Viktor Yushchenko spoke in January 2005 to the people of the nation regarding a significant change that had occurred in the country. The change had nothing to do with the usual government concerns or pronouncements regarding economic, military, or social policies. Instead, it was a celebratory statement that democracy had come to Ukraine, more than a dozen years after it left the Soviet Union. Yushchenko saw the European norms of individual freedom and equality for all citizens of a country, as now part of life in Ukraine, in contrast to the authoritarian, corrupt ways of the last president.

In his speech, although Yushchenko does not refer to the Orange Revolution by name, he describes its events, by which this latest phase of Ukrainian political history had come into being. The Orange Revolution of 2004–2005 began in response to clear electoral fraud that took place in the November 2004 presidential runoff election between Yushchenko and his opponent, Viktor Yanukovych. The massive antigovernment movement called the Orange Revolution forced a revote, which Yushchenko won (52% to 44%). Once elected, he gave this speech to thank the people who had made it possible.

Defining Moment

When the Soviet Union dissolved in December 1991, Ukraine took steps to become an independent country, specifically one not affiliated with the new Russian Federation. A mixed presidential-parliamentary system of government was established, with the president normally serving five-year terms. Leonid Kuchma served two terms (1994–2005), and while initially open to working with Western European nations, his authoritarian style (including media crackdowns) and the many scandals that surrounded him made him unwelcome in the West. As a result, Kuchma increased Ukraine's cooperation with Russia. Not running for reelection in 2004, he supported his prime minister, Viktor Yanukovych. Although the first round of voting was not marked by any significant

Viktor Yushchenko. Photo courtesy of the Government of Ukraine, via Wikimedia Commons.

problems, the second, runoff round was widely believed to be affected by fraud. The dramatic difference between preelection polls and the announced result caused major protests to occur in the capital of Kyiv and other cities.

The Orange Revolution, as it came to be called, began the day after the original runoff on November 21. While the demonstrations focused on Independence Square in Kyiv, there were supporting demonstrations throughout much of the country. Because of the history of corruption identified with the Kuchma regime, it was not hard for Ukrainian voters (and foreign election observers) to accept the idea that he and his prime minister had plotted to rig the second round of elections. Unofficial results showed Yushchenko winning by about eleven percent, while the "official" results had Yanukovych winning by three percent. Mass demonstrations were mounted to dispute the results, and legal proof of fraud was demonstrated in materials leaked by a member of the Ukrainian national police. As the Orange Revolution unfolded, the case claiming fraud was brought before the Ukrainian Supreme Court. In a surprising move, the court ordered a rerun of the second round of elections, for December 26, 2004. The results of that election were very different, with Yushchenko the clear winner. Once the results were verified, Yushchenko was declared president. His inauguration took place on January 23, 2005.

Yushchenko's inauguration speech served as a public affirmation of the new president's values and goals for the nation. It marked a very different approach to domestic and foreign policy for the Ukrainian state, as compared to that of his predecessor. Generally, this speech was received well, by both its primary audience, the Ukrainian people, and the secondary audience, the leaders of Western democracies. Although Yushchenko ended up being a one-term president, he did make efforts to fulfill some of the ideals outlined in his speech.

Author Biography

Viktor Andriyovych Yushchenko was born in northeastern Ukraine (Sumy Oblast) in 1954, with both of

The pro-Russia candidate, Viktor Yanukovych, was accused of rigging the initial election. Photo courtesy of the Government of Ukraine, via Wikimedia Commons.

his parents being teachers. A 1975 graduate of the Ternopil Finance and Economics Institute, he joined the state bank of the Soviet Union after having served an obligatory year in the military. After the dissolution of the Soviet Union, Yushchenko worked in the Ukrainian state bank, becoming governor of the National Bank of Ukraine in 1993. Having brought Ukraine's inflation under control, he was appointed prime minister by President Kuchma in 1999. Although voted out of this position by Communists and other conservatives in 2001, Yushchenko ran for the presidency as an independent in 2004. He survived being poisoned during the campaign. He ran on a platform of European Integration. During his presidency (2005–2010), his popularity plummeted, resulting in an electoral loss when he ran for a second term.

Historical Document

We have lifted the burden of the past from our shoulders. Nobody can order us how to live and whom to elect anymore. I have become the president of Ukraine by the will of the Ukrainian people....

Two months ago millions of people came to this square, to the squares and streets all over Ukraine. Our brothers and sisters, parents and children, friends and neighbors were standing day and night in the cold. Ukraine was devouring every word sounded here. The heart of Ukraine was beating here. Free people of the whole world, our compatriots dispersed in distant lands, were standing shoulder to shoulder with us. On Independence Square Ukrainians have risen as a modern Ukrainian nation. Stubborn resistance has stirred up our souls. All of us feel we are citizens. Our decency, generosity, and kindness have awakened. Armed with faith and will the people won a glorious victory. This is a victory of freedom over tyranny, law over lawlessness, and the future over the past. Each Ukrainian citizen has become the winner. We succeeded in holding a fair election on 26 December. We have freely chosen to go forward....

We, the Ukrainian citizens, have become a single Ukrainian nation. Nobody can separate us with languages, religion, and political views. We have a single Ukrainian fate. We have a single national pride. We are proud of being Ukrainians! We have already taken an irrevocable step to democracy. Only democracy guards the most valuable things for every person—family and children, peace and order, work, and well-being. Only in a democratic state are the highest values human dignity, freedom, equality, and solidarity. Only in a democratic Ukraine may the bright palette of languages, cultures, and views become the country's wealth. I pledge that every child will be able to learn the language of one's parents. Everyone will be able to pray in one's church. Everyone will be guaranteed the right to freedom of expression. We will listen to each other because there will be freedom of speech and an independent press. Everybody will be equal before the law. Independent courts will defend the rights of each person. I regard Ukraine as a state ruled by the law. We will establish democratic government—honest, professional, and patriotic....

Our way to the future is the way followed by a united Europe. We are people of the same civilization sharing the same values. History, economic prospects, and the interests of people give a clear answer as to where we should look for our fate. Our place is in the European Union. My goal is Ukraine in a united Europe. Ukraine has a historic chance to discover its potential in Europe. Our national strategy is to move toward our goal boldly, directly, and persistently. European standards will become a norm of our social life, economy, and politics. Every step to Europe opens up new opportunities for millions of Ukrainians.

Document Analysis

While speaking primarily to the people of Ukraine, Yushchenko here is also reaching out to the global community of nations. He emphasizes that a new day had arrived for Ukraine, one based on the democratic values of human dignity, equality, and freedom. The Orange Revolution had been successful, and now, Yushchenko believes, it is time for Ukraine to join with the Western European nations, as represented by the European Union (EU), rather than turn back to reliance on the Russian Federation.

Praising the people of Ukraine, Yushchenko begins the main part of his statement by mentioning the "millions of people" who demonstrated against the fraud in the original runoff in November 2004. He recognizes that this was the only reason he had been inaugurated as president, since his opponent, Viktor Yanukovych, had the majority of the vote in the November runoff, according to official results at the time. Because of the pressure exerted by the masses, and the level of fraud uncovered in court hearings, the Ukrainian Supreme Court had ruled that the runoff was invalid and so established a new runoff, which Yushchenko had won by almost seven percent. Because the people had stood firm in their demands for a fair and honest election, Yushchenko had won; thus, the people were heroes of freedom.

One point Yushchenko emphasizes is Ukrainian unity, which he sees as only possible through democracy. He believes this unity will bring together the "bright palette of languages, cultures, and views" that represent "the country's wealth." As the first national leader for whom Ukrainian (rather than Russian) was his native language, Yushchenko sought to bridge the Ukrainian/Russian linguistic divide within the country. Previous governments, going back to the time when Ukraine was part of the Soviet Union, often gave preferential treatment to Russian Ukrainians. Yushchenko promised equality for all.

The final point Yushchenko emphasizes is that a strong and prosperous future lay with Ukraine as it seeks not just close relations with the EU but full membership in this organization. While for centuries, Russia (and the Soviet Union) had had a predominant influence in Ukraine, the Ukrainian state was also sit-

After his man Yanukovych was driven out of Ukraine for good in 2014, Russian President Vladimir Putin would continue creating problems, annexing Crimea later that same year, before launching a full-scale war against Ukraine in 2022. Photo by Kremlin.ru, via Wikimedia Commons.

uated within Europe, and Yushchenko emphasizes that heritage as the foundation for creating a better future. Democracy, individual freedoms, and equality were social norms he believed had been chosen by the people of Ukraine in this election, and Yushchenko announced that he was dedicated to insuring the continuation of those European ideals throughout his presidency. The nation, under his leadership, would move "forward" by incorporating these ideals.

Essential Themes

With the modern state of Ukraine only slightly more than thirteen years old, Viktor Yushchenko was well

Pro-Orange Revolution demonstration in Brussels, Belgium, 1 December 2004. Photo by Steschke, via Wikimedia Commons.

aware that it was still in its formative years. He wanted to make certain that this new state would see itself as a democracy, with all the freedoms and equal rights that that entailed. Thus, he celebrated the free and fair runoff election which had been held in December 2004. The latter had occurred only because the people stood up to the government by not accepting the tyranny and the lawlessness of a rigged runoff in November. This is why he states that, "Each Ukrainian citizen has become the winner."

While the electoral results strongly reflected the regions (and ethnic composition of the regions' populations), Yushchenko believed that a democratic government could unify the country. This in turn could help overcome the threats by a few Russian-dominated regions in the east to leave Ukraine and join Russia, at least in Yushchenko's mind.

Finally, the election of Yushchenko, in his view, clearly demonstrated that there was a strong desire by the majority to move away from Russian dominance and to seek membership in the EU. With democracy not firmly established in Russia, and the Russian economy much weaker than that of Western Europe, Yushchenko's desire to be a part of a "united Europe" demonstrated a desire for Ukraine to be politically and economically a strong independent state. This he knew would not be possible with Russian dominance in Ukraine. Thus, he wholeheartedly turned to the West.

Speaking to the crowd at Independence Square, where the protestors had gathered just a few months prior to this speech, Yushchenko made it clear that the old order had ended. For him, Ukraine had fully moved into the twenty-first century as a European nation, reflecting the values of Western Europe. Looking to the east was a failed policy of the past for Yushchenko. He asserted that now there was the opportunity for a new way of life for the nation. However, his lack of strong political support in parliament created the conditions leading to failure for him and his ideals after taking office.

—Donald A. Watt, PhD

Bibliography and Additional Reading

Åslunc, Anders, and Michael McFaul eds. *Revolution in Orange: The Origins of Ukraine's Democratic Breakthrough.* Washington, DC: Carnegie Endowment for International Peace, 2006.

Beehner, Lionel. "One Year After Ukraine's 'Orange Revolution.'" *Council on Foreign Relations.* Washington, DC: Council on Foreign Relations, 2005.

D'Anieri, Paul. *Understanding Ukrainian Politics: Power, Politics, and Institutional Design.* London: Routledge, 2015.

Dickinson, Peter. "How Modern Ukraine Was Made on Maidan." *Atlantic Council.* Washington, DC: Atlantic Council, 2021.

Kuzio, Taras, ed. *Democratic Revolution in Ukraine: From Kuchmagate to Orange Revolution.* London: Routledge, 2009.

Miller, William Green. "The Orange Revolution and the Maidan Parliament." *Wilson Center.* Washington, DC: The Wilson Center, 2005.

Rennebohm, Max. "Ukrainians Overthrow Dictatorship (Orange Revolution), 2004." *Global Nonviolent Action Database.* Swarthmore PA: Swarthmore College, 2011.

■ Remarks by Yulia Tymoshenko after Her Release from Prison

Date: February 22, 2014
Author: Yulia Tymoshenko
Genre: speech

Summary Overview

When the Soviet Union dissolved in 1991, Ukraine held an official vote to become an independent country. The vote was 90 percent in favor of independence, and the government immediately took steps to make that a reality. Yet for the next nearly fifteen years, the nation's presidents, and their administrations, were plagued by scandals, corruption, and controversy. In 2004, then-president Leonid Kuchma, announced that he would not seek reelection. Two major candidates for the presidency emerged: Viktor Yanukovych and Viktor Yushchenko. Yanukovych was supported by Kuchma and had strong ties with the Kremlin, while Yushchenko held pro-Western and pro-European Union (EU) views.

The initial results in the 2004 election had Yanukovych as the winner, but the election was widely regarded as flawed and the results invalid. Massive protests emerged both in the capital city of Kyiv and in other cities in Ukraine, eventually forcing the Supreme Court to void the results of the election and order a runoff vote. Yulia Tymoshenko was a leading figure in the protests.

In the re-vote, the pro-Western Yushchenko achieved victory. The protests and demands for change that had helped bring him to office came to be called the Orange Revolution, after the color of the party he represented. Tymoshenko served as Yushchenko's prime minister both in 2005 and from 2007–2010. In 2010, after, the opposition party candidate Viktor Yanukovych was elected as president, Tymoshenko was jailed on charges that most outside observers considered to be politically motivated; she was not freed until 2014.

Defining Moment

By 2004, after many years of government scandals involving corruption at high levels, Ukraine seemed primed to erupt in the sort of popular protest that characterized the Orange Revolution. People were frustrated by the official corruption and lack of reform that had plagued their country for so many years, and in 2004 they expected to vote for change—only to see the election manipulated by the authorities in power; many voters faced intimidation as they went to cast their votes.

The Orange Revolution is called a bloodless revolution because, through street protests and civil demands, the system was changed. A second revolution, which came to be called the Revolution of Dignity, occurred in 2014, when the pro-Kremlin president at the time, Viktor Yanukovych, reneged on his promise to open Ukraine economically and politically to influence from the European Union (EU), with less reliance on Russia. The protests that occurred in this Revolution of Dignity were not entirely bloodless: more than a hundred people died in violent clashes between the police and protestors. Ultimately, however, Yanukovych was forced to leave the country in disgrace. The world watched as his former palace was entered by members of the public, who filmed and photographed the outsized, gaudy accommodations for all to see.

Author Biography

Often referred to as "Saint Yulia," Yulia Tymoshenko is a key figure in the struggle between the two main political and ideological forces in Ukraine. She was born in 1960, and holds advanced degrees in cybernetic engineering and economics.

Tymoshenko addressing Euromaidan with a speech, Kyiv, 22 February 2014. Photo by Mstyslav Chernov/Unframe, via Wikimedia Commons.

During her career, Tymoshenko has worked as a researcher, an academic, and a businessperson (in the gas industry). Her company helped to clear Ukraine's multibillion-dollar debt for natural gas from Russia and participated in international cooperation for machine building and construction. At the same time, was also accused of giving kickbacks to maintain her company's control over gas pipelines.

Tymoshenko was the first, and thus far only, female prime minister elected in Ukraine (2005; 2007–2010). By 2010 her alliance with Viktor Yushchenko had become brittle; she and Yushchenko both ran in the presidential election in 2010 against Viktor Yanukovych, splitting the vote and allowing Yanukovych to regain the office of president until 2014. This launched a bitter civil and political dispute as Tymoshenko's power bloc accused Yanukovych, once again, of widespread voting fraud and corruption. The Supreme Court reopened a criminal case against Tymoshenko that had been closed in 2004; she was jailed on those charges and other charges for the next four years. The reopening of the case was later determined to be illegal.

Upon her release, on February 22, 2014, she delivered the remarks that are reproduced here (in translation). Tymoshenko ran for president repeatedly but never won the office. She has been continuously active within the Ukraine parliament, especially since the Russian invasion of Ukraine in early 2022.

Historical Document

Remarks by Yulia Tymoshenko after Her Release from Prison

Kyiv, Ukraine

22 February 2014

[NOTE: On February 21st legislators voted to release former Prime Minister Yulia Tymoshenko from a prison hospital, where she was serving a seven-year sentence for abuse of power. One day later, on February 22nd, she gave the remarks below.]

By way of background, ten years ago, in November 2004, a rigged election gave victory to pro-Russian Viktor Yanokovych. The election campaign featured corruption, murder, the poisoning of the opposition candidate, pro-Western Viktor Yushchenko, and international concerns about the stability of Ukraine, even worries about the country's independent future. The polling results were not accepted by millions of Ukrainians. Popular protests began a process that eventually forced a second election won by Yushchenko. The protests were a grassroots, democratic, citizen's revolution demanding rule of law, accountability, openings to the West, and honest elections. The events became known in the media as the "Orange Revolution." The orange scarf came to symbolize the revolution (I proudly have one hanging over my desk).

Now, a decade later [i.e., 2014], a new revolution is underway. Yanokovych is again at the center of the controversy. This revolution may not be successful, although the tide of events seems to be turning favorably for the protestors. However, the future is still in doubt, especially if Russia sends in troops or the civil war breaks out. Crimea has already been annexed by Russia.

Appearing on February 22, 2014, at "Maidan Nezalezhnosti" (Independence Square) in Kyiv in a wheelchair because of health problems, Tymoshenko made a passionate speech to between 50,000-100,000 protestors.]

My dears, when I came to Kyiv I could not recognize Kyiv – burnt cars, barricades, but this is free country that you have given us as a gift. When I came to Kyiv, the first thing I wanted to do was to go to Hrushevskoho Street and touch the barricades where Ukrainian boys and girls were first ready to give their lives for Ukraine.

People who have been on Maidan and died here are heroes. Heroes will never die. They will always be with us. They will be our inspiration. Every official and every politician who will at least think of betraying you should see these boys in front of his eyes.

When snipers were shooting in the hearts of our guys, those are the bullets that will always wound us. If we do not take those (snipers) to court, we should be ashamed.

We could put an end to this dictatorship once and for all. Remember that you are the guarantor of victory. You cannot leave Maidan before we do what we came here to do. You are the force that can guarantee that. You have earned this with your patriotism and courage.

If somebody says that now you can leave, do not believe those people. You can't leave before everything is done.

No one but you could have done that. When our guys were covering themselves with wooden shields, this is the nation and the people that
cannot be put on their knees. No one will be building Mezhyhiryas again while
you have to gather kopecks for sick children. You will not let that happen.

I was praying to be part of you. We have to do a few things: We have to take Yanukovych and all his goons to Maidan. If you could have changed Ukraine, you can do anything. You were not happy about the agreement with Yanukovych and it is not working now.

When I saw AutoMaidan, I saw that we cannot be defeated. Many people are afraid to come to Maidan, they are looking for your protection. Not everyone has the strength to come to Maidan and sacrifice their lives. They
are scared and you are their hope.

We now have an open way to build Ukraine the way we want it. We know politicians are not trusted. Therefore we have to stand here till the end. You have deserved to run your own country. If government and parliament is composed without your participation, it will not be just.

From this time on there will be a different Ukraine. I will be a guarantor that you are not betrayed. Politics is sometimes a big theater.

I will be the guarantor that it is not that way. I am asking you to forgive me for all politicians regardless of political parties, positions. Politicians of today did not deserve you.

My dears, I feel what situation that you have lived in all this time and I'm proud of you. The liberation of Ukraine will be followed by the democratization in other post-Soviet countries. We are on the right path.

We will always be with you. We are one team. This revolution will be the beginning of changes in other post-Soviet countries. Now I will be doing everything so you would feel happy in your country. Glory to Ukraine!

[Source: denisegraveline.org/2014/07/famous-speech-friday-yulia-tymoshenkos.html]

Document Themes and Analysis

The Revolution of Dignity began in 2013 after then-President Yanukovych refused to sign a trade agreement and political affiliation with the European Union, instead creating closer ties with Russia. This was in direct opposition to the wants of the current parliament. The protests in favor of the signing soon broadened, with protestors calling for the resignation of Yanukovych and his government. Antiprotest laws worsened the situation, and a barricaded protest camp arose in Independence Square, where Tymoshenko gave her speech.

While the parliament voted to remove Yanukovych from office and the government resigned, Tymoshenko's remarks to emphasize that the battle has not yet been won. Even with the violence and death that occurred, the conflict, in her view, should and would likely continue. Yanukovych resisted his removal and sought help from Russia; Russia responded by calling the events a coup. As a result, pro-Russian counterprotests erupted, and additional territories declared themselves to be independent states, sparking an incipient civil war.

Tymoshenko ties this second revolution to the Orange Revolution of 2004. Because political conflicts throughout the period involved the question of Ukraine's ties with Russia versus the prospect of establishing stronger ties with the EU, connecting the two events gives greater weight to each. By portraying the conflict as a long-standing one, she may have inspired her listeners to think of themselves as part of an ongoing, historic struggle against an oppressive enemy. She calls those who have died heroes, saying that such heroes never die and will always be with the living.

Throughout the entire speech, Tymonshenko calls for her listeners to be brave in the face of what may come next. She addresses the destruction that had already occurred in Kyiv and recasts it as a struggle for freedom instead of a disaster to be feared. She calls for ongoing strength from her supporters as they continue to work toward a pro-Europe Ukraine.

Tymonhenko's speech is not inherently a call to action, but rather a call to readiness. While many famous speeches by world leaders were designed to inspire people to demand change and join movements, Tymonshenko's expresses pride and gratitude toward those who have already fought for change in Ukraine and urges people to continue the work they have started. One might say that her remarks are a reaction to events rather than a cause of them. Still, her speech is well known in Ukraine, where she is often considered a critical political figure who lead much of the ongoing revolution that is reshaping modern Ukraine.

—*Michael Shally-Jensen, PhD*

Bibliography and Additional Reading

Aslund, Anders, and Michael McFaul, eds. *Revolution in Orange: The Origin of Ukraine's Democratic Breakthrough*. Washington, DC: Carnegie Endowment for International Peace, 2006.

Kurkov, Andrey. *Ukraine Diaries: Dispatches from Kiev*. London: Harvill Press, 2015.

Wynnyckyj, Mychailo. *Ukraine's Maidan, Russia's War: A Chronicle and Analysis of the Revolution of Dignity*. Stuttgart, Germany: Ibidem-Verlag, 2019.

Arab Spring—and ISIS

In late 2010 in Tunisia, a revolt against government corruption and stasis sparked similar popular uprisings in predominantly Arab countries in North Africa and beyond. By 2011 the phenomenon had come to be known as the Arab Spring. Long-standing autocratic regimes fell in Egypt, Libya, Tunisia, and Yemen. At the same time, Libya and Syria erupted in civil war. In Syria, where the regime (aided by Russia) refused to give in to popular demands, the resulting war proved especially devastating, creating vast numbers of refugees and functioning as something of a proxy war between Russia and the United States (which favored regime change). In other nations, too, from the Gulf states to Iran, popular uprisings were contained or quelled. In Egypt, moreover, a backlash eventually took place, and a military regime took back control of the country in 2013. Yemen faced a similar fate as that of Syria, with Saudi Arabia and Iran fighting a proxy war between them there. Tunisia, where the Arab Spring first began, struggled with democracy for a decade before its citizens found it too slow and ineffective; in 2022 they voted to return to a more authoritarian form of government.

Amid the chaos left by the U.S.-led war in Iraq (2003–2011) and the Syrian civil war, a new threat emerged in the region, namely, the Islamic State (ISIS or ISIL), a militant jihadist organization seeking to establish a modern caliphate in the Middle East. Faithful supporters from around the globe heeded the call to revolution and traveled to ISIS's base in northern Syria to fight on the group's behalf. After yet another few years of war and devastation, extending from Syria to Iraq, ISIS was finally defeated by a U.S.-led coalition, in late 2017.

Tawakkol Karman—Nobel Lecture

Date: December 10, 2011
Author: Tawakkol Karman
Genre: speech

Summary Overview

The Arab Spring was not a singular event. The name refers to a series of revolutions and protests that began in Tunisia in late 2010 and then spread to countries in the region over the following year. The events were, in general, pro-democracy demonstrations largely led by the youth in the various North African and Persian Gulf countries that were involved. Most of the revolutionary activity and protests had faded out by 2012. Results of the protests varied in different countries; some countries experienced no substantial changes (e.g., Saudi Arabia, United Arab Emirates), others saw the overthrow of unpopular governments and the installation of more democratic governments (Tunisia, Egypt), while still others witnessed the overthrow of their governments and the creation of power vacuums that were filled by new hardline Islamist regimes. Some countries (Syria, Yemen) remain locked in civil war currently.

While there was a catalyzing moment for the Arab Spring (the self-immolation of Mohamed Bouazizi in Tunisia in December 2010), most countries that burst into revolutionary protests had already been experiencing unrest. Conflicts had been occurring over various charges of corruption in Tunisia since 2008, and demonstrations occurred against human rights violations in Western Sahara in late 2010.

In Yemen, protests began on January 27, 2011. The existing government was overthrown in 2012, but in 2014, Houthi forces overtook the capital city, Sanaa, and most of former North Yemen. A bitter civil war is ongoing. Saudi Arabian forces support the former Yemeni government as the true government of the nation, while, Iran, indirectly, gives its backing to the Houthis. Most experts consider the war to be an extension of the ongoing regional power struggle between Iran and Saudi Arabia. According to the United Nations, more than 150,000 people have been killed in fighting, and another 227,000 are dead because of famine and lack of healthcare facilities.

Tawakkol Karman, 2012. Photo by Frank Plitt, via Wikimedia Commons.

Defining Moment

Scholars have suggested several causes for the Arab Spring overall, such as the economic impact of the Great Recession of 2007–2009, persistent government corruption in the region, and the dissatisfaction of youth with their opportunities in their careers and personal lives. Most observers generally agree that social media influenced protestors' ability to both communicate and organize. Some note that access to social media probably also allowed users to witness what was being achieved by people in other countries, and pushed them to emulate those actions in their home countries.

The spark that lit the flame of revolution started in Tunisia. In December 2010, Mohamed Bouazizi was unable to find work. He began selling fruit at a roadside stand, which was then confiscated by a municipal official. An hour later, he doused himself in gasoline and set himself on fire. He died in January 2011. Protests over his death spawned more general protests against official corruption and economic distress in Tunisia, which inspired similar protests in other countries in the region.

Yemen had already been experiencing economic distress and civil unrest. Its economy was 75-percent oil based, but its oil reserves were starting to run out, and there was no clear replacement for this central source of income. A civil war was ongoing in Saana. Limited water reserves also were depleted. A 2009 paper from the Carnegie Endowment for International Peace stated that "Any single event—or more likely a confluence of worst-case events beyond the ability of the state to control—could lead to a further erosion of central government authority in Yemen and destabilization of the region" (Boucek 2009: 1). The Arab Spring seems to have provided the impetus to the destabilization predicted in this case.

Author Biography

Tawakkol Abdel-Salam Khalid Karman (b. 1979) is a Yemini novelist, journalist, and human rights activist. She cofounded and currently leads the group "Women Journalists Without Chains," and won the Nobel Peace Prize in 2011 for her work. She was the first Yemeni person, the first Arab woman, and the second Muslim woman to win a Nobel prize. Her protest work began long before 2010, focusing on the mistreatment of girls and women, the need for cultural change in Islam, and government corruption. She continues to work as an advocate in the region against many different issues, such as the U.S. drone presence and Saudi-led interventions in the country. In 2019, she was a target of a United Arab Emirates' surveillance system (Project Raven) that hacks into mobile phones and digital communications.

Historical Document

Oslo, Norway, 10 December 2011

In the name of God the Compassionate the Merciful

Your Majesties, Highnesses, Excellencies, Distinguished Committee of the Nobel Peace Prize, Arab spring and revolution youth in the arena of freedom and change, and all free people of the world,

Peace upon you from the Nobel Peace rostrum

With joy and pleasure I would like to express my gratitude for the honour I was given together with my peace fighter colleagues, Her Excellency the President Ellen Johnson-Sirleaf and Mrs. Leymah Gbowee, for this international award, which carries great moral and human meaning. Thank you for the award, which I consider as an honour to me personally, to my country Yemen, to the Arab women, to all women of the world, and to all people aspiring to freedom and dignity. I accept the award on my behalf and on behalf of the Yemeni and Arab revolutionary youth, who are leading today's peaceful struggle against tyranny and corruption with moral courage and political wisdom.

Alfred Nobel's dream of a world, where peace prevails and wars disappear, has not been achieved yet, but the hope to make it come true has grown large, and the effort to achieve it has doubled. The Nobel Peace Prize still offers this hope spiritual and conscientious momentum. For more than a hundred years, this award has stood as proof of the values of peaceful struggle for rights, justice and freedom, and also as proof of how wrong violence and wars are with all their backfiring and devastating results.

I have always believed that resistance against repression and violence is possible without relying on similar repression and violence. I have always believed that human civilization is the fruit of the effort of both women and men. So, when women are treated unjustly and are deprived of their natural right in this process, all social deficiencies and cultural illnesses will be unfolded, and in the end the whole community, men and women, will suffer. The solution to women's issues can only be achieved in a free and democratic society in which human energy is liberated, the energy of both women and men together. Our civilization is called human civilization and is not attributed only to men or women.

Ladies and Gentlemen,

Since the first Nobel Peace Prize in 1901, millions of people have died in wars which could have been avoided with a little wisdom and courage. The Arab countries had their share in these tragic wars, though their land is the land of prophecies and divine messages calling for peace. From this land came the Torah carrying the message: "Thou shalt not kill" and the Bible promising: "Blessed are the peacemakers," and the final message of the Koran urging "O ye who believe, enter ye into the peace, one and all." And the warning that "whosoever killeth a human being for other than manslaughter or corruption in the earth, it shall be as if he had killed all mankind."

However, in spite of its great scientific achievements, the history of humanity is stained with blood. Millions have fallen victims in the rise and fall of kingdoms. That is what ancient history tells us and what recent history confirms! Today's recent evidence tells us that the essence of messages calling for peace has repeatedly been trampled, and the human conscience has often been overrun by the voice of warplanes, rocket and missile launchers, bombs and all means of killing!

Ladies and Gentlemen,

Mankind's feeling of responsibility to create a decent life and make it worth living with dignity, has always been stronger than the will to kill life. Despite great battles, the survival of the human race is the clearest expression of mankind's yearning for reconstruction, not for destruction, for progress, not for regression and death. This tendency is strengthened day after day with all available means of communications, thanks to the rapid and astonishing development of information technology and the communications revolution. Walls between human societies have fallen down and the lives and destinies of societies have converged, marking the emergence of a new phase, a phase where peoples and nations of the world are not only residents of a small village, as they say, but members of one family, despite differences in nationality and race or in culture and language. All the members of this one family interact in all corners of our planet and share the same aspirations and fears. Despite all its missteps, humanity will go on in its march towards what is "beneficial to the people" and will make different cultures, identities and specific characteristics of civilizations come closer to each other on the road towards positive convergence and interaction, both in taking and in giving. Thus, understanding will gradually replace dispute, cooperation will replace conflict, peace will replace war, and integration will replace division.

One can say that our contemporary world, which has been refined and developed by expertise and long experience, good and bad, is marching with confident steps towards the creation of a new world and shining globalization. It will be a new and positive world with human prospects and globalization which will guarantee the values of freedom, truth, justice and cooperation to all human beings. It will be a world where all relationships, dealings and laws will be based on the prohibition of all forms and practices of exclusion and enslavement of man by man. This will mean a globalization with no policies of injustice, oppression, discrimination or tyranny, and a world full of partnership and cooperation, dialogue and coexistence, and acceptance of others. This will mean a globalization where resorting to the law of power and its might, against groups, peoples and nations, in order to deprive them of their liberty and human dignity, will disappear, once and forever. Am I dreaming too much ..?

I see on the horizon a glimpse of a new world, of a shining and flourishing globalization. I certainly see the end of a vicious and black history in which so many peoples and nations had experienced horror, tragedies, destruction and disaster. I certainly see the beginning of a humane, prosperous and generous history full of love and fraternity.

Ladies and Gentlemen,

Peace within one country is no less important than peace between countries. War is not just a conflict between states. There is another type of war, which is far more bitter, that is the war of despotic leaders who oppress their own people. It is a war of those to whom people have entrusted their lives and destinies, but who have betrayed that trust. It is a war of those to whom people have entrusted their security, but who directed their weapons against their own people. It is the war which today people face in the Arab States.

At this moment, as I speak to you here, young Arab people, both women and men, march in peaceful demonstrations demanding freedom and dignity from their rulers. They go forward on this noble path armed not with weapons, but with faith in their right to freedom and dignity. They march in a dramatic scene which embodies the most beautiful of the human spirit of sacrifice and the aspiration to freedom and life, against the ugliest forms of selfishness, injustice and the desire to hold on to power and wealth.

Ladies and Gentlemen,

Peace does not mean just to stop wars, but also to stop oppression and injustice. In our Arab region, there are brutal wars between governments and peoples. Human conscience cannot be at peace while it sees these young Arab people, who are in the age of blossoming, being harvested by the machine of death which is unleashed against them by the tyrants. The spirit of the Nobel Peace Prize is the spirit of peace, in which today we look forward in support of the aspiration of the Arab peoples for democracy, justice and freedom. If we support this spirit, the spirit of the Nobel Peace Prize, then we will prove to the despots that the ethics of peaceful struggle are stronger than their powerful weapons of repression and war.

Ladies and Gentlemen,

The revolutions of the Arab spring in Tunisia, Egypt, Libya, Yemen and Syria, and the movement towards revolutions in other Arab countries such as Algeria, Morocco, Bahrain, Sudan and others, in terms of motivation, driving power and objectives, didn't take place on isolated islands cut off from all the rapid and astonishing developments and changes which our world is witnessing. The Arab people have woken up just to see how poor a share of freedom, democracy and dignity they have. And they revolted. This experience is somewhat similar to the spring that swept throughout Eastern Europe after the downfall of the Soviet Union. The birth of democracies in Eastern Europe has been difficult and victory emerged only after bitter struggle against the then existing systems. Similarly, the Arab world is today witnessing the birth of a new world which tyrants and unjust rulers strive to oppose, but in the end, this new world will inevitably emerge.

The Arab people who are revolting in a peaceful and civilized manner have, for so many decades, been oppressed and suppressed by the regimes of authoritarian tyrants who have indulged themselves deeply in corruption and in looting the wealth of their people. They have gone too far in depriving their people of freedom and of the natural right to a dignified life. They have gone too far in depriving them of the right to participate in the management of their personal affairs and the affairs of their communities. These regimes have totally disregarded the Arab people as a people with a legitimate human existence, and have let poverty and unemployment flourish among them in order to secure that the rulers and their family members after them will have full control over the people. Allow me to say that our oppressed people have revolted declaring the emergence of a new dawn, in which the sovereignty of the people, and their invincible will, will prevail. The people have decided to break free and walk in the footsteps of civilized free people of the world.

All ideologies, beliefs, laws and charters produced by the march of humanity through all stages of its development and growth, as well as all divine messages and religions, without exception, oblige us to support oppressed people, be they groups or individuals. Supporting an oppressed person is not only required because of his need for support, but also because injustice against one person is injustice against all mankind.

Ladies and Gentlemen,

What Martin Luther King called "the art of living in harmony" is the most important art we need to master today. In order to contribute to that human art, the Arab states should make reconciliation with their own people an essential requirement. This is not merely an internal interest, but also an international one required for the whole human community. The dictator who kills his own people doesn't only represent a case of violation of his people's values and their national security, but is also a case of violation of human values, its conventions and its international commitments. Such a case represents a real threat to world peace.

Many nations, including the Arab peoples, have suffered, although they were not at war, but were not at peace either. The peace in which they lived is a false "peace of graves", the peace of submission to tyranny and corruption that impoverishes people and kills their hope for a better future. Today, all of the human community should stand with our people in their peaceful struggle for freedom, dignity and democracy, now that our people have decided to break out of silence and strive to live and realize the meaning of the immortal phrase of Caliph Omar ibn al-Khattab, "Since when have you enslaved people, when their mothers had given birth to them as free ones."

Ladies and Gentlemen,

When I heard the news that I had got the Nobel Peace Prize, I was in my tent in the Taghyeer square in Sana'a. I was one of millions of revolutionary youth. There, we were not even able to secure our safety from the repression and oppression of the regime of Ali Abdullah Saleh. At that moment, I contemplated the distinction between the meanings of peace celebrated by the Nobel Prize, and the tragedy of the aggression waged by Ali Abdullah Saleh against the forces of peaceful change. However, our joy of being on the right side of history made it easier for us to bear the devastating irony.

Millions of Yemeni women and men, children, young and old took to the streets in eighteen provinces demanding their right to freedom, justice and dignity, using non-violent but effective means to achieve their demands. We were able to efficiently and effectively maintain a peaceful revolution in spite of the fact that this great nation has more than seventy million firearms of various types. Here lies the philosophy of the revolution, which persuaded millions of people to leave their weapons at home and join the peaceful march against the state's machine of murder and violence, just with flowers and bare breasts, and filled with dreams, love and peace. We were very happy because we realized, at that time, that the Nobel Prize did not come only as a personal prize for Tawakkol Abdel-Salam Karman, but as a declaration and recognition of the whole world for the triumph of the peaceful revolution of Yemen and as an appreciation of the sacrifices of its great peaceful people.

And here I am now, standing before you in this solemn international ceremony. Here I am, in this unique moment, one of the most important moments of human history, coming from the land of the Arab Orient, coming from the land of Yemen, the Yemen of wisdom and ancient civilizations, the Yemen of more than five thousand years of long history, the great Kingdom of Sheba, the Yemen of the two queens Bilqis and Arwa, the Yemen which is currently experiencing the greatest and the most powerful and the largest eruption of Arab spring revolution, the revolution of millions throughout the homeland, which is still raging and escalating today. This revolution will soon complete its first year since the moment it was launched as a peaceful and popular revolution of the youth, with one demand: peaceful change and the pursuit of free and dignified life in a democratic and civil state governed by the rule of law. This state will be built on the ruins of the rule of a repressive, militarized, corrupt and backward family police rule, which has consistently brought Yemen to the edge of failure and collapse during the last thirty-three years.

Our peaceful and popular youth revolution is not isolated or cut off from the revolutions of the Arab spring. However, with all regret and sadness, I should note that it did not get the international understanding, support or attention of the other revolutions in the region. This should haunt the world's conscience because it challenges the very idea of fairness and justice.

Dear Ladies and Gentlemen,

Through you and your great universal forum, we send to the world a clear and expressive message in which we emphasize that:

– Our youth revolution is peaceful and popular and is rallied around by the people. It dreams of a free and democratic homeland with no room for tyranny, dictatorship, corruption or failure. I, on behalf of the revolutionary youth, pledge to all people in the world that we are committed to peaceful struggle as a strategic option, without deviation or retreat, regardless of the sacrifices and regardless of the extent of state repression, killing and violence.

– Our youth revolution is peaceful and popular and is motivated by a just cause, and has just demands and legitimate objectives, which fully meet all divine laws, secular conventions and charters of international human rights. Our revolution is determined to fully change the corrupt conditions and ensure free and dignified life, regardless of sacrifices and bitter sufferings, until the establishment of a democratic civil state, a state where the rule of law, equality and a peaceful transfer of power prevails.

– Our peaceful popular youth revolution has succeeded in attracting to its ranks and marches hundreds of thousands of women who have fulfilled, and still fulfil, a major, noticeable and effective role in its activities, and in leading its demonstrations even to the smallest details. Not tens, but hundreds of these women have fallen as martyrs or been wounded for the sake of the victory of the revolution.

– Because of the peaceful popular youth revolution, the voice and thundering march of young people have dominated and the voice of terror and explosive belts, which were employed by Ali Saleh as a justification for his rule, has faded away. The culture of peace is expanding and spreading, and it is finding a place in every neighbourhood and street where these young people walk demanding peaceful change and democracy.

– Our peaceful popular youth revolution has demonstrated that the values and objectives of freedom, democracy, human rights, freedom of expression and press, peace, human coexistence, fight against corruption and organized crime, war on terrorism, and resistance to violence, extremism and dictatorship, are values, ideals, demands and objectives of common human interest, and are cherished by the whole international community. These are not subject to division, selectivity or cancellation under the pretext of differences in human characteristics or the requirements of sovereignty in any way.

Distinguished Ladies and Gentlemen:

I would like to emphasize that the Arab spring revolutions have emerged with the purpose of meeting the needs of the people of the region for a state of citizenship and the rule of law. They have emerged as an expression of people's dissatisfaction with the state of corruption, nepotism and bribery. These revolutions were ignited by young men and women who are yearning for freedom and dignity. They know that their revolutions pass through four stages which can't be bypassed:

- Toppling the dictator and his family

- Toppling his security and military services and his nepotism networks

- Establishing the institutions of the transitional state.

- Moving towards constitutional legitimacy and establishing the modern civil and democratic state.

Thus, the revolutions of the Arab spring will continue through the effort of youth, who are ready and prepared to launch each stage and to fully achieve its objectives. Today, the world should be ready and prepared to support the young Arab spring in all stages of its struggle for freedom and dignity. The civilized world should, immediately after the outbreak of the revolutions of youth, commence the detention and freezing of the assets of the figures of the regime and its security and military officials. In fact this is not enough, since these people should be brought to justice before the International Criminal Court. There should be no immunity for killers who rob the food of the people.

The democratic world, which has told us a lot about the virtues of democracy and good governance, should not be indifferent to what is happening in Yemen and Syria, and happened before that in Tunisia, Egypt and Libya, and happens in every Arab and non-Arab country aspiring for freedom. All of that is just hard labour during the birth of democracy which requires support and assistance, not fear and caution.

Allow me, ladies and gentlemen, to share my belief that peace will remain the hope of mankind forever, and that the best hope for a better future for mankind will always drive us to speak noble words and do noble deeds. Together, we will push the horizons, one after another, towards a world of true human perfection.

Finally, I ponder myself standing here before you, in this moment, which every man and woman aspires to reach because of the recognition and appreciation is contains. As I do so, I see the great number of Arab women, without whose hard struggles and quest to win their rights in a society dominated by the supremacy of men I wouldn't be here. This supremacy has caused a lot of injustice to both men and women. To all those women, whom history and the severity of ruling systems have made unseen, to all women who made sacrifices for the sake of a healthy society with just relationships between women and men, to all those women who are still stumbling on the path of freedom in countries with no social justice or equal opportunities, to all of them I say: thank you ... this day wouldn't have come true without you.

Peace be upon you

Copyright © The Nobel Foundation 2011

Document Themes and Analysis

Given that Karman was accepting a prize for her work as an activist using peaceful tactics against human rights violations, it is not surprising that her talk focuses on the causes and benefits of peace. She focuses on the peaceful tactics taken by the Yemeni people, discussing how they have focused on nonaggressive action even in the face of deadly repression and oppression by "authoritarian tyrants." She provides assurances to the international community that the peaceful actions of those in Yemen will continue, even in the face of ongoing struggles in their country. This is all designed to contrast with the civil war and terrorist actions that had been occurring in Yemen at that time and would, unfortunately, continue in the future.

Karman also compares the events making up the Arab Spring to the struggles in Eastern Europe following the dissolution of the Soviet Union. In the latter case, former Soviet states struggled to find national identities and make decisions regarding whether to tighten their ties to Russia or focus more on Western connections. In many cases (notably, in the Balkans), violent conflicts erupted between different ethnic groups or nationalities, and between peoples and governments. Karman stresses that, in contrast to such violence, the Yemeni people are looking for peaceful solutions in the struggle against corruption in their country. She is clear about how such peaceful protests follow both international laws and moral or religious codes common around the world.

In her discussions of peace, Karman highlights that peace is about more than simply not experiencing war and overt violence; it is about removing oppression. She refers to what she calls the "peace of graves," where people are forced to submit to tyranny and corruption in order to survive. She includes the rights of women and youth in her discussion of the oppressed. (Trying to change policies that allow for child brides is one of the many issues she has focused on in her writings and work.) This is a broader definition of peace than is commonly used.

In much of her work, Karman has focused on the participation of young people. This was a theme throughout the Arab Spring; many of the revolutions were led by young people who were experiencing violent oppression and organized themselves to fight back. The participation of women too is an important element of Karman's work, living, as she does, in a country (and region) where women are generally given subordinate status.

Briefly, Karman notes that the fights in Yemen did not receive the same international attention as those in other countries, saying that this should "haunt the world's conscience." Indeed, Yemen had been in major conflict for more than three decades leading up to the 2011 revolution.

Unfortunately, Yemen continues to experience violent civil war to this day. Famine and economic crises threaten the country, which remains a proxy battleground for larger states such as Saudi Arabia and Iran. Without a peace settlement, along with other major changes, the Yemeni people will likely continue to exist in a state of deprivation and oppression, contrasting terribly with the hopes that Karman expressed in her Nobel lecture of 2011.

—Kay Lemay, MA

Bibliography and Additional Reading

Boucek, Christopher. "Yemen: Avoiding a Downward Spiral." Washington, DC: Carnegie Endowment for International Peace: Middle East Program, 2009. carnegieendowment.org/files/yemen_downward_spiral.pdf.

Brandt, Marieke. *Tribes and Politics in Yemen: A History of the Houthi Conflict*. New York: Oxford UP, 2017.

Clark, Victoria. *Yemen: Dancing on the Heads of Snakes*. New Haven, CT: Yale UP, 2010.

Kasinof, Laura. *Don't Be Afraid of the Bullets: An Accidental War Correspondent in Yemen*. New York: Arcade, 2016.

Egyptian President-Elect Mohamed Morsi's Acceptance Speech

Date: June 24, 2012
Author: Mohamed Morsi
Genre: address; political tract; speech

Summary Overview

In this speech, we can see the hopes of the Egyptian people expressed by their newly elected president, following the revolution of 2012 and the removal of Hosni Mubarak (in office since 1981) from the presidential office. The call for more equality between Muslims and Christians, men and women, political leaders and citizens is a strong theme throughout the work. However, we can also see the highly religious nature of Morsi's words, which possibly foretold the more religiously conservative track that his future policies would follow. In the moment that this speech was given, the Egyptian people were brimming with hope and promise for their country's future—as their protests had finally produced a significant change after thirty years of autocratic rule and repression of dissent. Mohamed Morsi was the fifth president of Egypt. He held office from June 30, 2012 to July 3, 2013 and was removed via coup d'état by General Abdel Fattah el-Sisi.

Defining Moment

This speech was a defining moment in the Egyptian Revolution of 2012. Having finally removed Hosni Mubarak, the authoritarian Egyptian president of thirty years, from power, Mohamed Morsi was the first democratically elected leader in over a generation. Part of the Muslim Brotherhood, an Islamic group founded in 1928 with a controversial place in the modern world, Morsi had been imprisoned twice under Mubarak's presidency for his leadership position within the Brotherhood and his anti-Mubarak politics. Though the Brotherhood originally declared that it would not put forth a candidate for the presidential race, Morsi was elected with over 51 percent of the vote (though voter turnout represented only 52 percent of the voting population).

This was the first time since the end of British colonialism that Egyptians had directly chosen their political representation. As important, this speech by the president-elect signaled to the people and the world that the protests, which had lasted from January 25, 2011 to February 11, 2011 and culminated in the resignation of Mubarak, had had a lasting impact on the political status of Egypt. In addition, with the deposi-

Mohamed Morsi, 2013. Photo by Wilson Dias, via Wikimedia Commons.

tion of Mubarak, the Muslim Brotherhood was able to move away from its time as an outlawed group and attempt to assert political control over the Egyptian government to reshape the political hierarchy. This reshaping was intended to bring together disparate groups within Egypt—Muslim and Christian, men and women, and regional political powers. Morsi and the Muslim Brotherhood had made a name for themselves as a reformist group strongly dedicated to charity and social work. It was these attributes which supporters hoped that Morsi would bring to Egyptian politics.

This was an unstable time in Egyptian history, rife with possibility but also careening toward the unknown and potentially dangerous lines of action. The military and old authoritarian policies of the government had maintained control for decades and would not be changed into something new and better overnight. Unfortunately, in the year that Mohamed Morsi spent as president, he was unable to significantly change the Egyptian state and instead fell into many of the same autocratic practices that previous presidents and military leaders had used. After ending many policies designed to check the power of the president, opposition forces together with the military overthrew Morsi, claiming that he failed to unite the Egyptian people under his presidency.

Author Biography

Muhammad Muhammad Mursi 'Issā al-'Ayyāt, more commonly known as Mohamed Morsi, was born in 1951 in El Adwah, Sharqia Governorate, Egypt. Not much is known about his early life before he studied engineering at Cairo University. He received bachelor's and master's degrees before attending the University of Southern California (USC), where he received a doctorate in 1982. He taught for a few years in California before returning to Egypt. Upon his return, he taught at Zagazig University and joined the Muslim Brotherhood, at least in part due to his experience in the United States, where he found that his values differed significantly from his American colleagues.

In 2000, he became more politically active—although his membership in the Brotherhood outlawed him from running for political office under Mubarak. As an independent, he pushed for more political freedom and the overturning of many oppressive measures that Mubarak used to keep power. During this time, he also supported many measures to restrict media and entertainment which he felt was contrary to his own moral beliefs. After being elected to a governing board of the Muslim Brotherhood, Morsi was arrested and imprisoned for seven months in 2006.

After his year in the presidency, Morsi was imprisoned and tried for a variety of international crimes, largely connected with his activities as a member of the Muslim Brotherhood. He was sentenced to death in 2015, but that ruling was overturned in 2016. While awaiting his retrial, Morsi remained in prison where the harsh conditions contributed to his death in 2019.

Historical Document

In the name of God, the most compassionate, the most merciful. Thanks be to Allah, prayers and peace be upon the messenger of Allah...

Egyptian people, you who today are rejoicing and celebrating the feast of democracy in Egypt, you who are standing in squares, in the Tahrir Square and in all the squares of Egypt, my beloved ones, my family and people, my brethren and my sons, who are looking forward to the future, you who want good, rebirth, development, stability, safety and security for our country of Egypt. My beloved ones, I address you thanks to God Almighty. We all thank God for reaching this historic moment, this moment which represents a landmark that has been written with the hands and wills of the Egyptians, their blood, tears and sacrifices, this moment, which we are all shaping with these sacrifices.

I would not have talked to you today as the first president elected by the free will of Egyptians in the first presidential elections after the 25 January revolution, I would not have been here today with you now amid this sweeping joy, which is sweeping all corners of our beloved homeland, I would not have been here but for God's help and these sacrifices, the precious blood of our honorable martyrs and our great injured men...

I promise them once again that this precious blood will not go in vain. Salute to the great Egyptian people, the best soldiers on earth, to the Armed Forces, to all its sons wherever they are, pure salutations from my heart to them and I bear them love that nobody knows except for God Almighty. I love them and appreciate their role and show keenness to strengthen them and keep them and this prestigious organization [the army] that we all love and appreciate.

And for the honourable policemen, the policemen who are my brothers and sons, some of whom mistakenly believe that I might feel less appreciation for them and that is wrong. Whoever commits a crime is punished according to the law. As for the honest policemen, who are the majority of my brothers and sons among policemen in Egypt, for those, I'm obliged to salute them because they have a big role to play in the future to maintain safety and security inside the homeland.

Due salutations, too, to all Egyptian judges, who supervised all the elections after the revolution and even to those who have not supervised the elections. All judges in Egypt should be appreciated, respected and loved, and they are the third authority that should always keep its head high, remain independent, possess its own will and work separately from the executive power, and my responsibility in the future is to make sure that judges truly and genuinely work separately from the executive and legislative powers…

Muslims and Christians alike, men and women, the old and the elderly and the young men, mothers and fathers, peasants and workers, public servants, teachers, university professors, businessmen, public servants, workers in the Public Enterprise sector and the government departments and the private sector, those who work in all state institutions, merchants, drivers, bus, trains, taxis, tok-tok cars, they are all my people, those who have professions, owners of small kiosks, owners of small shops, vendors selling goods on road pavements, the elderly, the students who go to public and private schools, those who have professions, everyone, I hope I don't ever forget anyone.

I address you all on this remarkable day in which I was chosen, thanks to Allah and your will, president for all Egyptians, and will stand at an equal distance from all Egyptians, everyone has his own value and standing, nobody is dealt with differently except on the basis of their giving to his country and the amount of respect they show for the constitution and law…

Egypt, which impressed the world with the queues of its voters, needs now to close ranks, unite the word, so that the patient, great Egyptian people can reap the fruit of their sacrifices in a better life, achieve social justice, freedom and human dignity, which are the basic slogans or the main goals that the throats of the revolutionaries kept repeating in all Egyptian squares on the 25th of January 2011, and which revolutionaries still repeat loudly in all the squares of the revolution, which is still continuing.

The revolution will continue until all its objectives are achieved. Together, we complete this march. The people have been patient, the Egyptian people have been patient and since then suffered disease, hunger, injustice, oppression, marginalization, the rigging of will and the rigging of elections. We used to look around in the world and say: when will Egypt, the Egyptian people, be the source of power? Today, you are the source of power as the world can see in this epic, in this great system through which we would take Egypt to a better future, god willing…

Egypt is for all Egyptians, all of us are equals in terms of rights…We are all Egyptians no matter what our viewpoints, we are all nationalists no matter what our parties and trends. We are all faithful to the revolution and to the blood of martyrs. There is no place for the language of collusion and there is no place for accusing each other of treachery…I invite you to prepare for a comprehensive project of rebirth, for the Egyptian rebirth, with the hands of all Egyptians. We Egyptians, Muslims and Christians, we Egyptians, Muslims and Christians, are advocates of civilization and construction…

I am intent with your help to build a new Egypt, a national country, a constitutional, democratic, modern country, and all my time will be dedicated to this big project which is based on our identity and reference. I will work hard with all of you to maintain Egypt's national security, with all its dimensions, whether at Arab, African, regional or international levels. We will maintain international charters and conventions.

We came to the world with a message of peace. We will maintain international charters and conventions and the commitments and agreements Egypt has signed with the world. We will also work to make the Egyptian system of ethics, and its civilizational identity, in addition to human values particularly in freedoms, respect for human rights, maintaining rights of women and children and abrogating all sorts of discrimination. We will establish, God willing, balanced relations with all world powers, we will establish balanced relations between us and other world countries based on common interests and mutual respect and benefits to all sides.

We will not allow ourselves to interfere in the internal affairs of any country in the same way that we will not allow any interference in our affairs and hence maintain our national sovereignty and the borders of the Egyptian state. Let everybody knows that Egypt's decision is made inside it, by the will of its sons, let everybody know that Egypt by our call for peace with all the world is capable by its people, men, people, armed forces, great history, of defending itself and preventing any aggression or thoughts of aggression against it or against its sons in any part of this world...

While we all are celebrating and rejoicing with this great democracy, with these elections, with the victory of the nation's will in the way that you are celebrating now. I reiterate what I have said before that I will not betray Allah in you, would not betray Allah in you and would not disobey Him in my country.

I set before my eyes God's saying: And guard yourselves against a day in which ye will be brought back to Allah. Then every soul will be paid in full that which it hath earned, and they will not be wronged. Repeat with me my beloved ones, with our will, our unity, our love for each other, we can shape the decent future for all of us. Some might not see that from outside the homeland or feel it is difficult for us to achieve that out of sympathy for us or for other reasons, however, we, God willing, can go ahead along this path to achieve a better future.

Allah guideth us all to the best of ways. My beloved ones, some see this, but we see it together close, God willing. Tomorrow is very soon. And Allah was predominant in His career, but most of mankind know not (Quranic verse). Peace and God's blessings be upon you.

[Source: www.wilsoncenter.org/president-elect-mohamed-morsis-first-speech]

Glossary

abrogating: evading responsibility; repealing or doing away with (a law)

public enterprise sector: a portion of the economy (a sector) made up of businesses wholly or partly owned by the state and controlled through a public authority

queues: lines of people

Quranic: based on or from the Quran, the Islamic holy book

salutations: greetings

sovereignty: authority of a state to govern itself or another state

tok-tok car: an open-sided, three-wheeled car that does not tilt; often used as taxis

Document Analysis

It is difficult to analyze a document objectively when you know the outcome of an event. Far too easily, events that have not yet happened will cloud a reader's understanding of a source documenting an earlier event. In the case of this speech, it is easy to see what happened afterwards and read those events into the words Morsi spoke in June 2012. But for Morsi, the Egyptian people, and the whole world, the future was wide open and this speech promised a freer, finally democratic Egypt.

Morsi begins and ends his speech with a similar theme, thanking Allah and the people for their support and envisioning a new period of "good, rebirth, development, stability, safety and security for our country of Egypt." This theme connects both Islam and the new political regime, a common feature in many governments. One of Morsi's goals for his presidency was to fulfill the Egyptian people's dreams during the protests, to have a "better life, achieve social justice, freedom and human dignity." Morsi, as part of the Muslim Brotherhood, believed that sharia law, laws and regulations based on religious law from the Quran, would work best for Egypt's new government. While not well understood outside of Muslim cultures, sharia law protects and supports life, property, family, and faith—many aspects of a better life.

After thanking the people for their votes, Morsi begins to address specific groups of individuals, including the army, police, and judges. This may seem an odd inclusion in such a speech, but one of the main reasons that the previous president, Mubarak, was ousted was because of his aggressive use of police force and his subordination of the justice system against Egyptian civilians. Morsi takes this opportunity to address an elephant in the room: military pressure and protests against police abuses were a major cause of the revolution, but that the same army, police officers, and judges were still needed and still part of the citizenry who were now under his rule. Moreover, they still had significant power. Morsi's position as the first freely elected president was quite tenuous and he had to find a way to bridge the deep divides among the Egyptian people. Morsi uses his words to call upon the best possible aspects of humanity, encouraging them to be "honourable" and "honest" so that they are "appreciated, respected and loved." In this way, he is trying to bridge the difficult and violent history of his country and find path forward that incorporates all his citizens and his goals for this country.

This speech highlights many of the ways in which Egyptians had suffered, first under colonial rule and then under the authoritarian presidency that had existed since 1952. Morsi speaks to all citizens of Egypt, from all genders, faiths, and social statuses, of a new Egypt, one in which their voice and their vote is heard and respected.

Essential Themes

The hope for the future envisioned by Morsi and the audience in this moment in time was profound. Freedom, equality, justice. People, especially those living through a revolutionary moment, can find the prospect of living those ideals to be enticing. But actually putting them into practice is hard—perhaps one of the hardest things that can be done. Mohamed Morsi, whatever his intentions were when he took office, was not able to put them into practice. Egyptian military leaders never lost power during or after the revolution; rather they remained a controlling presence, a ghost on the edges of the new political regime. In addition, revolutions create instability, as new rules and old institutions fight for control and people adapt to change. Given these circumstances, Morsi more and more quickly turned to the same tactics that had kept Mubarak in power—restrictive laws and harsh penalties for Egyptian citizens and less oversight for his own leadership. Violence broke out between different factions that had once been united in revolutionizing Egypt. In the end, the Egyptian Revolution of 2011 was ended by an inability to overcome the long-standing divides between not only the government and the people, but among the people themselves.

—*Anna Accettola, PhD*

Bibliography and Additional Reading

El-Bendary, Mohamed. *The Egyptian Revolution and Its Aftermath: Mubarak to Morsi.* New York: Algora Pub., 2013.

El-Sherif, Ashraf. "Egypt's Post-Mubarak Predicament." Carnegie Endowment for International Peace, 2014. www.jstor.org/stable/resrep12804.

Hessler, Peter. "Mohamed Morsi, Who Brought the Muslim Brotherhood to the Egyptian Presidency." *The New Yorker*, June 19, 2019. www.newyorker.com/news/news-desk/mohamed-morsi-who-brought-the-muslim-brotherhood-to-the-egyptian-presidency.

Shama, Nael. *Egyptian Foreign Policy from Mubarak to Morsi: Against the National Interest.* London: Taylor & Francis, 2013.

Islamic State—Proclamation of the Caliphate

Date: June 29, 2014
Author: Islamic State (ISIL/ISIS); delivered by spokesman Abu Muhammad Al-'Adnani
Genre: speech

Summary Overview

In 2013 a militant extremist group rooted in fundamentalist tenets of Sunni Islam and calling itself The Islamic State of Iraq broke its alliance with the better known al-Qaida terrorist network to become the Islamic State of Iraq and the Levant (ISIL, a.k.a. ISIS). The organization originated in Islamic resistance movements that were militarized in the face of the U.S.-led Western coalition that invaded Iraq in 2003. Following its split with al-Qaida, ISIL gained global prominence in 2014 when it captured large areas of Iraq and Syria and established a state based on its version of Islamic religious law (sharia). Spokesmen proclaimed that ISIL had established a modern caliphate that all Muslims should obey and that would eventually rule the world.

ISIL took control of territory through a strategy based on intimidation and violence. They executed thousands of prisoners of war, committed genocide against minority groups, and destroyed monuments and artifacts in their territory. ISIL also sought to control every aspect of the lives of civilians according to their version of sharia law. The group has been labeled a terrorist organization by most governments and international bodies. From 2015 to 2017, forces of the Iraqi government waged war against ISIL and eventually recaptured most of the territory under its control.

Defining Moment

ISIL's origins have been traced to the aftermath of the 2003 U.S.-led invasion of Iraq. In response to the invasion, small groups composed mostly of Sunni Muslims made attacks against U.S. troops, the official Iraqi government, and Shia Muslims. One of the original organizers of these attacks, Abu Musab al-Zarqawi, formed the groups into a force that waged a constant guerilla war against U.S. troops and the Iraqi government. In 2006, al-Zarqawi was killed by U.S. forces, but his organization continued to commit suicide attacks and recruit soldiers.

In 2010, Abu Bakr al-Baghdadi became the group's leader. In 2011, the group took advantage of the Syrian Civil War to set up organized guerilla institutions throughout neighboring Syria. The group eventually seized territory from the Syrian government and set up its own government in the eastern part of the country; all those under their rule were forced to obey their laws, dissidents were executed, and civilian property was seized. From this new base, al-Baghdadi continued to take over territory until the group had established a large state on the Syria-Iraq border.

ISIL gained worldwide recognition in 2014 when it launched a huge campaign in western Iraq and started calling itself the "Islamic State." ISIL won several battles against the Iraqi government, and its success prompted thousands of would-be *jihadi* soldiers to join the group from all over the world. Mosul, the second-largest city in Iraq, became ISIL's capital: fighters seized money from banks, executed Shia Muslims, and took control of all government buildings and airports. Thousands of civilians fled the city. On June 29, spokesmen for ISIL released a statement saying that they were establishing a new Islamic caliphate with al-Baghdadi as their leader.

Life in territory captured by ISIL was violently and strictly controlled. Women and girls were punished for leaving the house without full-body coverings and stoned for having contact with men; civilians and children were forced to watch public executions; entire minority groups were expelled or destroyed. ISIL financed its operations by extracting oil, selling stolen antiquities from museums, taxing non-Muslims heavily, and holding journalists and civilians for ransom. The group has been designated as a terrorist organization by most international governments. It has also been widely criticized by many Islamic religious leaders, who condemn the regime's violence and destruction as war crimes and misinterpretations of Islamic theology.

Author Biography

ISIL has also been known as the Islamic State of Iraq and Syria (ISIS) or Daesh, after its Arabic acronym. The leader of ISIL and self-proclaimed caliph of the Islamic State, known as Abu Bakr al-Baghdadi, was a militant from Iraq who took leadership of the group in the early 2010s. He gained prominence as a spokesman for ISIL in 2013, when he announced the official formation of the group to the international media. He later became the direct leader of ISIL and oversaw several councils that ran both the group's day-to-day operations and long-term strategy. He died in 2019 in connection with a U.S. special operations raid.

Abu Muhammad Al-Adnani (1977-2016), who delivered the speech proclaiming the caliphate, was one of al-Baghdadi's closest advisors and second-in-command of ISIL. Before his death in a U.S. attack, he was the group's main media spokesman and was known for his dramatic speeches that exhorted his listeners to violent action against non-Muslim cultures and people.

Historical Document

Proclamation of the Caliphate

Praise be to Allah, the Mighty and Strong. And may peace and blessings be upon the one sent with the sword as a mercy to all creation ... .

[It is said in Koran 24:55]: "Allah has promised those among you who believe, and do righteous good deeds, that He will certainly grant them succession to (the present rulers) in the earth, as He granted it to those before them, and that He will grant them the authority to practice their religion, which He has chosen for them (i.e. Islam). And He will surely give them in exchange a safe security after their fear—(provided) they worship Me and do not associate anything (in worship) with Me ... "

Succession, establishment, and safety—a promise from Allah reserved for the Muslims, but with a condition ... Having faith in Allah, keeping far from the gateways to *shirk* [polytheism] and its various shades, along with submitting to Allah's command in everything big and small ... Only after this condition is met will the promise be fulfilled ...

Allah ... also gave honor to the ummah ... [which] does not accept submission to anyone or anything other than Allah. It does not accept transgression nor oppression ... This is the ummah of Muhammad ... which, whenever it is truthful with Allah, He brings about His promise for them ...

Allah ... sent His Prophet ... while the Arabs were in the depths of ignorance and blinding darkness. They were the most naked, the hungriest, and the most backwards of peoples, sinking in depths of lowness ... This was the condition of the Arabs before Islam ... Then, when Allah blessed them with Islam and they believed, Allah unified them, united their ranks, honored them after their humiliation, enriched them after their poverty, and brought their hearts together, all through Islam. Thus, by the grace of Allah, they became brothers ...

Our dear ummah—the best of peoples—Allah ... decrees numerous victories for this ummah to occur in a single year, which He does not grant others in many years or even centuries ...

The time has come for those generations that were drowning in oceans of disgrace, being nursed on the milk of humiliation, and being ruled by the vilest of all people, after their long slumber in the darkness of neglect—the time has come for them to rise. The time has come for the ummah of Muhammad ... to wake up from its sleep, remove the garments of dishonor, and shake off the dust of humiliation and disgrace, for the era of lamenting and moaning has gone, and the dawn of honor has emerged anew. The sun of *jihad* has risen. The glad tidings of good are shining. Triumph looms on the horizon. The signs of victory have appeared...

Here the flag of the Islamic State, the flag of tawhid ... rises and flutters. Its shade covers land from Aleppo to Diyala. Beneath it, the walls of the *tawaghit* [tyrants] have been demolished, their flags have fallen, and their borders have been destroyed. Their soldiers are either killed, imprisoned, or defeated. The Muslims are honored. The kuffar [unbelievers] ... are disgraced. Ahl Al-Sunna [Sunnis] are masters and are esteemed. The people of *bid'ah* [forbidden religious innovation] ... are humiliated. The hudud [Koranic punishment] are implemented ... The frontlines are defended. Crosses and graves are demolished. Prisoners are released by the edge of the sword. The people in the lands of the State move about for their livelihood and journeys, feeling safe regarding their lives and wealth. *Wulat* [governors] and judges have been appointed. *Jizya* [the poll tax levied on non-Muslims living in Muslim lands] has been enforced. *Fay'* [a kind of booty taken from the Muslims' enemies] and *zakat* [alms paid by the Muslims] have been collected. Courts have been established to resolve disputes and complaints. Evil has been removed. Lessons and classes have been held in the mosques and, by the grace of Allah, the religion has become completely for Allah.

There only remained one matter, a *wajib kifaya* [collective obligation] that the ummah sins by abandoning. It is a forgotten obligation. The ummah has not tasted honor since they lost it. It is a dream that lives in the depths of every Muslim believer. It is a hope that flutters in the heart of every monotheistic mujahid. It is the *khilafa* [caliphate] ... the abandoned obligation of the era ...

Therefore, the shura council of the Islamic State studied this matter after the Islamic State—by Allah's grace—gained the essentials necessary for khilafa, which the Muslims are sinful if they do not try to establish. In light of the fact that the Islamic State has no shari'a[-based] constraint or excuse that can justify delaying or neglecting the establishment of the khilafa ... the Islamic State ... resolved to announce the establishment of the Islamic caliphate, [and to appoint] a khalifa (caliph) for the Muslims: ... the sheikh, the mujahid, the scholar who practices what he preaches, the worshipper, the leader, the warrior, the reviver, descendent from the family of the Prophet, the slave of Allah Ibrahim Ibn 'Awwad Ibn Ibrahim Ibn 'Ali Ibn Muhammad Al-Badri, [who is] Al-Hashimi Al-Husayni [and] Al-Qurayshi by lineage, Al-Samuraa'i [i.e. from Samarra in Iraq] by birth and upbringing, Al-Baghdadi [i.e., from Baghdad] by residence and scholarship. And he has accepted the baya' [pledge of allegiance]. Thus, he is the imam and caliph for Muslims everywhere. Accordingly, the Iraq and Sham in the name of the Islamic State is henceforth removed from all official deliberations and communications, and the official name is the Islamic State from the date of this declaration.

We clarify to the Muslims that with this declaration of khilafa, it is incumbent upon all Muslims to pledge allegiance to the caliph Ibrahim and support him ... The legality of all emirates, groups, states, and organizations, becomes null by the expansion of the caliphate's authority and arrival of its troops to their areas ...

The caliph Ibrahim ... has fulfilled all the conditions for caliphate mentioned by the scholars. He was given baya' in Iraq by the people of authority in the Islamic State as the successor to Abu 'Omar Al-Baghdadi ... His authority has expanded over wide areas in Iraq and Al-Sham. The land now submits to his order and authority from Aleppo to Diyala. So fear Allah, O slaves of Allah. Listen to your caliph and obey him. Support your state, which grows everyday—by Allah"s grace—with honor and loftiness, while its enemy increases in retreat and defeat.

So rush O Muslims and gather around your caliph, so that you may return as you once were for ages, kings of the earth and knights of war. Come so that you may be honored and esteemed, living as masters with dignity ... By Allah, if you disbelieve in democracy, secularism, nationalism, as well as all the other garbage and ideas from the west, and rush to your religion and creed, then by Allah, you will own the earth, and the east and west will submit to you. This is the promise of Allah to you ...

And a message to all the platoons and groups on the face of the earth, consisting of mujahidin and people working to support the religion of Allah and raising the Islamic banners—a message to the heads and leaders of these groups—we say:

Fear Allah with regards to yourselves. Fear Allah with regards to your *jihad*. Fear Allah with regards to your ummah ... We—by Allah—do not find any shari'a [-based] excuse for you justifying your holding back from supporting this state ... It is time for you to end this abhorrent partisanship, dispersion, and division, for this condition is not from the religion of Allah at all. And if you forsake the State or wage war against it, you will not harm it. You will only harm yourselves ...

As for you, O soldiers of the platoons and organizations, know that after this consolidation and the establishment of the caliphate, the legality of your groups and organizations has become invalid. It is not permissible for a single person of you who believes in Allah to sleep without having loyalty to the caliph. If your leaders whisper to you claiming it is not a caliphate, then remember how long they whispered to you claiming that it was not a state but rather a fictional, cardboard entity, until its certain news reached you. It is a state. Its news will continue to reach you showing that it is a caliphate, even if after time. And know that nothing has delayed victory and delays it now more than these organizations, because they are the cause of division and disagreements that ruin strength. Division is not from Islam at all ...

As for you, O soldiers of the Islamic State, then congratulations to you. Congratulations on this clear victory, congratulations on this great triumph. Today the unbelievers are infuriated in such a manner after which there will be no similar infuriation. Many of them almost die from anger and sorrow. Today the believers rejoice with victory from Allah, feeling great happiness. Today the hypocrites are degraded. Today the Rafidites [i.e. Shi'ites], Sahawat [awakening movement], and apostates are humiliated. Today the idols in the east and west are frightened. Today the nations of unbelief in the west are terrified. Today the flags of Satan and his party have fallen ...

Also know that one of the biggest factors that brought about this victory that Allah ... has blessed you with is your support of each other, the absence of disagreement, your listening to and obedience of your leaders, and your patience with them. So keep this factor in mind and preserve it. Unite with each other and do not disagree with each other. Accept each other and do not argue with each other. Be very wary of breaking the ranks ... And if anyone wants to break the ranks, split his head with bullets and empty its insides, whoever he may be ...

O soldiers of the Islamic State, there is one more matter that I wish to call your attention to. They [i.e. ISIS's opponents] will look for something to criticize and will attempt to raise misconceptions. So if they ask you, "How can you announce the caliphate when the ummah has not rallied behind you?" ... Then say to them [that] ... they have never united on a single issue, nor will they ever unite on any issue except for those whom Allah has mercy upon. Furthermore, the Islamic State will bring together those who want unity.

If they tell you, "You have stepped over them and acted on your own judgment. Why did you not consult the other groups, pardon them, and tolerate them?" Then say to them, "The issue is too urgent." ... And say to them, "Whom would we consult? They never recognized the Islamic State to begin with, although America, Britain and France acknowledge its existence. Whom would we consult? Should we consult those who have abandoned us? Those who have betrayed us? Those who have disowned us and incited against us? Those who have become hostile towards us? Those who wage war against us? Whom would we consult, and whom did we step over?" ...

And if they tell you, "We do not accept your authority". Then say to them, "We had the ability to establish the caliphate, by the grace of Allah, so it became an obligation for us to do so. Therefore, we hastened in adherence to the command of Allah ... And say to them, "We spilled rivers of our blood to water the seeds of the caliphate, laid its foundation with our skulls, and built its tower over our corpses. We were patient for years in the face of being killed, imprisoned, having our bones broken and our limbs severed. We drank all sorts of bitterness, dreaming of this day. Would we delay it for even a moment after having reached it?" And say to them, we took it forcibly at the point of a blade. We brought it back conquered and compelled. We established it in defiance of many. And the people's necks were violently struck, with bombings, explosions, and destruction ... Our caliphate has indeed returned with certainty ...

In conclusion, we congratulate the Muslims on the advent of the blessed month of Ramadan. We ask Allah ... to make it a month of victory, honor, and consolidation for the Muslims, and make its days and its nights a curse for the Rafidites, Sahawat, and the apostates ...

Glossary

Aleppo: a Syrian city, west of Iraq

apostate: one who disagrees with a religious position

baya: oath of allegiance

Diyala: a province in eastern Iraq

jihad: religious war

mujahid: one who wages *jihad*

tawhid: Muslim monotheism

ummah: the global community of Muslims

Document Themes and Analysis

The speaker of the 2014 Proclamation of the Caliphate begins by claiming that ISIL is the fulfillment of the Koran's promise of safety for Muslims. To support this claim, he points to ISIL's accomplishments: non-Muslims have been "disgraced"; Western symbols ("crosses and graves") have been destroyed; Islam is the only religion permitted. The last step, he says, is "the establishment of the Islamic caliphate". He names al-Baghdadi as the caliph and lists his ancestors and his piety as reasons for the appointment.

The speaker anticipates problems the caliphate will face. Soldiers and commanders might not accept the new state's orders, or foreign powers might refuse to acknowledge the caliphate because most Muslims do not support it. The speaker combats these claims by asserting again that the caliphate is "in adherence to the command of Allah" and by reminding the listeners of the war that ISIL waged in establishing its regime. The threat of violence, against both enemies and allies, runs through the entire proclamation. ISIL is praised for having "killed, imprisoned, or defeated" its enemies and for spilling "rivers of blood" on its way to establishing the caliphate; if any ISIL soldier disagrees with his commander, his fellow soldiers are ordered to "split his head with bullets."

ISIL's territory reached its greatest extent in approximately October 2014, when its self-proclaimed caliphate controlled approximately a third of Iraq and about half of Syria. From then, ISIL began to lose ground as the Iraqi army and other governments coordinated counterattacks. ISIL lost control of its base in Mosul in July of 2017 and the Iraqi government declared in December of 2017 that it had driven the organization out of the country. As of mid-2023, the group remained in existence, albeit in a much diminished condition.

—Hannah Rich, MA

Bibliography and Additional Reading

Cockburn, Patrick. *The Rise of Islamic State: ISIS and the New Sunni Revolution.* London: Leftward Books, 2020.

Laub, Zachary. August 10, 2016. *Council on Foreign Relations*: www.cfr.org/backgrounder/islamic-state.

Lawrence, Jessica. July 2, 2014. *ABC News Australia:* "Iraq crisis: Could an ISIS caliphate ever govern the entire Muslim world?" www.abc.net.au/news/2014-07-02/could-an-isis-caliphate-ever-govern-the-muslim-world/5559806.

McElroy, Damien. July 1, 2014. *The Telegraph:* "Rome will be conquered next, says leader of 'Islamic State.'" www.telegraph.co.uk/news/worldnews/middleeast/syria/10939235/Rome-will-be-conquered-next-says-leader-of-Islamic-State.html.

The Tunisian National Dialogue Quartet—Nobel Lecture

Date: December 10, 2015
Author: Tunisian National Dialogue Quartet
Genre: speech

Summary Overview

In the early days of the Arab Spring democracy movement (2010–2012), Tunisia seemed to be one of the biggest successes. The Tunisian movement focused on job opportunity, liberty, and social justice; protestors managed to overturn the Ben Ali regime—in power since 1987—in 2011. As in many other countries affected by the Arab Spring, however, the removal of the regime in power left a vacuum that was filled by other extremist actors. Government parties, including Ennahda and two affiliated parties that were called the Troika, focused intensely on Islamic law. They attempted to establish Islam as the national religion in the constitution and remove many of the legal rights of women, among other changes. Critics were concerned that they would attempt to incorporate sharia law into the constitution.

In response, four major groups in the country—the Tunisian General Labor Union (UGTT), the Tunisian Confederation of Industry, Trade and Handicrafts (UTICA), the Tunisian Human Rights League (LTDH), and the Tunisian Order of Lawyers—came together in 2013 to force a political transition to a more secular and democratic government. The group was referred to as the Tunisian National Dialogue Quartet. Through political and social practices, they managed a peaceful transition to a more equal form of government, with democratic elections held in 2014. However, events since 2019 have led to a destabilization of that peace and a return to less democratic rule.

Defining Moment

UGTT tried to force national reconciliation, threatening the strike of 500,000 members. They convened with the other three groups in 2012. Murders of opposition leaders led to calls for Ennahda to step down from its leadership position in 2013. Failure to respond led to a two-day strike by UGTT. Around 50 percent of the union's members struck, and protestors worked with the striking workers. Growing civil conflict led to the president halting all legislative proceedings (and thereby the congressional process).

In October 2013, UGTT again stepped into the process, making it clear that it sought a nonextreme, apolitical government. In 2014, the "big tent" secularist party Nidaa Tounes won enough seats in the Assembly to defeat Ennahda, effectively supporting a secular government in Tunisia.

In 2015, the four groups that made up the Tunisian National Dialogue Quartet were awarded the Nobel Peace prize; they were lauded by the international community as an example of how a government could peacefully transition into a new phase of leadership without bloodshed.

Author Biography

Tunisian General Labor Union (UGTT). This group is the national trade union in Tunisia. It was founded in 1946 and has more than 1 million members. It was the most politically active leading up to the National Dialogue, organizing its members in strikes and protests to help demonstrate the lack of support for the religious wing of the government.

Tunisian Confederation of Industry, Trade and Handicrafts (UTICA). This organization represents employers in the craft, trade, and industrial sectors in Tunisia. It was formed in 1947 and represents close to 150,000 businesses. Its members are organized in national and local associations, and it also supports members with professional structures.

The Tunisian National Dialogue Quartet visiting Vienna in March of 2016. From left to right Abdessattar Ben Moussa (Tunisian Human Rights League), Noureddhine Allege (Order of Lawyers), Houcine Abbassi (UGTT), Wided Bouchamaoui (UTICA). Photo by Bundesministerium für Europa, Integration und Äußeres, via Wikimedia Commons.

Tunisian Human Rights League (LTDH). This group monitors and defends human rights in Tunisia. The group was founded in 1976 and has fought against many causes in the country, including the death penalty and releasing Islamist individuals who had been imprisoned because of "acts of conscience."

Several of its leaders became ministers in the government in the 1980s.

Tunisian Order of Lawyers. All lawyers in Tunisia are part of this group, and the group itself is not affiliated with a political party.

Historical Document

Oslo, Norway, 10 December 2015

[On the behalf of the National Dialogue Quartet Houcine Abassi, Secretary General of The Tunisian General Labour Union, UGTT, Mohamed Fadhel Mahfoudh, President of the Tunisian Order of Lawyers, Abdessattar Ben Moussa, President of the Tunisian Human Rights League and Ouided Bouchamaoui, President of the Tunisian Confederation of Industry, delivered the Nobel Lecture on 10 December 2015 at the Oslo City Hall, Norway.]

His Majesty; Their Highnesses; The respected members of the Nobel Committee;

Ladies and Gentlemen,

We, the National Dialogue Quartet, consisting of the Tunisian General Labour Union, the Tunisian Union of Industry Commerce and Handicrafts, the Tunisian National Bar Association, and the Tunisian League for the Defence of Human Rights, we are greatly honoured to be awarded the 2015 Nobel Peace Prize which is the culmination of a long relentless struggle on the path of national liberation, construction of democracy and promoting universal values and principles. We are pleased to extend our sincere thanks and gratitude to the Nobel Peace Prize Committee and the Norwegian Parliament who, by giving us this award, have highlighted the Tunisian experience to the whole world. This will certainly give us more impetus to carry on our work for the benefit of our country.

This tribute is not only to us. It is indeed a tribute to all Tunisian political players who adopted an approach of collective agreement, and succeeded in putting the interests of their homeland and their people above their narrow partisan interests. It is a tribute to Tunisian women and Tunisian young people who revolted against discrimination and exclusion, and even challenged death in defending their civil rights and their right for freedom, dignity and decent life. It is a tribute to thinkers, intellectuals, trade unionists, law professionals, civil society activists, and our brave soldiers and security forces whose vigilance, sacrifices and contributions have shaped the exceptional Tunisian experience, as they were the safety valve against all attempts to blow up our modernist society gains, and attempts to damage our civil State and the real merits targeted by our revolution.

Your Majesties; Ladies and Gentlemen,

Before talking about the National Dialogue experience, let us emphasize that our euphoria and pride in this historic occasion should not veil our grief, sorrow and outrage about what has happened in many parts of the world. A few days ago, our capital Tunis and before that, Sousse, Bardo Museum, Beirut, Paris, Sharm el-Sheikh and Bamako have witnessed barbaric and atrocious terrorist incidents in which hundreds of innocent people were killed. The feelings of compassion and sympathy cannot prevent the grief and agony of the families of victims and others who fell in other cities around the world.

The tribute paid by the international community to the Tunisian national dialogue process confirms indeed that we share the same universal values of human rights which underpin human rights and reject all forms of intellectual and ideological isolationism. The progress in confronting all threats and risks to us around the world requires more solidarity, the build-up of a lasting and fair partnership among the peoples of the world, and searching for serious solutions to the problems which many countries are facing because of poverty. We are today in urgent need of a dialogue between civilizations, and a peaceful coexistence within the context of diversity and variation. We are today in urgent need to make the fight against terrorism an absolute priority, which means constant coordination and cooperation among all nations to drain out its resources and disconnect it from its incubator environment. Today, we need to accelerate the elimination of hot spots all over the world, and particularly to find a solution for the Palestinian cause and enable the Palestinian people to exercise self-determination on their own land and build their independent state.

This occasion is a tribute to a country with a long history and a civilizational legacy spanning more than 3,000 years, a country shaped over time by successive civilizations and characterized by an inherent belief in peace and moderation.

This historic occasion, which coincides with the anniversary of the Universal Declaration of Human Rights, is a tribute to the spirit of an inspiring revolution that the Tunisians led five years ago to protect their legitimate rights, to defend their freedom and dignity, a revolution in which all Tunisians shouted with one voice, "The people want" ... "The people want the right to liberty" ... "The people want the right to dignity" ... "The people want the right to work".

These slogans did have a magical impact. They inspired various peoples to rise up and claim their legitimate rights, and express their rejection of autocracy, injustice and oppression.

Your Majesties; Ladies and Gentlemen,

On the 17th of December 2010, the Tunisian Revolution erupted against poverty and marginalisation, and against development options that established exclusion and injustice between different regions and different communities. Its slogans were to claim economic and social rights outlined in three main demands: Job Opportunity, Liberty and Social Justice. It was demonstrated in social movements and young people's sit-ins, which all demanded a solution to the problem of unemployment, and an elimination of marginalisation. They demanded the right to proper development, fair distribution of wealth, and equality.

However, this uprising took an express and direct political turn after the escape of the hierarchy of power. It demanded the dissolution of all structures of the ruling party, suspension of the old Constitution of 1959, and the departure of the whole existing government. This situation left a great power vacuum that led the country into a serious crisis which could have had dire consequences. However, the established civil society – due to its deep roots in the community, its historic roles in the struggle for national independence and and its unwavering support of the causes of its people – moved from the very first days to secure the fulfilment of the aims of the revolution. In order to steer the transitional process in a democratic and constitutional direction, the High Commission for Achieving the Goals of the Revolution was established. The High Commission brought together all political, civil and social views and the most prominent independent national leaders. This helped fill the vacuum successfully and paved the way for the Constituent Assembly Elections of 23 October 2011.

The start was rather frustrating, as the almost consensual political scene that the country witnessed before the Constituent Assembly Elections changed into a new reality overwhelmed by dangerous violations and practices that deepened the trend of political polarisation and created a lot of confusion and concern about the future of governance in the country. This resulted in intensified polarisation between political factions, and the emergence of tension and alienation in the Community. So, chaos and lawlessness dominated the scene, which encouraged undermining the prestige of the State, and spurred the predominance of smuggling gangs, parallel trading barons, terrorist groups and religious extremism. This resulted in the assassination of human rights activist and political martyr Mr Chokri Belaid on 6 February 2013, followed by the assassination of the National Constituent Assembly Member, the martyr Mr Mohammed Brahmi on 25 July of the same year, and resulted in the fall of many martyrs among the security forces and army soldiers. The Tunisian Citizen became confused because of the lack of security, the deterioration of social and economic conditions, and the dominance of chaos in several aspects of Tunisian life.

Because of this tense situation and the escalation of the people's uprising in Tunis and many Tunisian cities, and after disruption of the role of the Constituent Assembly when some opposition deputies suspended their participation, the National Dialogue Initiative was launched after our four institutions unanimously agreed to sponsor it. The political stakeholders agreed that they needed to move ahead, and accepted the invitation to sit at the dialogue table in order to achieve the necessary consensuses that would ensure the completion of the transitional process which already exceeded its deadlines. This is what actually happened when all groups and factions agreed to sign our Road Map.

Your Majesties; Ladies and Gentlemen,

The Road Map included a series of consensual solutions for the contentious points. It stated the following:

Acceptance to form a technocrat government of professional experts headed by an independent national figure. The members of the government were not to run in the upcoming elections. Moreover, the existing government had to pledge to step down as soon as the new technocrat government was appointed.

The National Constituent Assembly was to resume its functions and determine its mandate and the ending of its proceeding.

Commencement of consultations on the independent figure who would be entrusted to form the government.

Agreement on a road map for completion of the transitional process that would set the timetable for the presidential and legislative elections. This timetable was to be announced to the general public after being signed by all parties. The roadmap agreement was to be issues under an act adopted by the National Constituent Assembly in a special meeting. Besides, there should be a provisional organization and review of the public authorities.

The National Dialogue was not an easy process. Indeed, some of its rounds were so difficult that we were forced to suspend it for nearly one month, after it was not possible to reach consensus on some points mentioned in the Road Map. However, we did not give up and kept on working as a quartet. We contacted the political parties and managed to get them together at the dialogue table. Thanks to this consensual approach that we adopted and sponsored with the support of all elements of the civil society, the transition path was successfully completed. Eventually, a provisional government of independent professional experts was formed, and a new constitution for the country was drafted and approved with a high level of consensus. The Independent High Electoral Commission was elected, and the electoral law was issued which led to the holding of legislative and presidential elections, thus producing a new Parliament, a new President and a Government that won the confidence of the majority of the people's deputies.

Thanks to this spirit, we, the sponsoring quartet, realised that the special characteristics of the transitional period cannot be dealt with in accordance with the process of elections only, as these remain fragile and exposed to various setbacks. Instead, the transitional period should be backed by a consensual legitimacy. Hence, we sought to convince everyone that the majority approach in the transitional period, in a community that is still taking its first steps towards democracy, may involve disagreement, tension and aggravation. It should presumably be backed by a political approach which provides the most possible consensus, thus ensuring the country's unity and solidarity. It is an approach of consensus based on constructive dialogue. Such an approach in transitional periods is characterised in exceptional cases with a mutual alignment of the people's consensual legitimacy and the electoral legitimacy which could be weakened or corroded, so that each legitimacy would not cancel the other. However, such an approach to the transitional process requires minimum pre-requisites which are available in Tunisia, but unfortunately did not exist in other Arab Spring countries.

Consensus requires well-planned preparation, genuine willingness for dialogue, pre-agreed controls of work and a framework in which ideas and viewpoints are shared by various political factions. In particular, a sponsor trusted and appreciated by all parties concerned should undertake the task of running and deepening the dialogue until it achieves its objectives.

Your Majesties; Ladies and Gentlemen,

We are proud that the Tunisian National Dialogue experience has received such unprecedented international sympathy and appreciation. This prompts us to persevere in this approach and adopt it as a strategic option for the management of our political, economic, social and cultural affairs. This is why we look forward to setting this experience, after its completion, as a role model for other peoples that are today facing difficult transitional processes, so that lessons could be learned to help solving their challenges in a similar way.

The successes achieved along the consensual transition path still need us to make tremendous efforts to fortify and consolidate them, so that they become a basis for new successes. We recognise that there are many challenges ahead of us, and there are still huge risks surrounding us.

At the political level, we are looking forward to completing the constituent path and organizing power and authority on a democratic basis, by finalizing the establishment of the remaining constitutional institutions necessary to consolidate liberties and resist the return of autocracy.

On the economic level, we have to create the conditions that ensure the return of the Tunisian economy to its normal state, and improve the overall climate for investment, and embark on approving the necessary repairs, with extensive consultation between the Government and the economic and social players, to preserve the interests of all groups and factions. This will contribute significantly to improving the stability of the country.

On the social level, we should work altogether to provide the elements of dignity and decent livelihood for all Tunisians wherever they are, and to eliminate poverty, deprivation and inequality between various groups. This requires that we address the problem of unemployment, and particularly the unemployment of university graduates.

On the security level, even if the security conditions get improved in general, and Tunisia makes progress in confronting terrorism and protecting our borders from smuggling, a huge effort must be made in order to make a quantum leap in the fight against terrorism and in dealing with the terrorist phenomenon. This will require extending the fight in various directions and disconnecting this phenomenon from its resources wherever they may be.

Your Majesties; Ladies and Gentlemen,

We recognise that the key to achieving stability in Tunisia lies in the creation of more job opportunities for our youth and in looking more after our inland regions, especially the border areas which have suffered for decades from marginalisation and in which our people are expecting after the Revolution to achieve better living conditions. This target requires the development of infrastructures and the improvement of basic life facilities such as health, transport and education, and requires putting heavy investments and exploring the possibilities of promoting minor projects, especially because these areas have a big civilization and traditional legacy that could be a springboard for the creation of many projects, whether in agriculture or in traditional industries, if only there is proper funding and an appropriate business environment.

We are well aware of all these difficulties, and fully aware of the challenges that lie ahead. We are determined to rely on ourselves in overcoming the difficulties, and we look forward to having the support of our friends all over the world. To everyone who believes in Tunisia, we say that we will continue working for our country and will keep our bet on dialogue and consensus as a suitable approach to overcome the difficulties regardless of their size.

Thank you, and may you always be a supporter of freedom and peace.

Copyright © The Nobel Foundation 2015

Document Themes and Analysis

The text of the National Dialogue Quartet lecture repeatedly refers to the concept of solidarity. The National Dialogue worked because it represented a large section of the population, not narrow special interests. People from disparate groups worked together to bring a peaceful transition of power to the country. The group applies this concept to other international problems, such as terrorism, suggesting that no one country can solve global issues on its own. Palestine and the ongoing conflicts there are specifically highlighted.

The lecture also discusses how important it is to have a process in place for what happens after a dictator is expelled, a regime is ended, or a group is removed from power. Without a plan determining what the next step will be, a power vacuum is created, and removing one dictator will simply lead to the rise of another. After the existing regime was ended in 2011, a new president stepped into place who created "dangerous violations and practices that deepened the trend of political polarization." The assassination of Chokri Belaid and Mohammed Brahmi in 2013 are cited as the beginning of a new process; it became clear that an organized discussion would be required to lead Tunisia forward on a secular, democratic path.

The Quartet is also clear that there is no point where this process is complete. Continuing to work together, with respect for other groups and people, is necessary for all members of society in order to allow the structure of a peaceful government to develop and grow.

The international community has widely hailed the National Dialogue in Tunisia as a demonstration of how the peacemaking process can be more effective than violence, and how a democratic change in power can occur. One key feature of the process was the requirement that, once the National Dialogue was complete, the existing party in the government would step down from its place and allow the new government to take leadership.

Unions and strikes were key elements to the success of the National Dialogue: without the huge membership of the UGTT and the ability of its members to halt economic activities if the government did not cooperate with conversations, it is unlikely that the transition would have been possible. The 2014 constitution therefore strengthened the laws around unions, giving them the unilateral right to strike and the ability to form new unions; under the previous laws, strikes were prohibited if they would affect "vital industries."

Some critics have expressed frustration that the government did not actually represent the working people who helped make the transition possible. The government in Tunisia was considered a technocrat government, where those who make the decisions have been selected on the basis of their expertise. While such an arrangement makes sense under certain circumstances, it also tends to lock nonexperts out of the ruling party, which means that those who have less economic and political power often are unable to be heard.

While the National Dialogue did lead to several years of peace in Tunisia, concerns arose about how the government would move forward after the COVID-19 crisis. The president died in 2019, and Kais Saled was elected president that October. As the COVID-19 pandemic crisis unfolded, however, Saled and his prime minister were in constant conflict, leading to government deadlocks that seriously impaired Tunisia's ability to respond to the situation and protect its people. Demonstrations began in 2021 over the issue, leading Saled to suspect parliament and dismiss the Prime Minister. Then, in 2022, he called for a same-day vote on a new constitution. Many in the opposition urged a boycott of the vote, resulting in a 30-percent turnout. The new constitution passed easily, and it gave substantially increased powers to the president. This event is now referred to as the "Tunisian self-coup." The Tunisian people have protested the change, and ongoing, sporadic protests continue. The UGTT initially supported Saled, but that relationship has now broken; the UGTT is now voicing concerns about whether Saled is committed to preserving the people's rights and freedoms.

—*Kay Lemay, MA*

Bibliography and Additional Reading

Bayat, Asef. *Revolutionary Life: The Everyday of the Arab Spring.* Cambridge, MA: Harvard University Press, 2021.

Chan, Sewell. "Nobel Peace Prize is awarded to National Dialogue Quartet in Tunisia." *New York Times,* October 9, 2015. www.nytimes.com/2015/10/10/world/europe/national-dialogue-quartet-tunisia-nobel-peace-prize.html.

Haloui, Yasmin. *Life in Revolution: Resistance & the Everyday in Tunisian Revolution.* Saarbrücken, Saarland, Germany: Lambert Academic Publishing, 2011.

Recent Revolutionary Disturbances

In recent years, Far-Right militia groups and white-supremacist organizations have gained greater prominence in the United States. For decades these were fringe organizations routinely renounced or kept at a distance by mainstream politicians, leaving them with little political influence. The spokespersons for such groups often follow an aggressive, neofascist line of argument in communicating their grievances in public. Social media has been key in spreading their messages. Often, however, they deny charges of racism or white supremacy, insisting that they are simply participating in identity politics to promote their group's interests. They blame liberal politics and "establishment" politicians for the "decline" of the country, and vow to "take it back" through direct action. Although there are differences among them, Far-Right groups generally oppose immigration, foreign aid, health mandates, affirmative action, the Black Lives Matter movement, and the federal government as a whole while supporting unrestricted gun rights, states' rights, a strong military, white Christian nationalism, and an "America First" foreign policy position. They tend also to be fueled by the notion that a secretive "deep state" runs the federal government, and by other unfounded conspiracy theories such as the idea that top Democrats operate a child sex ring. Many such ideas are associated with the influential political conspiracy movement known as QAnon, which arose on social media around 2017.

Most of these extremist groups were strong supporters of the presidency of Donald J. Trump. This relationship became especially apparent during the 2017 "Unite the Right" rally in Charlottesville, Virginia. The event brought together white nationalist and Far-Right organizations to protest the removal of statues of Confederate army figures such as Robert E. Lee. Carrying tiki torches and chanting "Jews will not replace us"—a reference to a fringe theory that Jews were secretly funding illegal immigration from Latin America in order dilute the U.S. white population—the Charlottesville marchers clashed violently with antifascist counterprotestors; one person was killed and nineteen injured. Asked to condemn the violence afterward, Trump offered only that in his view there were "very fine people on both sides" of the disruption. In later public appearances, he similarly refused to speak out against QAnon or the Far-Right vigilante group called the Proud Boys.

Shared interests between Trump and the Far Right came home to roost in the wake of the 2020 presidential election, which Trump lost to Democrat Joe Biden. Refusing to admit defeat, despite the certification of the electoral results by secretaries of state around the country, Trump convened a rally at the U.S. Capitol on January 6, 2021, as a way of disrupting the final certification by Congress that day. After the rally, armed mobs of antigovernment, pro-Trump extremists forced their way into the Capitol building, shouting "Hang Mike Pence" (the vice president) because of Pence's constitutional role in certifying the election count in Congress. It was only hours after the start of the violent rebellion that Trump, under pressure from top figures both inside and outside his government, advised the rebels via video that they should cease their insurrection.

With Biden in office, having been inaugurated on January 20, 2021, a (second) impeachment trial against Trump took place in the Senate. With the body being evenly divided between Republicans and Democrats, however, the vote at the end of the trial failed to reach the necessary two-thirds majority for conviction. (Republicans maintained that an *ex*-president could not be impeached no matter the charge.) In addition, a congressional investigation into the Capitol attack took place in 2021–2022 and concluded that Trump helped facilitate it, but no action was taken—largely because Republicans won control of that body in the 2022 mid-term elections.

Meanwhile, the U.S. Justice Department's prosecution of the January 6 offenders is ongoing. Over 1,000 individuals have been charged—some of them with "seditious conspiracy"—and nearly 350 have been convicted to date. A Special Counsel investigation into the past presidents and other Republican leaders' alleged roles in the attack also is ongoing.

In January 2023, a remarkably similar event took place in Brazil, in the capital of Brasília. In this instance, the Far-Right incumbent president, Jair Bolsonaro, had recently been defeated by his liberal opponent (and former president), Luis Inácio Lula da Silva, but refused to concede. As with the January 6 insurrection in the United States, rioters in Brasília invaded government buildings before the new president had been inaugurated, wreaking havoc but not threatening lawmakers: the buildings happened to be empty during a government intercession. Still, the invasion was viewed as an alarming attack on the democratic process in Brazil. Immediately afterward, authorities there launched prosecutions against the offenders.

■ Resolution Establishing the House Select Committee to Investigate the January 6th Attack on the U.S. Capitol

Date: June 30, 2021
Author: Nancy Pelosi
Genres: charter; legislation

Summary Overview

The House resolution examined here set up a bipartisan committee to investigate the role of violent political extremists in organizing and planning the attack on the U.S. Capitol on January 6, 2021. The attack took place in an effort to stop the certification of the November 3, 2020, presidential election, in which Democratic candidate Joe Biden defeated the incumbent Republican, Donald Trump. At the encouragement of Trump, a large crowd of Trump's supporters and adherents of the QAnon conspiracy theory marched from the site of Trump's speech, The Ellipse (just south of the White House), to the U.S. Capitol, breaching security barriers and eventually breaking doors and windows to enter the Capitol building. A joint session of Congress was taking place at the time, and congressmembers, together with Vice President Mike Pence, had to be rushed to secure locations to ensure their safety.

Less than six months after the attack, Speaker of the House Nancy Pelosi (D-CA) introduced H.R. 503, a resolution to establish a Select Committee to investigate the attack, the lack of sufficient Federal response to quell it, and the potential for future such attacks.

Defining Moment

On November 3, 2020, former vice president and Democratic challenger Joe Biden defeated the Republican incumbent president, Donald Trump in the U.S. presidential election. Biden won the popular vote convincingly, earning over 81 million votes compared with over 74 million for Trump. More importantly, Biden also won the Electoral College vote, which actually determines the outcome of the election, by a vote of 306–232. However, during August and September 2020, months before the election, Trump had made clear that he would not accept the result were he to be defeated by Biden. Immediately after the election, Trump made good on his earlier statements and initiated a series of unsuccessful legal proceedings to contest the elections in a number of swing states that Biden narrowly won.

On December 19, 2020, as the date for the Congress to meet to certify the election (January 6, 2021) approached, Trump issued a call on Twitter

Nancy Pelosi (D). Photo via Wikimedia Commons. [Public domain.]

A crowd-erected gallows hangs near the United States Capitol during the 2021 storming of the United States Capitol. Photo by Tyler Merbler, via Wikimedia Commons.

for his supporters to protest the election in Washington, D.C., tweeting "Big protest in D.C. on January 6. Be there, will be wild!" At noon on January 6, thousands of Trump's supporters gathered to hear his speech at the Ellipse, just south of the White House. Trump implored the crowd, stating, "it is up to Congress to confront this egregious assault on our democracy. And after this, we're going to walk down, and I'll be there with you...because you'll never take back our country with weakness. You have to show strength and you have to be strong. We have come to demand that Congress do the right thing and only count the electors who have been lawfully slated, lawfully slated."

After the speech, the crowd, without Trump, marched to and breached the Capitol building, engaging in a violent riot that forced congresspeople to flee and resulted in five deaths. In response, Pelosi and Democratic leaders in the House initiated impeachment proceedings against Trump one week later, though the Republican-controlled U.S. Senate acquitted him. (A majority of Senators voted to convict, but in this case a two-thirds "supermajority" was needed.) In an effort to hold those who planned and carried out the attack responsible for their actions, and to prevent future attacks, Pelosi introduced, and the House then passed, a resolution to form a select committee to investigate the attacks.

Author Biography

Speaker of the House Nancy Pelosi is a Democratic lawmaker who has been a congressperson since first winning election in 1987. She has led the Democratic caucus in the House, either as minority leader or as Speaker of the House since 2003. Often seen as a polarizing figure to Republicans, Pelosi has proven to be effective at moving Democratic-supported legislation

Tear gas outside the Capitol, January 6, 2021. Photo by Tyler Merbler, via Wikimedia Commons.

through the House during her two terms as Speaker (2007–11, and a second term when Democrats regained a majority in the House in 2019). Pelosi was instrumental in planning the 2019 and 2021 impeachment trials of President Donald Trump, the second one coming as a result of his actions that inspired and encouraged the January 6, 2021, attack on the U.S. Capitol.

Historical Document

Resolution Establishing the House Select Committee to Investigate the January 6th Attack on the U.S. Capitol

Whereas January 6, 2021, was one of the darkest days of our democracy, during which insurrectionists attempted to impede Congress's Constitutional mandate to validate the presidential election and launched an assault on the United States Capitol Complex that resulted in multiple deaths, physical harm to over 140 members of law enforcement, and terror and trauma among staff, institutional employees, press, and Members;

Whereas, on January 27, 2021, the Department of Homeland Security issued a National Terrorism Advisory System Bulletin that due to the "heightened threat environment across the United States," in which "[S]ome ideologically-motivated violent extremists with objections to the exercise of governmental authority and the presidential transition, as well as other perceived grievances fueled by false narratives, could continue to mobilize to incite or commit violence." The Bulletin also stated that—

(1) "DHS is concerned these same drivers to violence will remain through early 2021 and some DVEs [domestic violent extremists] may be emboldened by the January 6, 2021 breach of the U.S. Capitol Building in Washington, D.C. to target elected officials and government facilities."; and

(2) "Threats of violence against critical infrastructure, including the electric, telecommunications and healthcare sectors, increased in 2020 with violent extremists citing misinformation and conspiracy theories about COVID–19 for their actions";

Whereas, on September 24, 2020, Director of the Federal Bureau of Investigation Christopher Wray testified before the Committee on Homeland Security of the House of Representatives that—

(1) "[T]he underlying drivers for domestic violent extremism—such as perceptions of government or law enforcement overreach, sociopolitical conditions, racism, anti-Semitism, Islamophobia, misogyny, and reactions to legislative actions—remain constant.";

(2) "[W]ithin the domestic terrorism bucket category as a whole, racially-motivated violent extremism is, I think, the biggest bucket within the larger group. And within the racially-motivated violent extremists bucket, people

subscribing to some kind of white supremacist-type ideology is certainly the biggest chunk of that."; and

(3) "More deaths were caused by DVEs than international terrorists in recent years. In fact, 2019 was the deadliest year for domestic extremist violence since the Oklahoma City bombing in 1995";

Whereas, on April 15, 2021, Michael Bolton, the Inspector General for the United States Capitol Police, testified to the Committee on House Administration of the House of Representatives that—

(1) "The Department lacked adequate guidance for operational planning. USCP did not have policy and procedures in place that communicated which personnel were responsible for operational planning, what type of operational planning documents its personnel should prepare, nor when its personnel should prepare operational planning documents."; and

(2) "USCP failed to disseminate relevant information obtained from outside sources, lacked consensus on interpretation of threat analyses, and disseminated conflicting intelligence information regarding planned events for January 6, 2021."; and

Whereas the security leadership of the Congress under-prepared for the events of January 6th, with United States Capitol Police Inspector General Michael Bolton testifying again on June 15, 2021, that—

(1) "USCP did not have adequate policies and procedures for FRU (First Responder Unit) defining its overall operations. Additionally, FRU lacked resources and training for properly completing its mission.";

(2) "The Department did not have adequate policies and procedures for securing ballistic helmets and vests strategically stored around the Capitol Complex."; and

(3) "FRU did not have the proper resources to complete its mission.": Now, therefore, be it

Resolved,

SECTION 1. ESTABLISHMENT.

There is hereby established the Select Committee to Investigate the January 6th Attack on the United States Capitol (hereinafter referred to as the "Select Committee").

SEC. 2. COMPOSITION.

(a) Appointment Of Members.—The Speaker shall appoint 13 Members to the Select Committee, 5 of whom shall be appointed after consultation with the minority leader.

(b) Designation Of Chair.—The Speaker shall designate one Member to serve as chair of the Select Committee.

(c) Vacancies.—Any vacancy in the Select Committee shall be filled in the same manner as the original appointment.

SEC. 3. PURPOSES.

Consistent with the functions described in section 4, the purposes of the Select Committee are the following:

(1) To investigate and report upon the facts, circumstances, and causes relating to the January 6, 2021, domestic terrorist attack upon the United States Capitol Complex (hereafter referred to as the "domestic terrorist attack on the Capitol") and relating to the interference with the peaceful transfer of power, including facts and causes relating to the preparedness and response of the United States Capitol Police and other Federal, State, and local law enforcement agencies in the National Capital Region and other instrumentalities of government, as well as the influencing factors that fomented such an attack on American representative democracy while engaged in a constitutional process.

(2) To examine and evaluate evidence developed by relevant Federal, State, and local governmental agencies regarding the facts and circumstances surrounding the domestic terrorist attack on the Capitol and targeted violence and domestic terrorism relevant to such terrorist attack.

(3) To build upon the investigations of other entities and avoid unnecessary duplication of efforts by reviewing the investigations, findings, conclusions, and recommendations of other executive branch, congressional, or independent bipartisan or nonpartisan commission investigations into the domestic terrorist attack on the Capitol, including investigations into influencing factors related to such attack.

SEC. 4. FUNCTIONS.

(a) Functions.—The functions of the Select Committee are to—

(1) investigate the facts, circumstances, and causes relating to the domestic terrorist attack on the Capitol, including facts and circumstances relating to—

(A) activities of intelligence agencies, law enforcement agencies, and the Armed Forces, including with respect to intelligence collection, analysis, and dissemination and information sharing among the branches and other instrumentalities of government;

(B) influencing factors that contributed to the domestic terrorist attack on the Capitol and how technology, including online platforms, financing, and malign foreign influence operations and campaigns may have factored into the motivation, organization, and execution of the domestic terrorist attack on the Capitol; and

(C) other entities of the public and private sector as determined relevant by the Select Committee for such investigation;

(2) identify, review, and evaluate the causes of and the lessons learned from the domestic terrorist attack on the Capitol regarding—

(A) the command, control, and communications of the United States Capitol Police, the Armed Forces, the National Guard, the Metropolitan Police Department of the District of Columbia, and other Federal, State, and local law enforcement agencies in the National Capital Region on or before January 6, 2021;

(B) the structure, coordination, operational plans, policies, and procedures of the Federal Government, including as such relate to State and local governments and nongovernmental entities, and particularly with respect to detecting, preventing, preparing for, and responding to targeted violence and domestic terrorism;

(C) the structure, authorities, training, manpower utilization, equipment, operational planning, and use of force policies of the United States Capitol Police;

(D) the policies, protocols, processes, procedures, and systems for the sharing of intelligence and other information by Federal, State, and local agencies with the United States Capitol Police, the Sergeants at Arms of the House of Representatives and Senate, the Government of the District of Columbia, including the Metropolitan Police Department of the District of Columbia, the National Guard, and other Federal, State, and local law enforcement agencies in the National Capital Region on or before January 6, 2021, and the related policies, protocols, processes, procedures, and systems for monitoring, assessing, disseminating, and acting on intelligence and other information, including elevating the security posture of the United States Capitol Complex, derived from instrumentalities of government, open sources, and online platforms; and

(E) the policies, protocols, processes, procedures, and systems for interoperability between the United States Capitol Police and the National Guard, the Metropolitan Police Department of the District of Columbia, and other Federal, State, and local law enforcement agencies in the National Capital Region on or before January 6, 2021; and

(3) issue a final report to the House containing such findings, conclusions, and recommendations for corrective measures described in subsection (c) as it may deem necessary....

Glossary

DHS: Department of Homeland Security, the federal agency tasked with protecting Americans from foreign and domestic terrorism

USCP: United States Capitol Police, the police force tasked with protecting the U.S. Capitol

FRU: First Responders Unit, an elite portion of the United States Capitol Police tasked with protecting congresspeople, their staffs, and all people on the Capitol grounds

Document Themes

In the resolution, the select committee was tasked with investigating the facts and circumstances surrounding the attack, evaluate the response to the attack by various parts of the Federal government, and recommend actions that might prevent similar attacks against the nation's democratic institutions in the future. The committee would be made up of thirteen House members (seven Democrats, six Republicans), to be appointed by Pelosi in consultation with Republican Minority Leader Kevin McCarthy (R-CA). The measure passed the House by a vote of 222–190. All House Democrats voted in favor of the measure, and all but two Republicans—the exceptions being Liz Cheney (R-WY) and Adam Kinzinger (R-IL)—voted against the measure. Nineteen Republicans abstained from the vote.

In the aftermath of the passage of H.R. 503, the debate between Republicans and Democrats over the presidential election became even more contentious, with Republicans holding to Trump's unsubstantiated claims of fraud and Democrats continuing to focus on the efforts of the rioters on January 6 to overthrow a legal election. On July 19, Republican Minority Leader Kevin McCarthy selected five Republican lawmakers to serve on the committee, including Jim Jordan (R-OH), one of Trump's most vocal and polarizing supporters. Pelosi refused two of McCarthy's picks, Jordan and Jim Banks (R-IN), and McCarthy responded two days later by pulling all of his picks, leaving Pelosi with only two Republicans willing to serve at her request, with Liz Cheney (R-WY) and Adam Kinzinger (R-IL), who had both opposed Trump's actions on January 6, agreeing to serve alongside the seven Democratic members. As a result of their willingness to serve on the select committee, the Republican National Committee voted to censure both Cheney and Kinzinger.

After beginning its work on July 27, 2021, the select committee had, by February 2022, interviewed over 500 witnesses and obtained approximately 35,000 documents related to the attack. Many Trump administration officials, including Stephen Bannon, Roger Stone, Trump Chief of Staff Mark Meadows, National Security Advisor Michael Flynn, refused to testify, with some invoking their Fifth Amendment protection against self-incrimination and others, notably Bannon, being held in contempt of Congress. As of the end of February 2022, the investigation was ongoing but expected to wrap up after holding public hearings in mid-2022.

Vice-Chair Liz Cheney (R). Photo via Wikimedia Commons. [Public domain.]

—*Steven L. Danver, PhD*

Bibliography and Additional Reading

Ankel, Sophia. "Trump Promises 'Wild' Protests in Washington, DC, on the Day Congress Is Set to Finalize Election Results." *Yahoo News*, December 20, 2020. www.yahoo.com/video/trump-promises-wild-protests-washington-165055313.html.

Breuninger, Kevin. "Trump Refuses to Accept Election Results, Says It's 'Far from Over.'" *CNBC*, November 7, 2020. www.cnbc.com/2020/11/07/trump-refuses-to-accept-election-results-says-it-is-far-from-over.html.

Collinson, Stephen. "New Revelations Betray Depth of Trump's Post-Election Schemes." *CNN*, February 10, 2022. www.cnn.com/2022/02/10/politics/capitol-insurrection-donald-trump-republicans-congress/index.html.

Liasson, Mara. "Why President Trump Refuses to Concede and What It Might Mean for the Country." *NPR*, November 18, 2020. www.npr.org/2020/11/18/936342902/why-president-trump-refuses-to-concede-and-what-it-might-mean-for-the-country.

Liptak, Kevin. "A List of the Times Trump Has Said He Won't Accept the election Results or Leave Office if He Loses." *CNN*, September 24, 2020. www.cnn.com/2020/09/24/politics/trump-election-warnings-leaving-office/index.html.

Naylor, Brian. "Read Trump's Jan. 6 Speech, a Key Part of Impeachment Trial." *NPR*, February 10, 2021. www.npr.org/2021/02/10/966396848/read-trumps-jan-6-speech-a-key-part-of-impeachment-trial.

Sonmez, Felicia. "Pelosi Introduces Legislation That Would Establish Select Committee to Probe Jan. 6 Capitol Attack." *Washington Post*, June 28, 2021. www.washingtonpost.com/politics/pelosi-introduces-legislation-that-would-establish-select-committee-to-probe-jan-6-capitol-attack/2021/06/28/1d40b2c8-d852-11eb-9bbb-37c30dcf9363_story.html.

■ Summary of Terrorism Threat to the U.S. Homeland

Date: November 10, 2021
Author: Alejandro Mayorkas
Genres: government document; security advisory

Summary Overview

Since 2011, the U.S. Department of Homeland Security has managed what is called the National Terrorism Advisory System (NTAS). The NTAS issues alerts that are either "elevated" or "imminent," and includes specific information as well as an expiration date for any warning. In response to the 2015 terror attacks in Paris and San Bernadino, a third alert level, "intermediate," was added. In December 2015, the first bulletin was published. Bulletins discuss general trends and developments on terrorism threats that do not require a specific alert for that threat. The evolution of these warning systems is indicative of the constantly changing needs of counterterrorism efforts.

NTAS represents an updated version of the system created in 2002 by President George W. Bush following the 9-11 attacks on the World Trade Center and the Pentagon. That earlier system, called the Homeland Security Advisory System (HSAS), employed a set of color-coded warnings to indicate the level of potential threat of a terrorist attack. By 2004, however, the system faced criticism for lacking specificity and actionable content (and was the subject of jokes from comedians to Congress). Secretary of Homeland Security Janet Napolitano created a committee to evaluate the system and recommend changes. On January 27, 2011, Napolitano announced HSAS would be replaced with a new system, the NTAS.

Defining Moment

In March 2002, six months after the September 11 attacks, the Homeland Security Advisory System (HSAS) was created. President George W. Bush issued Homeland Security Directive 3 intending to provide information about "the risk of terrorist acts to federal, state, and local authorities and to the American people." The goal was to facilitate an informed government and citizenry and thwart further terrorist attacks. The U.S. attorney general managed the system until January 2003, when the newly created Department of Homeland Security (DHS) took over.

Inspired by the success of the forest fire risk system, the terror scale had five color-coded threat levels: The highest threat level, "severe," was red. This was followed by "high" in orange, "elevated" in yellow, "guarded" in blue, and "low" in green. According to the president's directive, "the higher the threat condition, the greater the risk of a terrorist attack."

HSAS threat levels were to be evaluated regularly and adjusted as needed. It was said that threat levels would adjust based on the degree a threat was "credible, corroborated, imminent, and grave." However, no criteria for determining the threat levels were ever published and the lack of transparency was criticized. Critics alleged that the lack of public criteria left the system open to manipulation by political machinations. In his book, *The Test of Our Times*, Tom Ridge said he was pressured by top aides to President Bush, including defense secretary Donald Rumsfeld and attorney general John Ashcroft, to raise the alert level on the eve of the November 2004 presidential election. This pressure led Ridge to leave the federal government for the private sector.

The system was also too vague to provide government, organizations, or individuals with enough information to understand, much less respond to, any threat. It became a favorite target of comedians and even appeared in a *Saturday Night Live* skit. In July 2009, DHS Secretary Janet Napolitano created a task force to review the HSAS. The task force confirmed that the HSAS the public had a "disturbing lack of confidence in the system" and agreed that "substantial reform" was required.

On January 27, 2011, Napolitano announced the HSAS would be replaced with a new National Terrorism Advisory System (NTAS). On April 26, 2011, the new NTAS replaced the old HSAS. Napolitano said, "Today I announce the end of the old system of color-coded alerts. In its place, we will implement a new system that's build on clear and simple premise: When a threat develops that could impact you—the public—we will tell you. We will provide whatever information we can so you know how to protect yourselves, your families, and your communities."

When DHS has information about a specific, credible threat, a formal alert will be issued with as much information as possible, including information such as geographic region, mode of transportation, critical infrastructure affected, protective actions authorities are taking, and steps for individuals to take. They also provide government agencies and emergency officials with threat assessments and news outlet and social networking resources to notify public.

The three alert levels are "elevated," "intermediate," and "imminent." The new system offers detailed alerts that include the threat level, plus details on the threat, duration of the alert, information on the affected areas and what steps are being taken to address the threat. These alerts are only shared publicly on social media and websites if there is a specific threat. The alerts have an expiration date unless new information allows for their extension. As of February 2022, no public alerts have been issued under this system.

The "intermediate" threat level was added to the NTAS on December 7, 2015. This new threat level was in response to a "new phase" of terrorist activity, which followed the 2015 terrorist attacks in Paris and San Bernardino. The Secretary of DHS for the Obama administration said that because of the continual threat, a high threat level was considered the "baseline."

In 2015, in addition to the adding a new threat level, the Department of Homeland Security modified the system by adding "bulletins" to the existing alerts. Bulletins discuss general trends and developments on terrorism threats that do not require a specific alert for that threat. The first bulletin was published in December 2015 after the terrorist attacks in Paris and San Bernardino and discussed self-radicalized groups. Between 2015 and February 2022, fewer than 20 bulletins were released.

Author Biography

Alejandro Nicholas Mayorkas was born in Havana, Cuba, on November 24, 1959. After the Cuban Revolution, his family moved to Florida and then California. Mayorkas attended Beverly Hills High School and attended college at University of California at Berkeley. He received his bachelor's degree with distinction in history in 1981. He received his law degree from Loyola Law School in 1985.

Mayorkas worked as a litigator in a private firm after law school. In 1989, as assistant U.S. attorney, he tried cases involving a wide array of federal crimes. From 1996 to 1998, he served as the chief of the General Crimes Section. In 1998, President Bill Clinton appointed Mayorkas as the U.S. attorney for the Central District of California, making him the country's youngest U.S. attorney.

Mayorkas joined the law firm O'Melveny & Myers as a litigation partner in September 2001. When Barack Obama was elected in November 2008, Mayorkas led the transition team responsible for the U.S. Department of Justice's Criminal Division. In 2009, President Obama appointed Mayorkas as the director of U.S. Citizenship and Immigration Services (USCIS). He then served as deputy secretary of Homeland Security (DHS) from 2013 to 2016.

In 2017, he joined the law firm of Wilmer, Cutler, Pickering, Hale, and Dorr. In November 2020, President-elect Joe Biden nominated Mayorkas as secretary of Homeland Security. Mayorkas received support from the Fraternal Order of Police, as well as former secretaries who served under President George W. Bush and Barack Obama. He was confirmed and sworn in on February 2, 2021. Mayorkas is the first Latino and immigrant confirmed to serve as secretary of Homeland Security.

Historical Document

Summary of Terrorism Threat to the U.S. Homeland

Department of Homeland Security
National Terrorism Advisory System Bulletin

November 10, 2021

Summary of the Terrorism Threat to the U.S. Homeland

The Secretary of Homeland Security has issued an updated National Terrorism Advisory System (NTAS) Bulletin regarding the current heightened threat environment across the United States. The Homeland continues to face a diverse and challenging threat environment as it approaches several religious holidays and associated mass gatherings that in the past have served as potential targets for acts of violence. These threats include those posed by individuals and small groups engaged in violence, including domestic violent extremists (DVEs) and those inspired or motivated by foreign terrorists and other malign foreign influences. These actors continue to exploit online forums to influence and spread violent extremist narratives and promote violent activity. The ongoing global pandemic continues to exacerbate these threats, in part due to perceived government overreach in implementation of public health safety measures. Further, foreign terrorist organizations and DVEs continue to attempt to inspire potential followers to conduct attacks in the United States, including by exploiting recent events in Afghanistan. As of November 10, 2021, DHS is not aware of an imminent and credible threat to a specific location in the United States.

Duration

Issued: November 10, 2021 04:00 pm
Expires: February 08, 2022 04:00 pm

Additional Details

Following the 20th anniversary of the September 11th attacks and the U.S. withdrawal from Afghanistan, violent extremist media branches of al-Qa'ida and its affiliates, as well as the Islamic State of Iraq and as-Sham (ISIS), have celebrated perceived victories over the United States and encouraged the use of violence by their followers and supporters to further their objectives. These foreign terrorist organizations will likely continue to maintain a highly visible online presence in an attempt to inspire U.S.-based individuals to engage in violent activity.

Through the remainder of 2021 and into 2022, racially or ethnically motivated violent extremists and anti-government/anti-authority violent extremists will continue to pose a threat to the United States. Pandemic-related stressors have contributed to increased societal strains and tensions, driving several plots by DVEs, and they may contribute to more violence this and next year. If a new COVID-19 variant emerges and new public health restrictions are imposed as a result, anti-government violent extremists could potentially use the new restrictions as a rationale to target government or public health officials or facilities. In addition, some DVEs have attempted to use the relocation of Afghan nationals to the United States to exacerbate historical DVE grievances over immigration and the American Muslim community.

Historically, DVEs and individuals inspired by foreign terrorist organizations have targeted crowded commercial facilities, houses of worship, and public gatherings, which have at times caused mass causalities. The continued reopening of commercial and government facilities and the potential for ongoing societal and economic disruptions due to the pandemic, as well as mass gatherings associated with several dates of religious significance over the next few months, could provide increased targets of opportunity for violence, though there are currently no credible or imminent threats tied to any dates or locations.

Foreign and domestic threat actors, to include foreign intelligence services, foreign terrorist organizations, and DVEs, continue to introduce, amplify, and disseminate narratives online that promote violence, and have called for violence against elected officials, political representatives, government facilities, law enforcement, religious communities or commercial facilities, and perceived ideological opponents.

Ideologically motivated violent extremists fueled by personal grievances and violent extremist ideological beliefs continue to derive inspiration from and obtain operational guidance, including regarding the use of improvised explosive devices and small arms, through the consumption of information shared in online forums. The use of encrypted messaging by violent extremists may obscure operational indicators that provide specific warning of a pending act of violence.

Law enforcement officials have expressed concerns that the broad sharing of false narratives and conspiracy theories that endorse the use of violence will continue to gain traction, resulting in individuals or small groups embracing violent tactics to achieve their desired objectives. DHS is concerned that increased acts of violence, as well as targeted attacks against law enforcement, may strain local resources and challenge the ability of law enforcement to maintain the safety and security of local communities.

How We Are Responding

DHS and the Federal Bureau of Investigation (FBI) continue to provide guidance to state, local, tribal, and territorial (SLTT) partners about the current threat environment. Specifically, DHS has issued numerous intelligence assessments to SLTT officials on the evolving threat.

DHS is engaging industry partners to help them identify and respond to the spread of disinformation, conspiracy theories, and false narratives on social media and other online platforms.

DHS has prioritized combatting DVE threats within its Homeland Security Grant Program as a National Priority Area and its Targeted Violence and Terrorism Prevention Grant Program.

DHS remains committed to working with our partners to identify and prevent all forms of terrorism and targeted violence.

How You Can Help

We all play a role in keeping our communities safe. Stay vigilant and say something when you see signs of suspicious activity.

Report suspicious activity and threats of violence, including online threats, to local law enforcement, FBI Field Offices, or your local Fusion Center.

If you know someone who is struggling with mental health issues or may be a danger to themselves or others, support is available.

Get engaged in prevention efforts in your community. Learn more about community-based prevention efforts that help individuals stay off the pathway to violence.

[Source: www.dhs.gov/ntas/advisory/national-terrorism-advisory-system-bulletin-november-10-2021]

Glossary

DHS: acronym for U.S. Department of Homeland Security, a federal agency created after the September 11, 2001, terrorist attacks to "prevent terrorism and enhance security, secure and manage U.S. borders, enforce and administer U.S. immigration laws, safeguard and secure cyberspace, and ensure resilience to disasters"

domestic violent extremists (DVEs): a term that the Federal Bureau of Investigation (FBI) and DHS say refers to "an individual based and operating primarily within the territorial jurisdiction of the United States who seeks to further their ideological goals wholly or in part through unlawful acts of force or violence"; the term "domestic terrorist" is used interchangeably with "domestic violent extremist"

SLTT: acronym for "state, local, tribal, and territorial"; typically used in reference to governments and their programs

the Homeland: the United States

Document Themes

The evolution of the color-coded HSAS into the bulletins and alerts of the current NTAS illustrate the constantly evolving landscape of counterterrorism efforts. Though the shock from the September 11 attacks has abated, there is no end in sight to the "long war on terror." The "threat landscape" today is far more complex than it was in 2001, making both acquiring and communication about intelligence gathering difficult. Terrorists, both domestic and international, continually transform their methods, targets, and tools. Government intelligence agencies are being pressed to change from their traditionally reactive stance to a more proactive way of gathering and sharing intelligence.

There is a fine line between cultivating a "culture of awareness" with meaningful warnings supported by hard evidence and causing a "senseless, unfocused nationwide response to unspecific threat criteria." Christopher Cox, the Chairman of the 2004 Committee on Homeland Security pointed out that "[k]eeping the American people at a high level of anxiety is not a sustainable strategy." Keeping the American people at a high level of anxiety is not a sustainable strategy. While the desire to create a "culture of awareness" was strong, so was the concern of playing into terrorist plans to destroy the American economy and way of life. Creating false threats and fearmongering offer an easy path to disrupting lives without much effort.

Advances in technology are providing many new avenues for terrorist groups to achieve their aims. For instance, advances in artificial intelligence are making it easier to create "deepfake" photographs, videos and audio recordings that are convincingly realistic and difficult to authenticate. The potential for deepfakes can be devastating—for instance, a video that looks like an invasion or a nuclear test. These developments create more pressure on American intelligence agencies, which are typically slow to respond to technological changes.

The costs of tools used by terrorists are also affected by advancing technology. The tools for espionage used to be very expensive and difficult to obtain, forcing the equipment out of the reach of even some countries' governments. Today technologies that could be used by terrorists such as satellite miniaturization and drones are affordable and easy enough for children to use.

Instead of focusing on the "hard targets" of the past, such as airports or embassies, which are difficult and expensive to breach, they are focusing on more "soft targets"—areas that are traditionally open and accessible, such as gatherings, festivals, and religious services. These are easier targets in terms of planning and execution. They are a challenge for law enforcement because by their nature they are open and accessible.

Social media has a major role in the fight against terrorism. Social media provides a nonphysical space for radicalization. Anonymous platforms and social media companies that do not have strong policing against hate speech can become a haven to those with extremist viewpoints. These sites make it easy for extremist movements to communicate and organize online, recruit new members, and inspire attacks.

"Lone actors" in terrorist actions often frequent extremist websites, which serve as a method of further radicalizing extremist beliefs. Many of them post on social media before carrying out an attack. For instance, Robert Bowers posted anti-Semitic comments against a Jewish group that aids refugees on the alt-right friendly website Gab before killing eleven people at the Tree of Life Synagogue in 2018. Brenton Tarrant, a white supremacist who killed fifty-one people in separate mosque shootings in Christchurch, New Zealand in 2019, livestreamed the attack on Facebook and published a manifesto online. These attacks also serve as inspiration for others that frequent these sites to commit terrorist acts.

Government agencies are responding to these technological imperatives. For instance, there are AI initiatives and digital innovation committees in the Central Intelligence Agency (CIA) and National Security Agency (NSA). The National Security Commission on Artificial Intelligence is working on using new technologies to "comprehensively address the national security and defense needs of the U.S." Many in the intelligence community are calling for a "wholesale reimagining of intelligence for a new technological era."

—*Noëlle Sinclair, JD, MLS*

Bibliography and Additional Reading

Fung, Archon, Mary Graham, and David Weil. *Full Disclosure: The Perils and Promise of Transparency.* New York: Cambridge UP, 2008.

George, Roger Z., and James B. Bruce, eds. *Analyzing Intelligence: National Security Practitioners' Perspectives.* 2nd ed. Washington, D.C.: Georgetown UP, 2014.

Martin, Gus. *Understanding Homeland Security.* 3rd ed. New York: SAGE Publications, 2019.

Ridge, Tom, and Larry Bloom. *The Test of Our Times: American Under Siege...And How We Can be Safe Again.* New York: Thomas Dunne Books, 2009.

Van Geel, Tyll. *Homeland Security Law: A Primer.* New York: Routledge, 2018.

■ Remarks by President Biden One Year after the January 6 Assault on the U.S. Capitol

Date: January 6, 2022
Author: Joseph R. Biden
Genre: speech

Summary Overview

January 6, 2021, was a historic day at the Capitol Building in Washington, D.C., as hundreds of rioters broke into the building, seeking to stop the certification of the election of Joseph R. Biden as president of the United States and Kamala Harris as vice president. The rioters attacked Capitol police, threatened legislators, and chanted "Hang Mike Pence"—President Donald Trump's vice president—because of Pence's role in carrying out the certification process. Over the course of the year following the event, President Biden had harsh words for the rioters and called for their prosecution; however, he seemed reluctant to clearly state the cause of the violence. On the one-year anniversary of the event, Biden spoke to the nation and directly attributed the attack to the former president (whose name he never used), Donald Trump. Biden outlined how Trump's lies and the misinformation spread by his supporters gave rise to the movement that culminated in the violent attack on the Capitol and Congress on January 6, 2021.

Defining Moment

Historically, American presidents often change the policies of their predecessors, but rarely do they speak out about their predecessor's personal choices and actions. Up until January 6, 2022, Biden basically followed this precedent and did not criticize Trump personally. In the months leading up to the 2020 election, Donald Trump had claimed that the election was not going to be fair, in that the Democrats and various other groups/forces would tamper with the vote. This was not based on solid evidence but helped to prepare his supporters for a possible loss, since the polls were tight between the two candidates. Once it was clear that Biden had won the 2020 election, Trump forcefully advanced the idea that Biden's supporters had cheated in various ways and the he (Trump) had actually won the election. This became known in media circles as "The Big Lie," and for more than a year after the election it was continuously repeated by Trump and his supporters. When Trump's lawyers tried to take legal action to block the results from being certified, filing numerous lawsuits in key states, the cases were quickly thrown out of court for lack of evidence and unsupported claims. Some state legislatures initiated recounts, and all official recounts demonstrated that Biden had won the states in question. This created a situation in which Trump's supporters, and seemingly Trump himself, believed that the only way Biden could be stopped from taking office was to interfere with Congress' final certification of the vote on January 6, 2021. This was precisely what the rioters were attempting to do when they assaulted the Capitol after hearing Trump speak nearby that same day. In his speech, Trump had made a number of provocative statements—"Never concede"; "fight like hell"; "walk down to the Capitol"; "we can't let this happen"—that suggested a link between what happened before and what happened during the riot.

While the Capitol Police made certain that members of Congress were safe, they were restrained in their use of force to repel those breaking into the building and vandalizing portions of it. This kept the number of casualties to a minimum, but it also made it more difficult for the police to deal effectively with the attackers until other federal departments sent reinforcements and the building was cleared. After this

"I have said it many times, and it is no more true or real than when we think about the events of January 6: We are in a battle for the soul of America. A battle that by the grace of God, and by the goodness and greatness of this nation, we will win." President Joe Biden in the Capitol Building, January 6, 2022. Photo courtesy of The White House, via Wikimedia Commons. [Public domain]

intense conflict, in which one rioter was killed and numerous police suffered wounds, the counting of the electors' votes and the certification of the election by the Congress continued. The Biden-Harris ticket was duly certified as the winner.

A year after the attack, Biden spoke to all citizens of the United States and called for unity against forces that would disrupt American democracy. This speech marked the anniversary of the attack and was a major change in the way Biden spoke about those who had encouraged the crowd to go beyond a peaceful demonstration to a riot and violent attack. With Trump still not accepting the outcome of the election, and claiming that the rioters were "special people" whom he respected, Biden was forced to ignore precedent and begin speaking directly about his predecessor and the harm he believed Trump had inflicted on the nation.

Author Biography

Joseph Robinette Biden, Jr. (born 1942) was elected the forty-sixth president of the United States in 2020. Born in Scranton, Pennsylvania, his family moved to Delaware while he was a youth. He graduated from high school there, then the University of Delaware, followed by the Syracuse Law School. In 1971 he was elected to the U.S. Senate, serving from 1972 until elected vice president in 2008. He was chair or ranking member of the judiciary and foreign relations committees. Serving as vice president from 2009 until 2017, he then defeated the incumbent president, Donald Trump, and became the president in 2021. Family tragedies have affected his career, as his first wife and a daughter died in an auto accident, when Biden had just been elected to the Senate and this started his lifestyle of commuting from Delaware to Washington each day, so he could help take care of his sons. When considering an earlier run for the presidency, Biden stepped aside due to one son having just died of cancer.

Historical Document

Remarks by President Biden One Year after the January 6 Assault on the U.S. Capitol

JANUARY 06, 2022

South Court Auditorium
Eisenhower Executive Office Building

9:16 A.M. EST

THE PRESIDENT: Madam Vice President, my fellow Americans: To state the obvious, one year ago today, in this sacred place, democracy was attacked—simply attacked. The will of the people was under assault. The Constitution—our Constitution—faced the gravest of threats.

Outnumbered and in the face of a brutal attack, the Capitol Police, the D.C. Metropolitan Police Department, the National Guard, and other brave law enforcement officials saved the rule of law.

Our democracy held. We the people endured. And we the people prevailed.

For the first time in our history, a president had not just lost an election, he tried to prevent the peaceful transfer of power as a violent mob breached the Capitol.

But they failed. They failed.

And on this day of remembrance, we must make sure that such an attack never, never happens again.

I'm speaking to you today from Statuary Hall in the United States Capitol. This is where the House of Representatives met for 50 years in the decades leading up to the Civil War. This is—on this floor is where a young congressman of Illinois, Abraham Lincoln, sat at desk 191.

Above him—above us, over that door leading into the Rotunda—is a sculpture depicting Clio, the muse of history. In her hands, an open book in which she records the events taking place in this chamber below.

Clio stood watch over this hall one year ago today, as she has for more than 200 years. She recorded what took place. The real history. The real facts. The real truth. The facts and the truth that Vice President Harris just shared and that you and I and the whole world saw with our own eyes.

The Bible tells us that we shall know the truth, and the truth shall make us free. We shall know the truth.

Well, here is the God's truth about January 6th, 2021:

Close your eyes. Go back to that day. What do you see? Rioters rampaging, waving for the first time inside this Capitol a Confederate flag that symbolized the cause to destroy America, to rip us apart.

Even during the Civil War, that never, ever happened. But it happened here in 2021.

What else do you see? A mob breaking windows, kicking in doors, breaching the Capitol. American flags on poles being used as weapons, as spears. Fire extinguishers being thrown at the heads of police officers.

A crowd that professes their love for law enforcement assaulted those police officers, dragged them, sprayed them, stomped on them.

Over 140 police officers were injured.

We've all heard the police officers who were there that day testify to what happened. One officer called it, quote, a med—"medieval" battle, and that he was more afraid that day than he was fighting the war in Iraq.

They've repeatedly asked since that day: How dare anyone—anyone—diminish, belittle, or deny the hell they were put through?

We saw it with our own eyes. Rioters menaced these halls, threatening the life of the Speaker of the House, literally erecting gallows to hang the Vice President of the United States of America.

But what did we not see?

We didn't see a former president, who had just rallied the mob to attack—sitting in the private dining room off the Oval Office in the White House, watching it all on television and doing nothing for hours as police were assaulted, lives at risk, and the nation's capital under siege.

This wasn't a group of tourists. This was an armed insurrection.

They weren't looking to uphold the will of the people. They were looking to deny the will of the people.

They were looking to uphold—they weren't looking to uphold a free and fair election. They were looking to overturn one.

They weren't looking to save the cause of America. They were looking to subvert the Constitution.

This isn't about being bogged down in the past. This is about making sure the past isn't buried.

That's the only way forward. That's what great nations do. They don't bury the truth, they face up to it. Sounds like hyperbole, but that's the truth: They face up to it.

We are a great nation.

My fellow Americans, in life, there's truth and, tragically, there are lies—lies conceived and spread for profit and power.

We must be absolutely clear about what is true and what is a lie.

And here is the truth: The former president of the United States of America has created and spread a web of lies about the 2020 election. He's done so because he values power over principle, because he sees his own interests as more important than his country's interests and America's interests, and because his bruised ego matters more to him than our democracy or our Constitution.

He can't accept he lost, even though that's what 93 United States senators, his own Attorney General, his own Vice President, governors and state officials in every battleground state have all said: He lost.

That's what 81 million of you did as you voted for a new way forward.

He has done what no president in American history—the history of this country—has ever, ever done: He refused to accept the results of an election and the will of the American people.

While some courageous men and women in the Republican Party are standing against it, trying to uphold the principles of that party, too many others are transforming that party into something else. They seem no longer to want to be the party—the party of Lincoln, Eisenhower, Reagan, the Bushes.

But whatever my other disagreements are with Republicans who support the rule of law and not the rule of a single man, I will always seek to work together with them to find shared solutions where possible. Because if we have a shared belief in democracy, then anything is possible—anything.

And so, at this moment, we must decide: What kind of nation are we going to be?

Are we going to be a nation that accepts political violence as a norm?

Are we going to be a nation where we allow partisan election officials to overturn the legally expressed will of the people?

Are we going to be a nation that lives not by the light of the truth but in the shadow of lies?

We cannot allow ourselves to be that kind of nation. The way forward is to recognize the truth and to live by it.

The Big Lie being told by the former president and many Republicans who fear his wrath is that the insurrection in this country actually took place on Election Day—November 3rd, 2020.

Think about that. Is that what you thought? Is that what you thought when you voted that day? Taking part in an insurrection? Is that what you thought you were doing? Or did you think you were carrying out your highest duty as a citizen and voting?

The former president and his supporters are trying to rewrite history. They want you to see Election Day as the day of insurrection and the riot that took place here on January 6th as the true expression of the will of the people.

Can you think of a more twisted way to look at this country—to look at America? I cannot.

Here's the truth: The election of 2020 was the greatest demonstration of democracy in the history of this country.

More of you voted in that election than have ever voted in all of American history. Over 150 million Americans went to the polls and voted that day in a pandemic—some at grea—-great risk to their lives. They should be applauded, not attacked.

Right now, in state after state, new laws are being written—not to protect the vote, but to deny it; not only to suppress the vote, but to subvert it; not to strengthen or protect our democracy, but because the former president lost.

Instead of looking at the election results from 2020 and saying they need new ideas or better ideas to win more votes, the former president and his supporters have decided the only way for them to win is to suppress your vote and subvert our elections.

It's wrong. It's undemocratic. And frankly, it's un-American.

The second Big Lie being told by the former President and his supporters is that the results of the election of 2020 can't be trusted.

The truth is that no election—no election in American history has been more closely scrutinized or more carefully counted.

Every legal challenge questioning the results in every court in this country that could have been made was made and was rejected—often rejected by Republican-appointed judges, including judges appointed by the former president himself, from state courts to the United States Supreme Court.

Recounts were undertaken in state after state. Georgia—Georgia counted its results three times, with one recount by hand.

Phony partisan audits were undertaken long after the election in several states. None changed the results. And in some of them, the irony is the margin of victory actually grew slightly.

So, let's speak plainly about what happened in 2020. Even before the first ballot was cast, the former president was preemptively sowing doubt about the election results. He built his lie over months. It wasn't based on any facts. He was just looking for an excuse—a pretext—to cover for the truth.

He's not just a former president. He's a defeated former president—defeated by a margin of over 7 million of your votes in a full and free and fair election.

There is simply zero proof the election results were inaccurate. In fact, in every venue where evidence had to be produced and an oath to tell the truth had to be taken, the former president failed to make his case.

Just think about this: The former president and his supporters have never been able to explain how they accept as accurate the other election results that took place on November 3rd—the elections for governor, United States Senate, the House of Representatives—elections in which they closed the gap in the House.

They challenge none of that. The President's name was first, then we went down the line—governors, senators, House of Representatives. Somehow, those results were accurate on the same ballot, but the presidential race was flawed?

And on the same ballot, the same day, cast by the same voters.

The only difference: The former President didn't lose those races; he just lost the one that was his own.

Finally, the third Big Lie being told by a former President and his supporters is that the mob who sought to impose their will through violence are the nation's true patriots.

Is that what you thought when you looked at the mob ransacking the Capitol, destroying property, literally defecating in the hallways, rifling through desks of senators and representatives, hunting down members of congress? Patriots? Not in my view.

To me, the true patriots were the more than 150 [million] Americans who peacefully expressed their vote at the ballot box, the election workers who protected the integrity of the vote, and the heroes who defended this Capitol.

You can't love your country only when you win.

You can't obey the law only when it's convenient.

You can't be patriotic when you embrace and enable lies.

Those who stormed this Capitol and those who instigated and incited and those who called on them to do so held a dagger at the throat of America—at American democracy.

They didn't come here out of patriotism or principle. They came here in rage—not in service of America, but rather in service of one man.

Those who incited the mob—the real plotters—who were desperate to deny the certification of the election and defy the will of the voters.

But their plot was foiled. Congressmen—Democrats and Republicans—stayed. Senators, representatives, staff—they finished their work the Constitution demanded. They honored their oath to defend the Constitution against all enemies, foreign and domestic.

Look, folks, now it's up to all of us—to "We the People"—o stand for the rule of law, to preserve the flame of democracy, to keep the promise of America alive.

That promise is at risk, targeted by the forces that value brute strength over the sanctity of democracy, fear over hope, personal gain over public good.

Make no mistake about it: We're living at an inflection point in history.

Both at home and abroad, we're engaged anew in a struggle between democracy and autocracy, between the aspirations of the many and the greed of the few, between the people's right of self-determination and self—the self-seeking autocrat.

From China to Russia and beyond, they're betting that democracy's days are numbered. They've actually told me democracy is too slow, too bogged down by division to succeed in today's rapidly changing, complicated world.

And they're betting—they're betting America will become more like them and less like us. They're betting that America is a place for the autocrat, the dictator, the strongman.

I do not believe that. That is not who we are. That is not who we have ever been. And that is not who we should ever, ever be.

Our Founding Fathers, as imperfect as they were, set in motion an experiment that changed the world—literally changed the world.

Here in America, the people would rule, power would be transferred peacefully—never at the tip of a spear or the barrel of a gun.

And they committed to paper an idea that couldn't live up to—they couldn't live up to but an idea that couldn't be constrained: Yes, in America all people are created equal.

We reject the view that if you succeed, I fail; if you get ahead, I fall behind; if I hold you down, I somehow lift myself up.

The former President, who lies about this election, and the mob that attacked this Capitol could not be further away from the core American values.

They want to rule or they will ruin—ruin what our country fought for at Lexington and Concord; at Gettysburg; at Omaha Beach; Seneca Falls; Selma, Alabama. What—and what we were fighting for: the right to vote, the right to govern ourselves, the right to determine our own destiny.

And with rights come responsibilities: the responsibility to see each other as neighbors—maybe we disagree with that neighbor, but they're not an adversary; the responsibility to accept defeat then get back in the arena and try again the next time to make your case; the responsibility to see that America is an idea—an idea that requires vigilant stewardship.

As we stand here today—one year since January 6th, 2021—the lies that drove the anger and madness we saw in this place, they have not abated.

So, we have to be firm, resolute, and unyielding in our defense of the right to vote and to have that vote counted.

Some have already made the ultimate sacrifice in this sacred effort.

Jill and I have mourned police officers in this Capitol Rotunda not once but twice in the wake of January 6th: once to honor Officer Brian Sicknick, who lost his life the day after the attack, and a second time to honor Officer Billy Evans, who lost his life defending this Capitol as well.

We think about the others who lost their lives and were injured and everyone living with the trauma of that day—from those defending this Capitol to members of Congress in both parties and their staffs, to reporters, cafeteria workers, custodial workers, and their families.

Don't kid yourself: The pain and scars from that day run deep.

I said it many times and it's no more true or real than when we think about the events of January 6th: We are in a battle for the soul of America. A battle that, by the grace of God and the goodness and gracious—and greatness of this nation, we will win.

Believe me, I know how difficult democracy is. And I'm crystal clear about the threats America faces. But I also know that our darkest days can lead to light and hope.

From the death and destruction, as the Vice President referenced, in Pearl Harbor came the triumph over the forces of fascism.

From the brutality of Bloody Sunday on the Edmund Pettus Bridge came historic voting rights legislation.

So, now let us step up, write the next chapter in American history where January 6th marks not the end of democracy, but the beginning of a renaissance of liberty and fair play.

I did not seek this fight brought to this Capitol one year ago today, but I will not shrink from it either.

I will stand in this breach. I will defend this nation. And I will allow no one to place a dagger at the throat of our democracy.

We will make sure the will of the people is heard; that the ballot prevails, not violence; that authority in this nation will always be peacefully transferred.

I believe the power of the presidency and the purpose is to unite this nation, not divide it; to lift us up, not tear us apart; to be about us—about us, not about "me."

Deep in the heart of America burns a flame lit almost 250 years ago—of liberty, freedom, and equality.

This is not a land of kings or dictators or autocrats. We're a nation of laws; of order, not chaos; of peace, not violence.

Here in America, the people rule through the ballot, and their will prevails.

So, let us remember: Together, we're one nation, under God, indivisible; that today, tomorrow, and forever, at our best, we are the United States of America.

God bless you all. May God protect our troops. And may God bless those who stand watch over our democracy.

Glossary

Capitol Police: a police department established in the early nineteenth century to safeguard Congress and the Capitol; it is under the control of Congressional leaders

Omaha Beach: the location where American troops landed in France during World War II

Selma, Alabama (Bloody Sunday—Edmond Pettus Bridge): Selma was the scene of many Civil Rights protests, and a march from Selma to Montgomery was organized for Sunday, March 7, 1965, which was brutally turned back by Alabama State Police at the bridge

Seneca Falls: reference to an 1848 conference to promote women's rights and suffrage

Document Analysis

Using the anniversary of the attack on the Capitol Building as the focal point for the speech, President Joe Biden calls for people to not only remember what they had seen on TV, but to understand the results of the government's yearlong investigation into the riot. Biden speaks about American democracy being under attack by the rioters, whom he clearly identifies as supporters of the former president, Donald Trump. Not only that, but for the first time in a systematic way, Biden argues that the attack was instigated by the former president, with Trump's "Big Lie" having convinced the rioters that they were patriots rather than criminals.

Although Trump, and his supporters, would dispute the statements made by Biden, and his interpretation of events, Biden bases his speech on facts that had been verified by independent researchers as well as the courts. At the heart of this speech is what Biden identifies as "the truth." This is that Trump "has created and spread a web of lies about the 2020 election." This was, according to Biden, the basis for the attack on democracy by the Trump supporters who rioted, attacked police officers, and rampaged through the Capitol on January 6, 2021.

Biden then goes on to outline and refute three parts of the post-January 6 Big Lie that Trump had been disseminating. Biden says that Trump was pushing the idea that the insurrection had happened on Election Day, not on January 6, a claim that would make Biden the insurrectionist and Trump the victim. This is an astonishing claim for any former president to make, even, perhaps, one so prone to untruths as Donald Trump. As for the accuracy of the election results, numerous recounts and court cases made it clear the outcome was accurate. Trump's unwillingness to accept his own defeat, and his ongoing effort to rewrite the history of the January 6 attack, clearly irk Biden and are founded on personal animosity, not legal evidence or concrete fact. Biden made it clear that the real patriots were the voters who went to the polls and cast their ballots, not the rioters who attacked the Capitol and tried to overturn an election.

Biden applauds the work of the various police who protected members of Congress and defeated the mob attacking the Capitol. He sees them as representative of America, not those who carried the Confederate battle flag into the Capitol while Trump watched on TV. Biden urges all citizens to work together as neighbors who know what truth is and uphold it, rather than separating themselves from one another through acceptance of the Big Lie. According to Biden, patriots are voters who participate in the democratic process, not those who violently attack American institutions because they lost the election.

Essential Themes

In this well-written speech, President Biden made it clear that the events on January 6, 2021, represented an attack on democracy in the United States, and that this was the result of former President Trump spreading "a web of lies about the 2020 election." Although the entire U.S. population and a few foreign leaders were the audience for the speech, Biden was focused on trying to sway political independents and moderate Republicans (not devoted supporters of Trump). Although the facts regarding what happened in 2021 were not generally in dispute, the interpretation of the events was; and so, throughout this speech, Biden tried to make his point clear that what happened a year earlier was totally un-American, nondemocratic and had been instigated by Trump, who was dissatisfied because he lost the election.

Although it is uncertain if Biden achieved his goal of changing people's minds, he clearly did go on record to lay the blame for the riot/insurrection at the feet of his predecessor. He did this in a dismissive manner, by never using Trump's name, only his title as the "former president." His forthright statement that the rioters were not patriots but rather were subservient to one man, made it clear that Biden was not going to allow history to be distorted by Trump and his supporters.

—*Donald A. Watt, PhD*

Bibliography and Additional Reading

Cillizza, Chris. "The Single Most Important—And Powerful—Line from Joe Biden's 1/6 Speech." *CNN Politics.* New York: Cable News Network, 2022.

Committee on Homeland Security and Governmental Affairs and Committee on Rules and Administration, Staff. *Examining the U.S. Capitol Attack: A Review of the Security, Planning, and Response Failures on January 6*. Washington, D.C.: U.S. Senate, 2021.

Raskin, Jamie. *Unthinkable: Trauma, Truth, and the Trials of American Democracy*. New York: Harper, 2022.

Wray, Christopher. "Examining the January 6 Attack on the U.S. Capitol." *FBI*. Washington, D.C.: Federal Bureau of Investigation, 2021.

■ Global Leaders Condemn Assault on Brazilian Government Buildings

Date: January 9, 2023
Author: Reuters News Service
Genre: news report

Summary Overview

Supporters of the losing right-wing presidential candidate in Brazil, Jair Bolsonaro, stormed government offices in the capital of Brasilia on January 8, 2023, just days after the winning left-leaning candidate, Luiz Inácio Lula da Silva, was inaugurated. The attack resembled the circumstances of January 6, 2021 in the United States when Congress was assaulted by Far-Right supporters of President Donald J. Trump. In each case, a losing presidential candidate claimed fraud and urged supporters not to accept the election outcome. The difference was that in Brazil, the attackers acted following the inauguration of the new president, and the government buildings they invaded were empty during a recess; in the United States, the attack took place during the last days of Trump's presidency, and a dual session of Congress was convened at the time—in fact, to authenticate the results of the election.

In countries where political differences have become polarized, election results can trigger claims of fraud and an unwillingness to accept the outcomes. Since elections are the core of a democracy, any attempt to deny the outcome is a challenge to the democratic system. The events of January 6 in the United States, and those of January 8 in Brazil, demonstrate the dangers inherent in a polarized democracy, where the electorate is sharply divided.

In this case of Brazil, the response by world leaders to the attack on government offices reflected the importance, in their view, of supporting democratic systems around the globe. In contrast, leaders of authoritarian regimes were less likely to comment on the attack, either because they supported Bolsonaro and his policies or because they do not support truly free elections in their countries. Leaders of democratic countries, on the other hand, were quick to condemn the attack because of the danger to democracy it represented and the challenge it posed to the maintenance of democratic institutions around the world.

Jair Bolsonaro. Photo by Isac Nóbrega/PR, via Wikimedia Commons.

Defining Moment

The attack in Brasilia, Brazil's capital, on January 8, 2023 was in response to the defeat of Brazil's controversial Far-Right incumbent president, Jair Bolsonaro, in elections held in October 2022. Bolsonaro had refused to concede and claimed that the election of the former president, Luiz Inácio Lula da Silva, was invalid. The latter figure, popularly known as Lula, had served time in jail on corruption charges, which were later annulled. The stark differences between the two candidates reflected the polarization of Brazilian politics in recent years. Lula and his successor, Dilma Rousseff, represented the Workers Party, which vowed to transform the nation by providing resources to the poor and protecting the ecology of the Amazonian basin, among other policies. Bolsonaro, with a military background and decades in Congress, was staunchly conservative and politically of the Far Right; his government openly harkened back to authoritarian military regimes of the past. Voters were asked to choose between two radically different paths for Brazil: one that allied with left-leaning governments in the region and sought a greater range of freedoms for the working poor, women, gays, and climate activists. The other side preferred a close relationship with the government of President Donald Trump in the United States and other authoritarian regimes around the world, claiming that Brazil needed strong leadership to keep it economically strong and prevent it from becoming a socialist nation.

Even before the election, Bolsonaro had claimed that the elections would be fraudulent. After losing by a margin of two percent (51% for Lula, 49% for Bolsonaro) following the vote, Bolsonaro requested that the electoral court invalidate all ballots submitted via voting machine. Encouraged by Bolsonaro, his followers protested that the election was stolen, much in the same way that followers of President Trump believed that the 2020 U.S. presidential election had been stolen. Bolsonaro and Trump exhibited many of the same characteristics regarding their approach to elections, hoping to limit votes cast through technological means and generally aiming to suppress access to the ballot. The inauguration of President Lula on January 1, 2023, sparked a riot not unlike that which

The attack resembled the circumstances of January 6, in the United States when Congress was assaulted by supporters of Donald Trump. Photo via Wikimedia Commons. [Public domain.]

occurred in Washington, DC, on January 6, 2021, shortly before Biden's inauguration.

In Brazil, thousands of Bolsonaro supports stormed the government's seat of power on January 9, 2023. The presidential palace, Congress, and the Supreme Court buildings were at the time closed, but they were nevertheless entered, vandalized, and sacked by a violent pro-Bolsonaro mob. The carpet in Congress was set afire, feces and urine were left, and pictures and objects were broken and smashed. Eventually, the police secured the area, and since then more than a thousand individuals have been arrested. Yet the image of Brazil's democratic institutions being attacked resulted in outrage both within the country and abroad.

The mob invades the National Congress. Photo by TV BrasilGov, via Wikimedia Commons.

Author Biography

Reuters is an international news service, now part of Thompson Reuters based in Toronto, Canada. The company was created by Paul Julius Reuter in London in 1851. Originally from Germany, Reuter founded a book publishing company in 1847 that published radical pamphlets. After the upheavals of 1848, Reuter moved to London and initiated the Reuter's Telegram Company in 1851. The agency saw the usefulness of the telegraph and, with reporters across the globe, expanded its reporting. In 1925 the Press Association of the United Kingdom acquired a majority interest in Reuters. The news agency was a pioneer in the transmission of news on the radio. In the 1960s Reuters was among the first news agencies to use computers to make electronic financial transactions and became a major financial services company. Reuters was acquired by the Thompson Corporation in 2008 and continues to provide text and photos internationally, making it one of the largest news organizations in the world. Because Reuters is a news-gathering organization, its reporting tends to be ideologically neutral as it feeds stories to newspapers and media companies that hold a variety of perspectives.

Historical Document

Global Leaders Condemn Assault on Brazilian Government Buildings

Supporters of Brazil's far-right former President Jair Bolsonaro on Sunday invaded the country's Supreme Court and its Congressional building and surrounded the presidential palace in Brasilia. Here are reactions from world leaders:

UNITED STATES PRESIDENT JOE BIDEN

"I condemn the assault on democracy and on the peaceful transfer of power in Brazil. Brazil's democratic institutions have our full support and the will of the Brazilian people must not be undermined. I look forward to continuing to work with @LulaOficial."

UNITED STATES SECRETARY OF STATE ANTONY BLINKEN

"We condemn the attacks on Brazil's Presidency, Congress, and Supreme Court today. Using violence to attack democratic institutions is always unacceptable. We join @lulaoficial in urging an immediate end to these actions."

MEXICAN PRESIDENT ANDRES MANUEL LOPEZ OBRADOR

"The coup attempt by the Brazilian conservatives urged on by the leadership of oligarchic power, their spokespersons and fanatics, is reprehensible and undemocratic. Lula is not alone, he has the support of the progressive forces of his country, Mexico, the American continent and the world."

WHITE HOUSE NATIONAL SECURITY ADVISOR JAKE SULLIVAN

"The United States condemns any effort to undermine democracy in Brazil. President Biden is following the situation closely and our support for Brazil's democratic institutions is unwavering. Brazil's democracy will not be shaken by violence."

ORGANIZATION OF AMERICAN STATES SECRETARY GENERAL LUIS ALMAGRO

"We condemn the attack on the institutions in Brasilia, which constitutes a reprehensible action and a direct attack on democracy. These actions are inexcusable and fascist in nature."

EUROPEAN UNION FOREIGN POLICY CHIEF JOSEP BORRELL

"Appalled by the acts of violence and illegal occupation of Brasilia's government quarter by violent extremists today. Full support to Lula and his government, to Congress and to the Federal Supreme Court. Brazilian democracy will prevail over violence and extremism."

INDIA PRIME MINISTER NARENDRA MODI

"Deeply concerned about the news of rioting and vandalism against the State institutions in Brasilia. Democratic traditions must be respected by everyone. We extend our full support to the Brazilian authorities."

PORTUGAL'S FOREIGN MINISTER JOAO GOMES CRAVINHO

"Without a doubt, former president Bolsonaro has responsibility. His voice is heard by these anti-democratic demonstrators. It would be very important if he had a message of condemnation in the face of the disorder that is currently happening in Brasilia."

CHILEAN PRESIDENT GABRIEL BORIC

"The Brazilian government has our full support in the face of this cowardly and vile attack on democracy."

COLOMBIAN PRESIDENT GUSTAVO PETRO

"All my solidarity to @LulaOficial and the people of Brazil. Fascism has decided to stage a coup. ... It is urgent for the OAS (Organization of American States) to meet if it wants to continue to live as an institution."

ARGENTINE PRESIDENT ALBERTO FERNANDEZ

"I want to express my rejection of what is happening in Brasilia. Mine and the Argentine people's unconditional support for @LulaOficial in the face of this attempted coup he is facing."

U.S. HOUSE MINORITY LEADER HAKEEM JEFFRIES

"The violent attack on the heart of the Brazilian government by right-wing extremists is a sad but familiar sight. We stand with the people of Brazil and democracy."

FRENCH PRESIDENT EMMANUEL MACRON

"The will of the Brazilian people and the democratic institutions must be respected! President @LulaOficial can count on France's unwavering support."

UNITED KINGDOM FOREIGN SECRETARY JAMES CLEVERLY

"The violent attempts to undermine democracy in Brazil are unjustifiable. President @LulaOficial and the government of Brazil have the full support of the UK."

VENEZUELAN PRESIDENT NICOLAS MADURO

"We categorically reject the violence generated by Bolsonaro's neo-fascist groups which have assaulted Brazil's democratic institutions. Our support for @LulaOficial and the Brazilian people who will surely mobilize in defense of peace and their president."

URUGUAY'S FOREIGN MINISTRY

"Uruguay condemns the episodes of violence against the institutions in Brazil and calls for respect for the rule of law, democracy and its government."

PERU'S FOREIGN MINISTRY

"The government of Peru energetically condemns the assault on the headquarters of congress, the presidency and the supreme court of Brazil and any attempt to disregard the legitimacy of the October 2022 elections. Our solidarity with President Lula and Brazilian democracy."

ECUADOREAN PRESIDENT GUILLERMO LASSO

"I condemn the actions of disrespect and vandalism perpetrated against democratic institutions in Brasilia, they attack democratic order and citizen security. I express my and my government's backing for the legal regime of @LulaOficial."

BOLIVIAN PRESIDENT LUIS ARCE

"We strongly condemn the assault on the Brazilian Congress, Palace and Supreme Court by anti-democratic groups. Fascists will always seek to take by force what they failed to achieve at the ballot box. Our solidarity with the Brazilian people and the president @LulaOficial."

PARAGUAYAN PRESIDENT MARITO ABDO

"We are concerned about what is happening in Brazil. The path should always be respect for institutions, democracy, freedom and non-violence."

U.S. REPRESENTATIVE JOAQUIN CASTRO

"Bolsonaro should not be in Florida. The United States should not be a refuge for this authoritarian who has inspired domestic terrorism in Brazil. He should be sent back to Brazil."

EUROPEAN PARLIAMENT PRESIDENT ROBERTA METSOLA

"Deeply concerned about what is happening at Brazil. Democracy must always be respected. The European Parliament is on the side of the Lula government and all legitimate and democratically elected institutions."

ITALIAN PRIME MINISTER GIORGIA MELONI

"What is happening in Brazil cannot leave us indifferent. The images of the irruption into institutional offices are unacceptable and incompatible with any form of democratic dissent. A return to normality is urgently needed and we express solidarity with Brazilian institutions."

SPANISH PRIME MINISTER PEDRO SANCHEZ

"All my support to President @LulaOficial and to the free and democratically elected institutions of the Brazilian people. We categorically condemn the assault on the Brazilian Congress and make a call for the immediate return to democratic normality."

CUBAN PRESIDENT MIGUEL DIAZ-CANEL

"We energetically condemn the violent and undemocratic acts in Brazil aimed at creating chaos and disrespecting the popular will which resulted in the election of President Lula."

COSTA RICAN PRESIDENT'S OFFICE

"The Government of Costa Rica regrets the attack on democracy in Brazil and calls for respect for the constitutional order of that country. We support the President @LulaOficial."

An example of some of the damage done inside the building. Photo by Agência Senado, via Wikimedia Commons.

Document Analysis

The attack on Brazil's Congress, Supreme Court, and presidential palace in Brasilia on January 8, 2023, was a shocking event that outraged many world leaders. The Reuters news article reproduced here captures the responses by twenty-six powerful political figures, ranging from presidents and prime ministers, government ministers, representatives of international organizations, and prominent politicians. Everyone quoted in the article condemns the violent attack in Brazil. With one exception, India's Narendra Modi, all those quoted are from the Americas or Europe. (There were no African leaders quoted in this report, nor any other Asian leaders.)

The language used by these leaders is similar: Ten condemn the attacks outright; twelve indicate their support for Lula and Brazilian democracy. The president of the United States, Joe Biden, is the first to be quoted in the article, reflecting the importance and power of that country in the hemisphere and in world affairs. In addition, there is a response from the U.S. Secretary of State, Anthony Blinken, and the White House National Security Advisor, Jake Sullivan. Representing the Democratic minority in Congress, Representative Hakeem Jeffries (New York) is quoted. There is no statement in the article from any U.S. Republican politician, likely because of the awkward similarity of this attack to that on the U.S. Capitol in 2021 by followers of former president Donald Trump. (Most Republican elected officials then, as now, maintained their support of Trump despite the historic breach.)

The various presidents and foreign ministers from the American states represent all of South America and one country, each, from the Caribbean and Central America: Mexico, Chile, Colombia, Argentina, Venezuela, Uruguay, Peru, Ecuador, Bolivia, Paraguay, Cuba, and Costa Rica. The Secretary General of the

Organization of American States, Luis Almagro, joined in the condemnation of the attack. By this time in early 2023, elections in Latin America had produced many left-leaning political leaders who did not approve of Bolsonaro or his policies. At the same time, it is notable that some of these countries' governments, such as those of Cuba and Venezuela, were (and remain) authoritarian regimes—albeit of the left.

The European leaders from Portugal, France, and the United Kingdom, along with Josep Borrell, the European Union Foreign Policy Chief, all affirm their support for President Lula and democracy in Brazil. The Spanish and Italian prime ministers, and the European Parliament President, Roberta Metsola, also voice their condemnation of the attack in Brasilia. It might be noted that the Italian prime minister, Giorgia Meloni, is herself from a hard-right party, but she has governed somewhat more moderately than observers had expected.

Leaders of China, Russia, Saudi Arabia, Egypt, South Africa, and other nations were not quoted in the article. It is not reported whether statements had been issued by representatives from these or other countries, but clearly these leaders felt no compunction to condemn the attack in Brasilia in the immediate aftermath of the event.

Essential Themes

As of mid-2023, democracy in many countries around the globe continues to be under attack, weakened, or is suffering from a loss of support. In the United States, hardcore followers of Donald Trump still believe in the former president's unfounded claims that he won the 2020 election, and consider Joe Biden as an illegitimate president. Some Republican members of Congress have expressed support for the January 6 rioters, and most of them refuse to say anything negative about the attack on the U.S. Capitol. Meanwhile, the elected president of Peru, Pedro Castillo, was removed from office by Congress after he threatened to dissolve that body. As a result, Castillo's followers protested, and deadly clashes with the police ensued. In Argentina, an assassination attempt on Vice President Cristina Fernández de Kirchner failed only because the shooter's gun jammed. Critics of Nicaragua's president Daniel Ortega, who was an antiestablishment revolutionary leader in the 1980s, have highlighted the authoritarian tactics that he has used to remain in power. Cuba remains a one-party (officially communist) state. And Nicolas Madura in Venezuela has overseen a weakening of institutional checks on his authority, as have leaders in Hungary, Poland, and Turkey. Narendra Modi in India has worked to stifle dissent and undermine opposition parties, even as he condemns, as illustrated here, attempts to disrupt the government in Brazil.

Strong leaders are seen by their supporters as the best way to ensure domestic tranquility, even at the cost of personal liberties. Bolsonaro in Brazil projected that image, and his defeat, and the many inflammatory comments he made about it, made his followers feel that the country was turning toward socialism and chaos. Activists among them rejected the ballot as the best way to resolve political differences and vented their frustration on the buildings representing the government. Whether the attack was encouraged by Bolsonaro, who was in the United States at the time, has been debated but not decisively proven or disproven. President Lula, once sworn into office, had his government pursue the attackers on legal grounds, and to date more than one thousand have been arrested. Their punishment could perhaps discourage others in Brazil from violent acts, as it is hoped that punishment of the January 6 attackers in the United States will do the same. Nevertheless, the images of rioters assaulting Brazil's democratic institutions produced a visceral response from leaders around the world. It seemed to signal that such attacks could occur not just in the United States or Brazil but elsewhere as well, and that leaders must stand up to condemn such violent, antidemocratic actions wherever they take place.

—*James A. Baer, PhD*

Bibliography and Additional Reading

Bianchi, Bernardo, Jorge Chaloub, Patricia Rangel, and Frieder Otto Wolf, eds. *Democracy and Brazil: Collapse and Regression*. Milton Park, Oxfordshire, UK: Routledge, 2020.

The Conversation. "Democracy under Attack in Brazil: 5 Questions About the Storming of Congress and the Role of the Military." January 8, 2023. theconversation.com/democracy-under-attack-in-brazil-5-questions-about-the-storming-of-congress-and-the-role-of-the-military-197396.

Lapper, Richard. *Beef, Bible and Bullets: Brazil in the Age of Bolsonaro.* Manchester, UK: Manchester University Press, 2022.

Picheta, Rob. "The Violent Attack on Brazil's Government Was Months in the Making: Here's What You Need to Know." *CNN,* January 9, 2023. www.cnn.com/2023/01/09/americas/brazil-congress-attack-explained-intl/index.html.

Wendling, Mike. "How Trump's Allies Stoked Brazil Congress Attack." *BBC,* January 9 2023. www.bbc.com/news/world-us-canada-64206484.

■ Chronological List

July 26, 1581: Dutch Declaration of Independence 3
1649: Resolves by the English House of Commons regarding King Charles I and the Authority
    of the People 23
1740: Reflection on the Glorious Revolution of 1688 29
March 5, 1774: John Hancock's Boston Massacre Oration 37
March 23, 1775: Give Me Liberty or Give Me Death 63
July 6, 1775: Declaration of the Causes and Necessity of Taking Up Arms 51
January 9, 1776: *Common Sense* 85
May 17, 1776: The Dominion of Providence over the Passions of Men 74
July 4, 1776: Declaration of Independence 98
1783: From the Commissioners for Negotiating a Peace with Great Britain 111
August 26, 1789: Declaration of the Rights of Man and of the Citizen 127
1790: *Reflections on the Revolution in France* 138
September 1791: Olympe de Gouges: Declaration of the Rights of Woman and of the Female Citizen . . . 153
1794: Maximilien Robespierre on the Ideals of the French Revolution 164
January 1, 1804: Haitian Declaration of Independence 181
1812: Cartagena Manifesto 190
February 15, 1819: Simón Bolívar: Address at Angostura 205
August 24, 1821: Treaty of Córdoba 212
1837-1838: Documents relating to the Canadian Rebellions, 1837-1838 .220
February 1848: The Communist Manifesto 270
January 7, 1852: Louis Kossuth-Speech at a Dinner Given in His Honor by the U.S. Congress
    in Washington, D.C. 281
June 25 and August 8, 1853: Karl Marx on British Rule in India 413
ca. 1857: Benito Juárez on *La Reforma* 233
1862 (reflecting on events of 1832): June Rebellion of 1832 as described in *Les Misérables* (1862) 255
April 7, 1868: Meiji Charter Oath 309
April 19, 1871: Manifesto of the Paris Commune 290
November 27, 1871: King Victor Emmanuel II: Address to Parliament 299
1887: John Morley on Irish Home Rule 343
March 25, 1895: Montecristi Manifesto 241
1902: *What Is to Be Done?* 371
1908: Proclamation of the Young Turks 589
October 5, 1910: Plan de San Luis de Potosi 325
November 25, 1911: Plan of Ayala 332
April 24, 1916: Proclamation of the Provisional Government of the Irish Republic 361
October 25 (November 7), 1917: Vladimir Lenin on the Tasks of the Soviet Government 389
1918: Soviets in Action 395
1918: Sun Yat-sen: "The Three Stages of Revolution" 463
1919: Government of India Act 424
March 1, 1919: Korean Declaration of Independence 315
March 1922: Mohandas Gandhi: Statement at Trial 443

July 19, 1936: ¡No Pasarán! ("They Shall Not Pass!")..........507
August 14, 1947: Jawaharlal Nehru's Speech on the Occasion of Indian Independence..........453
September 21, 1949: "The Chinese People Have Stood Up!"..........469
ca. 1952: Mau Mau Warrior Oath..........513
March 1954: CIA Summary of the Overthrow of Premier Mossadeq of Iran..........604
July 20, 1954: Geneva Accords on Indochina..........531
November 1, 1954: Proclamation of the Algerian National Liberation Front..........596
1956: "The Path of Revolution in the South"..........550
July 26, 1956: Gamal Abdel Nasser on the Nationalization of the Suez Canal..........614
October 22, 1956: Resolution of Hungarian Student Protestors..........641
February 27, 1957: Mao Zedong on Communism and Counterrevolution..........477
May 2, 1959: Fidel Castro's Speech at Twenty-One Nations Conference..........516
February 4, 1962: Second Declaration of Havana..........523
November 29, 1963: CIA Memo on National Liberation Front Methods..........559
December 23, 1966: Message from Ho Chi Minh..........566
July 27, 1968: The "Two Thousand Words" Manifesto..........648
January 27, 1973: The Paris Peace Accords..........571
June 30, 1973: Letter from a Chinese "Rusticant"..........491
January 6, 1977: Charter 77..........655
November 4, 12, 14, 1979; February 6, 22, 1980: Diary Excerpts of an American Hostage in Iran..........633
November 5, 1979: Ayatollah Khomeini on "The Great Satan"..........623
December 24, 1981: CIA Cable on the Situation in Poland..........663
November 12, 1986: Corazon Aquino on Achieving Peace through Peaceful Means..........685
June 3-4, 1989: U.S. Embassy Cables Concerning the Crackdown in Tiananmen Square..........497
November 10, 1989: Egon Krenz Letter to Mikhail Gorbachev..........670
December 25, 1991: Gorbachev's Farewell Address..........675
December 10, 1993: Nelson Mandela—Nobel Peace Prize Acceptance Speech..........692
1995 (concerning events c. 1975): Story from the Khmer Rouge Killing Fields..........581
September 1, 2003: Hugo Chávez Speech in Havana..........700
January 23, 2005: Inaugural Speech by Ukrainian President Viktor Yushchenko..........711
December 10, 2011: Tawakkol Karman—Nobel Lecture..........725
June 24, 2012: Egyptian President-Elect Mohamed Morsi's Acceptance Speech..........736
February 22, 2014: Remarks by Yulia Tymoshenko after Her Release from Prison..........717
June 29, 2014: Islamic State—Proclamation of the Caliphate..........744
December 10, 2015: The Tunisian National Dialogue Quartet—Nobel Lecture..........752
June 30, 2021: Resolution Establishing the House Select Committee to Investigate the January 6th Attack on the U.S. Capitol..........765
November 10, 2021: Summary of Terrorism Threat to the U.S. Homeland..........775
January 6, 2022: Remarks by President Biden One Year after the January 6 Assault on the U.S. Capitol..783
January 9, 2023: Global Leaders Condemn Assault on Brazilian Government Buildings..........796

■ Web Resources

Age of Revolutions
ageofrevolutions.com
Edited by several historians of revolutions, this site includes bibliographies, articles, links, and blog posts about the Age of Revolutions in Europe and beyond.

Age of Revolutions: Latin American Revolutions
ageofrevolutions.com/latin-american-revolutions
This website offers a good bibliography for students of revolution in Latin America. Also includes links and info regarding selected other revolutions.

Algerian War (GWonline)
gwonline.unc.edu/node/11722
GWonline, hosted by the University of North Carolina, provides a useful set of resources for students of the Algerian War (1954-62).

The American Revolution Institute
www.americanrevolutioninstitute.org
The American Revolution Institute of the Society of the Cincinnati is a great site for in-depth discussion of the Revolutionary War and, more broadly, life and culture in the American colonies towards the end of the eighteenth century.

Arab Spring: A Research & Study Guide (Cornell University Library)
guides.library.cornell.edu/arab_spring/home
This research & study guide includes background information plus separate tabs for Tunisia, Egypt, Libya, Yemen, Syria, and Bahrain.

The BCW Project
bcw-project.org
The BCW Project covers the British Civil Wars, Commonwealth, and Protectorate, 1638-60.

British Newspaper Coverage of the French Revolution
oldsite.english.ucsb.edu/faculty/ayliu/research/around-1800
Provides links to primary sources. Created by a University of California-Santa Barbara English Department program.

The Chinese Civil War (Alpha History)
alphahistory.com/chineserevolution/chinese-civil-war
Includes overviews, primary source documents, biographies, images, and more.

The Chinese Communist Party (Council on Foreign Relations)
www.cfr.org/backgrounder/chinese-communist-party
A short "backgrounder" on the Chinese Communist Party under Xi Jinping.

The Chinese Revolution (Alpha History)
alphahistory.com/chineserevolution
Includes overviews, primary source documents, biographies, images, and more.

The Cuban Revolution: Roots, Repercussions, Resistance: Digital Collections (Yale Library)
guides.library.yale.edu/c.php?g=296251&p=1974191
This set of digital resources includes links to primary source documents, on the Cuban Revolution.

Documenting Revolution in the Middle East (Center for Research Libraries)
www.crl.edu/focus/article/7437
A collection of online resources regarding the Arab Spring in the Middle East.

The End of South African Apartheid (ThoughtCo.)
www.thoughtco.com/when-did-apartheid-end-43456
An article on the end of apartheid in South Africa.

The English Civil Wars: History and Stories (English Heritage)
www.english-heritage.org.uk/learn/histories/the-english-civil-wars-history-and-stories
Provides facts, background information, and biographies relating to the English Civil Wars occurring between 1642 and 1651, including the overthrow of Charles I and the empowerment of Parliament.

EuroDocs: France 1789-1871
eudocs.lib.byu.edu/index.php/France:_1789_-_1871
Created by Richard Hacken, European Studies Bibliographer and Harold B. Lee Library of Brigham Young University, this site provides primary documents relating to France in the years 1789-1871.

Fall of Communism in Eastern Europe, 1989 (Office of the Historian)
history.state.gov/milestones/1989-1992/fall-of-communism
This article from the US State Department describes the fall of communism in Eastern Europe and features links to primary source documents. A table of contents provides access to related articles on the collapse of the Soviet Union, the breakup of Yugoslavia, and more.

The Glorious Revolution (UK Parliament)
www.parliament.uk/about/living-heritage/evolutionofparliament/parliamentaryauthority/revolution/
The UK Parliament presents this website devoted to the Glorious Revolution in England in 1688. Includes key documents, expert interviews, background information, and more.

The History Place: American Revolution
www.historyplace.com/unitedstates/revolution/index.html
Contains timelines and a picture gallery of George Washington.

Ho Chi Minh (1890-1969): Major Events in the Life of a Revolutionary Leader (Columbia University)
www.columbia.edu/cu/weai/exeas/asian-revolutions/pdf/ho-chi-minh-timeline.pdf
A detailed chronology of the life of the Vietnamese revolutionary hero Ho Chi Minh.

How Ukraine's Orange Revolution Shaped Twenty-first Century Geopolitics (Atlantic Council)
www.atlanticcouncil.org/blogs/ukrainealert/how-ukraines-orange-revolution-shaped-twenty-first-century-geopolitics/
An article about the Orange Revolution in Ukraine in 2004 and its significance for world affairs.

Indian Independence (National Archives of the United Kingdom)
www.nationalarchives.gov.uk/education/resources/indian-independence/
This website on Indian Independence includes numerous original documents along with an overview, teacher's notes, and links.

The Indian Independence Struggle (1930-1931) (International Center on Nonviolent Conflict)
www.nonviolent-conflict.org/indian-independence-struggle-1930-1931/
Covers the Indian independence struggle from 1930-1931.

Internet Modern History Sourcebook: 1848
sourcebooks.fordham.edu/mod/modsbook19.asp
Documents relating to the revolutions of 1848 in France, Hungary, and Prussia.

Internet Modern History Sourcebook: French Revolution (Fordham University)
sourcebooks.fordham.edu/mod/modsbook13.asp
Provides a considerable number of links to primary sources.

Internet Modern History Sourcebook: Middle East Since 1944 (Fordham University)
sourcebooks.fordham.edu/Halsall/mod/modsbook54.asp
Provides a wide selection of texts and images concerning modern Middle Eastern history.

Internet Modern History Sourcebook: 19th Century Latin America (Fordham University)
sourcebooks.fordham.edu/mod/modsbook32.asp
Presents a range of links to primary sources about revolutions and related events.

Irish Independence (National Archives of the United Kingdom)
www.nationalarchives.gov.uk/cabinetpapers/themes/irish-independence.htm
This website offers original documents and essays relating to early Irish nationalism, the Irish independence movement, war, and partition.

Liberty: The American Revolution (PBS)
www.pbs.org/ktca/liberty
Here, assorted web exhibits supplement specific individual television series and generally include a summary of each episode, interviews (often with sound bites), a timeline, a glossary, photos, and links to relevant sites.

Liberty, Equality and Fraternity: Exploring the French Revolution
revolution.chnm.org
This site, with more than 600 primary documents, is a collaboration of the Roy Rosenzweig Center for History and New Media (George Mason University) and American Social History Project (City University of New York).

The Mau Mau Rebellion (Boston University African Studies Center)
www.bu.edu/africa/outreach/teachingresources/history/colonialism/the-mau-mau-rebellion
A collection of resources relating to the Mau Mau Rebellion. Includes primary source documents, images, oral histories, and more.

Middle East & Islamic Studies (Columbia University Libraries)
library.columbia.edu/locations/global/mideast.html
A collection of websites and other useful tools and information, from Columbia University Libraries.

Middle East Research & Information Project
www.merip.org
Provides an informative website on Middle East politics, culture, and society.

1989 Twenty Years On: The End of Communism and the Fate of Eastern Europe (Ohio State University)
origins.osu.edu/article/1989-twenty-years-end-communism-and-fate-eastern-europe
An article on the end of communism and the fate of Eastern Europe.

100 Years of Irish Independence and Division (Ohio State University)
origins.osu.edu/read/100-years-irish-independence-and-division
Offers a brief overview of the Irish independence conflict along with images and a bibliography.

Our American Revolution (The Colonial Williamsburg Foundation)
www.ouramericanrevolution.org
Provides a good overview of the American Revolution through hundreds of primary sources and objects, including letters, flags, furniture, clothing, and more.

Red Dawn: Americans and the Bolshevik Revolution (BackStory)
backstoryradio.org/shows/russian-rev
In this podcast, the historians of BackStory look at the Russian revolution in October 1917. BackStory is a weekly podcast hosted by noted U.S. historians.

Religion and the Founding of the American Republic (Library of Congress)
www.loc.gov/exhibits/religion/rel03.html
Shows the role played by religion in the American Revolution by offering a variety of primary source documents.

Revolutions: Theorists, Theory and Practice (Pressbooks)
pressbooks.buffscreate.net/revolution/chapter/the-vietnamese-revolution
An examination of the Vietnamese Revolution as excerpted from the book Revolutions: Theorists, Theory and Practice, by Gregory Young and Mateusz Leszczynski.

Russian Revolution: February 1917 (Spartacus Educational)
spartacus-educational.com/RUSmarchR.htm
Includes an overview of the event, primary sources, student activities, and additional references.

Russian Revolution: October 1917 (Spartacus Educational)
spartacus-educational.com/RUSnovemberR.htm
Includes an overview of the event, primary sources, student activities, and additional references.

Sister Revolutions: American Revolutions on Two Continents (National Park Service)
www.nps.gov/articles/000/sister-revolutions-american-revolutions-on-two-continents-teaching-with-historic-places.htm
Provides helpful overviews and study guides based on a walking tour called "Statues of Liberators: Hispanic Heroes."

The South American Revolutions (Lumen Learning)
courses.lumenlearning.com/suny-fmcc-boundless-worldhistory/chapter/the-south-american-revolutions
Offers information and study guides for the key historical revolutions in this region.

Soviet History Internet Archive (Marxists Internet Archive)
www.marxists.org/history/ussr
Offers a useful collection of primary source documents concerning the early history of the USSR. Also includes pictures, maps, and links to related sites.

Spanish Civil War (1936-1939): Digital Primary Source Archives & Websites (Yale Library)
guides.library.yale.edu/c.php?g=296063&p=1973557
A collection of internet resources for students of the Spanish Civil War.

Spy Letters of the American Revolution (William L. Clements Library, University of Michigan)
clements.umich.edu/exhibit/spy-letters-of-the-american-revolution
The Gallery of Letters provides a brief description of each letter and links to more information about the stories of the spies in the letter or the secret methods used to make the letter.

TeachMideast (Middle East Policy Council)
teachmideast.org/background-context/history
Offers a range of resources for teaching and learning about the Middle East.

Vietnam's Misunderstood Revolution (Wilson Center)
www.wilsoncenter.org/blog-post/vietnams-misunderstood-revolution
An essay about the communist revolution in Vietnam, with links to related topics.

What is Important to Know About the Revolution of Dignity in Ukraine? (Ukrainer)
ukrainer.net/the-revolution-of-dignity
An article about the 2014 Euromaidan, or Revolution of Dignity, in Ukraine.

What to Read to Understand the 1979 Iranian Revolution (Brookings)
www.brookings.edu/articles/what-to-read-to-understand-the-1979-iranian-revolution
A list of books and articles recommended for students of the Iranian Revolution.

Bibliography

Abrahamian, Ervand. *The Coup: 1953, the CIA, and the Roots of Modern US-Iranian Relations.* New York: New, 2013.

Aburish, Said K. *Nasser: The Last Arab.* New York: Thomas Dunne Books, 2004.

Adel, Ezzat. "The Day Nasser Nationalised the Canal." *BBC News.* London: The British Broadcasting Corporation, 2006.

Akcam, Tanar. *The Young Turks' Crime against Humanity: The Armenian Genocide and Ethnic Cleansing in the Ottoman Empire.* Princeton, NJ: Princeton UP, 2013.

"American Political Writing, 1760-1769: A Declaration of the Causes and Necessity of Taking Up Arms". *Cambridge History of English and American Literature in 18 Volumes.* Bartleby.com, 2000.

Anderson, Kevin B. *Marx at the Margins: On Nationalism, Ethnicity, and Non-Western Societies.* Chicago: University of Chicago Press, 2010.

Ang, Cheng Guan. *The Vietnam War from the Other Side: The Vietnamese Communists' Perspective.* London: Routledge, 2002.

Ankel, Sophia. "Trump Promises 'Wild' Protests in Washington, DC, on the Day Congress Is Set to Finalize Election Results." *Yahoo News*, December 20, 2020. www.yahoo.com/video/trump-promises-wild-protests-washington-165055313.html.

Aquino, Corazon. *To Love Another Day: The Memoirs of Cory Aquino.* Edited by Lopa Rapa. Independent, 2020.

Arana, Marie. *Bolivar: American Liberator.* New York: Simon & Schuster, 2014.

Arirang News. "Korea's March 1st 'Samil' Movement hits 87th anniversary." *YouTube.* Seoul: Arirang News, 2016.

Arnade, Peter. *Beggars, Iconoclasts, and Civic Patriots: The Political Culture of the Dutch Revolt.* Ithaca, N.Y.: Cornell University Press, 2008.

Ash, Timothy Garton. *The Polish Revolution: Solidarity.* New Haven: Yale UP, 2002.

Asia for Educators. "Selections from A Program of National Reconstruction: 'The Three Stages of Revolution' (1918)" (Primary Source Documents with Questions) New York: Columbia University, 2018.

Åslunc, Anders, and Michael McFaul eds. *Revolution in Orange: The Origins of Ukraine's Democratic Breakthrough.* Washington, DC: Carnegie Endowment for International Peace, 2006.

Aslund, Anders, and Michael McFaul, eds. *Revolution in Orange: The Origin of Ukraine's Democratic Breakthrough.* Washington, DC: Carnegie Endowment for International Peace, 2006.

Baillie, Alexander Charles. *Call of Empire: From the Highlands to Hindostan.* Montreal: McGill-Queens University Press, 2017.

Bailyn, Bernard. *The Ideological Origins of the American Revolution.* Cambridge: Harvard UP, 1992.

Baker, Keith Michael. *The Old Regime and the French Revolution.* Chicago: University of Chicago Press, 1987.

Barnes, Jane and Helen Whitney. "John Paul II & the Fall of Communism." *Frontline.* Boston: WGBH Educational Foundation, 2014. Documentary.

Barthelmas, Della Gray. *The Signers of the Declaration of Independence.* Jefferson: McFarland, 1997.

Bartolovich, Crystal, and Neil Lazarus, eds. *Marxism, Modernity and Postcolonial Studies.* New York: Cambridge UP, 2002.

Baum, Richard. *Burying Mao: Chinese Politics in the Age of Deng Xiaoping.* Princeton, NJ: Princeton UP, 1996.

Bayat, Asef. *Revolutionary Life: The Everyday of the Arab Spring.* Cambridge, MA: Harvard University Press, 2021.

Beales, Derek, and Eugenio F. Biagini. *The Risorgimento and the Unification of Italy.* London and New York: Routledge 2002.

Beehner, Lionel. "One Year After Ukraine's 'Orange Revolution.'" *Council on Foreign Relations.* Washington, DC: Council on Foreign Relations, 2005.

Berkovitch, Sacvan. *The Puritan Origins of the American Self.* New Haven: Yale University Press, 2011.

Best, Geoffrey, ed. *The Permanent Revolution: The French Revolution and Its Legacy, 1789-1989.* London: Fontana Press, 1988.

Bianchi, Bernardo, Jorge Chaloub, Patricia Rangel, and Frieder Otto Wolf, eds. *Democracy and Brazil: Collapse and Regression.* Milton Park, Oxfordshire, UK: Routledge, 2020.

Bilefsky, Dan. "Ludvik Vaculik, Influential Czech Writer and Dissident, Dies at 88." *New York Times.* New York Times, 10 June 2015.

"Biography of Nelson Mandela." *Nelson Mandela Foundation: Living the Legacy.* www.nelsonmandela.org/content/page/biography.

Bischof, Günter, Stefan Karner, and Peter Ruggenthaler, eds. *The Prague Spring and the Warsaw Pact Invasion of Czechoslovakia in 1968.* Lanham: Lexington, 2010.

Bolton, Jonathan. *Worlds of Dissent: Charter 77, the Plastic People of the Universe, and Czech Culture under Communism.* Cambridge, MA: Harvard UP, 2012.

"The Boston Massacre." *The Coming of the American Revolution, 1764-1776.* Massachusetts Historical Society, 2008.

Boston Massacre Historical Society. Boston Massacre Historical Society, 2008.

Boston Tea Party Ships & Museum. Historic Tours of America, n.d.

Boucek, Christopher. "Yemen: Avoiding a Downward Spiral." Washington, DC: Carnegie Endowment for International Peace: Middle East Program, 2009. carnegieendowment.org/files/yemen_downward_spiral.pdf.

Bourke, Richard. *Empire and Revolution: The Political Life of Edmund Burke.* Princeton, NJ: Princeton University Press, 2015.

Bowden, Mark. *Guests of the Ayatollah: the Iran Hostage Crisis: The First Battle in America's War with Militant Islam.* New York: Grove Press, 2006.

Bowie, Robert R. & Richard H. Immerman. *Waging Peace: How Eisenhower Shaped an Enduring Cold War Strategy.* New York: Oxford UP, 1998.

Brandt, Marieke. *Tribes and Politics in Yemen: A History of the Houthi Conflict.* New York: Oxford UP, 2017.

Breen, Mike. "The March 1 Uprising: New Nation, New Leaders." *The Korea Times.* Seoul: Hankook Ilbo, 2018.

Brenner, Anita. *The Wind that Swept Mexico: The History of the Mexican Revolution of 1910-1942.* Austin, TX: University of Texas Press, 1984.

Brenner, Philip & Peter Eisner. *Cuba Libre: A 500-Year Quest for Independence.* Lanham, MD: Rowman & Littlefield Publishers, 2017.

Breuninger, Kevin. "Trump Refuses to Accept Election Results, Says It's 'Far from Over.'" *CNBC*, November 7, 2020. www.cnbc.com/2020/11/07/trump-refuses-to-accept-election-results-says-it-is-far-from-over.html.

"Brief Biography of Thomas Jefferson". *The Jefferson Monticello.* Thomas Jefferson Foundation, 2012.

Brittsan, Zachary. *Popular Politics and Rebellion in Mexico Manuel Lozada and La Reforma, 1855-1876.* Nashville: Vanderbilt University Press, 2015.

Brocheux, Pierre. *Ho Chi Minh: A Biography.* New York: Cambridge UP, 2007.

Brown, Judith M. *Gandhi: Prisoner of Hope.* New Haven, CT: Yale UP, 1989.

Buchenau, Jügen, and Timothy Henderson. *The Mexican Revolution: A Documentary History.* Indianapolis: Hackett Publishing Co., 2022.

Buckley, Chris. "Zhang Tiesheng: From Hero under Mao to 'Hero of Wealth'." *New York Times*, August 18, 2014.

Buckner, P.A. *The Transition to Responsible Government: British Policy in British North America 1815-1850.* Westport, CT: Greenwood Press, 1985.

Burke, Edmund. *Reflections on the Revolution in France.* Edited by J. G. A. Pocock. Indianapolis: Hackett Publishing Co., 1987.

Bushnell, David. *Simon Bolivar: Liberation and Disappointment.* London: Pearson, 2003.

Calvert, Jane E. "John Dickinson Biography." *John Dickinson Writings Project*. University of Kentucky, 2011.

———. *Quaker Constitutionalism and the Political Thought*. Cambridge: Cambridge UP, 2008.

Cameron, David R. "Lord Durham Then and Now." *Journal of Canadian Studies/Revue d'Études Canadiennes* 25:1 (1990).

CarbonBrief. "Explainer: 'Desertification' and the Role of Climate Change." August 6, 2019. www.carbonbrief.org/explainer-desertification-and-the-role-of-climate-change.

Carroll, Rory. *Comandante: Hugo Chávez's Venezuela*. New York: Penguin, 2014.

Carver, Terrell and James Farr, eds. *The Cambridge Companion to the Communist Manifesto*. New York: Cambridge UP, 2015.

Castro, Fidel. *Capitalism in Crisis: Globalization and World Politics Today*. Minneapolis, MN: Ocean Press, 2000.

Chan, Sewell. "Nobel Peace Prize is awarded to National Dialogue Quartet in Tunisia." *New York Times*, October 9, 2015. www.nytimes.com/2015/10/10/world/europe/national-dialogue-quartet-tunisia-nobel-peace-prize.html.

Chandler, David P. *The Tragedy of Cambodian History: Politics War and Revolution Since 1945*. New Haven: Yale UP, 1991.

Chasteen, John Charles. *Americanos: Latin America's Struggle for Independence*. New York: Oxford UP, 2008.

Cillizza, Chris. "The Single Most Important-And Powerful-Line from Joe Biden's 1/6 Speech." *CNN Politics*. New York: Cable News Network, 2022.

Clark, Victoria. *Yemen: Dancing on the Heads of Snakes*. New Haven, CT: Yale UP, 2010.

Cockburn, Patrick. *The Rise of Islamic State: ISIS and the New Sunni Revolution*. London: Leftward Books, 2020.

Collinson, Stephen. "New Revelations Betray Depth of Trump's Post-Election Schemes." *CNN*, February 10, 2022. www.cnn.com/2022/02/10/politics/capitol-insurrection-donald-trump-republicans-congress/index.html.

Committee on Homeland Security and Governmental Affairs and Committee on Rules and Administration, Staff. *Examining the U.S. Capitol Attack: A Review of the Security, Planning, and Response Failures on January 6*. Washington, D.C.: U.S. Senate, 2021.

The Conversation. "Democracy under Attack in Brazil: 5 Questions About the Storming of Congress and the Role of the Military." January 8, 2023. theconversation.com/democracy-under-attack-in-brazil-5-questions-about-the-storming-of-congress-and-the-role-of-the-military-197396.

Coogan, Tim Pat. *Ireland in the 20th Century*. New York: Palgrave Macmillan, 2006.

Cunningham, Philip J. *Tiananmen Moon: Inside the Chinese Student Uprising of 1989*. Lanham, MD: Rowman & Littlefield, 2008.

D'Anieri, Paul. *Understanding Ukrainian Politics: Power, Politics, and Institutional Design*. London: Routledge, 2015.

Darby, Graham, ed. *The Origins and Development of the Dutch Revolt*. London: Routledge, 2001.

De Krey, Gary S. *Restoration and Revolution in Britain: A Political History of the Era of Charles II and the Glorious Revolution*. London: Palgrave Macmillan, 2007.

Deak, Istvan. *Lawful Revolution: Louis Kossuth and the Hungarians 1848-1849*. New York: Columbia University Press, 1979.

"The Declaration of Arms". *Archiving Early America*. Archiving Early America, 2012.

"Declaration of Independence." *Charters of Freedom*. US National Archives and Records Administration, 2012.

Dedrick, Michael Robert. *Southern Voices: Biet Dong and the National Liberation Front*. Lexington: UP of Kentucky, 2022.

Dickinson, Peter. "How Modern Ukraine Was Made on Maidan." *Atlantic Council*. Washington, DC: Atlantic Council, 2021.

Dikötter, Frank. *The Cultural Revolution: A People's History 1962-1976*. New York: Bloomsbury Press, 2016.

Donagan, Barbara. *War in England 1642-1649*. Oxford: Oxford University Press, 2010.

Doran, Michael. *Ike's Gamble: American's Rise to Dominance in the Middle East*. New York: Free Press, 2016.

Doyle, William. *The French Revolution: A Very Short Introduction,* 2nd ed. Oxford, U.K.: Oxford UP, 2020.

Duiker, William J. *Ho Chi Minh: A Life*. New York: Hachette Books, 2000.

———. *Sacred War: Nationalism and Revolution in a Divided Vietnam*. New York: McGraw Hill, 1994.

Edgerton, Robert B. *Mau Mau: An African Crucible*. New York: Free Press, 1989.

Eizenstat, Stuart E. *President Carter: The White House Years*. New York: St. Martin's Press, 2018.

El-Bendary, Mohamed. *The Egyptian Revolution and Its Aftermath: Mubarak to Morsi*. New York: Algora Pub., 2013.

Ellis, Joseph J. *American Creation: Triumphs and Tragedies of the Founders of the Republic*. New York: Knopf, 2007.

El-Sherif, Ashraf. "Egypt's Post-Mubarak Predicament." Carnegie Endowment for International Peace, 2014. www.jstor.org/stable/resrep12804.

Elson, James M., ed. *Patrick Henry in His Speeches and Writings and in the Words of His Contemporaries*. Lynchburg, VA: Warwick House, 2007.

Erikson, Daniel P. *The Cuba Wars: Fidel Castro, the United States, and the Next Revolution*. New York: Bloomsbury, 2008.

Espiritu, Talitha. *Passionate Revolutions: The Media and the Rise and the Fall of the Marcos Regime*. Athens: Ohio University Press, 2017.

Eustace, Nicole. *Passion Is the Gale: Emotion, Power, and the Coming of the American Revolution*. Chapel Hill: University of North Carolina Press, 2008.

Fea, John. *Was America Founded as a Christian Nation? A Historical Introduction*. Louisville: Westminster, 2011.

Ferling, John. *A Leap in the Dark: The Struggle to Create the American Republic*. Oxford: Oxford UP, 2003.

———. *Setting the World Ablaze: Washington, Adams, Jefferson, and the American Revolution*. New York: Oxford UP, 2000.

Fischer, Louis. *Gandhi: His Life and Message for the World*. New York: Mentor Press, 1954.

Forester, Cecil Scott. *Victor Emmanuel II: And the Union of Italy*. N.p.: Simon Publications 2001.

Fowkes, Ben. *Eastern Europe 1945-1969: From Stalinism to Stagnation*. Harlow: Longman, 2000.

Fowler, William M. Jr. *The Baron of Beacon Hill: A Biography of John Hancock*. Boston: Houghton, 1980.

Franklin, Benjamin. *Autobiography of Benjamin Franklin*. ed. Charles W. Eliot. New York: SoHo, 2012.

Freedman, Russell. *Give Me Liberty! The Story of the Declaration of Independence*. New York: Holiday, 2000.

Fung, Archon, Mary Graham, and David Weil. *Full Disclosure: The Perils and Promise of Transparency*. New York: Cambridge UP, 2008.

Gaddis, John Lewis. *The Cold War: A New History*. New York: Penguin, 2005.

García De La Torre, Armando. *José Martí and the Global Origins of Cuban Independence*. Kingston, Jamaica: University of West Indies Press, 2015.

Gasiorowski, Mark J. *Mohammad Mosaddeq and the 1953 Coup in Iran*. Syracuse, NY: Syracuse UP, 2004.

Geggus, David Patrick, ed. *The Impact of the Haitian Revolution in the Atlantic World*. London: Reaktion Books, 2001.

George, Roger Z., and James B. Bruce, eds. *Analyzing Intelligence: National Security Practitioners' Perspectives*. 2nd ed. Washington, D.C.: Georgetown UP, 2014.

Geyl, Pieter. *History of the Dutch-Speaking Peoples, 1555-1648*. London: Phoenix Press, 2001.

———. *The Revolt of the Netherlands, 1555-1609*. Lanham, Md.: Rowman & Littlefield, 1980.

Ghosh, Durba. *Gentlemanly Terrorists: Political Violence and the Colonial State in India, 1919-1949*. New York: Cambridge University Press, 2017.

Girard, Philippe R. "Jean-Jacques Dessalines and the Atlantic system: A reappraisal." *The William and Mary Quarterly* 69.3 (2012): 549-582.

Githuku, Nicolas K. *Mau Mau Crucible of War: Statehood, National Identity, and Politics of

Postcolonial Kenya. Lanham, MD: Lexington Books, 2016.

"Give Me Liberty or Give Me Death!" *The Colonial Williamsburg Foundation.* The Colonial Williamsburg Foundation, 2012.

Glantz, Michael H. *Desertification: Environmental Degradation in and around Arid Lands,* Boca Raton, FL: CRC Press, 2020.

Gluckstein, Donny. *The Paris Communie: A Revolution in Democracy.* Chicago: Haymarket Books, 2011.

Gorbachev, Mikhail. *Memoirs.* New York: Doubleday, 1996.

Gott, Richard. *Hugo Chávez and the Bolivarian Revolution.* New York: Verso, 2011.

Greer, Allan. *The Patriots and the People: The Rebellion of 1837 in Rural Lower Canada.* Toronto: University of Toronto Press, 1993.

Guardino, Peter F. *Peasants, Politics, and the Formation of Mexico's National State: Guerrero, 1800-1857.* Redwood City: Stanford University Press, 2001.

Gullickson, Gay. *Unruly Women of Paris: Images of the Commune.* Ithaca: Cornell UP, 1996.

Haimson, Leopold H. "Russian Workers' Political and Social Identities: The Role of Social Representations in the Interaction between Members of the Labor Movement and the Social Democratic Intelligentsia." In *Workers and Intelligentsia in Late Imperial Russia: Realities, Representations, Reflections,* ed. Reginald Zelnik. Berkeley: University of California Press, 1999.

———. *The Russian Marxists and the Origins of Bolshevism.* Cambridge, Mass.: Harvard UP, 1955.

Haksar, Vinit. *Gandhi and Liberalism: Satyagraha and the Conquest of Evil.* London: Routledge, 2018.

Halberstam, David. *Ho.* Lanham, MD: Rowman & Littlefield Publishers, 2007.

Haloui, Yasmin. *Life in Revolution: Resistance & the Everyday in Tunisian Revolution.* Saarbrücken, Saarland, Germany: Lambert Academic Publishing, 2011.

Halsall, Paul. "Modern History Sourcebook: The Common Program of the Chinese People's Political Conference, 1949." *Internet History Sourcebook Project, Fordham University."* New York: History Department, Fordham University, 1998.

Hamnett, *Brian R. Juárez: Profiles in Power.* London: Longman, 1997.

Hanioglu, M. Sükrü. *A Brief History of the Late Ottoman Empire.* Princeton, NJ: Princeton UP, 2010.

———. *Preparation for a Revolution: The Young Turks, 1902-1908.* New York: Oxford UP, 2001.

Harding, Neil. *Lenin's Political Thought: Theory and Practice in the Democratic Revolution.* London: Macmillan, 1977.

Harkins, Susan Sales. *The Life and Times of Patrick Henry.* Hockessin: Lane, 2007.

Harsin, Jill. *Barricades: The War of the Streets in Revolutionary Paris, 1830-1848. New* York: Palgrave, 2002.

Havel, Václav. *Letter to Olga: June 1979-September 1982.* Trans. Paul Wilson. New York: Holt, 1989.

Hayes, Kevin J. *The Mind of a Patriot: Patrick Henry and the World of Ideas.* Charlottesville: U of Virginia P, 2008.

Heinl, Robert Debs, Nancy Gordon Heinl, and Michael Heinl. *Written in Blood: The Story of the Haitian People, 1492-1995.* Lanham, MD: UP of America, 2005.

Heller, Louie R. *Early American Orations, 1760-1824.* New York: Macmillan, 1902.

Hellyer, Robert, ed. *The Meiji Restoration: Japan as a Global Nation.* New York: Cambridge UP, 2019.

Henderson, Timothy J. *The Mexican Wars for Independence.* New York: Hill, 2009.

Herring, George C. *America's Longest War: The United States and Vietnam, 1950-1975,* 3rd edition. New York: McGraw Hill, Inc., 1996.

———. *From Colony to Superpower: U.S. Foreign Relations Since 1776.* Oxford: Oxford UP, 2008.

Hess, Gary. *Vietnam and the United States: Origins and Legacy of War,* rev. ed. New York: Twayne Publishers, 1998.

Hessler, Peter. "Mohamed Morsi, Who Brought the Muslim Brotherhood to the Egyptian Presidency." *The New Yorker,* June 19, 2019. www.newyorker.com/news/news-desk/mohamed-morsi-who-brought-the-muslim-brotherhood-to-the-egyptian-presidency.

Hillsborough, Romulus. *Samurai Revolution: The Dawn of Modern Japan Seen Through the Eyes of the Shogun's Last Samurai*. North Clarendon, VT: Tuttle Publishing, 2014.

"A History of Apartheid in South Africa." *South African History Online: Towards a People's History*. Available at www.sahistory.org.za/article/history-apartheid-south-africa

"Hobbes, Locke, Montesquieu, and Rousseau on Government." *Bill of Rights in Action* 20.2 (Spring 2004): n. pag.

Hoffman, Ronald and Peter J. Albert eds. *Diplomacy and Revolution: The Franco-American Alliance of 1778*. Charlottesville: UP of Virginia, 1981.

———. *Peace and the Peacemakers: The Treaty of 1783*. Charlottesville: University Press of Virginia, 1986.

Holmes, Clive. *Why Was Charles I Executed?* London: Hambledon Continuum, 2007.

Horne, Alistair. *The Fall of Paris: The Siege and the Commune*. New York: Penguin, 2007.

Hunt, Lynn. *The French Revolution and Human Rights: A Brief Documentary History*. New York: Bedford Books, 1996.

Husain, Iqbal, Editor. *Karl Marx on India: From the New York Daily Tribune (Including Articles by Frederick Engels)*. New Delhi: Tulika Books, 2006.

Ibárruri, Dolores. *They Shall Not Pass: The Autobiography of La Pasionaria*. New York: International Publishers, 1976.

Institute of Korean Independence Movement Studies. *The History of the Korean Independence Movement*. Cheonan City, Rep. of Korea: The Institute/Independence Hall, 2014.

Israel, Jonathan I. *The Dutch Republic: Its Rise, Greatness and Fall, 1477-1806*. Oxford, U.K.: Clarendon Press, 1998.

———. *Revolutionary Ideas: An Intellectual History of the French Revolution, from the Rights of Man to Robespierre*. Princeton, NJ: Princeton University Press, 2014.

Jackson, Alvin. *Home Rule: An Irish History, 1800-2000*. New York: Oxford UP, 2003.

James, Lawrence. *Raj: The Making and Unmaking of British India*. New York: St. Martin's Press, 1998.

Jansen, Marius B. *The Making of Modern Japan*. Cambridge, MA: Harvard UP, 2002.

"Jawaharlal Nehru (1889-1964)". *BBC—History—Historical Figures* (2014) www.bbc.co.uk/history/historic_figures/nehru_jawaharlal.shtml .

Ji Xianlin with Chenxin Jiang (trans.) and Zha Jianying (intro.). *The Cowshed: Memories of the Chinese Cultural Revolution*. New York: New York Review Books, 2016.

Johnson, Patrick. *Morley of Blackburn: A Literary and Political Biography of John Morley*. Lanham, MD: Fairleigh Dickinson UP, 2012.

Jones, Christopher D. *Soviet Influence in Eastern Europe: Political Autonomy and the Warsaw Pact*. Brooklyn: Praeger, 1981.

Kantowicz, Edward R. *Coming Apart, Coming Together: The World in the 20th Century*. Grand Rapids, MI: Wm. B. Eerdmans Pub. Co., 2000.

Karl, Rebecca E. *Mao Zedong and China in the Twentieth Century World.: A Concise History*. Durham NC: Duke University Press, 2010.

Karnow, Stanley. *Vietnam: A History*. New York: Penguin Books, 1991.

Kasinof, Laura. *Don't Be Afraid of the Bullets: An Accidental War Correspondent in Yemen*. New York: Arcade, 2016.

Kemp-Welch, A. *Poland under Communism: A Cold War History*. Cambridge: Cambridge UP, 2008.

Kerber, Linda K. "The Paradox of Women's Citizenship in the Early Republic: The Case of Martin vs. Massachusetts, 1805." *American Historical Review* 97.2 (1992): 349-78.

Kidd, Thomas S. *Patrick Henry: First among Patriots*. New York: Basic, 2011.

Knight, Alan. *The Mexican Revolution: A Very Short Introduction*. New York: Oxford UP, 2016.

Koenigsberger, H. G. *Monarchies, States Generals and Parliaments: The Netherlands in the Fifteenth and Sixteenth Centuries*. Cambridge, U.K.: Cambridge University Press, 2001.

Komisar, Lucy. *Corazon Aquino: The Story of a Revolution*. New York: George Braziller, 1987.

Koon, Helene. *Colley Cibber: A Biography*. Lexington: University Press of Kentucky, 2015.

Kossuth, Lajos, Francis W. Newman. *Selected Speeches of Kossuth.* London: Turner & Co., 1853.

Kramer, Mark. "The Kuklinski Files and the Polish Crisis of 1980-1981: An Analysis of the Newly Released CIA Documents on Ryszard Kuklinski." *Cold War International History Project: Working Paper #59.* Washington: Woodrow Wilson International Center for Scholars, 2009.

Kulke, Hermann, and Dietmar Rothermund. *A History of India.* 6th ed. New York: Routledge, 2016.

Kurkov, Andrey. *Ukraine Diaries: Dispatches from Kiev.* London: Harvill Press, 2015.

Kurla, Jon. "Patrick Henry (1736-1799)." *Encyclopedia Virginia.* Virginia Foundation for the Humanities, 30 Jan. 2012.

Kuzio, Taras, ed. *Democratic Revolution in Ukraine: From Kuchmagate to Orange Revolution.* London: Routledge, 2009.

Kyle, Keith. *Suez.* New York: St. Martin's Press, 1991.

Langley, Lester D. *Simón Bolívar: Venezuelan Rebel, American Revolutionary.* Lanham, MD: Rowman & Littlefield Publishers, 2009.

Lanning, Michael Lee. *The American Revolution 100: The People, Battles, and Events of the American War for Independence, Ranked by the Their Significance.* Naperville: Sourcebooks, 2008.

Lapper, Richard. *Beef, Bible and Bullets: Brazil in the Age of Bolsonaro.* Manchester, UK: Manchester University Press, 2022.

Larkin, Edward. *Thomas Paine and the Literature of Revolution.* New York: Cambridge UP, 2005.

Lary, Diana. *China's Republic.* Cambridge: Cambridge University Press, 2007.

Laub, Zachary. August 10, 2016. *Council on Foreign Relations:* www.cfr.org/backgrounder/islamic-state

Lawrence, Jessica. July 2, 2014. *ABC News Australia:* "Iraq crisis: Could an ISIS caliphate ever govern the entire Muslim world?" www.abc.net.au/news/2014-07-02/could-an-isis-caliphate-ever-govern-the-muslim-world/5559806

Le, Quynh. "Vietnam Ambivalent on Le Duan's Legacy." *BBC News.* BBC, 14 Jul. 2006. news.bbc.co.uk/2/hi/asia-pacific/5180354.stm.

Leffler, Melvyn P. *For the Soul of Mankind: The United States, the Soviet Union, and the Cold War.* New York: Hill & Wang, 2007.

Lendvai, Paul. *One Day That Shook the Communist World: The 1956 Hungarian Uprising and Its Legacy.* Princeton: Princeton UP, 2008.

Levine, Steven and Alexander Pantsov. *Deng Xiaoping: A Revolutionary Life.* New York: Oxford UP, 2015.

Liasson, Mara. "Why President Trump Refuses to Concede and What It Might Mean for the Country." *NPR,* November 18, 2020. www.npr.org/2020/11/18/936342902/why-president-trump-refuses-to-concede-and-what-it-might-mean-for-the-country.

"Liberty, Equality, Fraternity: Exploring the French Revolution." George Mason University Web site. chnm.gmu.edu/revolution.

Lih, Lars T. *Lenin Rediscovered: What Is to Be Done? in Context.* Boston: Brill Academic Publishers, 2005.

Limm, Peter. *The Dutch Revolt, 1559-1648.* London: Longman, 1999.

Linebarger, Paul Myron. *The Political Doctrines of Sun Yat-sen: An Exposition of the San Min Chu I.* (print original: Baltimore: The Johns Hopkins Press, 1937; second: Westport CT: Greenwood Press, Publishers, 1973.) Salt Lake City: Project Gutenberg, 2018.

Liptak, Kevin. "A List of the Times Trump Has Said He Won't Accept the election Results or Leave Office if He Loses." *CNN,* September 24, 2020. www.cnn.com/2020/09/24/politics/trump-election-warnings-leaving-office/index.html.

Lovatt Smith, David. *Kenya, the Kikuyu, and Mau Mau.* Herstmonceux, UK: Mawenzi Books, 2005.

Lynch, John. "Simón Bolívar and the Spanish Revolutions." *History Today* 33 Issue 7 (July 1983) www.historytoday.com/john-lynch/simon-bolivar-and-spanish-revolutions.

———. *Simón Bolívar: A Life.* New Haven, CT: Yale UP, 2007.

MacEachin, Dougland J. *US Intelligence and the Polish Crisis: 1980-1981.* Washington: Center for the Study of Intelligence, 2000.

Mahatma Gandhi Information Website. Mani Bhavan Gandhi Sangrahalaya www.gandhi-manibhavan.org/gandhicomesalive/speech3.htm.

Mahatma Gandhi One Spot Information Website. Bombay Sarvodaya Mandal-Gandhi Book Centre, Mumbai www.mkgandhi.org/main.htm.

Maier, Pauline. *American Scripture: Making the Declaration of Independence.* New York: Vintage, 1998.

Mailer, Gideon. *John Witherspoon's American Revolution.* Williamsburg, VA, and Chapel Hill, NC: Omohundro Institute/University of North Carolina Press, 2016.

Mandela, Nelson. *Long Walk to Freedom: The Autobiography of Nelson Mandela.* New York: Little Brown & Co., 1994.

Mansel, Philip. *Paris Between Empires: Monarchy and Revolution 1814-1852.* New York: St. Martin's Press, 2003.

Mao Zedong. *The Secret Speeches of Chairman Mao: From the Hundred Flowers to the Great Leap Forward.* Ed. Roderick MacFarquhar et al. Cambridge: Council on East Asian Studies/Harvard University, 1989.

Martí, José. *Selected Writings,* trans. Esther Allen. London: Penguin Classics, 2002.

Martin, Ged. *The Durham Report and British policy: A Critical Essay.* London: Cambridge UP, 1972.

Martin, Gus. *Understanding Homeland Security.* 3rd ed. New York: SAGE Publications, 2019.

"Marxism and Workers' Organisation: Writings of Marxists on Trade Unions, the General Strike, Soviets and Working Class Organisation." Marxists Internet Archive Website.

Mason, Laura, and Tracey Rizzo. *The French Revolution: A Document Collection.* Boston: Houghton Mifflin, 1999.

Matthews, Herbert Lionel. *Fidel Castro.* New York: Simon, 1969.

Maximin, Edward Francis. *Accommodation and Resistance: The French Left, Indochina, and the Cold War, 1944-1954.* New York: Greenwood Press, 1986.

Mayer, Robert. "Lenin and the Concept of the Professional Revolutionary." *History of Political Thought* 14, no. 2 (1993): 249-263.

McCullough, David. *John Adams.* New York: Simon and Schuster, 2001.

McDougall, James. *A History of Algeria.* New York: Cambridge UP, 2017.

McElroy, Damien. July 1, 2014. *The Telegraph:* "Rome will be conquered next, says leader of 'Islamic State.'" www.telegraph.co.uk/news/worldnews/middleeast/syria/10939235/Rome-will-be-conquered-next-says-leader-of-Islamic-State.html

McFarlane, Anthony. *War and Independence in Spanish America.* New York: Routledge, 2008.

McGarry, Fearghal. *The Rising-Ireland: Easter 1916.* New York: Oxford UP, 2010.

McGirr, Elaine M. *Partial Histories: A Reappraisal of Colley Cibber.* London: Palgrave Macmillan, 2016.

McLynn, Frank. *Villa and Zapata: A History of the Mexican Revolution.* New York: Basic Books, 2002.

McNamara, Robert, and Brian VanDeMark. *In Retrospect: The Tragedy and Lessons of Vietnam.* New York: Random House, 1995.

McPhee, Peter. *Robespierre: A Revolutionary Life.* New Haven, CT: Yale University Press, 2012.

McRae, Robert. *Resistance and Revolution: Vaclav Havel's Czechoslovakia.* Ottawa: Carleton UP, 1997.

Meier, Pauline. *American Scripture: Making the Declaration of Independence.* New York: First Vintage, 1997.

Meisner, Maurice. *Mao Zedong: A Political and Intellectual Portrait.* Cambridge: Polity Press, 2006.

Merriman, John. *Massacre: The Life and Death of the Paris Commune.* New York: Basic Books, 2014.

Middlekauff, Robert. *The Glorious Cause: The American Revolution, 1763-1789.* Oxford: Oxford UP, 2007.

Miéville, China. *October: The Story of the Russian Revolution.* London; Brooklyn, NY: Verso, 2017.

Miller, John. *The Glorious Revolution.* 2nd ed. London: Routledge, 1997.

Miller, William Green. "The Orange Revolution and the Maidan Parliament." *Wilson Center.* Washington, DC: The Wilson Center, 2005.

Milner, Laurie. "History: The Suez Crisis." *BBC*. London: The British Broadcasting Corporation, 2014.

Ministry of Foreign Affairs of the People's Republic of China. "Formulation of Foreign Policy of New China on the Eve of its Birth." *Ministry of Foreign Affairs of the People's Republic of China*. Beijing: Ministry of Foreign Affairs of the People's Republic of China, 2014.

Mintz, S. "Was the Revolution Justified?" *Digital History*.

Moorhouse, Geoffrey. *India Britannica*. New York: Harper & Row, 1983.

Morley, Imogen. "Anatomy of a Speech: ¡No Pasarán! - Dolores Ibárruri." *Language, Communication and Collaboration*. Berlin: Imogen Morley, 2017.

Morton, Desmond. *Rebellions in Canada*. Toronto: Grolier, 1979.

Morton, Grenfell. *Home Rule and the Irish Question*. New York: Routledge, 2016.

Muller, Dalia Antonia. *Cuban Émigrés and Independence in the Nineteenth-Century Gulf World*. Chapel Hill: University of North Carolina Press, 2017.

Navrátil, Jaromír, ed. *The Prague Spring 1968: A National Security Archive Documents Reader*. New York: Central European UP, 1998.

Naylor, Brian. "Read Trump's Jan. 6 Speech, a Key Part of Impeachment Trial." *NPR*, February 10, 2021. www.npr.org/2021/02/10/966396848/read-trumps-jan-6-speech-a-key-part-of-impeachment-trial.

Nehru, Jawaharlal. *Toward Freedom: The Autobiography of Jawaharlal Nehru*. New York: John Day Company, 1941.

Nelson, Cary. "The Spanish Civil War: An Overview." *Modern American Poetry: About the Spanish Civil War*. Urbana-Champaign IL: University of Illinois, 2001.

Nelson, Craig. *Thomas Paine: Enlightenment, Revolution, and the Birth of Modern Nations*. New York: Viking, 2006.

Ngor, Haing. *Survival in the Killing Fields*. New York: Basic Books, 2003.

Nguyen, Lien-Hang T. *Hanoi's War: An International History of the War for Peace in Vietnam*. (The New Cold War History) Chapel Hill, NC: University of North Carolina Press, 2012.

"The 1916 Rising". Department of the Taoiseach, Government of Ireland. www.taoiseach.gov.ie/eng/Historical_Information/State_Commemorations/The_1916_Rising.html .

"1916: The 1916 Rising—Personalities and Perspectives." The National Library of Ireland. www.nli.ie/1916/.

Norman, Jesse. *Edmund Burke: The First Conservative*. New York: Basic Books, 2013.

O'Brien, Connor Cruise. *The Great Melody: A Thematic Biography and Commentated Anthology of Edmund Burke*. Chicago: University of Chicago Press, 1993.

O'Day, Alan. *Irish Home Rule, 1867-1921*. New York: Manchester UP, 1998.

Office of the Historian. "The Chinese Revolution of 1949." *Milestones 1945-1952*. Washington, DC: Department of State, 2016.

Okey, Robin. *The Habsburg Monarchy, c. 1765-1918: From Enlightenment to Eclipse*. London and New York: Palgrave Macmillan, 2000.

Paine, Thomas. *Common Sense and Other Writings*. Ed. J. M. Opal. New York: Norton, 2012.

Phillips, Jak. "Top 10 Nobel Prize Controversies: Nobel-Winner Wrangling, Henry Kissinger." *TIME*. Time Inc., 7 Oct. 2011. content.time.com/time/specials/packages/article/0,28804,2096389_2096388_2096386,00.html.

Picheta, Rob. "The Violent Attack on Brazil's Government Was Months in the Making: Here's What You Need to Know." *CNN*, January 9, 2023. www.cnn.com/2023/01/09/americas/brazil-congress-attack-explained-intl/index.html.

Popkin, Jeremy D. *A New World Begins: The History of the French Revolution*. New York: Basic Books, 2019.

———. *You Are All Free: The Haitian Revolution and the Abolition of Slavery*. New York: Cambridge UP, 2010.

——— *A Short History of the French Revolution*, 7th ed. New York: Routledge, 2019.

Porter, Andrew, and Alaine M. Low, eds. *The Oxford History of the British Empire*, Vol. 3: *The Nineteenth Century*. Oxford, UK: Oxford University Press, 1999.

Powell, T. G. "Priests and Peasants in Central Mexico: Social Conflict during 'La Reforma.'" *The Hispanic American Historical Review,* vol. 57, no. 2, 1977, pp. 296-313.

Prados, John. *Vietnam: The History of an Unwinnable War, 1945-1975*. Lawrence: UP of Kansas, 2009.

Preston, Paul. *The Spanish Civil War: Reaction, Revolution, and Revenge* (revised and expanded edition). New York: W.W. Norton & Company, 2007.

Quirk, Robert E. *Fidel Castro*. New York: Norton, 1995.

Rabinowitch, Alexander. *The Bolsheviks Come to Power: The Revolution of 1917 in Petrograd*. Chicago: Haymarket Books, 2017.

Ramonet, Ignacio, and Fidel Castro. *Fidel Castro: My Life: A Spoken Autobiography*. New York: Scribner, 2009.

Raskin, Jamie. *Unthinkable: Trauma, Truth, and the Trials of American Democracy*. New York: Harper, 2022.

Read, Colin. *The Rising in Western Upper Canada, 1837-8: The Duncombe Revolt and After*. Toronto: University of Toronto Press, 1982.

———, and Ronald J. Stagg, eds. *The Rebellion of 1837 in Upper Canada: A Collection of Documents*. Ottawa: The Champlain Society and Carleton UP, 1985.

Reed, John. *Ten Days That Shook the World*. New York: New York: Penguin Classics, 2007.

Reeve, L. J. *Charles I and the Road to Personal Rule*. Cambridge: Cambridge University Press, 1989.

Rene, Helena K. *China's Sent-Down Generation: Public Administration and the Legacies of Mao's Rustication Program*. Washington: Georgetown UP, 2013.

Rennebohm, Max. "Ukrainians Overthrow Dictatorship (Orange Revolution), 2004." *Global Nonviolent Action Database*. Swarthmore PA: Swarthmore College, 2011.

Renwick, Danielle, and Brianna Lee. "US-Cuba Relations." *Council on Foreign Relations*. CFR, 4 Aug. 2015.

Riall, Lucy. *Risorgimento: The History of Italy from Napoleon to Nation State*. Basingstoke, U.K.: Palgrave Macmillan 2009.

Ridge, Tom, and Larry Bloom. *The Test of Our Times: American Under Siege...and How We Can be Safe Again*. New York: Thomas Dunne Books, 2009.

Robb, Graham. *Victor Hugo: A Biography*. New York: Norton, 1999.

Roberts, J. M. *The French Revolution,* 2nd ed. Oxford, U.K.: Oxford UP, 1997.

Rodriguez, Jaime E. *The Independence of Spanish America*. Cambridge: Cambridge UP, 1998.

Rosenfeld, Sophia. *Common Sense: A Political History*. Cambridge, MA: Harvard UP, 2011.

Ross, Stanley R. *Francisco I. Madero: Apostle of Mexican Democracy*. New York: Columbia UP, 1955.

Royle, Trevor. *The Last Days of the Raj*. London: Joseph, 1989.

Schapiro, Leonard. "Lenin's Intellectual Formation and the Russian Revolutionary Background." In his Russian Studies. New York: Viking, 1987.

Schiffrin, Harold Z. *Sun Yat-sen and the Origins of the Chinese Revolution*. Berkeley: University of California Press, 2010.

Schlesinger, Arthur M. *A Thousand Days: John F. Kennedy in the White House*. Boston: Houghton, 1965.

Schoenhals, Michael. "Original Contradictions: On the Unrevised Text of Mao Zedong's 'On the Correct Handling of Contradictions among the People.'" *Australian Journal of Chinese Affairs* 16 (1986): 99-112. JSTOR. 21 Dec. 2015.

Scurr, Ruth. *Robespierre: Fatal Purity*. New York: Metropolitan Books, 2006.

Sebestyen, Victor. *Twelve Days: The Story of the 1956 Hungarian Revolution*. New York: Pantheon, 2006.

———. *Lenin: The Man, the Dictator, and the Master of Terror*. New York: Pantheon, 2017.

Service, Robert. *Lenin: A Biography*. Cambridge, Mass.: Harvard UP, 2000.

Shama, Nael. *Egyptian Foreign Policy from Mubarak to Morsi: Against the National Interest*. London: Taylor & Francis, 2013.

Shepard, Todd. *The Invention of Decolonization: The Algerian War and the Remaking of France*. Ithaca, NY: Cornell UP, 2008.

Sherwell, Guillermo A. *Simon Bolivar, the Liberator*. Rockville, MD: Wildside Press, 2013.

Shin, Michael. *Korean National Identity under Japanese Colonial Rule: Yi Gwangsu and the March First Movement of 1919*. (Routledge Studies in the Modern History of Asia). London: Routledge, 2018.

"Shri Jawaharlal Nehru". *PMIndia*. www.pmindia.gov.in/en/former_pm/shri-jawaharlal-nehru/ .

Skilling, H. Gordon. *Charter 77 and Human Rights in Czechoslovakia*. London: Allen, 1981.

Slany, William Z. "Foreign Relations of the United States, 1955-1957, Suez Crisis, July 26-December 31, 1956, Volume XVI." *Office of the Historian: Department of State*. Washington: United States Department of State, 2018.

Slayikoya, Sara Popescu. "Causes and Effects of Desertification on People and the Environment." *Greentumble*, April 29, 2019. greentumble.com/causes-and-effects-of-desertification.

Smaldone, William. *European Socialism: A Concise History with Documents*. Lanham: Rowman, 2014.

Smith, Barbara Clark. *The Freedoms We Lost: Consent and Resistance in Revolutionary America*. New York: New, 2010.

Smith, David L. *The Stuart Parliaments: 1603-1689*. London: Arnold, 1999.

Snyder, Timothy. "Savagery." *The New Republic*. New York: The New Republic, 2012.

Solomon, Richard H. *Mao's Revolution and the Chinese Political Culture*. Berkeley: University of California, 1971.

Sonmez, Felicia. "Pelosi Introduces Legislation That Would Establish Select Committee to Probe Jan. 6 Capitol Attack." *Washington Post*, June 28, 2021. www.washingtonpost.com/politics/pelosi-introduces-legislation-that-would-establish-select-committee-to-probe-jan-6-capitol-attack/2021/06/28/1d40b2c8-d852-11eb-9bbb-37c30dcf9363_story.html.

Spence, Jack, and David Welsh. *Ending Apartheid*. New York: Taylor & Francis, 2014.

Spencer, Donald S. *Louis Kossuth and Young America: A Study of Sectionalism and Foreign Policy, 1848-1852*. Columbia, MO: University of Missouri Press, 1977.

Sperber, Jonathan. *Karl Marx: A Nineteenth-Century Life*. New York: Liveright, 2014.

Staten, Clifford L. *The History of Cuba*. Westport: Greenwood, 2003.

Stinchcombe, William C. *The American Revolution and the French Alliance*. Syracuse: Syracuse University Press, 1969.

Stone, Martin. *The Agony of Algeria*. New York: Columbia UP, 1997.

Sun Yat-sen. *Memoirs of a Chinese Revolutionary*. (original 1925) Agawam MA: Silver Street Media, 1912.

Sutton, Robert P. *Revolution to Succession: Constitution Making in the Old Dominion*. Charlottesville: U of Virginia P, 1989.

Szulc, Tad. *Fidel: A Critical Portrait*. New York: Avon Books, 1986.

Tait, L. Gordon. *The Piety of John Witherspoon*. Louisville: Geneva, 2001.

Thomas, Peter D. *Tea Party to Independence: The Third Phase of the American Revolution, 1773-1776*. Oxford: Clarendon, 1991.

Tracy, James D. *The Founding of the Dutch Republic: War, Finance, and Politics in Holland, 1572-1588*. Oxford, U.K.: Oxford University Press, 2008.

Traugott, Mark. *The Insurgent Barricade*. Berkley: University of California Press, 2010.

Tucker, Spencer C. *The Encyclopedia of the Vietnam War: A Political, Social, and Military History*. 2nd ed. Santa Barbara: ABC-CLIO, 2011.

Turner, Henry Ashby. *Germany from Partition to Reunification*. New Haven: Yale UP, 1992.

Ung, Loung. *First They Killed My Father: A Daughter of Cambodia Remembers*. New York: Harper Perennial, 2000.

Unger, Harlow G. *John Hancock: Merchant King and American Patriot*. New York: Wiley, 2000.

———. *Lion of Liberty: Patrick Henry and the Call to a New Nation.* Cambridge: Da Capo, 2010.

Unger, Jonathan. "China's Troubled Down-to-the-Countryside Campaign." *Contemporary China,* vol. 3, no. 2 (Summer 1979); pp. 79-92.

United Nations. "United Nations Conference on Environment & Development, Rio de Janeiro, 3 to 14 June 1992: Agenda 21." sustainabledevelopment.un.org/content/documents/Agenda21.pdf.

US Department of Defense. "Soldier Missing from Vietnam War Accounted For (Newton)." *Defense POW/MIA Accounting Agency.* Department of Defense, 8 Jun. 2015. www.dpaa.mil/NewsStories/NewsReleases/tabid/10159/Article/598458/soldier-missing-from-vietnam-war-accounted-for-newton.aspx.

Vaculík, Ludvik. *A Cup of Coffee with My Interrogator: The Prague Chronicles of Ludvík Vaculík.* Trans. George Theiner. London: Readers Intl., 1987.

Van der Lem, Anton. *Revolt in the Netherlands: The Eighty Years War, 1568-1648.* Trans. Andy Brown. London: Reaktion Books, 2018.

Van Geel, Tyll. *Homeland Security Law: A Primer.* New York: Routledge, 2018.

Van Gelderen, Martin. *The Political Thought of the Dutch Revolt, 1555-1590.* Cambridge, U.K.: Cambridge University Press, 2002.

VanDeMark, Brian. *Into the Quagmire: Lyndon Johnson and the Escalation of the Vietnam War.* New York: Oxford UP, 1995.

Várdy, Steven B. "Louis Kossuth. A Celebrated, Disillusioned Hungarian Revolutionary's Visit to Pittsburgh in 1852," *Western Pennsylvania History,* volume 91, no. 1, spring 2008; pp. 18-31.

Victor G. "On Lenin's Address to Petrograd Soviet," *Workers Vanguard* No. 861, 6 January 2005, www.icl-fi.org/english/wv/861/letter-lenin.html.

"Vladimir Lenin Works Index." Lenin Internet Archive Web site. marxists.org/archive/lenin/works/index.htm.

"Wars & Conflict: 1916 Easter Rising." BBC History. www.bbc.co.uk/history/british/easterrising.

Weigel, George. *The End and the Beginning: Pope John Paul II-The Victory of Freedom, the Last Years, the Legacy.* New York: Doubleday, 2010.

Wells, Tim. *444 Days: The Hostages Remember.* New York: Harcourt, 1985.

Wendling, Mike. "How Trump's Allies Stoked Brazil Congress Attack." *BBC,* January 9 2023. www.bbc.com/news/world-us-canada-64206484.

Wert, Michael. *Meiji Restoration Losers: Memory and Tokugawa Supporters in Modern Japan.* Cambridge, MA: Harvard University Asia Center, 2013.

Williams, Kieran. *The Prague Spring and Its Aftermath: Czechoslovak Politics, 1968-1970.* Cambridge: Cambridge UP, 1997.

Wills, Clair. *Dublin 1916: The Siege of the GPO.* London: Profile Books, 2009.

Wills, Garry. *Inventing America: Jefferson's Declaration of Independence.* New York: Vintage 2018 (reprint).

Wilson, David A. *Paine and Cobbett: The Transatlantic Connection.* Kingston, ON: McGill-Queen's UP 1988.

Wilson, George M. *Patriots and Redeemers in Japan: Motives in Meiji Restoration.* Chicago: University of Chicago Press, 1992.

Windrow, Martin. *The French Indochina War, 1946-1954.* Oxford: Osprey Military, 1998.

Witherspoon, John. *The Dominion of Providence over the Passions of Men.* 1777 Glasgow ed. Google Books, 2009.

Wolff, Barbara. "Was Declaration of Independence Inspired by Dutch?" University of Wisconsin-Madison News Web site. www.news.wisc.edu/3049.

Wolpert, Stanley. *A New History of India.* New York: Oxford University Press, 2009.

Womack, John. *Zapata and the Mexican Revolution.* New York: Vintage, 1970.

Wood, Gordon S. *Revolutionary Characters: What Made the Founders Different.* New York: Penguin, 2006.

———. *The Radicalism of the American Revolution.* New York: Vintage, 1993.

Wray, Christopher. "Examining the January 6 Attack on the U.S. Capitol." *FBI*. Washington, D.C.: Federal Bureau of Investigation, 2021.

Wynnyckyj, Mychailo. *Ukraine's Maidan, Russia's War: A Chronicle and Analysis of the Revolution of Dignity*. Stuttgart, Germany: Ibidem-Verlag, 2019.

Young, Eric Van. *The Other Rebellion: Popular Violence, Ideology, and the Mexican Struggle for Independence, 1810-1821*. Stanford: Stanford UP, 2001.

Zavitz, Erin. "Revolutionary Commemorations: Jean-Jacques Dessalines and Haitian Independence Day, 1804-1904." *The Haitian Declaration of Independence* 221 (2016).

Zobel, Hiller B. *The Boston Massacre*. W. W. Norton & Co., 1996.

Index

A

Act of Abjuration, 3, 8, 9
Adams, John, 49, 52, 53, 63, 69, 72, 96, 99, 103, 105, 111, 112, 113, 114, 118, 120, 123
Adams, Samuel, 37, 46, 49, 61, 98
African National Congress (ANC), 683, 692
Al-'Adnani, Abu Muhammad, 744
Algerian National Liberation Army, 587
Algerian National Liberation Front (FLN), 596-603
Algerian War, 596, 598, 603
Allied nations (or Entente powers), 315
al-Qaida, 744
"America First" foreign policy, 763
American independence, 85, 96, 122, 203
American Revolution, 35
Anglo-Persian Oil Company (APOC), 604, 623
Apology for the Life of Mr. Colley Cibber, An, 29, 30, 32
Aquino, Benigno, 685, 686
Aquino, Corazon, 685-691
Arab Spring (2010–2012), 587, 723, 725
armed personnel carriers (APC), 497

B

Battista, Fulgencio, 505
Battle of Monmouth (1778), 35
Bay of Pigs, 517, 523, 527, 560, 612
Ben Ali regime, 752
Berlin Wall, 639, 670, 671, 674, 676
Biden, Joseph R., 783
blood sacrifice, 361, 363, 367, 368
Boisrond-Tonnerre, Louis, 181, 183
Bolívar, Simón, 179, 190, 192, 205-211, 683, 701, 707
Bolshevik party, 371, 387, 389, 390, 402
Bolshevik Revolution, 371, 423
Bolsonaro, Jair, 764, 796, 797, 799
Bonaparte, Napoleon, 125, 181, 183, 191, 205, 212

Boston Massacre (1770), 35, 37-50
Boston Massacre Oration, 37-50
Boston Tea Party (1773), 35, 39, 63
Botha, P. W., 683, 692
Bouazizi, Mohamed, 725, 726
Bourbon Restoration, 253
British East India Company, 411, 413, 414, 422, 423, 424, 453, 454
British North America Act, 220
Burke, Edmund, 138
Bush, George W., 775, 776

C

Cambodian Genocide of 1975-1979, 581
Canadian Rebellions, 220-232
Cartagena Manifesto, 190-204
Castro, Fidel, 505, 516-522
Catholicism, 29, 33, 34, 214, 309, 359
Central Intelligence Agency (CIA), 498, 559, 560, 633, 663, 664, 781
Chanto, Sisowath Doung, 581, 583, 585
Charter 77, 639, 649, 655-662
Chávez, Hugo, 683, 700-708
Chinese Communist Party (CCP), 461, 469, 472, 477, 478, 483, 484, 491, 498
Chinese nationalist party, 469
Chinese People's Political Consultative Conference, 469, 472, 474
Churchill, Winston, 455, 560, 639
Cibber, Colley, 29, 30, 32
Cold War, 459, 498, 517, 521, 612, 615, 663, 671, 680
Committee of Public Safety, 164, 165, 175
Common Sense, 85-97
Communist Manifesto, The, 270-280
Communist movement, 270, 469, 475, 476, 680
Communist Party of Czechoslovakia, 648

Communist Party of the Soviet Union, 552, 639, 672, 676
Constitution of 1791, 125
Continental Congress, 35, 37, 39, 40, 47, 50, 51, 52, 53, 60, 63, 65, 69, 71, 72, 74, 75, 83, 85, 86, 87, 90, 99, 105, 111, 114, 467
counterterrorism, 775, 781
Cromwell, Oliver, 21, 27, 344
Cuban Revolution, 241, 242, 244, 249, 505, 523, 776
Cultural Revolution (1966-1976), 461, 470, 491, 492, 495
Czar Nicholas II, 369, 382, 395
Czechoslovak intellectuals ("Chartists"), 655

D

da Silva, Luiz Inácio Lula, 796, 797
de Gouges, Olympe (Marie Gouze), 153-163
de Klerk, F. W., 683, 692, 693, 694, 696
de San Martín, José, 179, 205
de Santa Anna, Antonio López (also Santa Anna), 179, 219, 233
Declaration of Independence, 3-19, 35, 40, 49, 52, 53, 75, 85, 86, 95, 96, 98-110, 127, 181-189, 206, 222, 223, 231, 315-322, 567
Declaration of the Causes and Necessity of Taking Up Arms, 51-62
Declaration of the Rights of Man and of the Citizen, 125, 127-137, 153, 154, 155, 156, 162
Declaration of the Rights of Woman and of the Female Citizen, 153-163
Democratic Republic of Vietnam (DRV, or North Vietnam), 532, 566, 567, 578
Dessalines, Jean-Jacques, 179, 181, 183, 188
Díaz, Porfirio, 240, 323, 325, 326, 328, 331, 332, 334, 335, 336, 337, 340
Dickinson, John, 51, 52, 61
Digital Archive of Cambodian Holocaust Survivors, 581, 582
Discourse on the Love of Our Country (1789), 138
du Motier, Marie-Joseph, 127
Durham Report, 220, 232
Dutch Declaration of Independence, 3-19

Dutch Republic, 3
Dutch Revolt of 1568-1609, 3
Dutch War of Independence, 3

E

Easter Rebellion, 361
Eastman, Max, 395
Eighty Years' War, 3, 18
Eisenhower, Dwight D., 523, 533, 571, 605
Ellipse, The, 765, 766
el-Sisi, Abdel Fattah, 736
Emmanuel, Victor, II, 299-305
Emperor Meiji, 309
Engels, Friedrich, 270, 271, 386, 415
English Civil War (1642-1649), 21, 23
English Revolution of 1688, 138, 151
European Union (EU), 709, 713, 714, 717, 722, 800, 804

F

February Revolution, 253, 390, 395, 687
Féin, Sinn, 341, 361, 367, 368
First Constitutional Era, 589, 590, 591, 594
First Indochina War (1946-1954), 529, 567
Francisco Madero Administration, 332
Franco-Prussian War, 257, 296, 297, 299, 301, 416
Franklin, Benjamin, 52, 53, 72, 86, 98, 99, 105, 111, 113, 114, 120, 123
French colonialism, 571
French Revolution, 19, 98, 112, 125
French Revolutionary Wars, 131, 253

G

Gandhi, Mohandas K., 411, 425, 443-452
Geneva Accords, 531-549, 550, 567, 571
Geneva Conference, 531, 533, 547, 576
German Democratic Republic (GDR, or communist East Germany), 670, 672, 673, 675
"Give Me Liberty or Give Me Death," 63, 65, 72
Glorious Revolution of 1688, 21, 29-34
Gómez, Máximo, 241, 242, 243, 249, 250
Gorbachev, Mikhail, 498, 654, 670-674, 675, 676, 680

Government of India Act of 1919, 424-442
Great Famine in Ireland (1845-1852), 341
"Great Satan, The," 623-632
Guevara, Che, 505

H
Habsburg scepter, 281
Haitian Declaration of Independence, 181-189
Hamid, Abdel, II, 589
Hancock, John, 37-50
"Hang Mike Pence," 763, 783
Harris, Kamala, 783
Havel, Václav, 655, 660, 662, 676
Henry, Patrick, 49, 53, 63, 64, 69, 71, 72, 99
Hessels, Andries, 3, 9
HMS *George* (1772), 35
Ho Chi Minh, 529, 531, 532, 533, 549, 550, 551, 559, 560, 561, 564, 566-570
Home Rule bills, 341
Homeland Security Advisory System (HSAS), 775
Huerta, Victoriano, 323, 326, 327
Hugo, Victor, 253, 255, 256
Hundred Flowers Campaign, 477, 478, 489
Hungarian Revolution, 281, 477, 489, 642, 646
Hungarian War of Independence, 281, 282

I
Ibárruri, Dolores, 507, 508
Indian independence movement, 443, 446, 453
Indian National Congress, 411, 425, 441, 443, 444, 445, 454, 455
Intolerable Acts, 35, 39, 49, 50, 98
Iran's Communist party, 604
Iranian Revolution of 1979, 623
Irish Home Rule, 343-360
Irish war of independence (1919-1921), 341
Islamic State (ISIL/ISIS), 744
Islamic State of Iraq and the Levant (ISIL, a.k.a. ISIS), 744

J
Jagiellon, Louis, 281
Jay, John, 111, 113, 114, 118, 120, 123

Jefferson, Thomas, 19, 49, 51, 52, 53, 61, 72, 96, 98, 99, 105, 107
Jinnah, Muhammad Ali, 411
Johnson, Lyndon, 560, 566, 569, 578
Juárez, Benito, 179, 233-240, 325
July Revolution of 1830, 255
June Rebellion of 1832, 255-269

K
Kai-shek, Chiang, 461, 469, 471, 474, 477, 478
Karman, Tawakkol, 725-735
Kenya African Union (KAU), 513
Kenyatta, Jomo, 505, 513, 515
Khmer Rouge, 529, 581-585
Khomeini, Ayatollah Ruhollah, 623, 624, 633
Khrushchev, Nikita, 477, 517, 527, 641, 642, 648
Killing Fields, 529, 581-585
Kimimasa, Yuri, 309, 311
King Charles I, 3, 21, 23-28, 94
King Charles X, 253, 255
King George III, 51, 52, 59, 65, 83, 85, 98, 106
King James II of England, 29
King Louis XVI, 111, 113, 127, 153, 164, 165
King Louis-Philippe I, 255
King Philip II, 3, 17, 19, 33
King Victor Emmanuel II, 299-305
King William III, 29
Kissinger, Henry, 571, 573
Korean Declaration of Independence, 315-322
Kossuth, Louis, 281-289
Krenz, Egon, 670-674
Kuchma, Leonid, 711, 717
Kuomintang, 461, 469, 471, 472, 474, 475, 476, 477, 478, 479, 489

L
L'Ouverture, Toussaint, 179
La Reforma, 233-240
Le Duan, 550, 551, 557, 558
Leadership of the Paris Commune, The, 290
Lenin, Vladimir, 369, 371, 389-394
Les Misérables, 253, 255-269
Liberal Party, 236, 237, 239, 240, 343, 346, 357

Liberator, The, 395, 408
Lilley, James, 497, 498
Livingston, Robert, 53, 99, 105, 111, 120
Louis XIV, 21, 29, 114
Louis XVI, 96, 111, 113, 120, 125, 127, 129, 151, 153, 154, 156, 164, 165
Low Countries, 1, 3, 10, 11, 14, 18

M

MacDonagh, Thomas, 361, 363, 366
Machado, Gerardo, 505
Mackenzie, William Lyon, 220, 231
Mackintosh, James, 138
Madera, Francisco, 323
Mandela, Nelson, 683, 692-699
Manifesto of the Paris Commune, 290-298
March First Movement, 315, 317, 321
Marcos, Ferdinand, 683, 685, 686
Marie-Antoinette, 129, 153, 154, 156, 164
Martí, José, 179, 241, 242, 243, 249, 250, 523
Marx, Karl, 270, 271, 280, 290, 298, 386, 393, 413-423
Marxism, 270, 271, 279, 280, 372, 373, 386, 387, 482, 483, 487, 505, 551
Mary II, 29
Mau Mau, 505, 513-515
Mayorkas, Alejandro, 775
McCone, John A., 559, 560
Meiji Charter Oath, 309-314
Meiji period, 307
Mexican independence, 212, 214, 218, 219, 239
Mexican Revolution (1910-1920), 323
Montagu, Edwin, 424, 425, 426, 443, 454
Montecristi Manifesto, 241-251
Morley, John, 343-360
Morsi, Mohamed, 736-743
Mossadegh, Mohammed, 587, 633
Mubarak, Hosni, 736

N

Nam-seon, Choe, 315, 317
Napoleon III, 253, 255, 257, 290, 299, 300
Napoleonic Wars, 125, 191, 253, 281, 299, 343

Napolitano, Janet, 775
Nasser, Gamal Abdel, 587, 614-622
National Assembly of France, 127
National Convention, 125, 129, 154, 164, 165, 175, 176, 177
National Liberation Front (NLF) or Viet Cong, 529, 559-565, 566, 596-603
National Terrorism Advisory System (NTAS), 768, 775, 776, 777, 779
Nationalist army, 507
Nazi Germany, 505, 596, 641, 653
Nehru, Jawaharlal, 411, 453-459
Ngo Dinh Diem, 529, 556, 559, 560, 571
Nicholas, Tsar, I, 281, 389
Nixon, Richard, 461, 517, 521, 571
¡No Pasarán! ("They Shall Not Pass!"), 507-512
nonviolent resistance movement, 411

O

Oath of Five Articles, 309
Óbregon, Alvaro, 323, 334
October Revolution, 280, 369, 390, 395, 397
Ode, Robert C., 633, 634
"On the Principles of Political Morality," 164, 165
Orange Revolution, 709, 711, 712, 714, 717, 719, 722
Organization of American States, 516, 523, 524, 799, 800, 804
Orozco, Pascual, 323, 334, 336
Ottoman Empire, 6, 8, 19, 45, 281, 282, 444, 587, 589, 590, 591, 592, 595, 614, 619

P

Pahlavi, Reza Shah, 587, 623
Paine, Thomas, 85, 86, 99, 138
Papineau, Louis-Joseph, 220, 231
Paris Peace Accords, 571-580
"Path of Revolution in the South, The," 550-558
Paul, John, II, 663, 668
peace of Karlowitz (1699), 281
Pearse, Patrick, 361, 363, 367
Pelosi, Nancy, 765, 766
Pence, Mike, 763, 765, 783

Peninsular War, 191, 205
Pentagon, The, 775
People Power Revolution, 683, 685, 686
People's Republic of China (PRC), 270, 461, 463, 468, 469, 470, 472, 474, 477, 478, 481, 491, 497
Perry, Matthew C., 307, 309
Plan de San Luis de Potosi, 325-331
Plan of Ayala, 332-340
Popular Front coalition, 507, 510, 511
Pot, Pol, 581, 584
Price, Richard, 138, 150, 151
"Provocative Answer to an Examination, A," 491

Q
QAnon conspiracy theory, 765
Qing (Manchu) dynasty, 461
Queen Elizabeth I, 8, 19, 29, 33, 142, 413, 424

R
Rajk, László, 641, 642
Reed, John, 395, 397, 398, 408, 409
Reflections on the Revolution in France (1790), 138-152
Republic of China (Taiwan), 461, 463, 467
Republic of the Seven United Netherlands, 3
Republic of the Seven United Provinces, 3, 8
Republic of Vietnam (RVN, or South Vietnam), 532, 566, 567, 578
Reuters News Service, 796
Revolution Society, 138, 148, 150
Robespierre, Maximilien, 164-178
Rusk, Dean, 559
Russian Revolution of 1917, 369, 477
Russian Social Democratic Labor Party, 371
Russian Social-Democratic Workers' Party, 369, 389, 390, 393
Russo-Japanese War (1904-1905), 307, 369, 395, 409

S
Second Declaration of Havana, 523-527
Second Virginia Convention, 63, 69, 70, 72
Secret Speech, 641, 642

Shah, Mohammad Reza, 587, 623
sharia, 742, 744, 752
Sieyès, Emmanuel Joseph (also Abbé Sieyès), 127, 129, 154
Sino-Japanese War (1894-1895), 307
Socialist Revolutionary Party, 369, 402, 403
Soviet invasion of Afghanistan, 633
Soviet Socialist Republics (USSR), 395, 670, 675
"Soviets in Action," 395-409
Spanish-American War of 1898, 190
Spanish Civil War (1936-1939), 505, 507, 508
Spanish Inquisition, 1, 7, 11, 17
Spanish-American War (1898), 179, 190, 241
Stalin, Joseph, 477, 641, 670
Stamp Act, 35, 47, 52, 63, 65, 71, 72, 98
Suez Canal Company, 614
Suez Maritime Canal, 614, 617, 620
Sunni Islam, 744

T
"Three Stages of Revolution, The," 463-468
"Two Thousand Words" Manifesto, 648-654
T'ieh Sheng, Chang (Zhang Tiesheng), 491, 492, 494
Takachika, Fukuoka, 309, 311
Takayoshi, Kido, 309, 311
Tayaert, Jacques, 3, 9
Ten Years' War, 241, 243
Thesiger, Frederic John Napier, 424, 426
Third War of Independence, 299, 300
Thirty Years' War, 3, 19
Tho, Le Duc, 571, 573
Tiananmen Square, 461, 497-503
Tito, Josip, 639
Townsend Acts (1767), 35
Treaty of Córdoba, 179, 192, 212-219
Treaty of Münster, 3, 18
Treaty of Westphalia, 3, 19
Tribune, The, 413, 422
Triple Entente (Russia, France, Great Britain), 389
Trump, Donald J., 763, 765, 767, 783, 784, 794, 796, 797, 803, 804
Tudeh Party, 604

Tunisian Confederation of Industry, Trade and Handicrafts, 752
Tunisian General Labor Union, 752
Tunisian Human Rights League, 752, 753, 754
Tunisian movement, 752
Tunisian National Dialogue Quartet, 752-761
Tunisian Order of Lawyers, 752, 753, 754
Twelve Years' Truce, 3, 18
Twenty-One Nations Conference, 516-522
Tymoshenko, Yulia, 717-722

U

U.S. Capitol, 763, 765-774, 783-795, 803, 804
U.S. Department of Homeland Security, 775, 779
Union of Hungarian University and Academy Students, 641
Union of Soviet Socialist Republics (USSR), 395, 670, 675
United Nations Convention Against Desertification, 700, 707
United Provinces, 3, 8, 10, 14, 15, 18, 29, 192, 206, 429, 440

V

Vaculík, Ludvík, 648, 649
Valcke, Jacob, 3, 9
van Dieven, Pieter, 3, 9
"Victory has been achieved," 469
Viet Minh, 529, 531, 532, 533, 549, 550, 561, 562, 563, 567
Vietnamese Communist Party, 550

Villa, Francisco "Pancho," 323, 334

W

Wilber, Donald N., 604
Witherspoon, John, 74, 75, 80, 83
Wojtyla, Karol, 663, 668
Wollstonecraft, Mary, 138
World Trade Center, 499, 503, 775
World War I, 307, 315, 360, 369, 390, 395, 409, 425, 426, 441, 511, 566, 567, 587, 589, 592, 604, 623, 624, 641
World War II, 317, 411, 461, 469, 470, 474, 475, 477, 498, 513, 516, 532, 550, 559, 571, 596, 598, 605, 623, 634, 641, 648, 653, 663, 664, 668, 670, 674, 676, 686, 793

X

Xiaoping, Deng, 461, 492, 497

Y

Yanukovych, Viktor, 709, 711, 714, 717, 718
Yat-sen, Sun, 461, 463-468
Young Turk movement, 589, 592
Young Turk Revolution, 589, 592
Young Turks, 587, 589-595
Yushchenko, Viktor, 709, 711-716, 717, 718, 719

Z

Zahedi, Fazlollah, 604, 609, 612
Zapata, Emiliano, 323, 332, 334, 336, 339, 340
Zedong, Mao, 459, 461, 469, 470, 471, 475, 477-490, 491

The Defining Documents Series

Defining Documents in American History: Themes
American Citizenship
The American Economy
Business Ethics
Capital Punishment
Civil Rights
The Constitution
Dissent & Protest
Domestic Terrorism
Drug Policy
Environment & Conservation
Espionage & Intrigue
The First Amendment
The Free Press
The Great Depression
The Great Migration
The Gun Debate
Immigration & Immigrant Communities
The Legacy of 9/11
LGBTQ+
Native Americans
Political Campaigns, Candidates & Discourse
Prison Reform
Secrets, Leaks & Scandals
Slavery
Supreme Court Decisions
U.S. Involvement in the Middle East

Defining Documents in World History: Themes
Asia
Genocide & The Holocaust
Nationalism & Populism
Plagues, Pandemics, and Public Health
The Middle East
Women's Rights

SALEM PRESS https://salempress.com (800) 221-1592

Defining Documents in American History: Eras
Exploration and Colonial America (1492-1755)
The American Revolution (1754-1805)
Manifest Destiny and the New Nation (1803-1860)
The American West (1836-1900)
The Civil War (1860-1865)
The Reconstruction Era (1865-1877)
The Emergence of Modern America (1874-1917)
The 1900s (1900-1909)
The 1910s (1910-1919)
World War I (1914-1919)
The 1920s (1920-1929)
The 1930s (1930-1939)
World War II (1939-1946)
Postwar 1940s (1945-1949)
The Cold War (1945-1991)
The 1950s (1950-1959)
The Vietnam War (1956-1975)
The 1960s (1960-1969)
The 1970s (1970-1979)
The 1980s (1980-1989)

Defining Documents in World History: Eras
The Ancient World (2700 B.C.E. - 50 C.E.)
The Middle Ages (476-1500)
Renaissance & Early Modern Era (1308-1600)
The 17th Century
The 18th Century
The 19th Century
The 20th Century (1900-1950)